TRANSFORM
YOUR LIFE, BUSINESS & HEALTH

Be Well

Dr. José Aguilar

Published by CelebrityPress®, Orlando, FL

CelebrityPress® is a registered trademark.

Printed in the United States of America.

ISBN: 978-0-9912143-9-6
LCCN: 2014942609

Most CelebrityPress® titles are available at special quantity discounts for bulk purchases for sales promotions, premiums, fundraising, and educational use. Special versions or book excerpts can also be created to fit specific needs.

For more information, please write:
CelebrityPress®
520 N. Orlando Ave, #2
Winter Park, FL 32789
or call 1.877.261.4930

Visit us online at: www.CelebrityPressPublishing.com

TRANSFORM
YOUR LIFE, BUSINESS & HEALTH

CONTENTS

CHAPTER 1

MASTERING YOUR MIND

BY BRIAN TRACY

Your mind is more powerful than you can imagine. You have within you, right now, the ability to overcome all your obstacles, solve all your problems and accomplish all of your goals, just by bringing the power of your mind to bear on the important parts of your life. When you master your mind and your deep unconscious abilities, you will move ahead faster and achieve more in a shorter period of time than perhaps you could even imagine today.

One of the keys to great success in life is to become very good at what you do, and concentrate on getting better and better. As a result, you will earn more and more and you will eventually rise to the top of your field. You will enjoy the respect and esteem of the people around you and you will enjoy the wonderful financial rewards that go along with the commitment to excellence in our competitive market society.

When I was a young man, after struggling for many years, I learned two things that changed my life. The first thing I learned was that *everyone* has the capacity to be excellent at something. One of the most important responsibilities of adult life is for you to choose your "area of excellence" and then to throw your whole heart into that area for a sustained period of time until you emerge in the top 10% of your field. No one else can do this for you, and without this commitment and this achievement, you will never accomplish what you are truly capable of.

The second thing I learned, which was even more important, was that everyone who is in the top 10% today was once in the bottom 10%. Everyone who is today leading their field was once starting off at the back of the field. Everyone who was at the front of the line of life today, started off at the back of the line.

For many years, I studied the biographies and autobiographies of great men and women, especially men and women who started from humble beginnings and rose to positions of power, prestige and leadership in their chosen fields. I found that all of these people have certain characteristics and qualities in common. And I also found that all of these qualities are learnable over time, if you know what they are and you know the steps that you need to take, to instill these qualities in yourself.

The philosopher Aristotle wrote that the aims and purposes of education are primarily to instill values, virtues and qualities of thinking in the minds of young people. Aristotle said that if young people grew up with the right way to think and respond to the world around them, they would enjoy lives of great accomplishment, prestige and esteem in their societies.

But, he asked, what if you have reached adulthood and for some reason you were not taught the essential qualities and mental thinking skills of highly successful people? Well then, Aristotle taught, the way that you develop the qualities that you recognize you need is to practice those qualities in every situation where those qualities are called for.

The Greek word for this approach to self-development is "Praxis." What the great philosophers, teachers and leaders found was that you can shape and sculpt your own character and personality by practicing the qualities that you most admire and aspire to having for yourself. For example, whenever you feel afraid in a particular situation, the quality of courage is required. If you practice being courageous, if you do the bold thing rather than the cowardly thing, you eventually develop the habit of courage in the face of fear and danger. And it is the same with any other quality.

The Law of Correspondence says that your outer world becomes a reflection of your inner world. The more that you develop and instill the key qualities of leadership and exceptional people into your own character and personality, the more your outer world of success, achievement and esteem will reflect what is going on inside of you.

In this chapter, I will give you some ideas about three key thinking skills and introduce you to all of them for your own information. Just remember that it is practice that enables you to develop the skills, not merely the learning of them, hearing of them or reading about them.

Let me start for a moment with the primary reasons for success in a fast moving, rapidly-changing society. In my estimation, they are focus, concentration, flexibility and anticipation.

Focus means that you have the ability to develop absolute clarity about what it is you want and where you are going. The lack of focus leads to fuzziness and confusion, the primary reasons that people underachieve and fail in life. The principle of concentration, which I will develop a little bit later, means that you develop the ability to discipline yourself to concentrate single-mindedly on one thing, the most important thing, and to stay with it until it is complete. With this ability, you can accomplish virtually anything. Without this ability, you will always have to work for someone else who has it.

The quality of flexibility is considered to be the most important single quality for success in the 21st century. Flexibility means that you develop the mental agility to move quickly with the winds of change, like a long-tailed cat in a room full of rocking chairs. Since everything is changing dramatically at a speed that has never before been experienced, the quality of flexibility enables you to abandon old unworkable ideas and embrace the new – on your journey toward the top 10% and the high levels of accomplishment of which you are capable.

The fourth quality is that of anticipation. This is something that is now taught in business schools under the title of "Crisis Anticipation." What this means is that you develop the ability to look down the road several months, or even several years, and accurately anticipate what is likely to happen both good and bad, if certain other things happen. By anticipating correctly, you also develop the ability to make plans and provisions to assure that you can maximize your opportunities and minimize any problems that occur.

As you can see, the qualities of focus, concentration, flexibility and anticipation are all attitudes of mind. They are all approaches to your life, people, work and relationships that enable you to be a master of the forces of change, rather than merely a victim of change.

The flipside of success, the reasons for failure, are primarily fuzziness or lack of focus, diffusion of efforts, lack of concentration, feelings of uncertainty, doubt, fear and anxiety. The reason that these qualities lead to underachievement is that they all diffuse your energies and disperse your attention. The inability to clarify your goals and objectives and concentrate single-mindedly on them, combined with fear and anxiety, causes you to drift endlessly, to go in circles, and never to accomplish anything worthwhile.

All growth in your personal character comes from your developing these new qualities that you need at a deeper and deeper level. In any group of people, the man or woman who is the most developed in terms of their qualities of character and personality will eventually rise to the top of that group. This must be your aim in everything you do.

The key principals of leadership and success that have been discovered in more than 3300 studies going back to 600 BC, are all qualities that you can program into your character as permanent guides for happiness and high accomplishment.

The first quality or principle is that of the "objective." In military terms, as well as in business terms, the principle of the objective requires that you are absolutely clear about who you are, what you want, where you are and where you are going.

The second principle of strategic thinking is the principle of the "offensive." This means that you continue to move out boldly in the direction of your dreams. You continually strive "to go where no man has ever gone before." You are intensely action-oriented and you make things happen rather than just waiting for things to happen.

The third principle or tool for mastering your thought is the principle of the "mass." This refers of course to your ability to concentrate your talents and abilities single-mindedly on one thing at a time. We will talk about this in a minute.

The fourth principle is the principle of the "maneuver." In military and business terms, as well as in your personal life, this refers to your ability to be creative, flexible, adaptive and adjustable to changing circumstances. All great battles, all great sports contests, are decided by the ability of one party to maneuver faster and in a more creative way than the opponent.

The fifth quality of superb thinking is the quality of intelligence. In military terms, this means to get all the information necessary about the positions and plans of the enemy before acting. In modern business terms, this means to understand the market thoroughly before launching new products and services. In personal terms this means that it is vital for you to become one of the most knowledgeable and skilled people in your field if you are going to enjoy the success that is possible for you.

The sixth quality or principle of success is "singleness of command." In military terms, this means that there is one person in charge. In business terms, this means that there is a clear hierarchy of command and control within an organization. Each person reports to only one person. In your personal life, this means that you are absolutely single minded in pursuit of your goals and objectives, rather than trying to pursue several different goals at the same time.

The seventh principle of success is that of "surprise." In military terms, this means that the successful general always does something that is completely unexpected and unanticipated by the enemy. In business terms, this means that you are always innovating and developing new, creative ways of attacking your marketplace. In your personal life, the principle of surprise is demonstrated when you move boldly out of your comfort zone and try completely different things from what you have done in the past. You know that "The more you do of what you're doing, the more you'll get of what you've got."

The eighth principle is that of "exploitation." In military terms this means aggressive follow-up and follow-through. In business this means that you sell all you can. You develop your markets fully. You do everything for your customers that you can possibly do, leaving nothing to chance. In your personal life, this means that you are totally committed to the full development of every aspect of your personality and your character. You never stop growing and becoming more and better.

The ninth principle is that of "security." In military terms security refers to the need to cover your base, to protect your back, to establish proper arrangements to assure that you are not caught off-guard by your enemy.

In business terms, this means that you never take a risk that you cannot afford to take, and that you continually do everything possible to assure the happiness and satisfaction of your best customers so that nothing happens to your business and to your cash flow.

In your personal life, the principle of security refers to your plans to adequately insure and provide against any untoward things that could happen to you or your family.

The tenth principle is the principle of "economy." In military terms, this means that you accomplish your objectives with the lowest possible expenditure of men and resources. In business terms, this requires that you are continually looking for ways to get the same results at the lowest possible cost. In personal terms, the principle of economy means that you are always looking for ways to achieve more with less, to reduce your costs of living and to do things in the most efficient way.

The eleventh principle of advanced thinking is the principle of "simplicity." In military terms, this means that the most effective plans are those that are the simplest and the least complicated to carry out. In business, the principle of simplicity demands that you always look for faster, easier, less complicated ways to achieve the same objective. In your personal life, the principle of simplicity can apply to many things, especially to simplifying your life so that you are doing a few things well rather than attempting to do many things, and doing many of them poorly.

These eleven principles are all vital to high achievement. The absence of any one of these principles can, in itself, be detrimental and even fatal to all your hopes.

All great business accomplishments are also based on the same eleven principles. Whenever you see a small business that grows rapidly and becomes a large business, you will find all eleven principles at work. Whenever you find an average person who begins to accomplish extraordinary things and achieve a wonderful life, you will find that they are consciously or unconsciously using all of these principles to a reasonably high degree.

We are living in an age of incredible opportunity and possibilities for the average person. Everything that you could ever want to know or want to become, you can learn by clearly specifying it in advance and then going to work on yourself and your situation. There are virtually no limits to what you can acquire, as long as you are clear about what it is you really want.

This brings us back to the first principle, the principle of the objective. The principle of the objective is the starting point of all great victories against overwhelming odds. And this does not simply refer to generals leading armies into battle. It refers to any entrepreneur, sales professional or businessman who is selling products and services in a highly competitive market.

I was discussing this principle with a group of entrepreneurs recently. I explained that all great victories are those that are won against overwhelming odds by superior thinking and deployment of resources. I then asked if they had any competition for their products or services in the local market. They all saw immediately that each one of them was competing with dozens, if not hundreds of other companies, all of whom were striving to get the same business. They were in the position of military commanders who were greatly outnumbered by vastly superior forces, fighting valiantly for market share, sales and profitability every single day. And you are exactly the same.

The principle of the objective means that you know exactly what it is you want to accomplish.

Some of the best questions that you can ask yourself repeatedly are questions such as, "What are you trying to do?" and, "How are you trying to do it?"

Asking yourself these questions, especially when things are not working out the way you anticipated, will help to clarify and focus your mind and thinking on your real objectives. "What are you trying to do and how are you trying to do it?" Another question you can ask to clarify your objectives is, "What are your assumptions?" "What are your conscious and unconscious assumptions? What are you assuming about the current situation that may or may not be true?"

Sometimes, people assume that, when they are negotiating with a customer for a product or service, the customer actually wants to buy the product or service from *them*. In reality, the customer could be negotiating with you for the sole reason of getting a lower price that he or she can use to buy the product or service that they want to from another company. What are *your* assumptions?

The rule is that errant or incorrect assumptions lie at the root of every mistake. What would you do, how would you change what you are doing if your current assumptions were wrong? What if the product or service that you are selling is not really appropriate for your current marketplace? What if your product or service was either overpriced or undervalued with the features and benefits needed by the marketplace today? If your product or service did not have the ability to achieve meaningful, competitive advantage in a tough market, what courses of action would that dictate to you and your company? What *are* your assumptions?

Another part of the principle of the objective is for you to think through who you really are. This is one of the most important questions you'll ever ask and answer, and accuracy is absolutely essential. Who *are* you? What do you believe in? What are your values? What do you stand for? What will you not stand for?

High performance only comes when your goals and plans on the outside are consistent and congruent with your values and beliefs on the inside.

Since you always accomplish on the outside what is consistent with the person you are on the inside, it is very important that you take the time to be absolutely clear about who you are, on the one hand, and what you really, *really* want on the outside. Only in this way can you master your mind and bring all your mental powers to bear on achieving on a high level.

Remember, the reason that most people fail is because they are fuzzy or unclear about what it is they really want and who it is they really are. Here's a question for you. What one great change would you make in your life today if you won a million dollars cash, tax free, in the lottery?

If you suddenly received a windfall of one million dollars cash, what would you do differently from what you are doing today? Whatever your answer to that question is, it can be very revealing in terms of what it is you really want, what it is you really believe in, what you stand for and most especially, the areas where you may be compromising yourself because of your perceived financial needs. How would you change your life if you had all the time and money in the world today?

The second principle I want to talk about is the principle of "intelligence." This means, as former President and CEO of ITT Corp., Harold Geneen said, "Get the facts!"

Geneen said that it was essential for you to get the real facts, the absolute truth, rather than the apparent facts, the assumed facts, the hoped-for facts or the wished-for facts.

Jack Welch, the former President and CEO of General Electric, perhaps one of the finest executives in America, says that the most important principle for leadership and high achievement is "The Reality Principle." The Reality Principle means that you see the world as it is, not as you wish it. You find out the actual reality of a situation before you make a decision.

The great majority of people in our society live in a world of delusion. They have wishes, hopes, fantasies and illusions about themselves and their world. Fully 90% of the population considers themselves to be in the top 10% of the population in terms of personality, intelligence, ability to influence others and attractiveness. Most people are highly deluded. However, this is not for you. Your starting point must be the solid foundation of truth and reality. You must absolutely refuse to delude yourself in any area.

The principle of intelligence means that you learn everything you need to learn about your work and your field. You read continually. You listen to audio programs in your car. You take additional courses. You subscribe to all the magazines and newsletters in your field and you read them from cover to cover.

The principle of intelligence means that you never stop learning, growing and absorbing new information and ideas in your field, because you know that one key idea is all that you need to give yourself a critical advantage in a competitive marketplace.

The third principle, the principle of the mass, or concentration, is the ability for you to set absolutely clear priorities on everything you do. The principle of concentration means that you have the ability to separate the vital and urgent from the unimportant and irrelevant. You have the ability to decide, in advance, the most important things that you could possibly be doing. You then have the discipline to do only those things until they are complete.

You have the willpower and mental strength to not give in to the temptation to clear up small things first. You always work from a list and you set priorities on the list before you begin. You always work on your highest value activities. You define the areas of your work and your life that are most important to your long-term success and you concentrate single-mindedly on those until you have mastered them and completed them.

The principle of concentration is so important that you cannot study it or practice it enough. You always ask yourself, "What is the most valuable use of my time right now?"

Every single day, you look into yourself and ask, "What can I, and only I, do, that if done well, will make a real difference?"

There are certain things that only you can do, and if you do them well, they will make a real difference to your life and work. Of course, if you neglect to do them, they will not get done and no one else will do them.

You have within you the mental abilities to accomplish extraordinary things. You have the ability to sit down and calmly think through your goals and objectives. You have the ability to develop absolute clarity about who you are and where you are going, and then to work in only those areas until you achieve the great things of which you are capable.

You have the unlimited ability to develop your intelligence to an extremely high level. You can learn anything you need to learn to achieve any goal you can set for yourself. You can develop any skill that can help you to move ahead more rapidly in your life. You can acquire any level of information. It is up to you to devote your life to continuous learning, because you know that continuous learning is the minimum requirement for success in any field.

Finally, you have the ability to concentrate single-mindedly on the most important things you can possibly do to achieve your goals. You have developed the self-discipline to hold your own feet to the fire. You have the inner resolve and the tenacity to stay with a major task until it is 100% complete. You know that, if you have every skill but the ability to finish your most important jobs, that all of your other skills will be ineffective.

This is a great world for us to live in. There have never been more opportunities or possibilities for you and I than exist today. But, throughout history, the men and women who have accomplished great things are those who have developed themselves to very high levels. The good news is that we all start off lacking these qualities and abilities. The even better news is that we can all learn and develop these qualities by clearly identifying them and practicing them until they become automatic. And when you master your mind and practice the principles of success practiced by the great men and women in history, your future will become unlimited.

About Brian

Brian Tracy is Chairman and CEO of Brian Tracy International, a company specializing in the training and development of individuals and organizations. Brian's goal is to help people achieve their personal and business goals faster and easier than they ever imagined.

Brian Tracy has consulted for more than 1,000 companies and addressed more than 5,000,000 people in 5,000 talks and seminars throughout the US, Canada and 55 other countries worldwide. As a Keynote speaker and seminar leader, he addresses more than 250,000 people each year.

For more information on Brian Tracy programs, go to: www.briantracy.com

CHAPTER 2

INTENTIONAL TRANSFORMATION

BY PAT STANGL

As an attorney, I take great pleasure in knowing I am able to help people through some of the most difficult times in their lives. Often, it's a time of change and transformation for them – a new lease on life so to speak. In my law practice I often hear things like, "I did not do what they say I did." "I am not guilty of what I am charged with…I will lose my job if… My spouse will leave me if…My reputation will be ruined if…" That is, if there is a conviction. These feelings spoken in a time of confusion, fear and emotional turmoil by clients who are charged with a crime, hang like a storm-laden cloud over their heads and are commonplace in my business, the business of being a trial lawyer devoted to defending those accused of crimes. I reassure them, "It will be OK; we'll get through this." As I look them in the eye I confidently state, "If you hire me I will do everything I can to help you."

It is vitally important for my client or potential client to truly feel my drive, determination and desire to help them and to provide them with the best possible representation. It is the same in any business, the customer must know that you care, they must know your passion for your given profession or line of work, and they must feel your commitment to them. First, however you must believe in yourself, because if you don't it will show and no one else will have confidence in your competence – no matter how good you may be at something.

Anytime you deal with people, you have the potential to influence their life and help them transform. I would like to share with you four very important principles that have allowed me to achieve a great deal of success in the people-helping business.

I. INTENDING GREAT RESULTS

When you have confidence in yourself and your particular skill set, you naturally and instinctively intend good results for your client and customers. The word intention can be defined broadly as a plan or a purpose. You plan on something happening, i.e., I plan to go to a movie this evening or my purpose is to get the best results for my client. When we think of intention, we often picture a kind of dogged determinism where we bite onto something, never letting go until we achieve the result we intend.

However, Dr. Wayne Dyer in his seminal book, *The Power of Intention*, defines intention differently; not as a dogged determinism but rather as a spiritual or energy source that can be harnessed to co-create your life. You can utilize this energy of intention to transform your business to achieve great results for your clients or customers. How do you do this? First, you need to get crystal clear about what it is you want to intend or achieve. Second, you need to take massive action; actually do something about it. If you want to achieve a particular result, you must take steps to manifest that intent. Intending a particular result is great, but without the right action it is a non-starter. Break down the goals which you intend to achieve into smaller achievable pieces and then build on those gains. Finally, you have to steadfastly believe and never waiver in that intention. You may suffer setbacks or it may seem that whatever you are intending isn't working or will never work, but you must continue to focus on that intention and think and act as if it has already happened. Visualize the new client or customer, visualize the new relationship, visualize the courtroom victory. The old saying, "As you think, so shall you go." is never more relevant than when dealing with the creative power of intention.

Let me give you an example. The year was 1993 and I was officially a lawyer for a little over two years when I started my own law firm. Mind you, I had no office, no money and no clients and, despite some experience in federal court, I had yet to try a federal case. That year

I was appointed by the court to represent a defendant in a federal fraud prosecution. My client was charged with submitting a false loan application for a federal loan by pledging collateral which was encumbered, meaning the collateral was not legally-owned outright by him. My client, a hardworking humble farmer, believed in good faith based upon representations made and documents provided to him by a cattle dealer, that he had in fact owned the collateral. However, through sleight of hand the seller retained legal ownership. The problem was my client signed the loan application and written in small print above the signature line was a statement that warned that it is a violation of federal law to make a false statement in a loan application. By signing the application the applicant was representing that the information provided in that application was true.

Now what? He signed the application and it was materially false. The case looked like a sure thing for the prosecution. I ran the case past my colleagues and the consensus was the same, don't try the case because you have no chance; plead him guilty and try to get him the best sentence. Yet, I couldn't. He was innocent. My client was steadfast and believed wholeheartedly that he owned the cattle. Indeed that was what he was told and if someone gives you their word and shows you legal papers it means something. In his mind it was simple; he did not submit a false loan application. The only chance we had was a good faith reliance defense – which luckily, under the charging statute, was a viable defense. Yes, we had a legal defense but that was a million miles away from a sure acquittal. Although at the time I didn't understand intention as I do today, looking back on that case I definitely intended a great result for my client. Despite the odds and what appeared to be all but a certain conviction for the government, I believed in my heart we could win. I wanted to win. I had to win or a great injustice would have occurred, an innocent man would have been convicted and sent to federal prison.

What did I do? Over the legal proceedings which ensued, piece by piece, bit by bit, I took massive action. I studied the Rules of Evidence like never before. I investigated. I interviewed witnesses. I dug. I read and then read more. I spent many late nights at the law library preparing for trial. I assiduously planned and wrote every question for each witness for direct and cross examinations, for my opening and my closing, and then I let go. I intended to win that case. I was confident I was as prepared as possible for trial. That is, as prepared as I could be for a lawyer with only one previous trial, an acquittal in state court. All I could do was everything I did for my client up to that point. After all, it was not my decision that would determine that humble farmer's fate.

We went to trial and as any trial goes it was a battle, up and down. My client testified and I was able to attack the credibility of the government's witnesses and the individual who sold the purported unencumbered cattle to my client. The case went to the jury. It was the longest wait of my client's life. The jury came back and the verdict was read. Not guilty! Looking back 20 plus years after the fact, it is clear to me that I intended a great result for that farmer and I applied massive action to that never wavering intent. Yes we had a few breaks along the way, but that is what can and will happen if you use the powerful energy force of intention to intend great results in your business and personal life.

II. MASTERING YOUR CRAFT

The word "master" has many definitions but the one most applicable to one's chosen profession or business is a person who is highly skilled or proficient or a person who has a particular expertise. I don't know if anyone ever truly masters their craft because when someone is a master it implies that there is nothing more. You did it, that's it. Rather, it is the intent to master one's craft, coupled with the desire for incessant improvement that results in proficiency and becoming highly skilled with a high level of expertise. Michelangelo once said, "If people knew how hard I worked to get my mastery; it wouldn't seem so wonderful at all." Simply put, there are no shortcuts or quick fixes. It requires commitment, very hard work and yes, there is that word again, "intention."

So how do you intend to become a master of your craft? Here are some guidelines. I suggest you read and absorb everything you can about your profession or business. You must make and take the time to learn and improve. In my field I am always reading books about trial tactics and strategies in addition to all the reading that is required in a trial practice including keeping up on changes in the law. As you work on becoming a master or expert in your field, learn from the best in your field and those who have gone before you. Attend seminars and conferences where the most successful people in your field will be speaking. Ask a lot of questions. People who excel at the highest levels in their field didn't get there by themselves and I have found they are more than willing to help, to answer questions and provide insight and guidance.

III. EXPERIENCE MATTERS

Pursuing the dream of mastering your craft requires time, practice and sacrifice. If you truly want to become the best in any field, you must make choices about how you spend your time. The only way to gain experience is to dedicate yourself to your work in your area of practice for an extended period of time. The trial I told you about earlier occurred over twenty years ago and since then I have tried many cases and in each of those cases I have worked to improve and master my craft but it is the collective experience of those individual cases which has pushed me further down the winding road on my journey of intending to master my craft.

Let me give you an example of the importance of experience. I recently tried a difficult case where my client was charged with driving while under the influence. While I intended to achieve a great result and win the case there were significant hurdles to overcome and I am not afraid to say we needed a little luck on our side. Indeed, the arresting law enforcement officer would testify that my client was driving a vehicle, registered to him, which he followed for approximately two blocks as he drove erratically through a hotel parking lot and exited onto a city street. After he stopped the vehicle my client allegedly alighted from it and took off running. My client insisted he was not the driver but rather his vehicle was being driven by an acquaintance he had met that evening who happened to be wearing a similar long sleeved shirt. I knew from handling hundreds of criminal cases that statements made by an officer in a police report and that officer's sworn testimony do not always match up with the physical evidence in the case.

While the State had a circumstantial case that put my client behind the wheel I hoped that what little physical evidence existed, namely the dispatch logs and photographs would show something different. I obtained the dispatch logs and they showed that the arresting officer never made his initial call into dispatch to report the incident of him following the vehicle until later that evening in direct contradiction of his trial testimony. Moreover, the officer could have activated his in squad camera and captured the whole event but inexplicitly did not. The same officer had taken numerous photographs of my client's vehicle but careful attention to detail demonstrated the photographs were taken before, not after, the initial dispatch call was made. Armed with the dispatch tape and the photographs, which the prosecution elected not to use, I waited patiently. On cross-examination, I was able to demonstrate that the officer was clearly mistaken about the events of the evening – which brought his whole testimony into question. Was his story about what had happened credible? The jury didn't think so and my client was acquitted of the drunk driving charges. My point is that there is simply no substitute for experience when it comes to the hard work of intending to master your craft.

IV. VALUE RELATIONSHIPS

Because of the 1993 case I mentioned earlier, I developed a professional relationship with the judge in that proceeding. It was a unique relationship because he had a reputation of being extremely hard on attorneys in the courtroom. He would seemingly pick on certain attorneys and I think he could sense their fear. If you were intimidated by him in any way, he knew it. Most attorneys did not like going in front of him but I loved it, and it seemed to all develop from that first trial I had with him.

In all the cases that I appeared before him after that initial trial, he knew I was always well prepared and he respected that. He would still "let me have it" every once in a while, because that's just how he was. He actually ended up helping me in that first trial when I was a young lawyer. You see, when you're a young lawyer, it's sometimes difficult to form questions that aren't objectionable. So, a lot of my initial questions were being objected to because they weren't in the proper form. He essentially did me a favor by calling counsel up to the bench and giving me a tip. He said, "The questions counsel is asking are relevant and appropriate, they just need to be phrased in a different way." That was a real learning experience that helped me in that particular case as well as in the hundreds of other cases in which I would subsequently be involved, and I will never forgot the value of what he did.

Appearing in front of that judge was not something most other attorneys valued. But, it's important to see the value and contribution of every person in your realm of connections. Learn from others, even if they are hard to understand or get along with. Value your relationship with them as well as with those that are more pleasant. Relationships give you the opportunity to grow and transform and also enable you to help and influence others so they can grow and transform.

My experience has shown me that transformation takes place when we

- Intend Great Results
- Master Our Craft
- Gain and Use Our Experience
- Value Relationships

By practicing these principles, Transformation is inevitable.

About Pat

Pat Stangl helps his clients tell their stories to judges and juries. As the sole owner of Stangl Law Offices, S.C., a statewide criminal defense and civil litigation law firm with offices in Madison and Northern Wisconsin, Pat focuses on defending those accused of crimes including those charged with driving while impaired. He has successfully defended numerous criminal cases including cases ranging in complexity from first degree intentional homicide to drug conspiracies, fraud, domestic and sensitive crimes to disorderly conduct. Having successfully defended over one hundred drunk-driving cases, he is well regarded by his peers as an excellent trial lawyer and has represented clients in civil and criminal cases in federal courts in Wisconsin, Minnesota, Indiana and California.

Pat also practices appellate law having argued in front of the Wisconsin Supreme Court and the United States Court of Appeals for the Seventh Circuit. He has a number of published appellate opinions in both state and federal Courts of Appeal. Articles about some of his cases have appeared in newspapers across the nation including *USA Today, The Wall Street Journal,* the *Chicago Sun Times, The Seattle Times,* the *Wisconsin State Journal* and many other publications and blogs.

Since 2012, Pat has been named yearly as one of the top 100 trial attorneys among all civil plaintiffs and criminal defense attorneys in Wisconsin by the National Trial Lawyers. The National Trial Lawyers is an invitation-only organization with membership invitations extended to the select most qualified attorneys from each state who exemplify superior qualifications of leadership, reputation, influence, stature and profile.

When he is not working, Pat loves spending time with his wife, Heidi, and their family and friends. Additional information about Pat and Stangl Law Offices, S.C. can be found at: www.stangllaw.com or by calling Pat's office directly at: 608-831-9200.

CHAPTER 3

PEOPLE ARE THE CATALYST

BY LOU RAY ROBINSON

What you leave behind is not what is engraved in stone monuments,
but what is woven into the lives of others.
~ Pericles

My road to West Point and ultimately as a coach and mentor has been an interesting one filled with increasingly transforming experiences across the globe. Growing up, I consistently faced people telling me what I could or could not do. Those encounters shaped me into a person driven to lead others to their best in spite of any obstacle. My journey started the year I was born, when my mother, a retired Army E-8, joined the Army. She was a single mother and I was the oldest of three. I held things together at home while she worked long hours giving us a greater opportunity than she had growing up poor. During our journeys across the globe, she stressed very important themes I have carried with me throughout my life:

1) Go to school, get good grades, go to college or join the Air Force

2) Nothing is more important than family, and

3) Take care of each other no matter what.

As long as I can remember, I've been taking care of people. I watched over my sisters, protected the bullied, tutored, and led, managed, and encouraged hundreds of people, creating plans for organizations around the globe. Creating these bonds to partner with others in their growth has been the core of my being my entire life. By the age of 18, I had lived in seven states and three countries. Adapting to such change in my life afforded me the increased opportunity to meet and help a diverse crowd of people and caused significant self-transformation.

At my third high school, I met a West Point cadet and one of many challenges to what I was capable of accomplishing. Instead of getting to know who I was on the inside, this fellow JROTC cadet did not like my outward achievements and told me I would never make it at West Point. I never planned to apply as I had aspirations to become an FBI agent not an Army Officer. Nevertheless, to prove him wrong, I did, and a recruiter convinced me that West Point was my best path to the agency. I joined the Law Enforcement Tactics Club, the Rifle Drill Team, became a powerlifter, and after being on the Color Guard, became Captain of the Color Guard in my final year. Before graduating with a B.S. in Computer Science, I tutored and guided many in math and computers. As an officer, I inspired soldiers to many achievements, led the officer strength-building program, and built long lasting relationships with many across the globe. Promotions led me to varying experiences including leading a team responsible for the entire fiber backend in Korea, and supporting military intelligence operations at Fort Hood, TX. I led teams of ten, thirty, and a hundred people. In each experience, I practiced and developed my relational skills. My military experience led me to the Pentagon as a member of the global strategic planning team for the Air Force Chief Technical Officer. Here I found myself training officers and continuing my passion to help people. It is during my time at the Pentagon that I decided to pursue more formal mentorship training. I decided to pursue a Master's degree to develop a roadmap to help others achieve their aspirations.

Even at such a high level in my career, I continued to face judgments from others who assumed that just by looking at me, I could not be a representative in a group of high ranking civilian officials. I happen to be far more diverse than what labels like Veteran, or Army Officer or West Pointer might say about me. One boss told me he never met a West Pointer he liked. Later, he retracted his statement. I happen to be a Seminarian preparing for Ordainment (the initial path I took to develop my passion for mentorship) and receive questions about how I could be a soldier and a minister simultaneously. In many contexts people assume who I am, where I belong, or what I can do or am capable of – based on a label. At eighteen, an adult who should have been encouraging and mentoring me asked me why I, as an African-American, would join an Army for a country that did not accept us. I simply told her if one of us does not try to succeed, how could any of us? Once, I met either Simon or Garfunkel, who asked me how I could be a woman in the military. As a peace promoting team, I can only assume they asked for that reason. At the Pentagon, a Colonel wrote me a seven-page letter detailing how women could not preach. I honestly respect that he cared that much to mentor me, but he was wrong in two cases. Not only was my goal to counsel soldiers which Army Chaplains do 80% of the time, he was incorrect in his reasoning. We can be pretty strong too! I recall amazement at my ability to do seventy-two push-ups and ninety sit-ups in two minutes in the military, and I would always respond with the fact that my mother could do 100 push-ups in two minutes far surpassing me!

Maybe when you read about my West Point or military experiences you thought I was a woman. Maybe you thought I was strong. Maybe neither crossed your mind. Maybe it was strange for you to hear that I was in seminary or thought it was strange someone would dare tell me who I couldn't be. Even as a 0.01% minority at West Point in the 90s, I was hired at the Pentagon by a 1972 graduate and found myself making the same assumptions that I have encountered in my career while I looked for a tall blond haired blue-eyed interviewer who was a minority himself. No affiliation can fully define the whole of who I am, who anyone is nor what you or I can offer. Moving from place to place and working with people from all around the globe, transformation was continuous. I have overcome adversities and learned from my failures and successes to get the results I have achieved. These experiences helped me understand people at a deeper level and, as a result, I developed a specific skill set that has given me the ability to guide people towards their personal goals and synch them with their organization's goals. This linkage is one of the cornerstones to sustainable organizational success regardless of size, profit or non-profit status, or location.

There was an important lesson in my own false assumptions teaching me to help people learn more about who I really am by getting to know who they really are. I started to teach others how to do the same as it is in the resulting relationship that organizations can finally create passion within people to drive towards organizational goals. Most people can resonate with what my family tried to teach me about taking care of others. The bonds formed in healthy or strong relationships are the bonds that cause people to rally behind each other and support each other in the good times and bad. If there is a person or group of people in your life that will back you up or that you would back up or help through most storms, that connection is the type of bond that helps drive teams, and thus, organizations on towards their vision.

This is the message for this chapter. As you try to maintain control of your business or whatever goal you are pursuing and you let those goals control or guide your path to success, there is a cornerstone to success that must accompany you on that path. Without it, the ground you gain can be for naught when you find yourself searching for the missing tool that will clear the rest of your path to success. That tool is the skill that builds mutually supportive relationships with people whose relationships will carry you through your journey. The practice to effectively build relationships on a deeper level with others is a skill you must continuously build. These experiences can leave leaders blind to diverse thoughts, innovations, or hidden contributions that we never tap into as leaders focus on the business and forget to grow people and grow with people. Therefore, in summary of my experiences above, I have defined five simple points you can refer to along your path to achieving your goals. These points will help you maintain the type of relationships that will allow you to tap into a wealth of insight, support, and sustainable actions that you can build your goals upon:

1. Be ***in Communication*** with the people around you to start to get to know who they are and what diverse ideas they can contribute to the overall goal in partnership with you.

2. Be ***in Connection*** with the wants and needs of others and, as much as you can, provide for those needs, showing them that who they are matters— igniting the will to support the very organization (family) that supports them.

3. Be the **_Encouragement_** people need to do great things so that you can maintain that connection.

4. Be **_in Collaboration_** with the people you work with, especially those that work for you, inspiring their need to feel like they are a part of accomplishing something great and, thus, tap in to what each person can uniquely offer.

5. **_In Compromise_**, be willing to settle. If, for example, you can get three of your top five by giving others three of their top five, then go for it, creating a win-win situation that strengthens that bond you are trying to achieve with others.

Whether you find yourself at the very bottom of an organization or at the top, at home, or even in a short-term relationship you can apply these five points. This is a long-term, life-long strategy you implement on your team, in your organization, or in your group. Remember, in the toughest of times they will always follow who they believe in, because in consistently implementing these five points over time you give them the passion to act and partner with you. They will have your back, and in giving what they can give of themselves, you will find the missing ideas, innovations, or work ethic that will take you to that next level. No one can believe in a person nor follow that person around blind corners if they cannot connect. Connection is the precursor to trust. People are social beings and must be able to connect with others on some level in order to gain trust. Communication, connection, collaboration, and compassion cannot occur if you treat a person as if they are expendable and treat your interaction with them as a temporary necessity on your way to achieving your goals. Not only can you destroy their spirit to stand behind you, the mission, or the task at hand, it can cause an unexpected detour when you arrive on top with no one to sustain you there. Compassion is not on my list because I cannot teach you to have compassion for others as this comes from within. If you are a person of compassion, combine what you have learned about compassion to the points. If you are not, learn and apply some of the key concepts from key writings about transformational or spiritual leadership. The best instruction I have found in this area comes from authors Jim Kouzes and Barry Posner in their 1999 work *Encouraging the Heart: A Leader's Guide to Rewarding and Recognizing Others*.

These skills are only a catalyst of success. You must build strengths in the other pillars of leadership success that you will find as you study and practice other transformational leadership skills. As you continue to develop your relational skills with others consider that ultimately supporting the greater good of others will ultimately rally others towards your own goals. Some may get lost in imitation thoughts that they alone created their success. Success cannot be sustained alone. Life was not meant to be tackled alone. Woven fabrics are strong because of how they are interlaced, and so the same with what results from mutually-supporting relationships. I have learned not to linger in any discouragement resulting from those who are not receptive to my attempts to connect. Every attempt to connect or build relationships may not be successful, however, as a long-term plan, the amount of successes will give you the stepping stone for the support you need. Use connection failures as opportunities to build your relational skills. As I have found great success in helping others achieve their own goals, I hope that my insights will help you because as you help others achieve, you will achieve.

About Lou Ray

Lou Ray Robinson is a Veteran Army Officer currently working to build a business coaching platform that will benefit businesses in the areas of people growth. Lou Ray is a graduate of the United States Military Academy at West Point with a degree in Computer Science.

Lou Ray is highly relatable due to an eclectic and diverse background that includes being a mentor for a group of people with the highest suicide rate in the country, learning to read Hebrew, Greek, and French, and even powerlifting. Lou Ray is also a Seminarian finishing up her final two courses for her Organizational Leadership Master's Degree in order to pursue other interests outside of the coaching platform. These interests include Chaplaincy in the Army Reserves and leadership over a large organization. Well-traveled across 39 States and 9 countries, including assignments in Korea, Fort Hood, and at the Pentagon, Lou Ray's experience generates a unique combination of expertise that includes over 16 years of substantial leadership experience.

Lou Ray's passion is to help individuals achieve their best in spite of the current circumstances they may find themselves in. Lou Ray's slogan is *People First, Mission Always*.

You can connect with Lou Ray at:
mail to: TheRobinsonSolution-Transformed@yahoo.com
www.linkedin.com/in/louray/
www.TheRobinsonSolution.com

CHAPTER 4

FROM CATERPILLAR TO BUTTERFLY: MY LIFE-CHANGING TRANSFORMATION

BY JANETTE GLEASON

January 4, 2010, I remember the day vividly. Our Christmas tree was still up in our living room, evergreen wreaths and other decorations adorned our walls, and new toys sprinkled the rooms in our house. While the kids were still basking in the glow of their Christmas wishes coming true, I held anxiety in the pit of my stomach, but tried to keep a happy face. With the economic uncertainty, our family-owned small business (financial planning and tax preparation) took a hit like many other small businesses across the country at that time. Christmas was anything but merry for me that year. With our debt climbing from medical bills, household expenses and small business needs, I was overwhelmed with wondering how we would manage to keep it all going. As a stay-at-home mom, it started to bother me that I couldn't contribute to my family's financial stability.

As I went about caring for our three young children and keeping our house in order that day, a man knocked on our front door. Deep down I knew who it was, but I didn't want to face the music. Keeping my chin up, I opened the door and awaited the bad news as he started to look around the inside of our home, taking it all in and surveying all that he could see. "How can I help you?" I bravely asked him. "Ma'am, your house was sold at auction today. I am now the owner. I'm ready to take possession and expect you to be completely moved out in two weeks or else I will take legal action." He handed me some papers from his attorney mandating that we leave the house in good condition.

There we were at rock bottom—feeling hurt, ashamed and hopeless. We had only a hundred dollars in our bank account, nowhere to live, and no reasonable way out of this mess. My husband, Joe, and I gave up control to a higher power to keep our family safe and provide us a new opportunity for growth.

Within a week, we had completely moved out of the house, fixed up our little rental house and began a new chapter together as a family…One that would bring me closer to my husband and to our children…One that would reveal our true friends and the forces working behind the scenes to change everything for me. It was a new chapter that would lead to some unexpected, **life-changing transformations** – for our business and for me personally.

> *Just when the caterpillar thought the world*
> *was over, it became a butterfly.*
> ~ Proverb

Out of necessity, we turned to the resources we had – our persistent attitude, our business and our database. Throughout the years, we had spent hundreds of thousands of dollars acquiring the names of our leads, prospects and clients. As we could no longer afford to spend $10,000 per month on marketing and advertising, we were forced to get creative and resourceful! We had current tax and financial clients who loved us and also had collected the names of so many who indicated interest in our services at one time. I thought, "Let's see what happens if we turn our attention to them!"

I began to tinker with Infusionsoft, the sales and marketing automation software program we had been using for a couple of years, and quickly realized we were only skimming the surface of the software's true capabilities. I watched every tutorial and video in Infusionsoft's online help center and participated in many of the educational webinars to learn how to apply all of its features in our small business. My husband affectionately referred to me as his "mad scientist" while I was conjuring up new follow-up sequences and automated email campaigns while also creating systems for our office procedures.

Joe and I immediately began to see things turn around in our business, and I had a brand-new hobby! It was an exciting new hobby that had me waking up in the middle of the night to head to my computer to implement as much as I could. I had fallen in love with marketing and this amazing software program.

Within 30 days, we had created effective new marketing campaigns and had automated processes for our tax practice. By utilizing only email marketing, we were able to fill more than 800 tax appointments. That tax season, we had nearly doubled our revenue and had slashed our marketing budget down to $500 per month.

Feeling a spark of hope and an enormous sense of pride, I decided to enter Infusionsoft's "Ultimate Marketer" contest. I had seen advertisements for the contest and thought, "Why not? I've accomplished so much in such a short amount of time. I'd love to share my story with Infusionsoft!"

I began to practice positive thinking and visualization to create a mindset for winning. As I filled out responses in the contest application, I poured out my heart writing about the wonderful results we were experiencing by utilizing Infusionsoft and lifecycle marketing strategies. I explained how Infusionsoft had given me hope again and expressed my heartfelt gratitude for those life-changing turn of events. I felt incredibly blessed to be given the opportunity to continue to stay home with our children and be able to work and contribute to our small business in a way that wasn't possible before. I submitted my application with various samples of our marketing and crossed my fingers!

When I received the call from Infusionsoft telling me I was one of three finalists who would be presenting at its annual conference, I couldn't believe this was actually happening to me! I knew that preparing my presentation was going to be one of the most important things I would ever do and that I would be there for a greater purpose. If a stay-at-home mom could learn this software, implement these marketing strategies and see quick results, surely anyone could!

I felt compelled to inspire the thousands of small business owners at the conference to take action just as I had done. While I didn't walk away as the "Ultimate Marketer 2011" that year, I won just the same. A new opportunity and business was born for me - one that would transform my life forever.

Other small business owners began to approach me, asking if I could help them like I helped my husband with his business. What first began as a hobby turned into part-time work, then full-time, and is now a full-fledged business with a team in place! I have worked with hundreds of small business owners in a wide variety of industries to revamp their marketing and implement campaigns in Infusionsoft.

> *We delight in the beauty of a butterfly, but rarely admit*
> *the changes it had to go through to achieve that beauty.*
> ~ Maya Angelou

Over the years, Joe and I have enhanced our customer nurture campaign for our tax preparation and financial planning business. Now I teach my clients these same simple, yet effective strategies and present at workshops and conferences to help other small business owners implement them as well! I specialize in helping my clients keep top-of-mind awareness with their leads, prospects, customers and referral partners so they are the first people their contacts think of when they are ready to buy or refer. Here are the tactics:

1. **Monthly Nurture Emails**: I encourage my clients to send monthly holiday greetings to their databases. A simple "Happy Thanksgiving" email with a favorite recipe or a "Happy Valentine's Day" note with a special poem is a great way to stay in touch with their prospects and clients all year long. Making these communications entertaining and personal helps my clients' contacts get to know them better and feel connected.

2. **Printed Newsletters**: Small business owners can build trust with their contacts by sending a monthly printed newsletter delivered right to the mailboxes of their prospects and/or clients. One of my coaches taught me that 60% of the newsletter content should be non-industry specific. Including highlights from a recent family vacation, thoughtful recipes, comics, games and puzzles helps prospects and clients know, like and trust the small business owner better.

3. Events: Hosting events for prospects and/or clients regularly can keep them educated about services, products or trends and lets them know how much they are appreciated. An event could be a promotion, a sale, a webinar or an in-person gathering. The sky's the limit! Most of all, have fun and enjoy the time spent building these important relationships.

4. Birthday Greetings: Saying "Happy Birthday" to customers with a special email, a card or even a personalized gift can make a huge and lasting impact. They will appreciate being remembered on their special day!

5. Special Touches: Letting customers know how much they're appreciated is easy with special touches such as a welcome gift, a new customer kit or a postcard reminder. Joe and I send our new clients a delicious box of brownies to welcome them into our family of clients. Unexpected gifts and touches can go a long way towards solidifying relationships with new and existing customers.

You, too, can implement these tactics into your marketing strategies. Once you do, you will begin to see results within a few months' time. From the work I've done with my clients, I can tell you that it typically happens in four to six months. After hitting that mark, your business will grow noticeably.

We do not need magic to transform our world. We carry all the power we need inside ourselves already. We have the power to imagine better.
~ JK Rowling

As for my personal transformation, I've learned some key techniques to keep me focused on my goals and to create what I want to experience next.

Here are some tips to help you clearly identify your desires and how to achieve them:

1. Focus: Set goals by getting super-focused about the experience you'd like to create next. I make long-term plans for the future, but I set goals that can be achieved within six to 12 months. That makes it easier to focus and more realistic to achieve them. Create notebooks, posters and vision boards with words and pictures describing your heart's desires.

2. **Gain support**: You cannot create alone! Get support and advice to achieve your goals by joining a mastermind group for business advice and accountability, hiring coaches to keep you motivated and moving in the right direction, and finding peers to encourage and uplift you.

3. **Repeat positive affirmations**: Since thoughts become things, be careful about the thoughts you choose and the words you speak. I make a conscious effort to think positive thoughts by reading daily affirmations and listening to upbeat and inspiring songs.

4. **Practice visualization**: Each night as you are falling asleep, imagine yourself experiencing the life you want to live or achieving your goal. The most important thoughts you have each day are the ones you hold in your mind right before falling asleep. These are the thoughts that stay with you all through the night while you rest and sleep. They become deeply ingrained in your subconscious mind.

5. **Stay grounded**: In this day and age with so much technology, distractions and stress, it's important to stay grounded. I recommend getting regular exercise, taking walks, washing dishes, dancing and cooking to stay grounded and connected with the earth.

6. **Say the Ho'oponopono prayer**: Live with forgiveness by saying this Hawaiian prayer to make things right with your current problems or troubled relationships. Hold that person or situation in your mind and say, "I love you. I'm sorry. Please forgive me. Thank you." You will notice how problems get resolved easily or correct themselves with very little or no effort by you.

7. **Express gratitude**: Practice expressing your gratitude daily. Say "thank you" often through your words and actions. Whether you write a thoughtful email, send a handwritten card or give a shout-out to someone on Facebook, remember to let others know how thankful you are for them!

A wonderful blessing that has emerged from my recent transformational experiences has been having the opportunity to inspire and motivate others to achieve their goals, to create their dream lifestyles, too!

I feel so incredibly blessed to be living my dream lifestyle as a mompreneur. As a stay-at-home mom AND an entrepreneur, I am living the best of both worlds! Each day is a wonderful adventure filled with love, gratitude, success, joy and hope.

About Janette

An award-winning entrepreneur, Janette Gleason takes great pride in empowering people to create their dream lifestyles. After the small business she and her husband, Joe, owned faced financial struggles, Janette turned things around with the help of Infusionsoft, a sales and marketing software program. Within 30 days, she completely overhauled the business's marketing strategy using the Infusionsoft applications. Her creativity and results-driven campaigns led her to be named one of Infusionsoft's 2011 Ultimate Marketer Finalists as well as its 2013 Big Drive Winner.

In addition to being the founder and CEO of Gleason Consulting Group, LLC, Janette and Joe own and manage three other small businesses: Gleason Financial Group, LLC; Gleason Tax Advisory Group, LLC; and Gleason Investment Advisory Group, LLC. With a strong background in database marketing, she assists her companies and other small business owners with creating campaigns and systems that nurture prospects and help retain existing clients.

Janette grew up in the suburbs of Chicago and attended Augustana College in Rock Island, Illinois, where she graduated *Magna Cum Laude*, earning her Bachelor of Arts degree in Elementary Education and Spanish. After her 10-year teaching career, Janette became a stay-at-home mom to care for her family and support her autistic son. Now as a Mompreneur, Janette balances her work and family life so she can enjoy the best of both worlds.

Today, Janette strives to help others, particularly women and mothers, to find their heart's desire and to create their dream lifestyle. In addition to being a co-author of *Transform,* Janette is the author of *Confessions of a Mompreneur: My Journey from Stressed-Out, Stay-at-Home Mom to Successful Entrepreneur.*

Janette currently resides in Surprise, Arizona, with Joe, their three children and their dog, Buddy. When she isn't running one of their small businesses, consulting with clients or being "Mom," Janette enjoys reading, sewing, traveling and spending time with friends and family.

To learn more about and connect with Janette:
Visit http://www.janettegleason.com
Find her on Facebook at: www.facebook.com/gleasonconsulting
Follow her on Twitter @janettegleason

CHAPTER 5

PREPARING FOR A TRANSFORMED ECONOMY

BY DENISE LONGSHAW

Being a long time follower of Brian Tracy, when I received the invitation to co-author a book with him I was ecstatic! Brian is my idol. I have been reading his books and listening to his audio recordings since I was a teenager. My immediate thought was to find the very first audio cassette, The Psychology of Success that I listened to when I was first introduced to Brian's work back in 1989. I was excited when I found the cassette, but to my dismay I could not find a cassette tape player to listen to it. This dilemma made the topic of this book even clearer. Things change and the world has transformed. No longer are there cassette players and change is taking place in almost every aspect of our lives at a very rapid pace. Are you prepared for all the transformation that is taking place? Are you prepared to transform along with it?

My goal and purpose in my profession is to help pre-retirees and retirees through this transformation process by assisting them with developing the proper financial strategy that will enable them to enjoy a successful retirement. I began my financial services career in 2003 as a Financial Advisor with VALIC Financial Advisors, working primarily with State of Florida employees who are members of the Florida Retirement System (FRS). Always seeking to improve and expand in my profession, I went on to gain a broad knowledge of the industry by working with a variety of well-respected companies.

I then combined my accumulated knowledge and established my own firm, the Longshaw Financial Group, to better serve my clients. I established my own financial practice to fulfill a growing need among Baby Boomers who seek a solid retirement strategy and a personalized approach to financial planning to help them achieve the financial security and independence they desire. The Baby Boomer generation is a unique group in that they have probably seen more financial change in a relatively short period of time than any other generation.

As you know simply by your daily participation in the country's economy, the financial world of the 2000's is so much different than it was even in the late 1900's. There have been huge changes in how retirement planning is done, and I suspect in the next ten to twenty years we will see even more unique changes to this very important area of people's lives. Let's consider some of the important national financial transformations that have taken place and how we must transform to face these changes.

THE SOCIAL SECURITY DILEMMA

Have you ever considered how the Social Security system has transformed since its inception? When the Social Security Act was passed in 1935 as part of President Roosevelt's "New Deal" with America, it was based on certain mathematical and demographic information that needed to remain fairly constant in order for the plan to have longevity. When it was first implemented those that drafted the numbers based them on expected birth rates and life expectancies.

Following is some of the information that led the proponents of this legislation to believe in this program. In 1935 there were 42 workers putting money into Social Security for every one that was drawing money out. That seemed to work well. Another astounding fact is that the government established retirement age at 65 when the average life expectancy at that time was only 62. If someone did live until they were 65, it was highly unlikely they would live too many years beyond which also safeguarded the system. No one ever anticipated people living into their 80's and 90's when this law was enacted.

How has Social Security transformed? According to the Social Security Administration website, today there are only 3 people contributing to

Social Security for every 1 person drawing money out. It is projected that in 10 years that ratio will be 2 to 1. Additionally, people can now begin drawing Social Security at age 62 if they choose to do so. So the ratio of people contributing to people drawing money out is extensively narrower, retirees are withdrawing money from the system earlier, and people are living much longer.

Add to this scenario that Social Security is actually costing the Federal Government over $700 billion a year which is equivalent to an astounding 20% of their budget. Yes, Social Security has changed. In fact, did you know that the Social Security program was never designed to be a retirement program; it was originally simply an insurance program in case people happened to live beyond the age of 65.

What does all this information mean for us today? Simply this; the Social Security program is in deep trouble and we need to take that into consideration when planning for retirement. People once depended on Social Security to sustain them. However, that can no longer be the strategy for retirement. It may be a factor in the strategy, but it is inevitably becoming less of a factor than in times past.

THE GREATEST CHALLENGE IN THE HISTORY OF THE UNITED STATES

Within the last fifty years, the world has transformed from the advent of women's liberation with mothers in the work force to globalization and technological changes at lightning speed. In fact, it is almost impossible to keep up with the transformation. However, there is one important change that occurred and it is still occurring. Unfortunately, many people do not seem to realize the severity of the situation and how it can affect them. The situation I am referring to is America's Debt Crisis!

America has transformed! Do you remember when American was the largest lender nation? Now America is the largest borrower. As of this writing, the U.S. national debt stands at $17,515,512,933,376.00 and will be substantially higher by the time this book is published.

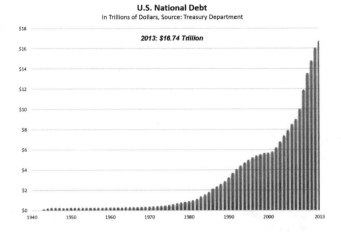

U.S. National Debt
In Trillions of Dollars, Source: Treasury Department

2013: $16.74 Trillion

In 2012, I met Mr. David Woods, the former comptroller of the United States Accounting Office. For several years now Mr. Woods has been sounding the alarm about the U.S. Government debt and the trillions of dollars of unfunded debt. This is a man that has personally given oversight to the financial statements of the government. It is astounding to watch our debt rise continuously. If you haven't seen the debt clock yet I encourage you to see the numbers for yourself at: www.usdebtclock.org. The debt clock is explicit evidence that we face an impending crisis in the near future.

When someone is in debt they reduce their spending, increase their revenue or, as a last resort, file bankruptcy. It is plausible but unlikely that the U.S. Government will file bankruptcy. It is also unlikely that it will cut spending, because of the promised benefits and unavoidable strain that the aging population will put on the system as 77 million baby boomers file claims for social security and escalating health care costs as demand for Medicare benefits increase. In addition, the government must pay the interest, not the principal, on the debt to our creditors (countries such as China and Japan) and this could account for about one-third of our country's spending. Therefore, the most likely answer is Higher Taxes! The Government will very likely raise taxes in the near future. This is perfect timing for Uncle Sam but very unfortunate for Baby Boomers who will be tapping their retirement accounts and must pay taxes on these distributions that have been growing tax deferred for up to the last thirty or more years.

I would like to impress upon you to really pay attention because it is pertinent that you begin to prepare now. It is important that you transform your thinking, transform your actions, and transform your life now as you brace for the impact of Higher Taxes!

TAX DEFERRED INVESTING – GOOD OR NOT SO GOOD?

One thing that many people that are saving for retirement have in common is the majority of their retirement savings are in a tax-deferred vehicle, such as a 401k, 403b, 457 plan, IRA, SEP etc. The historical Wall Street strategy and industry norm has been to encourage investors to enroll in their employer's tax deferred retirement plan because when you retire you will be in a lower tax bracket.

As a retirement consultant, my primary clients are baby boomers and Florida public sector employees. My experience has been when I help clients to retire, most often, they are not in a lower tax bracket because they need to live on the same amount of income they had before they retired. Realizing this, I had to transform my practice and strategies to teach my clients how to transform along with these changes so they can have a secure retirement future and prepare for the tax impact that could be brewing.

It is very important for retirees to understand that, by law, they must begin at age 70½ taking a Minimum Required Distribution from their tax deferred retirement accounts even if they don't need the money. The government requires you to take at least a minimum distribution based on a predetermined formula. This distribution has an impact on retirees in two ways. First, it reduces the amount of their investment. Secondly, the distribution is taxable at the current tax rate.

If the owner of a tax deferred account passes away, the money in that account will go to the designated beneficiary. That beneficiary will then be responsible for paying the taxes on the distribution received based on their tax bracket. Keep in mind that if a beneficiary receives a lump sum payment from a tax deferred account, it will likely boost them into a higher tax bracket and they will have to pay taxes on the distribution based on that higher tax bracket. However, if it was in a tax-free account, it would be free and clear for the beneficiary. No income tax payment would be due.

Since there is now a great likelihood that the tax rate for retirees may very possibly increase in the not too distant future, a larger portion of their spendable income will be lost. If you have to begin taking money from a taxable account, and your tax rate is higher, then your spending power will be diminished. That is why I encourage people to consider tax-free accounts.

Tax consideration as it relates to retirement planning is crucial when developing a long-term financial strategy. There are specific strategies that pre-retirees and retirees need to consider when they are still in the accumulation phase of their life as well as when they begin drawing money from their retirement accounts. In the present day economy, I strongly believe people need to think about investing in tax-free vehicles as part of their retirement portfolio. A correct retirement strategy will enable them to maximize the use of their money for the longest period of time possible with the ultimate goal of never running out of money in their lifetime.

THE PERFECT STORM

There is a perfect storm brewing. Baby Boomers are beginning to retire at the astounding rate of 10,000 per day. Not only are they beginning to draw money from the market to support them during their retirement years, but also they are now tapping into their Social Security benefit that they have contributed to for the past 45 years. This is placing a tremendous burden on the potential endurance of the Social Security system. Add to this the growing national debt, which will very likely result in an increase in taxation. Consider the risk of inflation, a 3% annual inflation rate equates to a 30% loss of purchasing power within 10 years. Some economist are predicting future hyperflation. An increase in the rate of inflation can have a devastating effect on the income of a retiree. This is a game changer. Our nation has never experienced a phenomenon like this in its entire history. The convergence of these factors is creating an environment for the perfect storm that will have a tremendous impact on every person in the country.

PREPARING FOR THE STORM

So, where do you turn for help in preparing for this inevitable storm that is brewing? Keep in mind that properly preparing for this storm will require extensive planning and forethought. What you do with your money has to be about planning, not just putting money into an account.

When I first entered the financial services business I was trained to sell product. I was instructed to have a transaction orientation. However, as I matured in the business, I learned the difference between simply making an investment transaction and developing a retirement planning strategy. It was an eye-opening transformation for me. I learned how I could better serve my clients and direct them to make wise investment decisions based on what was going to be most beneficial to them in the long term. Find an advisor who will look at your entire financial picture and one who understands how to structure a portfolio with the proper mix of taxable, tax-deferred and tax-free accounts.

Unfortunately there are many financial advisors that are simply transaction oriented and don't take into consideration the potential tax ramifications for the client or their heirs. A transaction-based advisor will simply be looking for money to roll over into another account. It is imperative that you stay away from transaction-oriented advisors.

You may ask, "How can I know if someone is a transaction based advisor?" I would suggest asking the advisor questions about tax-deferred versus tax-free investments and why the investment he or she is recommending to you is in your best interest. A transaction-oriented advisor will likely not have straight answers to your questions. While this isn't a foolproof methodology, it may help you discern what type of advisor you are talking to. It is also a good idea to find out who successful people you know are using as their tax advisor and why they are using them. Keep in mind that just because someone is using a financial advisor, in itself, doesn't make the advisor good or bad. But the experience others have with an advisor may be some of the best information you can receive in your quest to find a qualified advisor. Ask questions about why they use their advisor and listen for reasons surrounding tax-deferred investing and tax-free investing.

Finally, it is extremely important to work with an advisor who understands the strategies of retirement distribution planning. Many times the advisor who helped you to accumulate your assets may not be the advisor who is trained to help with distribution planning.

I believe the perfect storm is brewing. I don't know exactly when the impact will take place or the extent of the damage that will be left in its path, but I do know the time to prepare is now. With the proper planning I'm very confident you will weather the storm and be a survivor.

About Denise

Denise Longshaw began her financial services career in 2003 as a Financial Advisor with VALIC Financial Advisor. She worked primarily with State of Florida employees who are members of the Florida Retirement System (FRS). Always seeking a better approach, a better method, a better answer and the best results for the clients she serve, Denise gained industry wide experience working with companies such as InvestaCorp, Planmember Securities, ING Financial Partners and Bencor Retirement Group.

Denise observed throughout the years that many people make financial decisions with incomplete information or a limited knowledge of how money works. She believes a retirement plan cannot be a ten-minute conversation with a bank teller or fifteen minutes to enroll in an employer's 401k or 403b plan. She believes it is an advisor's responsibility to thoroughly understand the goals and dreams of the clients they serve and advisors should focus on doing investigational work first to get a genuine understanding of a client's needs and to provide solutions rather than to sell products.

Today, she is the President and Founder of LONGSHAW Financial Group, a financial services firm located in Broward County, Florida. LONGSHAW Financial Group was founded to fulfill a growing need among baby-boomers who seek a solid retirement strategy and a face-to-face, personalized planning approach to help them achieve financial security and independence. Longshaw Financial Group begins with a clean slate to design a custom fit retirement plan for each client. The firm works exclusively for clients and not for financial companies or brokerages.

In addition to working with private individuals, Denise continues to work with members of the Florida Retirement System and is sought after by many FRS Deferred Retirement Option Program (DROP) participants and Investment Plan members for her guidance, her solid judgment and specific recommendations based on her client's goals and wishes.

Denise is an Investment Advisor Representative with Global Financial Private Capital, LLC, an SEC Registered Investment Advisor that brings institutional level wealth management practices and pricing to individuals. She is supported by a Financial Planning team and insurance specialists to help clients achieve their financial goals. Denise holds a bachelor's degree in accounting and is certified as a Chartered Retirement Planning Counselor through the College for Financial Planning. She is a current member and past board member of the Broward Chapter of the National Association of Insurance and Financial Advisors, and also, a member of Kiwanis International. She lives in Fort Lauderdale with her 11-year-old son, Jonathan.

CHAPTER 6

SELF-EXPRESSION
—HOW TO TRANSFORM EACH MOMENT OF YOUR LIFE

BY DAVID ZEMA

"Seen This Morning - Those passing by the old red brick school house at Third and Wood Street in the small town of Belle Vernon, Pennsylvania wondered why a group of young children were gathered by Mrs. Biagini's kindergarten class window with curious looks on their faces." ~ An Imagined Newspaper Story.

It was a bright, sunny, spring day when, at the age of 5, I discovered my ability to make people laugh. A few weeks earlier at the hobby store next to where I lived, I saw a gag milk carton that made the sound of a cow mooing. Enthusiastically, I saved up my allowance to buy the maniacal moo machine and waited for the right moment to create complete commotion at school.

The little rectangular red milk carton looked just like the real thing complete with a cartoon drawing of an unusually cheerful cow. But unlike real milk containers, when turned upside down to pour the imaginary liquid this unique flask triggered a loud unrelenting mooing sound effect.

All morning, I eagerly anticipated our lunch break. As soon as the teacher announced that it was time for lunch, I quietly and mischievously strolled to the refrigerator and grabbed the convincing yet counterfeit carton of milk from my little blue lunch box. Right on cue, as they heard the sound of the longhorn, my teacher and classmates ran to the nearest window to see the moo cow they expected to be there.

If my classmates had turned around, they would have noticed me watching them - trying to contain my laughter as I pumped the little red carton again and again.

At first, my teacher and classmates experienced a moment of surprise followed by confusion then disappointment when they didn't see the howling heifer. As soon as I revealed the source of the mooing to them, they began to laugh. Watching them realize they had been fooled, yet seeing that they could still enjoy the moment along with me, was the real payoff for yours truly.

Although, I discovered my knack for being funny that day, it wasn't until much later that I realized how natural positive self-expression can help to turn around our most difficult experiences at every moment – should we allow it to.

My expression of fun and joy seemed to come naturally and was shared on both sides of my family. My father, his father and my maternal grandfather told jokes and stories regularly. One of my aunts on my father's side had the most infectious laugh that I had inherited as well. My maternal Grandmother and Grand Aunt were regarded by all as the most fun-loving people in our family.

To balance my nature, my mother was more reserved, thoughtful, analytical, and could sometimes be reflective and introverted. Nevertheless, she was also very determined and persistent. Those were good qualities for me and my siblings to observe and emulate as well.

Little by little, I grew as a young performer, writer, producer, director and promoter. I was always learning how to express each emotion and communicate every nuance.

In grade school, I asked my best friend, Lonnie, to work with me on writing, producing and performing a two person show. Then we promoted the idea to our teacher and she allowed us to do our two person mini extravaganza for the class just before the holidays. The play was well received and the audience chuckled throughout. The show was so successful that we were asked to do another play the next year. Later, in junior high school we took over the entire gym for another holiday spectacle – which filled the space with laughter.

However, my growth as impresario was abruptly interrupted by an upsetting and startling discovery. Besides, my childhood expression of my natural personality became subdued as well.

Quite by accident, I found out that for many years my father was involved in an ongoing relationship with a girlfriend while still being married to my mother. At the time, I was still very young and wasn't sure how to handle the situation. After all, I wasn't sure if my mother knew about my father's extra marital affair. I didn't know how to speak to my mother or my father or his girlfriend about my feelings or their situation.

My reactions at the time were anger, confusion, resentment and betrayal. I withdrew from reality and became very introverted. My internal world became shame-based and I only allowed myself to see things through my small window of embarrassment. In my thoughts and in my relationship with others, I was stuck replaying the same emotions again and again.

No matter what happened to me during those days in my young life, I had the same reaction. Most of the time I was angry, easily frustrated, filled with uncertainty and dread. My nickname could have been "Johnny Sour Note."

Worse yet, because I was so wrapped up in my own negative emotional world, I became disconnected from people and events in the world beyond my mind. Everything that occurred went through my destructive internal filter, causing me to unconsciously intensify my own pain.

Most notably, during those years I was completely unaware that I was suffering from past events and behaviors of other people over which I had no control. My recovery from my emotions about the discovery of my family's secret, and progress in developing my personal expression of personality, would have been quicker had I realized these past events and the people involved were outside of my scope of influence.

Yet, one of the only traits that protected my emotional well-being was that I still had the desire to see other people smile and laugh. Since I harbored such humiliation every waking moment, I had nothing to hold me back. So, I became the subject of the joke and didn't feel any additional degradation at all.

Actually, during those uncertain and trying times, making others smile or laugh at my expense became the best way to lift myself out of my depression. Creating laughter is still how I shift gears from personal pain to a better mood to this day. Somehow using my ability to make others laugh helped me to get the courage to continue on my quest to find the best way to express myself and explore my talents. Later I found out upon hearing many comedians interviewed, that they became addicted to their ability to make others laugh at an early age too.

But at the time I felt incomplete as a person. My personality teeter-tottered between unhappiness and ridiculousness – like it was a satirical version of Dr. Jekyll and Mr. Hyde and there was no end in sight. These impulsive mood swings made it difficult to make any real sustained progress toward becoming the fully functioning creative individual that I wanted to be.

My instincts drew my attention to creative areas of expression including writing, photography, film and video, public speaking and oral interpretation. I was also drawn to technical areas and teaching as well. Because I was stuck in a mental malaise, I felt lacking in these areas and couldn't see through my own miasma far enough to develop my skills.

About the time I began college, my older brother Gary who had recently moved to New York City had a terrible accident – which caused him to lose his right arm. I went to visit him that summer and was amazed at how quickly he had adjusted to the circumstances. He was a musician and composer. During this time he became even more involved in his most natural form of self-expression – creating music. I learned from him how important it is to continue exploring the constructive natural desires you have to express yourself—no matter what difficulties you may face.

I returned to my next semester at Cal U. of Pennsylvania as an inspired person determined to move away from my internal struggles and be an active participant in the present moment.

My opportunity to explore the moment came one day in Dr. Blout's public speaking class; we were discussing the upcoming Homecoming Queen election. As I read the rules, I noticed that it didn't require the applicant to be a female and joked that I would be eligible to run. Some of my classmates agreed and challenged me to run. So I did.

Not long after that, I got a dose of self-awareness when I told one of my friend's about my brother's accident. He thought I was joking! I couldn't believe that people perceived me as being nothing but a shallow prankster.

That's when I decided to lift myself out of my depression and to become a complete person. I wanted to people to know that I was much more than a grumpy guy who played practical jokes for no reason. However, the Homecoming Queen campaign was underway and would certainly continue the perception that I was only a superficial foolish person.

Perhaps it was too late for me to become more than the class clown, because I already had a well-known local photographer who shot pictures of the other candidates do my headshot as well. I printed posters that wisecracked "Forget the Face, Remember the Name." They were already plastered all over campus. Who would believe that I didn't just do this as some silly stunt?

How would I ever convince people that I was more than just another smiling face? Would they accept me for what I truly stand for? Or would they reject me?

At that moment, I realized that one of the best ways to get people's attention is through humor and controversy. With that thought in mind, I calmed down and wrote out ideas to turn what started out on a whim into something constructive for all involved.

After a heated campaign, I won. Many people expected me to stop there. Certainly, the college wanted me to admit that it was all a joke and to quit. No way! Now I had the opportunity to express my message. So, I felt that I couldn't quit and have self-respect, let alone gain the respect of others.

Then I expressed to everyone that I believed that the role of Homecoming Queen could be used to promote the college. Many agreed when I pointed out the flimsy requirements to run for queen. They listened when I suggested that the Homecoming Queen and the ceremony could be used to promote the college academically, and not just as another beauty pageant.

I achieved my goal to be perceived as a thoughtful person. More importantly, people were thinking and speaking about the roles of men and women in our generation.

To continue to promote my ideas about role models, the next year I asked Kitty Dasta, a 34 year old mother of four children who I met during my campaign, to run for homecoming queen. Of course, I managed her campaign and she won the title by a landslide. At the ceremony, I proudly turned over the crown to Kitty who could continue carrying the torch as an enlightened example of an ideal persona for our generation. Of course, we got even more favorable media attention that year for the college.

I felt so alive and enjoyed working on those two homecoming events. I learned to deal with my emotions and adversity as well. During this time I also met a young woman named Judy who became my lifelong friend and companion. By following through with my ambitions and beginning a path of self-discovery and learning, I found the encouraging nature in my experiences and met many wonderful friends.

In many ways I realized that I was lucky to have a supportive family, even if it was dysfunctional. My teachers, friends and classmates also enjoyed and encouraged me to explore and express my talents. Far too often, I witness parents, teachers and other adults consistently limiting self-expression in children, younger people and even adults. Of course, guidelines must be spelled out for appropriate expression in social situations. But I believe that we must help ourselves and our community to learn how we can use self-expression to become the best we can be.

For example, I recently saw a commercial for an insurance company that follows a young man throughout his day. First we see water pouring on his head as he walks down the street. Afterward, he moves a nearby flower pot so that it can receive the downpour and continues on his way. Next he helps an older street vendor lift her cart onto the sidewalk. A dog begs for a scrap of food as he eats lunch at a sidewalk cafe. The young man gives him a chicken wing instead, as the cook who is watching shakes his head as if to suggest he doesn't understand. A mother and her young daughter sit peacefully on the sidewalk with a sign saying "funds needed for education." He reaches into his wallet to find only two bills. He gives them both to the little girl as a nearby vendor shakes his head in dismay. When the young man reaches his home, he quietly places a bunch of bananas on his elderly neighbor's door. She slowly opens the door and discovers the fruit but he is gone. We hear the announcer say, "What does he get in return for doing this every day?"

As time goes on, the plant flowers, the dog adopts him, the girl goes to school because of his help, the old neighbor lady discovers him and gives him a hug, and the street vendor gives extra helpings while he helps her. The narrator tells us that he gets nothing from this and no one will know about it. However, the voice goes on to say that the young man feels many emotions, witnesses happiness, reaches a deeper understanding, feels the love, and most importantly, receives what money can't buy – a world more beautiful. Then the voiceover asks, "What do you desire most?

As a coach, I have seen many people stuck expressing the same emotions or stopping their own progress. Helping them to discover their blocks and create ways to overcome them and to see their own strengths, has been my most rewarding experience in life.

At the time of this writing, it has been about 40 years since these events occurred, but I remember them clearly because they shaped my future. Now my brother and I have discovered that we are eligible to be Italian citizens. Accordingly, our next transformation will be as dual citizens with new challenges of traveling, learning a new language and culture. With all of the lessons that I have learned available to help me make new discoveries, I am filled with wonder, awe and a sense that it will be an even greater exploration period in my life. I look forward to how I will transform myself through expressing my natural qualities during the next years of my life.

About David

David Zema helps people learn to stay in touch with their true self and how to express those core elements that define who they are so that they can create authentic communication. Being part of the baby boom TV generation, David became interested in media at an early age. While still in college, David engineered his first campaign using media exposure to call attention to his message.

David believes that by finding and staying in touch with your best self, you will find a never-ending source for the most natural trusted qualities needed to deliver your message. David's media business focuses on helping his clients create marketing messages. Also, he facilitates the definition of their own core strengths enabling them to easily draw from their treasures for every part of their life, career, or business. By staying close to their real self and desires they will be perceived as trusted, capable connections and attract clients, allies, partners and more business. David has developed an exclusive method that he calls UMAP or Unique Marketing and Promotion, which shows his clients how to trigger their core strengths to kick into high gear whenever they are needed to produce positive results.

David enjoys working with everyone from people just starting out to established professionals. Clients include companies such as Verizon, CBS Radio, Fuse TV, Discovery Networks, corporate executives, lawyers, doctors, dentists, business owners, actors, television and radio personalities, chefs, authors, teachers, and children.

David is a graduate of California University of Pennsylvania where he majored in media communication. David is the president of David Zema Enterprises, Inc., where along with writing, producing and voicing marketing messages, he runs presentation skills seminars through his Voice Of Success Programs division.

David has been chosen as one of America's PremiereExperts™ and has been quoted in the *Pittsburgh Post Gazette, Wall Street Journal, Atlanta Constitution,* and *Backstage,* and published articles in theatrical trade papers *Soul of American Actor* and *Showbusiness.*

Prior to working on this book, David contributed as a voice over expert to four books on acting by Glenn Alterman, *Promoting Your Acting Career: A Step-By-Step Guide to Opening the Right Doors, An Actor's Guide–Making It in New York City, Secrets to Successful Cold Readings,* and *100 Acting Jobs for Actors.*

David has been seen and heard thousands of times in many commercials and programs on television, the internet, radio and telephone.

You can connect with David at:
info@davidzema.com
www.facebook.com/dzevos
www.about.me/davidzema

CHAPTER 7

HOW A SMALL-TOWN DENTIST IN RURAL AMERICA GENERATED 549 NEW PATIENTS FROM A THREE-HOUR EVENT WITHOUT ANY MARKETING!

BY DAROLD D. OPP, DDS

Does generating 549 new patients from a patient appreciation event sound too good to be true? Jerry Jones, one of the best marketers in dentistry, touted this success story as "the non-marketing marketing wonder of dentistry!" during his 2013 Dental Office: IMPOSSIBLE marketing extravaganza held in Scottsdale, Arizona.

Before we delve into this marketing wonder, let me introduce myself. My name is Dr. Darold Opp, and I practice family dentistry in Aberdeen, South Dakota. I live in rural America. I am an average dental clinician. I have a great team, and we have a unique business model. My collections in 2011, 2012, and 2013, during one of the most challenging economies in history, averaged over $3.3 million—$1.3 million in hygiene and $2 million in restorative dentistry. Here is where it gets really interesting. I do not do any of the following procedures: oral surgery including implants, orthodontia, sedation, sleep apnea, TMJ, dentures, full mouth crown and bridge, and upper molar endodontics. A number of dentists at the 2013 Jerry Jones event asked me, "What is your secret?"

My simple and honest answer? A patient appreciation event! But not just any event, mind you. Our SmilePalooza celebration is so unique that my local newspaper called it "South Dakota's Version of Disney World."

Our event has grown each year, and so have our results. In 2010 we generated 147 new patients and $165,588 in direct revenue. In 2011, 172 new patients and $181,425 in revenue. In 2012, 230 new patients and $206,116 in revenue. In 2013, we created a customized pre-event and post-event marketing campaign for the first time, and our numbers skyrocketed: 232 new patients and $397,594 in annual revenue with a lifetime value of $1,160,000. All accomplished with our three-hour SmilePalooza event.

Here is the crazy part: We began SmilePalooza in 2008 with no intention of it being a new patient magnet. My hope and desire was to create a simple appreciation day for my own patients. But when you live in a small community and have an event in a public venue, it is extremely hard not to open the day to everyone. Hesitantly, that is what we did, and our first-year attendance was eye-popping. We were expecting 300 people, and more than 3,000 attended. We had ordered 900 hot dogs, and we ran out in the first hour. We were frantic, to say the least!

Hot dog shortages aside, our inaugural event was a resounding success. We registered 850 children that first year and stopped counting because we ran out of registration stickers. Of those 850 kids, 87 percent were not our patients, so we realized that opening our event to the public was a great idea after all. SmilePalooza was truly a serendipitous new patient magnet. We did not create any post-event marketing with offers to entice attendees to come to our office until 2013. We know at least 549 new patients came unsolicited during 2010-2012. We failed to track adequately in 2008 and 2009, so our new patient numbers actually far exceeded the 549 we counted.

Here is where it gets really interesting. After our 2008 event, we saw a surge of families come into our office stating that SmilePalooza was their main referral source. We couldn't believe this was happening simply because of a three-hour event, so we decided to host another event the following year, thinking we would "debunk" what had happened in

2008. We were in for another surprise. More than 4,000 people attended in 2009, and the kid count was even higher than in 2008.

I must admit that the idea of an appreciation event did not originate with me. One of my marketing mentors is Dan Kennedy. Dan is considered to be the world's greatest marketer and millionaire maker. He loves event marketing and believes it is one of the top means of creating practice buzz and reciprocation. You may wonder how reciprocation relates to marketing. Robert B. Cialdini, Ph.D., the foremost expert on social psychology in the world, has written a classic book entitled "Influence: The Psychology of Persuasion." In this book he writes about six principles of influence that permeate every society. The first principle is reciprocation: If you do a kindness for another, they will feel an obligation to return the favor. The incredible success of SmilePalooza in securing new patients was simply the principle of influence at work. And work it did!

So, what makes SmilePalooza such a unique event? First of all, no one else is doing one similar. When we began thinking about having an appreciation event for our patients, I did exhaustive research both offline and online about how to market an event like this, and I came up empty. I could not find anything like it outside or inside dentistry. That was frustrating. How in the world would I even begin to try planning such an endeavor? But as they say in business, you are either a pioneer who paves the way or you are a settler who reaps the efforts of others. We weren't given a choice. We had to be pioneers. Our long history of working with children in the office and creating innovative ideas that give us staying power in the community was in our favor. We already knew what kids and their families enjoy.

And so we created SmilePalooza to be a one-of-a-kind, fun-filled family extravaganza. Imagine with me an afternoon in the park where 4,000 people gather to see Super Heroes and Disney Princesses come to life, the Tooth Fairy and Tooth Man welcoming old and new friends, multiple inflatable bounce houses, 20-foot-tall walking puppets roaming the park, and the world's largest bubble tower filling the sky. Plus we have fire trucks, clowns, circus animals, live music, dance contests, horse races, celebrities on stage, crazy activities for all ages, shirt cannons, snacks and drinks, and tons of prizes. And the best part—all the laughter, all the screams of joy, all the pictures, and all the family memories are FREE!

Google "SmilePalooza 2013" and see for yourself why it has become the #1 free kids' event in dentistry.

One of the rewards of SmilePalooza has already been discussed: new patients. And that is very significant! It is no secret that in 2008 the economy went south in a big way. Roger P. Levin, DDS, a well-recognized dental consultant, wrote in the May/June 2013 Dental Business Review that a shocking 75 percent of practices had declined in the preceding four years, not only in income but in new patient numbers as well. In the same newsletter, a roundtable of practice analysts was asked to name the #1 area of concern in the dental practice. They all echoed the same thing: having trouble filling hygiene schedules. My current dental consultant, Mike Abernathy, DDS, wrote in his new book, "The Super General Dental Practice," that the economic downturn of 2008 has drastically changed the business of dentistry and it may never be the same again. Dr. Abernathy goes on to say that we need to be very creative and innovative about the type of dental services we offer, and we also must do everything in our power to keep satisfied patients in our practice and to find new ways to create a competitive advantage.

Speaking of competitive advantage, if I asked you what sets you apart from the dental practice next door or down the street, what would your answer be? In my small rural community of 26,000, there are 18 dentists. For 24 years of my dental career, I was frustrated by trying to separate myself from the crowd. In the consumer's mind, which is the only perception that really matters, I was no different from the guy next door. Look at any yellow pages ad or, better yet, any website, and you will be hard-pressed to decide what differentiates Doctor "A" from Doctor "B".

SmilePalooza was truly serendipitous, not only because it has generated hundreds of new patients over the past six years, but also because it has given us a unique competitive advantage that has placed my office into the top "mental real estate" of the moms in my community. Why is that so important? Moms schedule 92 percent of all dental appointments. In addition, Sally Hogshead in her book, *Fascinate: Your 7 Triggers to Persuasion and Captivation* writes about a study in which more than 1,000 people were asked "What is your #1 fascination in life?" Ninety-six percent responded with "my children." For any family dentist reading those words, this should be an "aha!" moment. The incredible success of SmilePalooza was in part orchestrated by the planning that my team leader and I did, but as Dr. Cialdini revealed in his research on the principles of influence, we were fortunate to target the two most critical pieces of our event's success, moms and their children.

While increasing patient numbers and prospective income was the first reward from our event, there were so many more than we ever anticipated. For example, what business, including dentistry, would turn away free publicity? For six years running, our local newspaper has covered SmilePalooza as a news story, complete with eye-catching photographs and the reporter's commentary. Having our story become one of the top views of the day and remain in the top 10 researched for several days after the event was invaluable. The headline *South Dakota's Version of Disney World* would have cost thousands of dollars to buy as ad space, so the free price tag made it even more priceless!

Increased name recognition in the community helps place you and your practice into an additional position of influence, something that Dr. Cialdini calls social proof/authority. In 2010 our practice won the prestigious ABBY award, which is the highest honor for community involvement in our city. No other dentist has won the award in its 20-year history, and we were blessed to overcome all odds, coming in ahead of 3M, a company of 750 employees, and Avera Health, Aberdeen's largest employer, with a team of more than 1,300. Not a bad accomplishment for an office of 10! In 2012 we were awarded The Hometown Hero award for our commitment to SmilePalooza and the numerous other projects we undertake to better our community. I say these things not to impress you but to impress upon you that anyone can accomplish similar things, if not more, simply by creating a niche that is unique.

In 2013, I came to the conclusion that if we wanted to take our SmilePalooza event to the next level, then we needed to leverage ourselves through the power of networking. Our positive reputation in the community had grown, and it had caught the attention of other businesses, allowing us to garner sponsorships for our event. Through a simple, well-crafted appeal letter, we raised over $19,000 in cash donations and in-kind gifts, literally eliminating all of our hard costs for SmilePalooza. We were able to generate $397,594 in new patient revenue with minimal or no financial costs of our own. Who wouldn't like that return on investment? And there's more! Sponsorships also allowed us to expand our influence into our sponsors' networks when they personally invited their clients to the event, leveraging even more "dental ambassadors" for SmilePalooza for years to come.

Now we are adding another feature to SmilePalooza, and it's one that has us extremely excited. Make-A-Wish®, the charitable foundation that grants wishes to children who are sick, is becoming actively involved in pre-promotion as well as participating in the event itself. Considering our focus on making a difference for moms and their children, partnering with this charity makes all the sense in the world. Plus, here is another piece of information that I find interesting: 68 percent of moms prefer to go to a dentist who is committed to a cause. Interesting data! Make-A-Wish includes references to our partnership on all its social media sites and is providing ongoing promotions up to the day of the event. Can you ever have enough people singing your praises? Not in today's economy!

Another new feature relates to our registration process on the day of the event. We obviously give people the opportunity to preregister on a SmilePalooza website prior to the event, but the vast majority of families sign in on site. New technology has allowed us to instantly merge attendees' names into a database that immediately starts our marketing program the second they hit the submit button. Strike while the iron is hot! In addition, the attendees have the opportunity to sign up for a free computer-based loyalty program that has weekly interactive contests, free games, and other goodies that allow us another opportunity to stay engaged with potential new patients throughout the course of the 12 months leading up to the next year's event.

We have created an extensive marketing program that keeps SmilePalooza actively working throughout the year. Through scripted emails, recorded radio ads, follow-up postcards, and personalized thank-you notes, we are able to reach a "warm" lead (someone who has attended our event) with our marketing efforts. One cannot overestimate the importance of repeated contacts to the same leads. A commonly-accepted marketing principle is that it takes as many as seven positive touches to get a prospect to become a buyer. If the event is our first impression with an attendee, every contact beyond that moves us one step closer to success.

By now you may want to ask me "How in the world does the average dentist attempt to accomplish everything you have mentioned?" It is all about the power of SYSTEM (Save-Your-Self-Time-Energy-Money). Since we were the pioneers of this type of event marketing, you can become the settler who reaps the rewards of all our heavy lifting. In the introduction I mentioned the Dental Office: IMPOSSIBLE marketing seminar. Many of the top marketers in dentistry presented at this meeting, and it was there that the SmilePalooza Event-In-A-Box coaching program was shared for the first time. Clients are already on board, and excitement continues to grow for those who want to create the #1 niche for attracting moms and their children to their practices.

As Dan Kennedy says, "Small hinges swing big doors." SmilePalooza may be only one small hinge of your marketing strategy, but as you have seen from the results, it swings a BIG REVENUE DOOR!

Here's to our continued success in the best profession in the world!

About Darold

Darold D. Opp, DDS, is a family dentist in Aberdeen, S.D., population 26,091. He has a single doctor practice that produces $3.4 million a year without comprehensive crown and bridge, oral surgery, dentures, implant surgery, TMJ, sleep apnea, and sedation dentistry. Dr. Opp went from $500,000 in debt in 2010 to recreating lifetime savings and ready to retire in four years using the strategies in this chapter.

For more info, contact Dr.Opp via his informative webinar at: www.3HourFamilyDentalMarketing.com.

CHAPTER 8

PERSEVERANCE PAYS OFF

BY DAVID ALTENBERN

My story is one of perseverance pays off, starting with a great belief in myself, and the following lessons of life and business. Hopefully, it will inspire at least one person to become all that they can be.

To be more specific, I went from being on top of the world and living life large in my dream house on a lake with a pool and the owner of a thriving law firm, to a life of internal strife as a result of the premature 2006 death of my beautiful daughter, then going on to a life of *"escape"* in Saint Thomas, Virgin Islands, followed by making a *"hard comeback"* to where we are today – *positively touching more lives than ever in our thriving Houston, Texas law firm* that handles major personal injury matters, along with Family law and Business cases. In short, *my life story is a true testament to that old adage that God works in mysterious ways.*

Then again, it is my firm belief that we are not here to understand everything that comes our way. Rather, we are here to always make the best choices possible from the circumstances that we face.

The eternal truth is that we never really know when...or how...God or "Angels on Earth" will touch us, teach us, and turn us in to new directions for our happiness and success. We should live our lives by the lesson of the *Serenity Prayer* –

> *"God, grant me the Serenity to Accept*
> *the things I cannot change;*

The Courage to Change the things I can;
and the Wisdom to know the Difference."

There is also that special poem *"Don't Quit"*:

"Don't quit when the tide is lowest,
for it's just about to turn;

Don't quit over doubts and questions,
for there's something you may learn;

Don't quit when the night is darkest,
for it's...I"

In summary, I went from very difficult feelings to now networking with hundreds of professionals, owners, and key managers of businesses weekly, with more time now than ever for daily trips to Lifetime Fitness, and enjoying nightly television with my wife, all with more energy and while helping serve more clients than ever.

As the coffee cups to our new clients profess, *"We work hard for Justice our Clients Deserve"…"Earning Client Trust…and Opponent Respect… One Case at a Time."* We also like to think that our *connections* and *experience* make a difference. My experienced legal assistants, especially the very dedicated Laura, have kept us going strong. Hiring, training, supervision, effective delegation, and direction of your "professional team" simply is important. We like to think of ourselves as the "A-Team" and we take a very personal approach to our team/family.

Now please don't misunderstand. It is not my message that *all good comes about by pure luck or fate or destiny.* Rather, it is that by following certain *fundamental keys to success*, you can best balance your physical, emotional/spiritual, and business interests.

You may wonder if there is one key or secret to success? *My answer is no.* The truth is that there are *several fundamental principles* that can best position ourselves for success.

First, **proper foundations** are important. For most of us, that involves a great belief in ourselves, strong family support, an excellent education, and positive role models/mentors along the way. Sports played a big part of growing up. As one coach told our team… *"the true value of sports* *lies in the lessons taught about life, leadership, teamwork, learning to win, learning to lose with the right perspectives, and most importantly, learning to think large and outside of yourself."* Wanting to be a lawyer, I also liked reading Hardy Boys mysteries and law-related books and taking psychology and communication courses in school. I attended great colleges at Michigan State University (Criminal Justice Major), and The University of Texas School of Law. Working in your field early in life also helps, like clerking and being an assistant investigator for a great law firm. A legendary trial lawyer once told me, *"A lawyer's credibility is what it's all about for success in trials, as well as following the old adage about preparation, preparation, and more preparation."* *These words made lasting impressions upon me.*

Second, the **right attitude** and **approach to communication** are *essential* to success. To begin with, *people tend to best learn one of three ways* – First, some learn best by *visual* ways; Second, others learn best in an *audible* fashion; Third, some learn most in an *emotional/kinetic* way. So if we communicate that our audience can *"see, hear, and feel"* our message, we will greatly improve our relationships. My father always told me that, no matter my specific education focus, learning as much as possible about communication and psychology serve me well in life. Studies also show that the most successful people *network* and *exercise* more than others, and I definitely endorse those findings.

The principles of **primacy and recency** should help *structure* our *communications*. In addition, *actions to follow our promises always speak louder than words alone.* Finally, recent neuropsychology research concludes that people tend to make decisions on the basis of subliminal concerns regarding the safety and welfare of themselves and their immediate family. Therefore, by making our appeals to others with this in mind (in addition to *emotional* and *rational appeals)* can best achieve our goals.

Third, being **positive, balanced, and always looking for self-improvement** is what all of us should strive to do. Taking an approach that we are *"always learning"* is an important *attitude for success*. We should always read, watch, and listen to as much self-improvement wisdom and meaningful news that we can stand. *Music* alone can be a valuable and great teacher—just listen to the words of Rascal Flatts' *"My Wish"* or Lee Ann Womack's *"I Hope you Dance."*

Fourth, learning from **role models** is important. My father's *intense work ethic and discipline* that led him to early retirement and financial independence, as well as my mom's *great compassion*, and *my wife Linda being my greatest cheerleader* has always kept me going strong. One special Valentine's gift of years ago – a crumpled coffee cup – had this memorable *"I Love You, Despite Your Imperfections."* Learning from great trial attorneys has also helped me. Finally, I am also a disciple of the *BNI* way of *"Givers gain."*

We should regularly make "to do lists" and then prioritize the items. We also need to focus our efforts as follows:

1. Identify the real prospects of your business;

2. Build rapport;

3. Make your appeal (on how you can help and/or be a resource);

4. Overcome obstacles (timing, price, service, and other details);

5. Close the deal.

Fifth, the **determination, vision, and perseverance** to succeed, along with regular *a) self-assessment* and *b) self-redirection are cornerstones to success.* As they say, *"it's not where you start, but rather, where you finish in life."* It is good to remember we need to pass through a few storms in life to get to the rainbows. Finally, it is the *proper mastery of the distinct stages of successful sales and goal setting* as espoused and taught by Brian Tracy that distinguishes the most successful people from others.

We need to become the person that many others come to know, like, and trust before we can be truly successful. Another important lesson is the "24 Hour Rule": we should not make significant decisions, absent necessity, before 24 hours from when we find ourselves faced with the critical choice. We simply tend to make better decisions when we follow this rule.

Acting with great professionalism, energy, passion, focus, communication, and actions of a leader will be noticed by others. One of the most important lessons of "servant leadership" is also "seeking to understand before you seek to be understood" or listening first before you try to persuade.

As a sports advertisement once stated, in order to become a champion, you need "Hard Work, Practice, Intensity, and Passion," and most important, the ability to "Repeat." Learning to be "out of the box" and with risks calculated/reward analysis will also help distinguish you along the way. Helping someone or imprinting memorable words of wisdom onto others has priceless rewards. "Spreading goodwill" to all that you touch, irrespective of the income, is always a good thing. The value of the proper timing and tone to effective communication is often underestimated in my experience.

As for using psychology to our success, the people with whom we deal all want a few basic things. First, they want to feel good about the person with whom they deal and about the money they spend. Second, they want to feel like they obtain a real deal on their decisions - in terms of value, convenience, and/or price. "Another day in Paradise" attitude breeds success. Finally, the word "help" is probably the most important single word in generating success - knowing when and whom to ask for help, as well as being known as the "resource person" who gives help is invaluable.

To best network, we need to learn to ask questions and be an active listener. A most important network question is "Do you know someone who does _____?" In this way, we open the brain of our audience to their entire "sphere of influence" (including themselves) as opposed to the less effective, and more narrow question "Do you do _____?" The art of asking interesting and open ended questions, along with the art of storytelling (to help make memorable impressions), are a couple keys to our growth.

In closing, my perspective is that *everyone* is fully capable of achieving their full potential of happiness and success by following the guiding principles as outlined above. Simply put *"perseverance pays off"* – so long as we maintain a firm belief in our self-worth and talents and we continually work at self-improvement, always engaging in hard work, practicing focal analysis with regularity, and dedicating ourselves to overcome the storms that will undoubtedly come our way. With these approaches, we can all truly achieve our highest potential and our version of the American Dream.

We all have valuable viewpoints to share with others. Hopefully, you have enjoyed mine. My wish is that you too live the life that you have always wanted, and *that in some small way, this story contributes to making a positive difference.*

About David

David Altenbern was born in Freeport, Illinois. He graduated from Palatine High School outside of Chicago, Illinois in 1974. He then graduated from Michigan State University with a Criminal Justice, B.A. degree in 1978, followed by graduating from the University of Texas School of Law with a J.D. degree in 1982. During a summer while in law school, David then graduated from the U. S. Navy Officers School in Newport, Rhode Island. David was also recognized into the "Order of Barristers" in law school (a top 10 advocate out of a graduating class of 500).

David then started his law practice in 1982 with the Anchorage, Alaska law firm of Bankston & McCollum, becoming a partner of the firm in four years in 1986. David, however, then decided to return to Houston, Texas where he was with the law firm of Morris & Campbell for two years before starting his own law firm in 1988.

David has been recognized by his peers and *H-Texas Magazine* as one of the "Top Lawyers for The People", "Personal Injury and Family Law-2003 forward" and "Top Lawyers" (all categories of law-2005 forward), as well as being the first *"Ask the Expert"* in Personal Injury Law, by the first ever *Lawyers of Houston* legal directory in 2011 (Publisher-Mylo Media). Throughout his legal career, David has focused his law practice in the fields of Personal Injury, Family Law, and Business Law.

David has been a member of the American Association of Justice (AAJ), the Texas Trial Lawyers Association (TTLA), and the Houston Trial Lawyers Association (HTLA) and the Houston Bar Association (HBA). He is also rated in the top category of "Excellent" by AVVO, a national attorney rating organization.

David is involved in his local community by serving as an elder to Memorial Lutheran Church, an Ambassador to the Houston West Region and President of his West Memorial Chapter of BNI (Business Network International), President of his gated neighborhood Crestwater Homeowner's Association, a member of the Christian Business Fellowship Association (CBFA), a member of the Better Business Bureau (BBB) and a member of the Board of Directors of Joe Joe Bear Foundation (a nonprofit organization that provides teddy bears to children in hospitals who suffer from cancer or other terminal illnesses). David has also helped organize a few golf tournaments over the years.

David's personal interests are watching college and pro sports, playing golf, playing Texas Holdem poker tournaments, watching Survivor, watching movies and all types of travel, especially taking cruises.

David has been married twenty years to his wife and legal assistant Linda, with six children and ten grandchildren between them. David and Linda met in Houston, Texas twenty-five years ago when they worked for different law firms. They have travelled throughout Mexico and the Caribbean, and lived for one year in Saint Thomas, Virgin Islands after the untimely death of daughter Christi.

Tel. (713) 961-8012
Fax (713) 961-8022
email: davidalt22@hotmail.com
website: www.attorneyaltenbern.com

CHAPTER 9

MIND YOUR Ps & Qs TO POLISH YOUR EXECUTIVE SKILLS AND SHINE IN BUSINESS

BY BARBARA HINES

My early education was at the feet of a disciplined and strict Army officer father and his quintessential Army wife who together embodied 'duty, honor and country'. They raised their tribe of children to behave in public, dress well, speak courteously (Yes, Sir) and be respectful of position. This firm boundary of good manners and sturdy work ethic surrounded a fun, creative and carefree childhood filled with my stay-at-home mother's artistic activities and my dad's entertaining, loving and protective nature. Minding your Ps and Qs for me meant paying attention to the details while having fun.

As a female Army Brat in the 1960s, I was also expected to get an excellent education (the real purpose of which was to nab a suitable man rather than have a career), to be brave and adapt to change with many household moves, to use good manners to build successful relationships and to participate in and support the community.

As life happens, I was propelled to address all of the above as a teenager when several accidents within a few years claimed the lives of my brother, sister, cousin and dear father, leaving us devastated and at a very loose end, until an old family friend with a big military future married my mother and moved us to Washington, DC. My way of coping with a new life and family was to stay very busy. Within months, I was fortunate enough to be selected to serve as one of the first female Pages in the U.S. Senate, breaking a nearly century and-a-half tradition.

In one fell swoop, my life changed drastically; I finally had something exciting to care about, so willingly adapted to change, embraced education albeit on a huge new learning curve supported by my new father's diplomatic job, started a promising career as a female icon (who knew?), really enjoyed the 'start-up' aspect of this new enterprise, discovered I was ambitious and good at noticing details, built new relationship skills using polite manners, and helped others while becoming part of a lifelong community that includes the likes of Bill Gates. This story pretty much sums up my career supported by a formal university education, on-the-job training in a household that regularly held diplomatic events and a variety of high stakes work experiences.

By minding your Ps and Qs (paying attention to details) and continuously challenging, learning and adapting, especially to new technologies and fluctuating staff environments, you too will be able to polish your executive relationship building, communication and negotiating skills to shine in business by acting to connect, interacting to communicate and interconnecting to collaborate:

1. PROFESSIONALISM & QUESTIONS TO CONNECT

'Acting' with professionalism firstly means using the skill, good judgment, and polite behavior that is expected from a person who is trained to do a job well. This is your individual action to polish your skills to create a winning, balanced and successful business future with persistent investigative actions to connect:

- Research potential clients and reasons to work together - Do your homework and be resourceful. As Thomas Edison said, 'Genius (i.e., success in business) is 1% inspiration and 99% perspiration,' so put in the effort to find opportunities and ways to help the people with whom you wish to connect.

- Understand goals - Based on your research, ask yourself what dynamic changes will affect a person or business for the better and determine how you can help them achieve it. Find the need, and fill it with factual and useful information.

- Develop a networking strategy to connect - People buy people so it helps to meet someone through trusted mutual contacts whether through a colleague, group or network event. So buy that ticket or ask to be introduced, and position yourself to successfully connect.

- Establish relationship trust with empathy, humor and common experience - It takes only 7 seconds to know if you will do business with someone, so take a deep breath and pay attention when saying hello with a firm handshake and smile. Say their name and use simple manners - 'please' and 'thank you'. Compliments help break the ice but only if genuine. Take notice to identify personal or business conversational topics such as hobbies or events in which they invest, use professional verbiage and open body language, speak in the positive and act with kindness, dress appropriately, remember the nose knows, maintain an arm's distance of space, have a funny and safe (non-political / non-religious / non-sexual) joke ready to tell, relate common human experiences, give knowledge and find an opportunity to mention or demonstrate that you are committed to being accountable.

- Ask questions, listen and paraphrase for clarity - We have two ears and one mouth for a reason. Ask a question and give the gift of your full attention and eye contact to let people speak and fully answer the question without interruption, which is usually a good provider of more information than originally requested. Listening and paraphrasing questions for clarification help you narrow down the goals and real concerns to address.

- Demonstrate how your proactive leadership and ideas create opportunities to solve business problems - Conversation is a dynamic opportunity to explore challenges and solutions to problems. In one prepared sentence, relate an example of how you applied your skill successfully to accomplish a goal that a business was concerned about achieving, and perhaps what innovation you injected to design a new, more efficient way around a problem that led to success for the person, business or member community.

- Relate your credentials - Find an opportunity to mention a place where you worked, person you helped, school you attended or a relevant course you took to share your credentials to do the job that may be on offer.

- Gain commitment to work with you - As every salesman knows, you must always ask for the order because you have nothing to lose but if you get a negative reply, let them off the hook graciously, with humor even, offer your business card and promise to help anytime. You never know what the future holds or when opportunity will knock. The best you can do is lay out the red carpet and open the door with a smile. Remember, rejection only means you've eliminated something that doesn't work to get closer to a more defined opportunity.

2. PROFILE & QUALITY TO COMMUNICATE

Once you've made a good contact, use your connecting skills to 'interact' with well-written and efficient communications for a win-win relationship. There has never been an easier time than in today's social media frenzy to craft your unique personal message and publicize it over many channels, but it is important to be clever about managing time, expectations and the written word. Communicating your message, profile, measure of excellence and suitability for purpose will help drive business to your door, so minding these Ps & Qs will help:

- Think before you speak - Refrain from saying anything out loud or in writing that you would not wish to see on the front page of a newspaper or go viral - On the first day of my first job as a Page, my female colleague and I were barred from the Cloakroom and therefore from doing our jobs by Senators who were unaccustomed to having girls around to see them tuck in their shirts, smoke cigars, curse and tell jokes. The Equal Rights Amendment had recently passed in the House of Representatives but not yet in the Senate. Spurred by Washington Post reporters who chased us to contest this infraction, my colleague asked me to join her in complaining in public via an interview, which I refused as I wanted to have a second day on the job. That weekend, her picture and story were on the front page of the Style section and we once again had the use of the Cloakroom, but it crippled her senior relationships. I admired her guts but, agree or not, preferred to use diplomatic backchannel communications to achieve the goal.

- Nurture Relationships - Good business karma says 'act to help' with thoughtful intent and there are many channels to court and communicate with new contacts, the most popular being LinkedIn.

Ask for referrals to make contacts and nurture them. If you see an article or hear of a morsel of interesting and useful information, send a quick note to help a potential client stay in the loop, look good at work, say happy birthday or to congratulate them on a job well done. If your gesture is appreciated or reciprocated, you've set the scene for success. This investment applies to internal contacts as well, especially your boss, as sooner or later you will likely need their help.

- Use Spellcheck and manage expectations - When communicating in writing, nothing screams 'unprofessional' or 'dinosaur' more than sloppy inattention to spelling and grammar. If you wouldn't say it, avoid writing it, and avoid writing it if you would only say it privately. Writing is easy to misinterpret so use positive language that outlines benefits, breeds confidence, clearly states the intention of the communication and manages expectations such as a deadline for action or when to expect a follow up call, and do what you say you will. Taking the time to write a considered message will leave a good lasting impression and save time pursuing business or back-pedalling from mistakes. By the way, if you do make a mistake, apologize quickly, take responsibility and feedback and perhaps offer compensation. Rarely, whether in or out of your control, there may be nothing you can do that will satisfy some customers, so it may be best to move on or, if possible, hand the relationship to a colleague.

- Communicate Brand - Your brand is your signature so it is important to reflect it in a positive light in all interactions. Ensure your website and social media profiles are factually accurate, professionally written, authentic in colour, style and content, consistently updated with clear concise messaging, have keywords optimized for SEO and offer sharing and feedback options. People like to share stories and experiences that build trust and establish mutual benefit to create synergies, build influence and give customers an enjoyable experience of working together.

3. PARTNERSHIP & QUANTUM ENERGY TO COLLABORATE

To give your business a quantum leap to the next level, it is highly beneficial to develop 'interconnectivity' synergies and focused energy to create win-win-win partnership situations where your relationship wins, your company wins and your project wins:

- Source potential partners - Start with logical industry or repeat supporters with a vested interest and customer base that buy your products or services. Reading industry literature, joining industry groups and attending events will develop your database and identify new entrants. Reports that affect your industry may be available from financial services for example that may be open to partnering in exchange for publicizing the report. Be resourceful and brainstorm.

- Create business-funding partnerships to support project or events - This requires resources, excellent preparation, collaboration and teamwork, and the better you prepare and set up the project, the easier it becomes to execute. Involving more people of course requires increased safety awareness, project quality, clear contracts, improved cost controls, timely issues resolution and commitment guided by the mantras of 'on time and within budget' and 'under promise and over deliver'.

- Match strategy - Matching corporate strategy to event or service strategy, balancing rights and responsibilities with desires, and aligning these to measurable tasks that consider risks, are the keys to securing partners. Clearly worded helpful information that starts with the end goal in mind and fairly treats all offers, will guide your vision and influence a positive outcome.

- Sell - Selling is often a lengthy process of research that considers price, benefits, buy-in from multiple stakeholders, exclusivity, marketing goals, product education, speaker participation, optional extras and possible internal staff competing priorities which you may need to dig deep to understand. Once a proposal is developed and sent, use the personal touch to call at a convenient time or meet in person to respectfully guide them through their options to create tailored 'outside the square' opportunities to interconnect.

The entire Ps & Qs process from connection to interaction to interconnectivity is a constant and balanced refinement of price and benefits to structure a customer proposal that creates a winning partnership, enjoyable experience and a feeling of importance and future business community success. The challenge is yours to polish your executive relationship building, communication and negotiating skills to shine in business.

About Barbara

Barbara Hines helps people and businesses identify and build executive, B2B and industry relationships that advance business goals to raise professionalism, profiles and partnership profits. Her skills were honed over the past 30 years while setting up offices or projects for the U.S. Congress, White House, Pentagon, U.S. Embassy in Vienna and not-for-profits in Washington, DC; businesses and PR companies in New Zealand; and for local government and associations in Australia.

Barbara specializes in developing and managing 1) business relationships to identify and increase professional connections, 2) executive communications and social media skills to raise individual and company profiles, and 3) collaborative sponsorships of events and conferences to increase partnership profits, all with a sense of fair play to build business community spirit in a constantly learning and changing environment. She holds a Bachelor's Degree in Marketing, Graduate Certificate in Business & Event Management and is in perpetual social media and technology training.

She is author of the e-book, *20/20 Hines Sight - 20 Business Lessons Learned in 20 Years*.

Contact info: www.barbarahines.org, Info@barbarahines.org

CHAPTER 10

TRANSFORMATION OF THE HEART

BY AL BARBOUR

"My friend, we have a problem." Those are words that can overwhelm you, especially when they come from your physician after an examination and receiving the corresponding test results. The doctor was talking, but my mind was racing. I was only grasping a few words at a time; "Cardiomyopothy; irregular heartbeats; heart failure." I had known something was wrong with my heart for a while, but now it had a name and a diagnosis.

My family doctor made the referral to the cardiologist—a visit and a problem I really didn't want to face. But there I sat on the exam table in my new cardiologist's office as he showed me the x-rays of my heart. Dilated Cardiomyopothy is an insidious disease—an enlarged heart. Simply put, the larger your heart becomes, the less efficient it becomes. The less efficient it becomes, the more fatigued you feel with increased shortness of breath, swelling of the legs, ankles and abdomen. The heart cannot pump the blood, so the blood does not get the oxygen it needs. So, basically, you begin to suffocate from the inside out.

As most people do in today's information-driven world, when I initially received my diagnosis, the first thing I did was get on my computer to Google "cardiomyopathy." What I read about the condition scared me to death.

At that time I weighed about 260 pounds on a 5' 10" frame. I was enjoying life. I had my golfing buddies and every weekend was filled with golf and beer. My wife and I would often have friends over for cookouts and get-togethers. We were living for today and having a large time.

When the diagnosis of cardiomyopathy entered my life, rather than meet it head on, I took a detour for about 10 years. My cardiologist told me to lose weight, quit drinking beer, begin exercising, and take my medications. Basically, he wanted me to take better care of myself. I was at a distinct crossroads in my life that I didn't want to face. In fact, I even turned away from my wife and family, from the people who loved me most. Rather than sharing with them my medical condition, I downplayed it and joked about it.

Not heeding my doctor's advice, I doubled down on beer and food. As a result, my weight ballooned up to 300 pounds and I remember joking, "With proper medication you can live any way you want." I continued to meet with my cardiologist but it was like I was playing games with him. He would tell me what to do, and then I would do what I wanted. At a time in my life when I had a wife and family who loved me and could have offered me the support I desperately needed, I shut them all out and continued to live as if nothing was wrong. Sometimes the easiest person to deceive is yourself, and I was living proof of that.

On Mother's Day in 2000, I got up and told my wife, "Let's get dressed and surprise my parents at church." They were going to a small church in a poor side of town where my mother had grown up. The people were mostly mill workers who worked at a local textile mill. The preacher was a man who had dedicated his life to God and that community for many years. I don't remember the sermon, but when the invitation came from the pastor for anyone who wanted to rededicate their life to the Lord, I stood silent. I distinctly remember the choir echoing the most beautiful sound I had ever heard. I had been raised in a Christian home, baptized at the age of twelve, but when I went to college, I left the church and had turned away from God. Now, instead of going to church for the right reason, I was there only to please my mother on Mother's Day. Every ounce of my body wanted to step out, walk down the aisle and ask Jesus to forgive me and to take me back. Yet I held onto the back of the pew, my knees shaking and not being able to breathe. I left that day and allowed that opportunity to pass. For the next several years I went through a very dark time in my life. There seemed to be absolutely no joy in my life. I just went through the motions.

One day, I remember riding in my golf cart when a group of geese flew overhead. I could hear their wings beat the air and could hear their distinct honking as they graced the sky. I remember saying, "God, I don't deserve to be able to speak to You. But thank You for letting me see how great Your creation is." At that moment I felt a warmth inside me that I had not felt in many years. It was then that I began to realize there was something missing in me. There was a hollowness I couldn't fill. Several weeks later, on a Sunday morning, I told Susan, my wife, to get up. She inquisitively asked, "Why?" I quickly replied, "We're going to church." To which she questioned again, "Why?" I said, "Because nothing else is working." I had reached the end of my struggle and I knew I needed an answer that was bigger than I was.

When we walked into Temple Baptist Church that morning, a feeling of joy came over me. Words cannot express the feeling of happiness I experienced that day. Maybe it was because two of the greatest blessings of my life were about to happen. The first was that I was going to be in church for the right reason, to worship God with my father, mother and wife. The second was that my wife, Susan, would accept Jesus as her Lord and Savior and join the church. God had blessed me with a wife who loved me, supported me, and now was following me into the church.

We immediately joined the church and later I became a Sunday school teacher for a men's adult class. Our marriage grew stronger and sweeter and I saw my wife in a new light. A real transformation had taken place in my life.

But the cardiomyopathy was still there and my heart began to fail in January 2011. By June of that year, I began to vomit. The doctor said I was entering the final stages of heart failure. My cardiologist told me he had done all he could for me and referred me to UNC Heart Transplant Center.

There is a process to qualify for a heart transplant that begins with a series of tests and a review panel to determine if you are a candidate. After being deemed a qualified candidate, on July 7, 2011, I entered

UNC Hospital and checked into the Heart Transplant wing. To be listed as A1, you have to be receiving two types of medication. This is done through a peripherally inserted central catheter or PICC in one arm and another in your neck. Both have lines that go directly to each side of your heart to pump the necessary drugs to stimulate your heart to beat. I was also hooked up to three or four monitors and all other sorts of wires – making even the slightest movement quite an ordeal.

Then you wait. And you think. It begins to dawn on you that you're waiting for someone else to die so you can have their heart and live. Lying on your back, looking up at the ceiling only reinforces your feeling of complete and total helplessness. Before, time seemed to pass so quickly; but lying there in such a vulnerable state caused time to just stretch out before me. Days seemed to lose their meaning. The reality of my situation began to settle in; either I would get a heart or I would die. Time was not on my side.

I was a Christian believer, a Sunday School teacher, a Deacon at my church, yet I was afraid. Each morning, a parade of doctors would come by and check my status. Each day became another day on the waiting list. After several weeks, my heart continued to decline and the medication was failing. The situation was looking very bleak to say the least.

I was reading my Bible daily, and one day read Psalm 16: "Keep me safe, O God, for in you I take refuge." The words took root in my heart as if the Holy Spirit planted them there. Later that Friday, my doctor told me I was running out of time and they would have to do something. They were contemplating putting me on a heart machine. The transplant coordinator came by and I asked where I stood on the donor list. She told me I was 20th in the Southeast. Needless to say, I was devastated. Later that evening after my wife and mother had left for the day, I wept uncontrollably. I had reached the end. I remember opening my Bible up to Psalm 16 again, "Keep me safe, O God, for in you I take refuge."

I realized then that there was part of me that I had never surrendered to God. Part of me was still trying to take care of me. I prayed, "I cannot handle this anymore. Let me abide completely in You." Instantaneously, peace came over me. At that very moment I knew and understood it was all right. No matter what happened, whether I lived or died, it was going to be OK.

The next day at 5:30 in the afternoon, the head transplant nurse came to my room and told me they had a heart for me in Orlando, Florida. They were going to fly down that night, harvest the heart, and put it into me at 4:30 Sunday morning, July 24, 2011.

My brother was there when I got the news about my new heart. He immediately called his wife and I called mine. They picked up my mother and came to the hospital. People from the church also came to my room that evening as I was being prepared for surgery. My room was full of friends and family laughing, talking and praying. Fear was not present at the time I had feared the most. The thoughts about when they would split open my chest, take out my heart and put another one in always kept me up at night. But it turned out to be the most peaceful experience of my life. If you ever wondered if prayer works, I'm here to tell you it does! Many people were praying for me and I rode those prayers that night, down to the operating room.

God guided the hands of the surgeon and I rode those prayers back to the recovery room. When I awoke from the surgery, the first words I said to my wife were, "I can breathe again." I stayed in the hospital seven more nights before being released.

I wish I could say that closeness with God never changed, but it seems that the stronger we get, the less we think we need God. I came to realize that drifting from God is not because God moves away from us, it's because we move away from Him. God gives us all a choice. Just as in any relationship, we have to work on our relationship with God, not once a week, but daily. Unfortunately, I came home with a new heart and renewed health, but with the same mind and the same weaknesses. After a few months I had drifted back to eating the wrong foods and my closeness with God was not the same.

There's a passage in the book of Colossians that says, "Whatever you do, work at it with all your heart, as if working for the Lord." This verse resonated with me and I wrote it down on a yellow legal pad so I would remember it. I asked myself, "How can I translate this verse to relate to every aspect of my life; God, family, friends, career, people in my career, people God puts in my path, and even myself?"

First, I purposed to make God part of everything I do in my daily life, not just part of Sunday. Secondly, I determined to start every morning asking God to use me for His purpose that day and to help me see what He would have me see, hear what He would have me hear, feel what He would have me feel and do what He would have me do. Third, I pledged to give thanks throughout the day. The simple fact that Christ is for us is enough to outweigh any bad day.

Further, I have committed myself to the following 10 Daily Resolutions. I find these resolutions influence not only my personal life, but also the way I conduct my business and relate to others.

1. I will put the interests of others before my own (Philippians 2:3)

2. I will speak less and listen more. (James 1:9)

3. I will pray without ceasing for the spiritual needs of others, no matter their plight, background or circumstances. (Philippians 4:6-7)

4. I will put the needs of my family above my own. (1 Timothy 3:5)

5. I will not let success or failure enter into my consideration. (Colossians 3:23-24)

6. I will not be judgmental of others. (James 1:12)

7. I will lead a quiet life, take care of my business and work as long as God gives me the privilege. (1 Thessalonians 4:11)

8. I will not worry about tomorrow, but rather, live each day as if it could be my last. (Matthew 6:24)

9. I will get up each morning knowing I am one step closer to my home in heaven. (Philippians 3:12-14)

10. I will give thanks at the end of each day for God's faithfulness and forgiveness. (Ephesians 2:8)

I have thankfully experienced two major transformations; one physically and one spiritually. Interestingly, the physical heart I received enabled me to continue to live my physical life like everyone else. I no longer weigh over 300 pounds, I weigh 171 pounds and I run/walk 5 miles a day. Thankfully, I can do whatever I want physically because of the generosity of a family in Orlando who went through the very painful loss of a 25-year-old family member. That heart enabled me to breathe and physically live again. But, the transformation that took place in my spiritual and emotional heart changed how I look at life, people, relationships, work and everything that I encounter on a daily basis.

Both transformations were vital to me. Christ died for my sins, another man died that I might continue to live. God has a purpose for each one of us. If you want to transform your life, help someone else transform theirs and your life will change forever.

About Al

In 1986, Al founded Barbour Tax and Financial Services. The mission of Barbour Tax and Financial Services is to help retirees and soon-to-be retirees achieve their financial dreams through low risk investments, comprehensive financial planning, and tax minimization strategies. Financial planning is more than having a great stock or bond, it's more than having your money locked away in a low interest rate CD. A sound financial plan is one that helps you achieve your financial goals while accounting for all aspects of life; including taxes, Social Security, Medicare, and Risk Management—including planning for the unexpected and the inevitable.

Our holistic approach looks at all aspects of our clients' lives and takes in to account not only the hard cold logic of finance, but the human aspects of what it'll take to give our clients peace of mind.

Just as every person is unique so is every financial strategy. Our office lives by Colossians 3:23, " Whatever you do, work at it with all your heart as if working for the Lord."

Al teaches Sunday School to seniors and participates in mission trips to the Navajo Indian Reservation in New Mexico. As a heart transplant recipient, he volunteers with the North Carolina Organ Donor Association, speaking from personal experience about the impact of this life-changing gift. Al and his wife Susan enjoy traveling, working in their yard and spending time together.

CHAPTER 11

EMBRACING CHANGE AND TRANSITION

BY BRIAN BLACK

As I lay in bed, my mind began to race thinking about what the doctor was going to say about my newborn son. It had only been a couple of hours since Caden was born, but I knew something wasn't right. They had kept him in the nursery for an extended period of time throughout the night and most of the next day. During that time, the doctor informed us that Caden was going to be transported to another hospital two hours away for testing and further evaluation. As we got up early the next morning to make the trip, I still knew nothing about his condition. My only concern was getting to the hospital and finding out what was going on. My anxiety continued to escalate the closer I got and did not know what to expect when I saw him.

After going through the check-in process, I made my way up the elevator following the NICU (Neonatal Intensive Care Unit) directional signs on the wall. It was a maze that seemed to go on forever. When I arrived at the nurse's station, I told her that I was here to see Caden Black. I showed her my wristband and they allowed me through the doors. Because of the risk of infection, I had to put on a sterile gown over my clothes and wash my hands in a sterile sink with soap and water for at least thirty seconds – which seemed like an eternity. The nurse led me over to where Caden was lying in a crib wrapped up in blankets with a baby cap on his head. When I saw him, I was overtaken by the heart monitors, IV's, and feeding tube that was attached to his small cheek and that had been inserted into his nose. The first thing I noticed was that he was so weak that he couldn't grip my finger like a normal newborn. His lack of muscle tone was so severe that he couldn't even smile or hold his eyes open. He was unable to eat on his own and received the nutrition he needed through his feeding tube. As I sat and watched him sleep, I felt helpless not being able to help him in any way.

After seventeen long days of Caden's short life, he made enough progress where he was able to go home. Days later, I received a phone call from his doctor and vividly remember standing over his crib when receiving a final diagnosis. The conversation was short, but he informed me that Caden had what they call Prader-Willi Syndrome (PWS). The characteristics of PWS is low muscle tone, short stature, cognitive disabilities, problem behaviors, and chronic feeling of hunger that can lead to excessive eating and life-threatning obesity.

I began to struggle with the question of "Why Me?" My thought was that this experience is something that was supposed to happen to everyone else, not Brian Black. This is not what I had written in my "blueprint" for my life. My son was supposed to be the strong little guy that hit home runs and ran up and down the basketball court. He was going to be the star soccer player and be the fastest kid on the block. Academically, he was going to make good grades and excel in everything. However, that was not going to be the ultimate plan. My blueprint was changing and my life was about to be transformed forever.

That was eleven years ago, and I have learned more from Caden than he will ever learn from me. Even though he still has challenges ahead of him, I take one day at a time and dwell on what he CAN do instead of thinking about what he CAN'T. He does what he can with what circumstances he has been given. He has achieved MUCH more than I ever imagined at this point in his life, and I'm confident he will continue to thrive because of his desire to overcome his disability. One thing is for sure: Caden is going to make a difference in the lives of others and is going to excel in what he does in his own unique way.

So, how have I learned to embrace this type of change and transition in my life? Well, I definitely don't have all the answers, but I've come to realize that learning is an option. Therefore, I've tried to look back and learn from different experiences where I've gone through adversity and apply them to my life.

I want to share five words that I've used to help me find value in who I am, and experience victory in what I do. I believe these words define what we must learn in order to build a foundation for adjusting to change and reaching our full potential.

THE 5 D'S OF DIRECTION

(1). Desire: "Getting What You Want"

We all desire something in our lives. Last year I wanted to challenge myself to compete in what they call a "sprint triathlon." Now, this is not the Ironman that you often see on television, but a shorter version that consists of swimming, biking, and running a shorter distance. I knew it would be a big commitment, but I had the desire to discipline myself and be consistent in my training. After 4 months of preparation for the competition, I felt as if I was ready. I studied the race map in detail and developed my plan. As the gun fired and I went into the water to begin my swim, I was unable to see anything! Although my goggles were in place and I felt prepared, I began to panic. It seemed as if everyone was trying to swim on top of each other as I was kicked and pushed around in the water. Understand, I had read about strategy for the different stages of the race, but nowhere did it say that I might drown during the swim! As I tried to survive, it began to make sense. Training in the clear pool where I could see everything was much different than swimming in the open water.

After swallowing half the river, I finally made it to what they call the "transition" area where you prepare for the next stage of the race. I had all my gear organized on a towel beneath my bike that was on the rack and ready to go. I put on my helmet, shoes, and jersey and was off. As I began pedaling and increasing speed, I noticed that I had more energy. What was different and why all of a sudden did I feel more focused? The answer is that my "transition" to the bike and the run had been perfect. I was ready for the changes and made the adjustments I needed to make. Unlike the water, I had a clear vision of where I was going. I knew that with my desire to finish, I would be able to pace myself to the end.

Every day we get up and go in some direction. Whether it is left, right, or straight ahead, there is a course. However, from the very beginning I was thrown off my course, and wasn't able to recover. I will be the first one to admit, that it was a bad experience. However, through experiencing one bad thing, I was still able to make the transitions I needed in the middle of the race to conquer the course. The question is, "Are you change ready? Do you have the desire to make transitions in your life?"

(2). Dedication: "Forget It and Drive On"

F.I.D.O.... Don't be mistaken, I'm not referring to a dog here! I'm talking about being determined to achieve something, and if you fail, "Forget It And Drive On." I took this a step further when I was playing college baseball at Baylor University. Under the bill of my hat I wrote the initials F.I.D.O. to help me remember that if I made an error during the game or struck out, I needed to forget about it and take advantage of the next opportunity. While playing for Baylor, I estimated that I played in close to 275 games. During a game, I would normally get four times to bat, which means that I had 1,100 at bats during my career. Let's assume that the pitcher threw me an average of four pitches every time I went to bat. That results in being thrown 4,400 baseballs while trying to get a hit! You're now probably wondering how many of those baseballs did you actually hit! Well, if you know anything about baseball, you know that you are considered to be a successful hitter if you can get a hit three out of every ten times. That leaves seven times where you're either going to strike out or not get a hit. It can be frustrating, especially if it happens seven times in a row! I've been there and if you think about it too much and let it get in your head, things may only get worse. So, I had to have a short memory and remember that if I didn't do as well as I wanted on the first time I went to bat, that I had three other chances throughout the game. That's where F.I.D.O. became part of my mental game, and it was just as important as the physical. It would remind me that regardless what happened on the field, I had to keep a level head in order to perform for the entire nine innings of the game. I had to be dedicated to go out every day and keep swinging the bat and never giving up. Still today, every time I walk in my office, I see my hat in a glass case and it reminds me of the many times I had to look under it and read those four letters to have the dedication I need to succeed in all that I do!

(3). Determination: "One Foot In Front Of The Other"

I remember when Caden was two years old. We had him riding a horse to increase the strength of his spinal column and create better balance.

Because of his weakness, Caden didn't walk for the first time in the living room like most kids. He walked for the first time after getting off a horse! It was an alternative way to help him create the balance and strength he needed to accomplish a task. He had to put one foot in front of the other in order to begin building the muscles in his legs. He showed determination that he wanted to overcome the inability to walk. Determination is a powerful tool and it must be a mental part of who we are in order to achieve the goals that we have. Where there is a will, there is a way!

(4). Discipline: "Getting Where You Need To Go"

Without discipline, you have nothing. If you have no mission, you go nowhere. Without implementation of thoughts and ideas, there will never be action. Without action, you will only waste your time. It's like training for a marathon. You become disciplined to work out every day, but after the race you quit your routine. At that point, you find yourself starting over 6 months later when you could have just maintained the shape you were in. Believe me, I've been there, done that, and it makes no sense!! Maybe it's something different for you, but I'm sure you can identify! If you are going to get what you want out of life, you have to figure out what you need, and discipline yourself to get where you want to go.

(5). Destination: "The Journey"

Without a doubt, I know that my life is eternal and my destination is well beyond this earth. However, there are many in this world that seek to find purpose each and every day and they can't find it. I truly believe that if you can take responsibility for who you are, have confidence in what you do, and find the hope that is going to get you where you want to go, you will be able to navigate your way down a road that leads you to getting the most out of the gifts and talents you have been given. The fact is that life is not a smooth highway, it is more like a country road with bumps and holes in it. The goal is understanding how to sustain the bumps and not get "stuck" in the holes. If we don't acquire the skills to do those things, there is going to be a rough road ahead. But remember, just because you see a sign that says SHARP CURVE 300 FT. AHEAD doesn't mean you're going to end up in the ditch unless you don't know how to make the turn!

Whether it is a career, a relationship, or circumstances we experience in our lives, we will continuously experience change and transition on a daily basis. It's not a matter of if; it's a matter of when. Personally I've experienced all three. I've been laid off from my job, gone through a divorce after sixteen years of marriage, and have a child with special needs. I didn't plan on those things being a part of my "blueprint" for life. After these types of life changes, many people ask themselves, "Where do I go from here?" I believe that we must focus on answering the question of, "Where do I **GROW** from here?" What will be your destination?

The choice is yours!

About Brian

Brian Black is a Certified Professional Coach and Master Practitioner in administering the Energy Life Index Assessment developed by the Institute of Professional Excellence in Coaching (IPEC). As a graduate of Baylor University, he completed his undergraduate degree in Health & Human Performance where he played baseball as a student-athlete. Brian went on to earn his Master's Degree in Educational Psychology from Baylor and resides in Waco, Texas where he is CEO/ Founder of Brian Black Coaching. He is recognized as being one of America's Premier Experts in coaching the leaders of today to embrace change and transition in the new emerging generation of those who have primarily been educated by the internet. He is a member of the International Coach's Federation (ICF) and acts as a public speaker, conducts workshops, and works with clients one-on-one within his practice.

After two years in private practice as a counselor, Brian spent twelve years in the corporate world working for some of the largest Fortune 500 medical device companies in the world. He spent his time primarily in sales with Johnson & Johnson and Pfizer. In addition, he spent several years in the private business sector working for several start-up medical device companies. Brian holds his Real Estate license in the state of Texas and has spent time working in that market as well.

Over the past two years, he has stepped out of corporate to pursue what he feels is a calling to use the gifts, talents, and experience he has to help others identify who they are, define what they want to do, and help them get to where they want to go. Brian believes that whether it is a career, relationship, or circumstances in life, learning to embrace change and transition will define your self-growth and development.

Brian can be reached at: brian@brianblackcoaching.com or directly by phone at: (254) 495-2527. You can visit his website at: www. brianblackcoaching.com.

Be sure to follow Brian on Twitter @Bblackcoaching
"Friend up Brian on Facebook: Facebook.com/BrianBlackCoaching

CHAPTER 12

THE TRANSFORMING POWER OF A SMILE

BY BRIAN BERGH, DDS, MS

Every time you smile at someone, it is an action of love,
a gift to that person, a beautiful thing.
~ Mother Teresa

Think back to when you were a child and someone smiled at you. You probably smiled right back, didn't you? Children smile about 400 times every day. And it's been shown that 50% of people will return a smile, even to a total stranger.

What is it about a smile that is so important? And why as adults have we seemed to forget how to smile? Did you know that adults typically only smile 20 times each day? A far cry from when we were children. What happens to us as we get older?

Human emotions, including happiness, have been studied for years. In particular, smiling has been studied extensively.

Smiling has a huge impact not only on your health, but it can also enhance the success and quality of your relationships, both business and personal.

A study at UC-Berkeley looked at yearbook senior photographs. The broadness of the students' smiles was measured and compared to the success of their marriages and also how much impact they had on others.

Those with broader smiles had both more successful marriages and greater impact on those around them. Makes sense, doesn't it? Smiling is the universal language of love and caring.

Another study, from Wayne State University, looked at the pictures on baseball trading cards from the 1950's. Again, the broadness of the players' smiles was studied and shown to have a great impact on their future success. This time on how long they would live. Those who had broader smiles lived over seven years longer! When you first think about it, it doesn't make sense that smiling would increase lifespan almost 10 percent. Continue reading, and you will discover some of the reasons why this happens.

Smiling people are perceived as looking younger than people with neutral expressions, by at least three years. So smiling regularly can both extend your life and make you look younger at the same time. Maybe a simple smile is the fountain of youth.

Another study at Penn State University showed that people who smiled appeared more likable, more courteous, and more competent. All three are important in future success.

Human emotions play a big part in our everyday interactions. When we meet someone for the first time, we are judged within the first few seconds. How we present ourselves, our dress, our confidence and our appearance in that first encounter will likely determine the future of that relationship. There are no second chances to make a good first impression.

To be successful in today's world, gaining the extra edge is critical. Those who smile and show a genuine enjoyment of what they are doing, the project they are working on, are felt by others to be easier to work with. And people are more inclined to be cooperative with someone who smiles. How much does a smile cost? Nothing, nada. Looking at the return on investment from a smile, it could possibly be the best investment you could ever make.

Imagine you are meeting someone for the first time. You approach that individual and they look at you with no facial expression, no smile. What is your reaction? You're probably not very excited to continue that relationship, and it would take a lot of time to overcome that poor introduction.

Now, imagine a different scenario. One where the same individual greets you enthusiastically (not too enthusiastically, though), with a big, genuine smile. Totally different experience, right? How likely are you to want to continue that relationship? If you're like most people, you are very likely to want to move forward in that relationship.

This is the power of a genuine smile.

A study, reported in *Neuropsychologia*, showed that our brains may very likely be programmed to pay attention to smiling faces. People were asked to look at photos of smiling and neutral faces. When the pictures were shown again, it was clear that the individuals with smiling faces were better recalled than those who were not smiling. We all know that messages seen over again stick better in our brains. Think of the repetition of products that we see on commercials and other advertising and marketing material. Don't you begin to feel more familiar and more comfortable with a product or service the more times you see the advertisements? When we meet someone for the first time and smile in the interaction, we will likely be remembered at a subsequent meeting. With trust being paramount in creating and maintaining a personal or professional relationship, being remembered and recognized will help increase that trust, increasing future opportunities.

A genuine smile has major health benefits, also. We've already seen that those who smile broadly will live longer and look younger. Smiling also lowers heart rate, reduces stress (by increasing endorphin production), creates a better mood and increases productivity. Smiling also reduces physical and emotional pain and boosts our immune system, relaxing our bodies and allowing the immune system to react quicker and more effectively.

What can you do if you don't feel like smiling? What if you're "down in the dumps" and just don't want to smile at anyone? Charles Darwin, in his Facial Feedback Response Theory, theorized that facial expressions don't necessarily function to show your mind's mental state, but that facial expressions can actually determine your mental state. In other words, by smiling, you make yourself want to smile. You've no doubt heard the phrase "fake it, 'til you make it" many times, I'm sure. The mere act of setting the stage for the feeling you'd like to have will create that actual feeling.

Dr. Michael Levis at Cardiff University used botox injections on individuals to keep them from being able to frown. The people in the study reported feeling happier and less anxious. Now, I'm not saying you should go to this extent, but it does show how much our external expressions have on our internal state of mind and feelings.

If you listen to Brian Tracy speak about self-confidence, you'll hear him tell you that one of the best things you can do is to say over and over again "I like myself, I like myself." There is tremendous power in this short and simple statement. The same can be said about your smile. Speaking the same words, but substituting "smile" for "myself" will give you a great start in confidently showing your smile. "I like my smile, I like my smile." You can even say "I love to smile, I love to smile" and change your state of mind.

But sometimes even great self-confidence can't overcome the appearance of a smile. We can do everything in our own power to improve our smile and appearance, yet we can still be self-conscious about our smiles. And each and every day we don't smile to our fullest, we are losing opportunities for success.

A recent study looked at both professional and personal success based on the whiteness of the teeth. People who had whitened their teeth were more likely to be hired and were also more likely to be offered a higher salary than those who hadn't whitened their teeth. Imagine that, whiter teeth can improve your chance of getting a job and increase the wage you'll be paid. This study also showed that there was greater interest in continuing a personal relationship with people who had whitened their teeth. Individuals with whiter teeth are also more likely to have greater financial and professional success and are thought to be more trustworthy.

So what if you are self-conscious about your smile? You're embarrassed to smile because of the way your teeth look. Maybe your teeth dull and discolored, or maybe your teeth are crooked and mal-aligned, or maybe you're missing some teeth. Many people are in this position. They wonder what can be done, what their options are. The great news is that you have several options to change all of these.

Whitening teeth has never been easier than it is today. With multiple options, anyone above a certain age can whiten their teeth. Many products, including whitening toothpastes, whitening strips and other teeth whitening products can be purchased over the counter. These products offer an easy way to whiten and brighten your teeth in the privacy of your own home. The amount of change can be slight, but enough to make a noticeable change in the appearance of your teeth. Whitening kiosks are present in many malls across the United States and can make greater changes in the appearance of your teeth. For significant changes in the coloration of your teeth, a dental professional would be the best professional to see. From take-home teeth whitening kits, to in-office treatments, the amount of whitening done by a dentist can be much greater than using over-the-counter products. And the dental professional can monitor the health of your teeth at the same time.

Whitening your teeth will make them look more attractive and healthy. But what if your teeth are crooked or you have missing teeth? These are procedures that should be done by a dental professional, your dentist or orthodontist.

Today's orthodontic treatment to align and straighten teeth is more popular with adults than at any time in history. Many adults did not have the opportunity to have their teeth straightened when they were children. We also see adults who have had previous orthodontic treatment and teeth have shifted due to varying factors. With the current advances in orthodontic treatment, the stigma of having traditional metal braces is a thing of the past. There are more options for a more cosmetic appearance of braces than ever before. Clear aligners, clear braces and concealed braces (braces behind the teeth), provide adults with more choices to align their teeth without the look of traditional metal braces. There are even tooth-colored wires available to help reduce any metal appearance of the braces. And adult treatment can be done quicker and more comfortably than in the past, too. Advances in the orthodontic field are creating more and more options for adult cosmetic orthodontics every year. And not only are well-aligned teeth more attractive, they are also healthier.

Cosmetic dentistry is another option for people with chipped or worn down teeth and severe discoloration of the teeth. Veneers (thin tooth-colored porcelain covers) or crowns can change both the shape and color of the teeth. These changes can be almost instantaneous, often taking less than one to two weeks.

You can now see how much your smile can transform you; not only in your personal life but also your professional life. And your smile will not only transform you, but will transform those you come in contact with, too. If you have something of value to give or sell to others, one of the best ways to begin is with a smile. That smile will help get you in the door and will allow you to have influence over others; the opportunity for you to change the world around you.

The "Butterfly Effect" is a theory that when a butterfly flaps its wings, there is a small change in the environment around the butterfly. With the proper conditions, that simple flutter of the butterfly's wings could eventually cause a full hurricane on the other side of the world. Think of the power a smile, your smile, could have on the world. Just like the butterfly, your smile could cause a transformation half-way across the world. We can never fully know what change can happen because of our actions. Think of the changes you would like to see in your life, the lives of your family and friends, the world. And start each interaction with one of the most powerful expressions you can ever use – your smile. The value of a beautiful and healthy smile can really be considered priceless when you look at the opportunities that smile will bring to your life and others around you.

About Brian

Dr. Brian H. Bergh is a 2nd generation orthodontist following in the foot-steps of his father, Dr. Harold Bergh. Dr. Brian Bergh started in the orthodontic field at the tender young age of 13 working for his father as a lab technician. His love for orthodontics continued to grow as he continued to work in his father's office through high school and college. Dr. Bergh graduated from Loma Linda University Dental School in 1990 and served as president of his dental class for two years. He was elected to the OKU Dental Honor Fraternity, an honor reserved for the top 10% of dental students nationwide. Dr. Brian Bergh entered the University of Southern California graduate orthodontic program by invitation and earned his Master of Science Degree in Craniofacial Biology and Certificate in Orthodontics in 1992.

Dr. Bergh maintains an active role in our local community, as well as in the dental field. Dr. Bergh has served as President of the Glendale Academy of Dentists, the USC Orthodontic Alumni Association, the Glendale Healthy Kids and the Glendale Noon Rotary Club. Dr. Bergh also spent several years as a regional editor for the Pacific Coast Society of Orthodontics Bulletin. Dr. Bergh has served as a Clinical Professor at the USC School of Dentistry, where he's lectured and instructed dental students in Orthodontics. He currently holds study clubs instructing general dentists and dental hygienists about Orthodontics and Invisalign.

Dr. Bergh believes that education is the key to providing the best orthodontic treatment available. He routinely earns over 75 (3 times the required amount) hours of continuing education credits each year, with more than half of those hours concentrating on the Invisalign Treatment System.

Dr. Bergh has been recognized as one of America's Top Dentists for several years and also voted Best Orthodontist in Glendale and the Foothill area many times. His office has received the Talk of the Town 5-star award for outstanding customer service for the past 5 years in a row. Dr. Bergh was recently recognized by *Los Angeles Magazine's* 2014 Southern California Super Dentists.

Dr. Bergh is married to his lovely wife, Tina, who he met through the orthodontic profession. They have 3 children, Kaila, Kaigan and Bryley, a wild and spirited Poo-chon named Maddi and 4 Koi fish in their backyard pond. Dr. Bergh loves to go to Magic Mountain and ride the coasters, to Dave & Busters to play the video games and to the movies to see the latest comedy films.

CHAPTER 13

AIM HIGHER FOR SUCCESS

BY CARL J. BLACKBURN, O.D.

Looking around the room, I was able to associate names with two of these familiar faces, Warner Roberts, a local TV personality and Herb Kelleher, the co-founder of Southwest Airlines. We were all gathered at The Houstonian Hotel to hear a speech by W. Clement Stone. I was very glad to have been invited but I had no clue why I had been invited. I was a subscriber to Stone's magazines, *Success Unlimited* and *PMA Advisor*, maybe that was the reason. Whatever the reason, I was there to thank him; it would probably be my only chance to ever see him in person.

We had been close friends for many years but he didn't know it. We first became acquainted when I started professional school. A friend gave me a copy of *Success through a Positive Mental Attitude* by Napoleon Hill & W. Clement Stone. I had never read anything about how to become successful. For the first time, I took step back from my life and examined where I was going with my life. I was determined to begin using these principles of success to improve my life, to improve my chances of success. For the first time, I understood that if I was going to become successful, I needed to take control of my mind and direct my thoughts toward success. My first goal was to graduate from professional school and I did.

After graduation, I was employed by several established practitioners. I learned a lot from them. Eventually, when I thought I had enough "activity knowledge," I purchased an optical franchise. I built my optical franchise into one of the highest volume locations and eventually opened several other franchise locations. Sixteen years following my graduation, I had gained a lot of valuable experience running high volume optical franchises, had been President of our state association, had run a marathon, had a paid-for home with a Porsche in the garage, and had two loving daughters and a beautiful wife. I was coasting along thinking I was successful.

One day, while talking with one of the founders of the optical franchises, I made several suggestions on how we could improve our business. I offered these suggestions to him on a fairly regular basis but very few of them were ever put into place. After listening to my suggestions and probably tiring of hearing them, he said, "If you are so damn smart, how come you aren't rich?" He said it in jest but that thought stuck in my mind. He was a multi-millionaire and he was measuring success quite differently than I had been.

I kept thinking about what he said and realized that I was in a rut, certainly it was an affluent rut but I knew I needed a new challenge. I thought, maybe I haven't been aiming high enough. Owning a franchise has some very positive attributes but it also has some negative aspects. You have agreed to run your business by their operating system. Creativity and innovation are usually not a big part of any franchise system.

I started thinking about going into another business but rejected that idea. It would have been very foolish to throw away my 16 years of optical experience. My first employer had a full surface optical laboratory. During the five years I was affiliated with his practice, I had learned how to manufacture glasses. Thoughts of creating a new optical concept with an in-house optical laboratory had been popping into my mind for several years but I had never acted on the idea.

So I stepped back and started looking at the optical business with a very critical eye. How could it be improved? What are some important patient problems that could be made better? If I could design the perfect optical business what would it look like? What do patients complain about? Maybe I could speed up the manufacture of glasses so that patients could get their new glasses in a few hours instead of waiting for a week. Maybe our location should be open from 10am until 8pm...six days a week so that patients would have access without needing to take off of work…and be more accessible. Maybe we should have a super large selection of eyeglass frames with each category displayed in a different department. Maybe we should have optometrist's and ophthalmologist's offices located nearby. I could visualize our new optical superstore concept in my mind.

I considered every option I could think of…all towards the goal of opening the best optical that had ever been created. I immediately started putting together a plan of action on a yellow legal pad. I ordered my action plan with the highest priority items first…and I refined and worked on my plan every day. Some 14 months after I began my plan, we opened the first 1-hour optical superstore in a mall location. It was a brand new eyewear and eye care concept. Would eyewear customers like our new superstore? Would it be successful? We had taken a big risk.

The night before our grand opening, we were discussing our prospects and I observed that if we could just gross $3000 the first day, we might be successful. We had to remain open until 9:30pm that first night, but we did make $3000. Customers loved our concept…after selecting their eyewear, some watched through the windows as we fabricated their lenses; others left with pagers and went shopping until we paged them when their new glasses were ready. We were surprised at the volume of business we started doing…the first year we grossed over $2.5 million. We were the highest grossing optical in the USA.

We began making plans to expand our Eye+Tech optical superstore concept. We started construction on three locations. As we were nearing completion, misfortune struck, our financing fell through. We were suddenly scrambling to make payments so that we could get these new locations open. I sold my franchises, invested my savings, maxed my credit cards…raising just enough money to just get the doors open. We were in a serious financial situation.

My Eye+Tech financial mess was the reason why I was at the Houstonian Hotel meeting. My financial mess was why I wanted to personally thank W. Clement Stone. During those months and months of financial anxiety, every night, for me to keep a positive mental attitude, I reread *Success through a Positive Mental Attitude*. I thought about the principles and concepts found in that book. I knew that with PMA I could attract solutions to my financial problems. Eventually, we thought up some successful promotions that improved our cash flow. Our patient volume began growing. We started making money. We began to work our way out of our financial problems but we still had a long way to go.

Trying to raise additional funding, we put together a presentation binder and started visiting different venture capital groups. We took a lot of time with our presentation binder with bios, photos, expansion plans and projections. We knew the optical business and we wanted our presentation binder to reflect our experience, abilities and prospects. Unfortunately, we really had no luck with the venture capital people. They wanted a lot more of the company than we were willing to give.

One day, in my office, the telephone rang. When I answered, a gentleman told me his name and said he would be in Houston in a few days that he was with a company that had some interest in the one-hour optical superstore business. We set up the meeting and thanks to our presentation; we had a new partner, The Gillette Company. They purchased a 40% interest in our company plus agreed to fund our expansion plans.

Gillette was a great partner. We started opening stores and in a few years we had built and opened 22 Eye+Tech optical superstores in six states; Texas, New Mexico, Colorado, Arizona, California and Washington. I was the Chairman of the Board and the CEO of the company.

It was during that time that the Houstonian Hotel meeting occurred. At that meeting, during a break, I approached Mr. Stone, introduced myself, and told him my story about starting Eye+Tech. I discussed how I had gone through some very tough times getting started and keeping it going. How by reading his books and articles, he had helped me to control my thoughts. How PMA had put me and kept me on the road to success. How we were now enjoying great success, opening stores and making money. I told him how I felt without his help I couldn't have made it and that I wanted to sincerely thank him for all he had done for me. When I finished, his eyes sparkled, and with a big smile and his booming voice, he congratulated me and shaking my hand, said, "I bet you would like to hug me for that." I said that I believed that I would and...I did...and we both laughed and had a celebration of success.

I didn't realize it at that time, but about 2 years after my conversation with Mr. Stone, I would undergo another severe test. We had continued building and opening Eye+Tech stores. We had developed a system where in 90 days after signing the lease we could have a store up and running. We had 38 stores, when Gillette came to me with some bad news. They were undergoing a takeover attempt and wanted to sell all of their investments except the razor blade business. They needed the cash to buy their own common stock.

With that conversation, I had gone from opening and managing 38 Eye+Tech stores to trying to sell the entire business. I wasn't happy about that but I was determined to get the job done. By controlling my thoughts and always keeping a Positive Mental Attitude, I changed my focus towards making the best of our situation.

In 6 months, I was able to find a buyer and close the deal. Despite the fact that a leading investment banking firm had valued our company at $18 million, I sold Eye+Tech to a large optical corporation for $32 million.

It was just 7 years from the day I first started creating the Eye+Tech concept until we sold the company. Those thoughts, ideas, plans plus a lot of hard work by me and my Eye+Tech colleagues were worth $32 million. My goal in aiming higher had been achieved.

I want to share some ideas to help you achieve success:

1. Never be satisfied at where you are in your life. Always be progressing towards some greater goal…always be aiming higher.

2. Look at your business or profession with a very critical eye. Ask yourself, how can your customer's experience be improved? Search for ideas to improve some aspect of your business. Look for ways to do something to better serve people. Become a leading expert in your field.

3. Immediately begin writing down all of the ideas that come to you. Keep them organized by category. Remember everything that exists today, first started as someone's thought or idea. Ideas are always out there but you must tune yourself into them. If you are creating, the ideas will come to you. Immediately write down and act on these ideas.

4. Develop a written plan of action. Prioritize the items in your plan. Associate a time schedule with each item in your action plan.

5. Put aside everything in your life and focus solely on following each part of your plan towards success.

6. Expect that something unexpected could happen and if it does, work your way through the problem by controlling your thoughts with PMA.

7. Read personal development and positive motivational books and articles. Listen to audio tapes. Attend and learn from seminars. Keep your mind charged with PMA.

I wish you well on your journey to success…I only ask one favor…

That you begin your success journey at this very moment!

About Carl

Carl J. Blackburn, O.D. was an undergraduate at the University of Oklahoma and received his Optometry degree from the University of Houston / College of Optometry.

Carl is a member of the Texas Optometric Association, the American Optometric Association and the Energeyes Association. He is licensed by the Texas Optometry Board as a Therapeutic Optometrist and an Optometric Glaucoma Specialist.

Carl is a member of the Optometric Business Academy Advisory Panel. He was a lecturer from 2006 until 2010 at the Optometric Business Academy's Elite Seminars. He frequently contributes practice management and motivational articles to Foresight and the Acuity in Business optometric publications and the Energeyes Association's website and newsletter. He lectures nationally on practice management: *Dynamic Growth in an Optometric Practice – Getting to the Next Level.*

Carl J. Blackburn is a Professional Development Consultant for a leading contact lens manufacturer. He conducts national seminars to help Doctors understand techniques that will help them build their contact lens practices.

Throughout his optometric career, Carl has been recognized as a practice management innovator. In 2006, he was named *Innovator of the Year* by the Optical Division of Walmart. For his work in creating Eye+Tech, the one-hour optical superstore concept, he was featured in management guru Tom Peters' video series, *The Next Step – Innovation in Customer Service.*

He is currently working on a book about the discovery of some secret manuscripts attributed to Thomas Aquinas.

CHAPTER 14

SALES PROMOTION: TRANSFORMING YOUR BUSINESS FROM SURVIVAL TO THRIVING

BY DANETTE GOSSETT

My first encounter with marketing occurred when I was 14 years old and was asked to participate in a focus group. I, of course didn't know what a focus group was at that time. Turns out it's a guided group discussion about a product, service, ad campaign, political campaign or just about anything you'd like feedback about. Would you buy the product if they said this, use a service if you heard a particularly phrased testimonial, or even as simple as choosing one color over another? My first focus group experience was to comment about the new design of a soda can. I found it fascinating.

The president of the marketing research company was my church youth group leader, so I was asked to participate in many groups over the next few years. And I became more and more intrigued by all the elements that went into marketing a product or service.

I started working for the company the summer after I turned 16 and for all the summers and breaks through college. I conducted telephone surveys (this was when you really didn't mind someone calling you and asking questions – people wanted to talk to me); I did on-site intercepts (asking people questions in a mall or in front of a theme park) and even door-to-door surveys.

In college I studied marketing management and market research and after graduation headed to New York City to work on Madison Avenue in some of the best-known advertising agencies. I was fortunate to work on many well-known national brands developing not only advertising campaigns, but also direct mail and sales promotion programs.

Initially, I resented working on the non-advertising marketing initiatives because I thought they were not as important or impactful (or as much fun as shooting on location in Hawaii) as a television commercial.

After many years in the "business" I came to realize that my early training in all marketing tactics, and especially sales promotion, was going to be the key to my long-term success. I learned how a fully-integrated marketing campaign could literally transform a company from survival to thriving.

I've learned that most people are confused about what "marketing" is. When I introduce myself the first response is, "Oh, you must be in Public Relations," or "You must be with an advertising agency." I've never been in PR and while I do advertising within a sales promotion program at times, I'm not an advertising agency, so that confuses people even more.

Basically, marketing is everything your company does to attract business. From the development of the logo and business card and website to advertising campaigns, public relations, social media, collateral materials, direct mail, sales promotions and more.

Of course, there are businesses that specialize in one or several or all of those marketing tactics. They are there to help you maximize your budget and make sure you are utilizing the best tactics for your business success.

Over the years I have narrowed my focus to mainly concentrate on sales promotion programs.

Why? I've always found that sales promotion is a key component of most marketing plans and I can be very creative in their development.

Sales promotion by nature is designed to change the buying behavior of a target audience to purchase something NOW, not in the future. In other words, it's a short-term incentive designed to create an immediate need and transform the "looker" into a buyer.

For example, how many times have you opened your Sunday newspaper to see a coupon for something you don't necessarily need right now, but the offer enticed you to buy now. I recently responded to a "60% off framing for this week only" offer. It was on my list of to do's but it didn't have to happen right away. That was an effective sales promotion in reaching me and getting me to respond immediately.

So how do you develop an effective sales promotion that reaches your target customers and transforms them into happy customers now?

First, you need to know who your best customers are. The loyal most profitable customers are the ones that you want to profile, not just someone that shops your loss leaders every week. If you don't have your customer profile defined, then it's time to develop a clear understanding of your best target customer including their basic demographics, psychographics as well as what they buy, at what price, when and how often.

Understanding your target customer will help you in developing an effective sales promotion that will "speak" specifically to their needs and thereby increase your overall response rate and sales.

Sales promotions are an effective means for bringing in new customers, moving customers away from the competition, getting loyal customers to buy more or try another product or service, stimulating business during slow times and many other needs that require a change in the customers' behavior.

For instance, you have a sales plan with a quarterly sales goal and at the start of the third month of the quarter your sales are flat. What do you do?

An effective sales promotion can bring a quick traffic-building boost to your quarter. How many times have you seen an automobile dealer running specials at the end of a quarter? Maybe a special financing deal, special sale price if purchased before the 1st or low down payment offer, all designed to get their target customers in the door to buy now. That's a sales promotion offer.

What about attracting a new audience to your business? Not long ago we developed a promotion to bring more group meeting business to a cruise line. Their research indicated it was a good fit for their business, but this audience had been solicited several times before with little or no success.

We determined this target needed a longer explanation to achieve the level of understanding of the benefits the cruise line could bring to their group meetings. Because of the message length, we decided to use direct mail to deliver the promotional offer. It included a multi-level box, gift and an offer of a free cruise so they could experience all that the cruise line had to offer their group meetings.

It was very well received, achieving an 8% response that ultimately translated into more than $10MM in sales. It was their highest return on investment (ROI) of any promotional offer that year.

As you can see, a sales promotion can be extremely varied. They can include:

- *Buy-One-Get-One Free Offers:* BOGO's – many retailers utilize this offer regularly
- *Discount or Money-Off Coupons or Vouchers:* In the newspaper, flyers, downloadable from a website; $1.00 off your next purchase
- *Gift with Purchase:* Buy a full size, get the travel size free; buy a razor get a shave cream sample for free
- *Free Promotional Gift:* Your logo-branded promotional gift; stop by our trade show booth and receive a free calculator, travel mug, USB
- *Free Samples:* Tastings of food or drink at supermarkets; free sunscreen at festivals; hand sanitizer at the mall
- *Website or Social Media Efforts:* Like our page and get a free upgrade or discount
- *Joint Promotions:* Buy a theme park ticket and get a discount or upgraded hotel stay; rent an SUV and get a free ski or bike rack
- *Sweepstakes:* Prizes are given by the luck of the draw when participating, think free Superbowl tickets when you enter a drawing

- *Contests:* Create a recipe and be entered into a chance to win a new Kitchen – you have to "do" something to be entered, just entering a drawing is a sweepstakes
- *Cause-related efforts:* A wine company donates 50% of the proceeds to a charity
- *Finance deals:* 0% financing for 5 years on selected vehicles; lower down payment
- *Upgrades:* Rent an economy car for 7 days and get upgraded to mid-size
- *Service offers:* Free delivery; free training

However, be careful that sales promotions are not your only marketing tactic, because constantly running a sales promotion can have an impact on your overall brand image.

The long-term benefits of a well-thought out and executed sales promotion program can build your short term sales success, help to bring in new customers and build on your desired brand image. However, on the negative side, a poorly-managed promotion could negate your long-standing positive brand position.

For instance, you introduce a sales promotion with a limited time restriction "for this week only" offer. If you repeatedly extend the time restriction then your customers will realize that the sale price is just the new price thus negating the purpose of the promotion, bringing in immediate sales. It can also alter the perception of your company and the quality of your products or services, effectively changing your company to being seen as a strictly "discount" brand. Now, you can run a weekly promotion, just make sure it's a different product or service being offered each time.

Are you ready to boost your sales and transform your business from survival to thriving? Here are 3 promotional tactics that have proven to be effective for a wide variety of businesses, big and small:

1. Create An Added-Value Promotion
This strategy can utilize any number of the various tactics listed above. For this to be most effective it's best to know what your competitors are offering and go bigger. Maybe you don't want to discount or discount as much as your competitor and get into a

pricing war. So an alternative is to add value. In other words, giving your customers something they would value, want or need when they make their purchase. For instance, a gift card (dollar amount would be dependent on the value of the sales item of course), free delivery, tickets to a local event, movies, e-books, music downloads, free gift (not necessarily a sample size, but something that would complement what they are purchasing). For example, with gas prices so high today many retailers are offering a free gas card with purchase. A friend of mine is now a new and loyal customer of one retailer because of that very sales promotion.

2. Give a Surprise Reward

This is similar to the added value promotion and could be many of the same items but the "gift" is a surprise your customers receive with their purchase. This promotion is not communicated ahead of time, hence the "surprise". Being a surprise engages customers and thanks them for their business and loyalty. It gives you an opportunity to exceed their expectations thus thwarting any of your competitor's future promotional efforts to steal your now more loyal customers. My friend with the gas card now shops regularly at that retailer and is constantly telling me of the upgrades or free gifts she receives with purchase. The advertised free gas card promotion brought her in and the surprise "rewards" are keeping her more loyal. I asked if she'd keep going back if the gas cards are eliminated, she said "absolutely."

3. Social Media is Talking

As we all know, social media can be a highly effective way to reach your customers. So why not get them talking about you! You may have an active social networking community that can help extend your message to an even broader audience. Are you using it? Are you familiar with Facebook, Twitter, Instagram, Pinterest, YouTube, Google+, Foursquare, Flickr, WhatsApp or any of the almost daily-added options? If not, it's time to get your feet wet! I am sure we've all seen some of the recent campaigns that moved events from social media to the evening news! The possibilities are endless. We had a national ice cream brand recently give free samples away at a local outdoor mall. It was only mentioned on twitter and they had people lining up for blocks and it made the evening news. At the event they gave coupons for a discount on the next purchase. I am sure the promotion was duplicated in many markets and was quite successful in increasing sales.

For any promotion, just make sure it's something that makes sense for your customer. Think about what would motivate them to purchase from you and you are on your way to transforming your business to greater success.

About Danette

Danette Gossett resides in Coconut Grove, Florida, just south of downtown Miami. She is the founder of Gossett Marketing Communications, Inc. and co-founder of Promotions Resource LLC.

Danette brings more than 30 years of experience developing advertising campaigns, direct marketing programs and sales promotions to her clients. Prior to starting her companies, she worked for New York advertising agencies including Saatchi & Saatchi & Lowe Marschalk. Her corporate experience included National Advertising Director for Avis Rent a Car Systems, Inc., and Director of Marketing Services for Royal Caribbean Cruise Line.

Her company, Gossett Marketing has been working with a wide variety of national and Florida-based clients for more than 20 years. They specialize in building loyalty, growing sales and incentivizing action that delivers results through sales promotions, promotional products, incentive programs and direct mail.

Gossett Marketing is a WBENC nationally-certified Woman-Owned Enterprise.

Her partnership venture, Promotions Resource LLC with Kevin Danaher, recently launched a new authority website: www.SalesPromotions.org. This marketing resource network is designed to assist businesses in understanding and creating effective sales promotions to increase sales now.

Danette has won a number of industry awards and recognition: EXPY Award from the National Association of Experts, Writers & Speakers, Gold Effie for Advertising Effectiveness, Hot Creative from Direct Magazine, Outstanding Woman Business Owner of Miami Dade County by the National Association of Women Business Owners, Bronze Award for Best Blog from the Promotional Products Association International, Top 100 Minority Business of Miami-Dade County by the Greater Miami Chamber of Commerce and the Decade of Excellence from the Women's Business Development Council of Florida.

Danette is active in the community as well, a past Chair of the Coral Gables Chamber of Commerce, past President of the Foundation of the Coral Gables Chamber of Commerce, Mentor for the University of Miami School of Business, Trustee and member of the Board of Directors of the Greater Miami Chamber of Commerce and Chair of the Good to Great Awards for the Greater Miami Chamber of Commerce.

For more information visit the websites: SalesPromotions.org, GossettMktg.com and InterestingMarketingTidbits.com.

Also, please follow them on Twitter at @Marketngtibits and @SalesPromoOrg.

CHAPTER 15

IT'S ONLY HALFTIME—
THE 7-STEP PLAYBOOK TO
TRANSFORM YOUR LIFE

BY DR. ANDREAS BOETTCHER

Having been an entrepreneur since my early 20's, I had the good fortune of experiencing a great deal of success as a chiropractor, real estate investor, network marketer and Ironman triathlete. Life was great and exciting, having built several million-dollar businesses by the age of 38. However, in 2009, with the downturn in real estate and some tough decisions, I reset every aspect of my life. Essentially, I lost everything, went through a divorce, and even underwent emergency back surgery in less than a year; turning me from "Ironman" to "aluminum man" seemingly overnight. I had no choice but to reinvent myself professionally…but how? I had no working capital, a severe back injury and not to mention just moved to a new state.

This is when I discovered the key to dealing with these challenging times in life. It is to focus on positive knowing, not just positive thinking. After all, I was successful before and knew that I could do it again. That's positive knowing – using your knowledge and experience to catapult you to a new level of success. Never to be stripped away. Unless you allow some event, circumstance or person to take it? Only you hold that power.

IT'S ONLY HALFTIME

We all have opportunities in life that resemble halftime at your favorite sporting event. While the crowd is enjoying the halftime entertainment, the players are taking that time to ReSet, ReFuel, and ReCommit. "Halftime" is an opportunity for new decisions and new actions for a life and business you love. Whether you are up by 20 or down by 20, how will you come out of the tunnel for the second half?

It's Only Halftime is a story of transformation and reinvention. It's about embracing change and overcoming complacency. It's about living your true purpose in life and not living life as if it were a dress rehearsal.

In just a moment I will share with you my abbreviated 7 Step Playbook to Transformation. My own transformation has me working with some of the biggest brands and success experts in the world today. Leading me exactly where I want to be, helping people like you around the world live their true passion in life and amplifying their own voice, experience and expertise into profits and opportunity for those they serve.

Achievement comes down to the 4 D's – which are the foundation to the 7 Step Game Plan. To properly execute the Game Plan, you will need a:

1. Desire for a new future or result

2. Decision to make it happen

3. Discipline to see it through

4. Determination to Finish Strong

Let's put on our game face and get it done!

7 STEP PLAYBOOK TO TRANSFORM YOUR LIFE

I. Get clear on what you want.

Clarity is arguably the single most important word on the road to transformation. Fully 80% of your success comes from being absolutely clear about what you want to accomplish, even if you're not sure how. The best part about declaring halftime is having the opportunity to decide right now what you want. Then ask yourself, "Is what I'm doing right now bringing me closer or further away from my goal?"

Regardless of your story as it reads today, what will your new story be for the future? What do you want? Dream as if there are no barriers, no limitations and no possibilities of failure. What would you do differently? Write them down now in the present tense, as if they were already true.

Now the question is, are you willing to put the work in to make it happen? Success always looks easy from the outside but the journey is filled with obstacles, challenges, roadblocks and lessons. Remain clear and keep your eyes on the prize. You can have just about anything you want as long as you are willing to play 'all-out' but you must know your "end zone."

II. Why are you not there yet?

Is it a lack of desire, time, energy, education or resources? Maybe other commitments, another job, or naysayers are in your way? Is it someone else's fault, something you feel you deserved but didn't get? Be honest with yourself and do not hold back. Begin writing down a list of all the reasons you are not there yet.

After you make your list, go back and look at all your responses. I'm willing to bet every single one of them is just an excuse!

Accept responsibility for your situation, whether it's your fault or not. Only then can you possess the power to transform. Continue to make excuses and those excuses, people or circumstances will forever hold you down and frankly, crush your dreams. Remember, declaring halftime is an opportunity to ReFocus your thinking and actions!

Success shows no prejudice toward your background, circumstances, or education, and it certainly doesn't care about your excuses. All success cares about is how bad you want it. Everything else is commentary. Best part, you get to define your own success. If you have a desire to change with a strong enough WHY to support it, anything is truly possible. Now take that list of excuses and get rid of them for good.

III. Define your WHY before even thinking about HOW!

The biggest mistake I see people making on the road to achievement is jumping into the HOW before knowing the WHY. The HOW is where the work is, where the hurdles show up, where the doubt sets in and where we get swept into the details that tend to derail us from our goals. Have you ever suffered from "someday I'll get to it" or "someday the timing will be just right?" Let me guess, you likely have goals fitting into the "someday" category, don't you?

Have you ever tried before and failed? Have you given up or quit on a goal all together? Have you ever procrastinated on what you should do and fallen into your proverbial comfort zone instead? These are all sure signs your WHY was simply not strong enough. I would even challenge you by saying it simply wasn't a priority.

It is absolutely critical you become crystal clear as to WHY you want to achieve your goal. Your WHY can't simply be to "make more money" or "lose weight." That is not a WHY. It's a weak prayer at best and will falter at the first sign of prevailing winds. We've all heard the story of a mother lifting a car to save her child. That's a WHY! A WHY produces immeasurable strength and taps our Inner Drive that no adversity can overcome. The deeper the emotion attached to your WHY, the greater the meaning and commitment you'll have for seeing your goals through.

IV. Draft your team! But be careful whom you let in the "locker room."

Whatever you do, don't try to do it alone. The proper support is critical to your success. So be very careful whom you'll let into the "locker room." I think of it like all the crazy media surrounding your favorite sporting event. All the silly questions they sometimes ask, along with the naysayers and their negative comments. Sometimes the team just needs to shut the locker room door and tune it all out. You need to do the same. Who will you let into your "locker room?"

I can't tell you how many times even close family thought I was crazy for choosing to become a chiropractor. They would say, "Why do you want to become a quack?" "Why don't you become a real doctor?" Funny how their minds changed when I became one of the most successful chiropractors in the country and then had the nerve to ask if they could borrow money from me. Or how many times I heard people say to me, "You're crazy for wanting to do an Ironman; why would you want to do that?" Only to have them later be inspired to buy some running shoes.

Be careful whom you share your dreams with and always seek counsel not opinion. Far too often we ask opinions of those that have never achieved anything. They live a life by default instead of a life by design. Certainly they are good people and that lifestyle may make them happy. But if you are looking to break free, seek out those who are doing what you want to achieve. Find a mentor, a coach or someone who will support your vision and goals while leading you in the right direction.

V. Time to "Get in the Game!" A plan without action is a plan to fail.

Now that you are clear on what you want, why you want it, and are done with any excuses, it's time to kick it off! This is where so many aspiring entrepreneurs, or anyone with a dream, get hung up – in all the details! They get so busy planning and planning that they forget to get in the game and kick it off!

Throughout my Ironman career I would often meet people inspired to do the same or even your local 5k. Their heart was in the right place, they were motivated for change and had a powerful reason for wanting to do it. However, they got so busy preparing, they became distracted. They would have to buy the right shoes, get the right clothes, buy a workout journal, find a coach, and buy all kinds of ridiculous sport drinks and so on. Not that some of these aren't important, but after watching them prepare for sometimes weeks at a time, I would often find myself asking them, "When are you going to start running?"

Winners are predisposed to action, even when they don't have all the answers. There will always be details to sort out when you're on the field. But if you never get in the "game," you'll never score any points— much less have any W's in the win column. Develop your plan yes, but don't forget to action that plan in the process. So let's get out of the locker room and get in the game!

VI. Fuel your Body and Mind!

I learned this lesson early on from my grandfather, who I called Opa. My Opa lived an incredible quality of life, never needing prescription medications or doctor visits, even up until the day he passed away. He lived by eating food out of his garden that would rival any Whole Foods grocery store and he exercised daily, walking his German Sheppard nearly 5 miles every night. He also rode his bicycle nearly 70 miles every Sunday, leaving many behind – including me as 16 year-old varsity soccer player. He was in his late 70's at that time. He also never watched TV, listened to the news or liked hanging around "old people" because they were all too negative for him.

He was guardian to his mind and body. I learned and decided then, this is how I wanted to age. How do you want age?

Today's life arena requires more focus, energy, discipline and endurance than ever before to remain sharp and focused. As entrepreneurs and anyone undergoing transformation, we are competing in the modern world of life, balancing career, business, family and health, so that we may enjoy the rewards of our labor for years to come and with those we love the most. Decide today and then ask yourself, "Is what I'm doing today supporting my visions for health and vitality for the future?" If not, what are you going to do about it?

VII. Visualize your Success...daily!!

The inspiration behind ever attempting my very first Ironman Triathlon hit me while being a spectator at the Arizona Ironman in 2005. The stands around the finish line were packed with friends and family cheering on their loved ones. The energy was palpable as I watched these incredible athletes, one by one, complete a race, in what to many, is unachievable. A full Ironman, 140.6 miles all in one day, with only 17 hours to finish. This is a 2.4-mile swim, followed by a 112-mile bike ride and then a 26.2-mile run. Athlete after athlete from all walks of life crossed the line in sheer joy, pride and an indescribable sense of achievement. Many, exhausted by the long grueling day, suddenly found a burst of energy to cross the white finish line; a white line that requires months and years of preparation to cross. It requires a relentless commitment with long, lonely hours of what can feel like endless hours of training. ...All for one moment in time to hear the voice of Ironman announcer, Mike Reilly, utter those words every aspiring Ironman wants to hear, their name followed by "...you are an Ironman!"

I can feel the chills now as I hear these words permanently etched in my memory as one of the most crowning physical achievements of my life. Every detail is as vivid as if I were sitting there today! I rehearsed that image over and over and over again as I was inspired to hear Mike utter my name at that very stage the following year. I watched every Ironman race I could, many times over, inspired by everyday people like you who have dreams, and more importantly, the courage to achieve them. Participating were individuals with some of the most incredible challenges imaginable; cancer survivors, amputees, paraplegics, widowers, survivors of horrific accidents, just to name a few. Out there, grinding it out despite their circumstances, when they truly have every excuse to eat bon bons on the couch and let life pass them by. But they don't. Instead, they decided this is my life, this is my time and no one is going to ever take that away from me. They decided to leave their old story behind to tell a new story – a story of perseverance and victory.

What is your "white line?"

Going for your dreams and being an entrepreneur will always have its challenges and its ups and downs. It's all part of the journey of transformation, but it's the journey that makes life so exciting and incredibly rewarding - as long as you never lose focus and hope.

When the bottom fell out on me in 2009, I was tested like never before, but as a result grew stronger in the process - like working a muscle in a gym or training for a race. As one of my favorite lines in the movie Shawshank Redemption states, "Hope is a good thing, maybe the best of things and no good thing ever dies."

So even when your current circumstances and true potential may temporarily be veiled in a sea of challenge, uncertainty and fear, embrace who you are and who you aspire to be, but NEVER settle for where you are.

Believe it's Possible, See it Through and Finish Strong!

Dr. Andreas

About Dr. Andreas

A professional speaker and master trainer with over 20 years' experience as an executive and serial entrepreneur, Dr. Andreas Boettcher has delivered over 1,000 presentations and shared the stage with such luminaries and best-selling authors including Brian Tracy, Dr. Deepak Chopra and Tony Robbins. He continues his work with Mr. Tracy today as both a colleague and friend, leading and training his team of Certified Trainers.

His methodology for sales success, called "Prescription-Based Selling" is a nod to his earlier career as a chiropractic physician/CEO of a multi-disciplinary wellness center, which he and his then partner built from the ground up, generating $1.7 million in annual revenues in just five short years. He speaks openly and with first-hand knowledge of the numerous challenges yet exceptional rewards of entrepreneurship. However, many believe that his greatest professional strength is his ability to teach his clients to connect with their authenticity, amplify their voice and turn their passions into profits.

As former Director of Sales for Peak Potentials Training, Andreas led all aspects of sales, building a new, million-dollar sales team from scratch while overseeing millions of dollars in offers presented from the stage. Working from his core belief that selling is a process and that everything we do involves selling, in some form, Andreas strips away the fear and "pushiness" often associated with sales transactions, transforming them into an opportunity for both parties to win.

He offers workshops and trainings for professional sports teams in the NBA, NHL, NFL and MLB, teaching relationship-based selling skills in order to customize the fan experience while building long-term relationships. In addition to Dr. Andreas' own business success, his trainings, products and services have generated well over $20,000,000 and counting in gross revenue for his clients and audiences.

In his personal life, Andreas has competed in over 50 triathlons and three Ironman distance events. The lessons gained from his experience and discipline as an athlete transcend into compelling stories of inspiration, motivation and commitment for any individual or organization looking to improve performance and leadership. But it's his trademark blend of unbridled drive, humility and authenticity that keep him in high demand as a motivational speaker and master trainer, empowering thousands both on and off-stage.

Entrepreneurs, service professionals and experts all over the world credit Andreas for helping them speak more confidently, sell more genuinely and serve more fully. Visit: www.DrAndreas.com to learn more about Andreas, his speaking engagement availability, programs and trainings.

CHAPTER 16

LIVING YOUR JOURNEY AND USING LIFE'S TURNING POINTS AS THE KEY TO FUTURE SUCCESS

BY ELIZABETH WEIHMILLER

"We learn something from everyone who passes through our lives...
Some lessons are painful, some are painless...but, all are priceless."
~ Unknown

How well is your life progressing along the journey your inner self envisioned? Grab a piece of paper and take a moment to look back on your life up to this point.

- What do you see as the key events in your life?
- Are there points in time that really stand out?
- What would you consider to be your turning points?

Our past can really help us excel and move into our future. We can't live in our past because then we are not moving forward. The past is the tool and textbook for our future. We can't predict the future, unfortunately, but we can take and learn from the lessons of our past. Just like we can use textbooks to learn from history, you can use your past as the textbook of your life. A key point to remember, however, is to not live in the past, for then you will get stuck and won't be able to fully embrace the future and your true destiny and life path.

Have you ever considered that we achieve success and fulfill our potential through transformation.

I'd like to share my journey to this point, some of the lessons I've learned, and how they've helped in my evolving transformation. Pinpointing these has helped me move into the future. You yourself may have had similar experiences or they may trigger memories, good or bad, that may have taught you different lessons. It's about looking honestly at ourselves. When we give ourselves the respect to admit as humans that we make mistakes, we can learn from them. That can only make us stronger, building us into the unique individuals we are.

1. Inner Strength

My parents divorced when I was three years old and I spent time going back and forth between my Dad's house and my Mom's house. Over time both of my parents found someone else and both remarried. Now, like Cinderella, I truly gained a step-mom who was not the nicest and that's being polite. She wanted to be in control of everything, she wanted to become my mom. Thanks, but no thanks! I already had the most amazing mom a girl could ask for. As things developed, some events occurred one weekend when I was at my dad's house and my stepmom had my dad and I sit down so she could have a talk with me about whatever I had done to piss her off this time, but this time it really pushed her over the edge. I ultimately ended up getting kicked out of the house. My mom was called and I was brought home. I was seven years old. My mom had taught me to be and respect myself and hold on to what I believed and I did in this case. I was told I was not welcome back until I apologized. I didn't apologize because I didn't feel I had done anything wrong and did I mention I was seven. No seven-year old knows everything. I think that is why they call it growing up and maturing. Let me also mention this happened again when I was nine. This situation taught me to have inner strength, because it is inner strength that will give you the ability to move forward and believe in yourself.

2. Determination & Sticking to Gut Decisions

Lets jump ahead to middle school. I had not hit my stride in elementary school and was labeled, because of that, as not one of the brightest or even most motivated students. Well in the public school systems, it follows you as you progress to higher grades. I was lumped in classes in middle school with people that just didn't care and were considered troublemakers. They would ask me and try to bribe me to do their homework. This got me thinking about the education I was getting versus the one I wanted. There was a private school near my house and we drove by it regularly, it just called to me. I couldn't tell you what called to me, but it was an intuitive hit that I needed to go there. It didn't hurt that their mascot was the Husky and I happened to have a Husky. I approached my mom and stepdad to talk about applying to the school and what they thought about the idea of switching schools. They supported and encouraged me to follow what I sensed was best for me. Now, my step mom got wind of this and decided I should be applying to and looking at all the other private schools in the area (and there are more than a few). This made me want to rebel and not apply to the school I wanted to go to. Thankfully, my mom is amazing and said I should still apply and that I didn't need to apply to any others. She said this way I wouldn't regret not applying but that if I was accepted I could then decide whether I wanted to go or not. To this day I remember how excited I was when I received the call that I had been accepted. I ended up going to the private school and it was the best decision I ever made. This was the first time I experienced how fantastic a tool my intuition is.

3. Perseverance because Everything happens for a Reason

End of my junior year of high school, my family – my mom, stepdad and I - decided to move to Phoenix, Arizona (yes, I really did have a choice in the matter). We did things differently in my house than most. However, senior year of high school, my life was changed forever. Sonny, my stepdad, was an amazing stepdad. I couldn't have gotten any luckier when he and my mom married. He was always there for me and I knew I could turn to him when I needed help. He passed away fours days after Christmas 2006. This was quick and unexpected, as he was diagnosed with a completely metastasized cancer of unknown origin, just three week prior to his death. This taught me a lot and honestly really put things in perspective. This experience made me realize that each day is really a gift and you don't know what the next hour, day, week, month, or year holds but persevering through what life throws at you is the only way to grow and learn. These moments can only strengthen you – and yes, in the moment it will likely not seem like it at all. Everything happens for a reason; it may not be until a few years down the road, however, that the reason reveals itself. To be honest "everything happens for a reason" is not only my favorite saying, but it is also my least favorite saying as well. Every time something happens I tell myself this and it really helps calm me down and remind me to just take a deep breath and continue on my journey.

4. Confidence

Following my intuition again, I ended up going to a relatively small university tucked in the mountains of Flagstaff, Arizona. Northern Arizona University had a unique class in its business school called Bizblock. In this class you worked with your team to create a business including the full business plan and all the research and work that goes with it. This was all leading up to the end of the semester when we would be competing to present our business idea to a group of venture capitalists. We made it! Of ten business ideas we were one of the four selected. This class taught me I was capable of more then I ever imagined and it was just the tip of the iceberg. It also made me realize that I was not cut out for and didn't want to go into the "normal corporate 9-5 world." I wanted to do more and have a greater impact.

5. Taking Risks and Intuition

After graduating college a semester early, I decided to join Strategic Alignment Partners as an entrepreneur, because I was being drawn to it. The company stood for what I wanted. I didn't listen to the naysayers and didn't want to kowtow to what they thought I should do with my life because that was just it! It wasn't their life. It's funny how everyone wants to give advice on other people's lives, but won't take advice for their own. I knew that I got bored easily and this was a fantastic opportunity with no chance of being bored. I recognized it would take hard work with no guaranteed income every two weeks. But, I recognized I would get paid in other ways, including the learning, opportunities and networks I'd have. I also chose this path because I knew it would challenge me and that I'd constantly be "pushed off" the proverbial cliff, making me stronger and transforming me in new ways and going to new levels.

6. Using Tools to Grow

I learned a valuable lesson that you always need to be growing and pushing yourself to new levels by learning from all sources. The most important part of learning is to really get to know yourself, because until you know yourself and transform yourself, nothing else will really matter. I found unique ways of delving "deeper" into who I am and what I am meant to do in this life. Some of the tools that I have really found to be the most helpful for me are TriMetrix® HD, Numerology, Astrology (which is very different from what you see in the paper), and a unique amazing belief-changing process. These have each helped me objectively understand some things that had already happened in my life. For example, while I connect with lots of people quickly, I've never felt like I fit in. I now understand that's part of my journey and purpose. I often take and refer to these insights at least every two months to remind myself of my gifts and talents and what I need to avoid to keep me on track on my journey.

Numerology has given me a better understanding of my life path and destiny as well as things I need to work on at different points in my life. My deep dive into Astrology, including the north node, planets, signs, and houses have shown how a person can understand their special talents that can be turned into professional success as well as self-defeating tendencies that could hold you back from fully achieving your life purpose. Ultimately, it provides a true, deeper understanding of yourself, your hidden talents, and the pesky negative influences that could distract you from achieving your true-life purpose.

The final thing that has had a significant impact on my transformation and moving to higher levels is the ability, through a very cool process, to change ones subconscious and unconscious beliefs. I have been able to shift my mindset in ways that stick and that have allowed me to begin moving towards my purpose and not holding myself back. Sometimes you need to be open to more unconventional ways that really "pin you down" as to your strengths and areas to improve on to really move to the next level.

I would rather know the opportunities for growth than be the person sticking their head in the sand and continually getting hit over the head with the lessons that need to be learned.

Which person would you rather be? As they say, knowledge is power.

Life is all about turning points. You may not know them as they are occurring, but if you take the time to go back and reflect, it will help you recognize those crucial turning points of your past, but most importantly what you are truly capable of. If you take advantage of all the tools available to you – not just the ones mentioned above, but all possibilities – there truly are no limits to what you can achieve and where you can go.

As Nido Qubein said: *"Your present circumstances don't determine where you can go; they merely determine where you start."*

About Elizabeth

Elizabeth Weihmiller has a passion for helping others overcome limiting beliefs, fulfill their potential and achieve their unique success. She has had the unique advantage of learning, growing and uncovering her unique gifts early as a result of challenging situations that she has faced. These include her parents divorce at a young age, a difficult stepmom, her adored stepdad's unexpected death, winter break her senior year in high school right after moving to a new city with no support network, switching schools several times as her own choice, meeting executives of clients while young, overcoming the naysayers on her goals and dreams and overcoming her own insecurities and lack of confidence in herself. The coaching and mentoring she has received, including from her Mom, Boss and three-time best selling author Gayle Abbott, has helped her continuously evolve on her journey.

She knows that when you discover your strengths, potential hindering factors, purpose and destiny, you can more easily move along your unique path. You can take action to minimize potential hindering factors and can change limiting unconscious or subconscious beliefs. She uses all she has learned about the esoteric sciences to help others progress along their path.

Elizabeth's goal is to give the advantage she has had to others who have big dreams, feel they are missing something in their life, are blocked by feelings of limitations or who even just want to go to the next level without the normal way of having older adults dictate to them or tell them what to do. She is passionate about using new, 'outside the box' ways of doing things and moving to higher levels of consciousness, while still being grounded and aware of the practical realities of the world.

Elizabeth is a graduate of Northern Arizona University (Go Lumberjacks!) with a degree in Business Management and certificates in Economics and Human Resources. She is a Certified Behavioral Analyst, Certified Values Analyst, TriMetrix® HD Certified, and EQ Certified. She also has certifications in PER-K and PSYCH-K.

She joined Strategic Alignment Partners, Inc. full time upon graduation after really weighing the pros and cons of taking a "normal" corporate job versus the life of an entrepreneur. Since joining, she has played a crucial role in helping take the company to new levels, bringing in new ways of doing things and delivering exceptional levels of client service. She has grown up around business and attributes her love of business and entrepreneurism to this fact, even though she swore she would never go into the "family" business. She loves cars and airplanes and in her spare time loves spending time with her two Siberian Huskies – Mystic and Snowball, reading, travelling, learning new things, hanging with friends, working out, and anything that can be done in the majestic outdoors.

Contact Information:
eweihmiller@strategicalignmentpartners.com
(571) 346-7667

CHAPTER 17

CHOOSING THE LIFE YOU DESIRE

BY CHRISTINE SPRAY

Sometimes people look at me and think I have had everything given to me and that life has always been some form of perfect. If you have had any level of success, no doubt others have thought the same about you. What people don't often realize is that many successful people have a story of transformation and sometimes the transformation is quite dramatic.

In a leadership workshop I did a few years ago, I led the group through a lifeline exercise where you plot out your life experiences which made you who you are today. Part of this exercise was to draw a picture of yourself in 30 seconds. That day, for the first time since grade school, I drew a picture of myself. It was a smiley face with a tear coming out of one eye. Very few people know why there was a tear in my picture, but it was part of my transformational story.

The information I share with you in this chapter is very personal. There is a risk to vulnerability. But I'm willing to take that risk to demonstrate how your life can be transformed. Mine was, and I know yours can be too!

TRANSFORMING A LIFE OF GRIEF TO AN ATTITUDE OF GRATITUDE

My life has been filled with tragedy, sadness, and despair. However, I have chosen to not stay there. Instead, I made choices that would take

159

me from the conditions from which I came to the places I desired to be. Instead of tragedy, I choose triumph. Instead of sadness, I choose gladness. Instead of despair, I choose hope. Instead of being a victim, I am a victor. Instead of living in grief, I have an attitude of gratitude. You see, life can be what is dealt to you or what you decide it will be. It is what you want it to be and only you can make that choice for yourself.

Some people feel comfortable living in negativism, drudgery and an overall depressive state. Oh, they will complain about it until the cows come home, but they won't do anything about it. They sometimes enjoy the attention it brings them. But not this woman! I refuse to live with a victim mentality. Instead, I choose to live a life of blessing and I look at every tragedy or negative circumstance that has every occurred in my life as an opportunity to gain greater appreciation for all the great things in my life. No sitting in the muck and mire of life for me. I choose blessing!

TRANSFORMING FROM FEAR TO FAITH

To say that I grew up in a dysfunctional family is an understatement. As long as I can remember, I lived in fear. I no longer allow fear to dominate my life, but I distinctly remember that, while growing up, I feared my mother, my past, my present, my future, and life in general. Even though my personality is one to love and trust everyone, to this day there are occasionally circumstances that will bring back those feelings of fear and anxiety.

Probably because I grew up in a household of overwhelming lack, I have always had this almost overwhelming fear of becoming homeless and having to live on the streets. In our home, we seemed to lack everything, from not having food, to not having money to pay the electric bill. This fear of living on the streets actually served as a major driving force and motivation for me to go to college so I could obtain a good job and take care of myself.

I knew I could not go on allowing fear to be such a controlling part of my life. To deal with this issue, I decided to research fear to understand what I could do to overcome it. One of the research tools I used in my quest for an answer was a Concordance – which is a dictionary of sorts. You can look up a word and it will give you every place in the Bible where that word is used. I used that Concordance to look up the word "fear" many nights. I would then look up the specific verses in the

Bible to see what it said about the subject. The exercise enabled me to overcome my fear by learning that if I truly had faith, I could not have fear.

I made a decision to focus my attention on faith and the knowledge that I did not have to live in fear. By faith I was able to accept the difficult times of my childhood, leave them behind and focus on what I knew I was capable of doing in the future. I was no longer bound by the fears that haunted me for so many years.

TRANSFORMING FROM BEING FATHERLESS TO THE FATHER THAT COUNTS

When I was five years old I received a school assignment to go home, find out what my daddy did for a living and then come back to school the next day to share that exciting information with the entire class. You may find this odd, but until that time, I did not know I was supposed to have a dad. That day I ran excitedly from the school building to the car where my mother was waiting to pick me up. Jumping up and down with the excitement of a super-charged five year old with a new discovery, I blurted out, "Mommy, Mommy, Mommy…I have a daddy…I have a daddy!! Take me to see my daddy!" I was so anxious to find out who he was and what he did so I could tell all my friends in school.

Within a few seconds my mother dashed to pieces my new-found hope of a daddy when she said, "You don't have a daddy. He was killed in a car accident." In just seconds I went from total euphoria thinking I had a daddy I never met, to total despair to find out he was killed.

When I was eight years old, my mother took me, my sister and my brother to the cemetery to see where my dad was buried. She shared with us what really happened – and that he was murdered. It was a very vague story and my young mind didn't fully comprehend the scattered details. That's really all I ever knew about my father or the circumstances that surrounded his death. It was just never discussed.

As you can imagine, growing up without a father was difficult. A single mother trying to raise three children was an extreme challenge. There were many days I wondered about my father, what he would have been like, if he would have taken me on walks, or if I would have been a "daddy's girl." I later learned that my father passed while my mother was pregnant with me. I also was told that he thought he was having another little boy and wanted to name me Christopher, so my mom came as close as she could by naming me Christine. Even though I never met him, I still miss my daddy to this day.

The good part of my childhood was that my mother took us to church. There, I learned about faith and that there was a God to whom I could turn. I grew to understand that we all have a choice about the way we live our lives and that there would always be someone who was worse off than we were. I also learned about another father, a heavenly Father. While I still miss my daddy greatly, I take great solace that I know the Father that counts.

I understand that not everyone who reads this will be able to identify with this aspect of my transformation from being fatherless to knowing what I term, the "Father that counts." But it has great meaning to me and has been instrumental in setting my course in life. This relationship is the basis of my faith, my attitude of gratitude as well as every other aspect of the life I now am privileged to enjoy.

TRANSFORMING FROM BEING FINANCIALLY CHALLENGED TO FINANCIAL FREEDOM

While growing up, my family was very poor. If we had food, it was often the same meal every day and I never had money for lunch. Anything I needed I would have to earn money to buy. I started working when I was 14 years old, and helped pay the rent and basic utilities. In high school I would leave school at 1 p.m. to go to work to support our family. I left home while still in high school to live with affluent families where I would house sit, clean pools, take care of their dogs, wash their cars and water their plants on a daily and weekly basis.

I did not grow up in an environment that was conducive to producing successful offspring. I remember looking at other families that had beautiful homes, nice cars, designer clothes, and were polished. I couldn't buy the houses, cars or clothes, but at a young age I taught myself how to make my own clothes and even give myself French manicures that were better than a professional salon manicure. To this day, I do my own nails 95% of the time – it's just a carry-over from my childhood – and let's face it, I save time and money.

When I was 13 years old, I remember seeing a commercial on television about a cassette tape called, "Where There's a Will, There's an A." I used my life savings at the time to buy the tape. Just from hearing that simple commercial, for some reason I believed if I could make good grades, I could do anything and have anything in life. No one ever told me to get good grades or encouraged me educationally; I was just driven to get A's. I was always stressed because I had to work so much and it took away from my time to study.

Growing up in financial hardship was not easy by any means. It was difficult to see my friends at school wearing designer clothes and driving expensive cars when I had none of that. Yet my circumstances enabled me to be resourceful and something as simple as a phrase like, "Where there's a will, there's an A," became motivational. I was able to extract from my meager surroundings and circumstances the resourcefulness and the motivation to become better than my past.

Even though I could have fallen into the downward spiral of poverty, I chose to go in the opposite direction, using my circumstances as motivation to become better and to desire success. Even to this day, I believe where there is a will, there is not just an "A," but there is a way! I have followed the way to financial freedom because of the choices I've made in my life and by refusing to allow my past to dictate my future.

TRANSFORMING FROM SICKNESS TO HEALTH

I have had a number of physical problems throughout my life, but I refuse to allow those issues to stifle my personal growth or my physical activity. I've had three pre-cancer surgeries, surgery on both ankles and knees, broken ribs twice, a broken neck, I wasn't able to have children, and I live with a condition called neurocardiogenic syncope (a brief loss of consciousness caused by a sudden drop in your heart rate and blood pressure, which reduces blood flow to your brain). While that's quite a list, I choose to feel blessed in my health. I'm blessed to be cancer-free. I'm blessed to have nieces and nephews.

You can dwell on the list of ailments, or you can focus on where you're blessed. I could tell a lot of stories about my illnesses, surgeries and hospital stays, but I choose to talk about being cancer-free and my participation in various sports, like riding my bike and raising money for Multiple Sclerosis for more than 20 years. I take care of my body with proper nutrition and regular exercise; I have transformed from sickness to health and that's the way I choose to live!

TRANSFORMING FROM DYSFUNCTIONAL RELATIONSHIPS TO DYNAMIC RELATIONSHIPS

As I mentioned previously, to say that I grew up in a dysfunctional family is an understatement. No father, very little money, forbidden to talk with anyone about our problems, working since the age of 14 to support my family, and the list goes on and on.

Add to this dysfunction, when I became old enough to date, well, let's say I dated some real "toads." I knew I needed to seek out relationships that were healthy, but how?

As I progressed through college then into the workforce, I formed relationships with individuals who were successful. I had friends with designer clothes and expensive cars while in high school, but I never knew what success was supposed to look like or how it was to be achieved.

As I worked hard, I was able to see what success looked like up close. Today I enjoy serving and working with chief executives and business leaders who want to go to the next level. I work with clients across the country, helping them develop strategic plans and influencing the growth potential of their companies. I facilitate professional development workshops training professionals on how to develop long-term relationships, build their business and ultimately increase revenues across diverse industries. Additionally, I've started two successful businesses, I am a national keynote speaker, a best-selling author, an executive coach, a trainer, a consultant, and a chair and national speaker for Vistage International.

Today, I am part of a cohesive family that I have created with my husband and soul-mate. I am not poor. I treat people with dignity. I am making a difference in the lives of others. I went through a metamorphosis; a transformation. It was long and grueling. It took a lot of time and effort. But I made the transition. Has it always been easy? Not at all. I have had the rug pulled out from under me multiple times. But each time I have gotten back up and have stood strong, like the sunflowers grown in the Netherlands, the tallest in the world. Through hard work and right choices, I have been able to leave behind the dysfunctional relationships and create dynamic relationships.

No matter what your circumstances may be, I am confident you too can transform into the person you want to become. Don't wait to enjoy life, make the most of every day. It's your life; don't ever give up. Make it the best one possible. If I can be successful, anyone can.

About Christine

Christine R. Spray
Founder & President, Strategic Catalyst, Inc.
Founder & President, National Business Development
Association
Chair & National Speaker, Vistage International

Christine Spray is a nationally-recognized business development keynote speaker, best-selling author, consultant, trainer and coach. Spray serves as a CEO and business advisor with a passion for helping people and companies grow. She has led numerous organizations' efforts in new business development, strategic marketing, employee retention and professional development programs, client relations and operations.

Spray launched Strategic Catalyst, Inc. after working in public accounting and industry in senior leadership roles with start-up, restructuring and growth responsibilities. She recognized that by aligning business goals with marketing, human resource and business development strategies, organizations could leverage new business opportunities for far greater results. With 20 years of experience, she has created proven programs for management in the area of new business strategy by implementing Individual Revenue Assessments, Business Development Programs, Strategic Business Development Plans, and Accountability Models.

In addition, Spray launched the National Business Development Association (NBDA) to fill the need for a national trade association to provide best practices to individuals whose primary responsibility is generating business for their organization. NBDA provides a vibrant learning community where members can stay on top of industry trends and continually hone their skills through targeted professional development. Members of NBDA strongly believe in order to be a successful business development professional, you must focus on others and their needs before focusing on yourself. You will find this philosophy at the center of everything that is taught at the NBDA.

Spray also serves as Chair and National Speaker for Vistage International, the world's leading chief executive organization; its affiliates have more than 16,000 members in 16 countries. In her Vistage leadership role, she provides monthly professional development programs and one-on-one coaching for CEOs to help them become better leaders, make better decisions and therefore achieve better results.

Spray's Leadership:

- Former Chair, Women Energy Network's Advisory Council
- Former Board Member, Women Energy Network
- Former Committee Chair, Emerging Women Leaders of the Greater Houston Partnership
- Former Committee Chair, University of Houston Alumni
- Former President, Association for Accounting Marketing
- Former Co-Chair, Kay Bailey Hutchison Texas Governor Race
- Former Nominating Chair, Leadership Council American Lung Association
- Former Board Member, Houston Health Charities of Texas
- Former Board Member, Houston Strategic Forum
- Former Board Member, MIT Enterprise Forum
- Former Board Member, YMCA Camping Services
- Former Delegate, American Society of Women Accountants
- Former Chairman, Small Business Committee GSWCC
- Former Co-Chair, Shaker Committee GSWCC

Spray's Acknowledgements:

- Chair Excellence Award, Vistage International
- 50 Most Influential Women, Houston
- Rookie of the Year, Vistage International
- Entrepreneur of the Year, Houston Technology Center
- Top Ambassador, Greater Houston Partnership
- Lifetime Member, Greater Houston Partnership
- Mover & Shaker, Greater Southwest Houston

Spray holds a Bachelor of Science in Biology from the University of Houston and is a Graduate of Coach University.

For more information about Christine Spray and her companies, please visit: www.strategiccatalystinc.com and www.nbda.co or call 832-380-8224.

CHAPTER 18

BE UNIQUE, MOTIVATED AND SUCCESSFUL

BY JAMES BENNETT

I'm often asked how I've managed to create success in life while marching resolutely to the beat of a different drummer, and I invariably point out that any success I have flows directly from my commitment to being myself. Plenty of people extol the virtues of conforming to a program, plan, template or rulebook. I'm just not one of them. And while millions of people spend hours each week watching their favourite TV Reality shows, you'll find me in the blissfully independent pursuit of my goals. The idea of watching someone else create their dream home, body, relationship or business has never made sense to me. We all get the same 24 hours: I spend mine designing and living a world that is uniquely my own.

In my view, Reality TV isn't too far removed from Romans days when slaves, animals and Christians fought for their lives. Although the stakes were much higher then, the concept is similar: put on a show to funnel people's attention where you want it to go. Today's programs are dictated by vast commercial interests and I'm concerned that they affect everything from our workplace conversations to our cultural values. And, sadly, the images they present as "Normal" are usually anything but; do they celebrate the viewer's strengths or subtly reinforce a sense of inadequacy?

I've long been a fan of personal development expert Jim Rohn, who once said, "Make a plan for your life or risk being part of someone else's." As I tell my clients, no one else will care as much as you do about your results, so make sure that the life you create is one that you actually want to live.

I committed early to this path. My father died when I was four years old and my mother, quite naturally, felt completely unprepared for life as the widowed mother of three boys under the age of 10. Although she remarried, the marriage did not last, and it wasn't long before we were living in poverty and worried about the future. As a teenager, I had my share of deprivation and my peer group wasn't filled with people determined to create massive success in life. It's easy to take on the belief systems of the people around us and we tend to become "the average" of the people with whom we surround ourselves. I was an independent kid who wasn't content to take what life dished out, however. I wanted to play with possibilities that extended beyond the envelope of my world. And to do that, I had to get over my fear of living full out to the edge of my capability. It wasn't easy. And it has been worth it!

Today I get enormous satisfaction out of helping entrepreneurs power forward in their own businesses as well. There is no place for fear in the running of a successful business—as former U.S. President Franklyn D. Roosevelt said, "We have nothing to fear but fear itself." But we are often flooded with negative economic news, and even the most positive thinkers among us have no doubt struggled at times with doubts about the future. Which points to another reason for forging an independent path: it allows us to keep negative news and views at arm's length, so we ourselves don't become pessimistic.

I believe it's important to question the prevailing wisdom about most things. For example, do we need an Ivy League education in order to be successful? I think not! History is full of stories about people who built massively successful businesses with no university education at all—people like entrepreneur Richard Branson, Apple co-founder Steve Jobs, and Dave Thomas, founder of Wendy's restaurants. And we all know about the successes of Walt Disney, Thomas Edison, Colonel Sanders and Albert Einstein. They may not have had a degree but they certainly were original thinkers!

But how can entrepreneurs guarantee success?

As a business coach, I obviously favour the idea of hiring someone to help you generate better results. Coaching works. If you're wary of the concept I invite you to look at it this way: many people will gladly hire a golf pro to improve their golf game, or a tennis instructor to improve their strokes. So why hesitate to hire a business mentor, especially when the implications of poor business results are significantly more serious than bad golf scores!

So what else can you do to contribute to your own unique success? Here are a few ideas:

I. Embark upon a Relentless Search for Knowledge

The Internet has revolutionized the way we do business and we now live in a world where we are competing with people around the world. And while our competition has increased, the size of our potential market has, too. Advancements in technology have connected us in ways we could never have imagined just a few decades ago. We need to learn how technology can help our businesses. And how it can hurt them.

But technology isn't the only topic entrepreneurs should be following. I firmly believe that you can never know too much about the world and the people with whom we share it. Learning keeps us sharp and one of my mottos is: "What If?" We know that the average person uses only five per cent of their mental capacity. What if I could use even one per cent more? Or better yet, what if I could learn one per cent more than what I currently know, or what if I could apply even one per cent more of what I know? Can you imagine the possibilities that line of thought might generate? What do I need to learn in order to make that happen?

II. Avoid the News

Although I am an avid reader, I generally stay away from the news, whether it's coming at me from a newspaper, magazine, online platform or radio. News outlets are organized around negative information. If something bad happens, you'll hear about it. If something good happens, it usually doesn't make the cut. What that means is that we are exposed to a vision of reality that is skewed to disaster. Does that help us maintain a positive outlook or make sound decisions based on the whole picture? No! But it does provide us with a perfect scapegoat if things go wrong. How can we be expected to thrive if the economy is bad? Well, actually, some businesses do very well when the economy is doing perceptively poorly. Shouldn't yours?

Anyone willing to adapt quickly and seek out opportunity can enjoy unlimited potential for growth and wealth, no matter what economic challenges seem to be presenting. You might have to work hard or change how you operate in order to make that concept bear fruit. But it's possible. Information is valuable, of course, and I suggest to my clients that they find an online platform that presents a balanced synopsis of what they need to know.

III. Focus

How is it that such a small and simple word can represent such a challenge for so many people and businesses? It really is a great question and one that a mentor of mine once qualified by saying "If you try to be all things to all people, you will end up being nothing to anyone." The most successful people in business are able to maintain a laser-like focus in everything they do. You won't find them wasting time with activities that don't bring them closer to their goals, and they never perform low value-add tasks that they can delegate to others in their organizations.

How do they maintain this focus? Most successful people I know write down what they want to achieve, and review the list at least once a day to ensure they stay on task. If they determine that something has shifted, they modify their actions to stay on track.

What you focus on tends to grow!

If your business is in its start-up phase, or you are redefining an existing business, you can improve your focus by zeroing in on who your ideal customer is. Is it a man or a woman? How old are they? Where do they live and what do they do for a living? Do they take public transit to work or do they drive a car? What kind of car? These criteria are all important because buying decisions are based in emotion and the more you know about your ideal customer, the better able you are to identify their emotional triggers. Miss this piece and you lose your chance to connect and, ultimately, to make a sale.

Business owners at any stage of the success cycle can also increase their focus if they get into the habit of establishing weekly planning sessions to pinpoint all the activities that will bring them closer to their goals.

If an action doesn't bring you closer to your goals, you really need to question why you are doing it. There are only so many hours in a day and you need to ensure you use them wisely.

IV. Commit to Excellence

What sets your business apart from other every other business around the world? That's a key question, and for 99% of the business people I've coached, the answer lies in their commitment to excellence and the way they "Wow" their clients.

So how do we reach this superior level of excellence? There are a number of ways to do this and they all begin with you. In order to function at your peak level of performance, it is important that you treat your body and mind like the superior, finely-tuned machine that it is. You would never put regular gas into a high performance vehicle, would you? Your body needs the same consideration. It's important to eat high quality, nutritious foods and exercise both your body and your mind regularly. Leaving out this piece will lead to low energy, slow response times and a lack of the kind of sparkle that attracts positive attention.

It's also important to be active in personal development. The world's best in any field invest more in their training and development than they do in actual execution. For example, a professional golfer will put their entire life on hold while they prepare for a pro tournament that lasts just a few days. They'll engage a coach, sink thousands of practice putts and spend untold hours on the driving range. An Olympic sprinter will hire a coach, lift weights, extend their cardiovascular fitness, pay careful attention to their diet, and work on their mindset. All for a race that lasts less than 10 seconds.

In most fields, successful people spend about 80% of their time training and 20% executing. Success requires a lot of commitment. If it seems as though you are too busy to make time for more training and development, I invite you to consider this: most of us work at about 50% of our capacity and many of us are not exactly efficient when it comes to using our time.

Could you listen to an MP3 or a CD while you are commuting to work or while exercising? Could you wake up a half hour early every day to squeeze in time for a little reading? Over even just a few months you can leverage small amounts of time into big gains in knowledge and understanding if you are dedicated and consistent. Imagine the benefits over a decade! You could learn about best practices in your industry and develop your management and leadership skills. You could learn about, and implement, more advanced accounting and operational procedures. You could improve your marketing strategy.

And you could figure out how to "WOW" your customers with exceptional customer service. That's a crucial aspect of ensuring that when people think about the kind of product or service you offer, your business is top of mind. If you are diligent, people will feel that your product is so valuable that the cost is almost irrelevant. You have no doubt heard the old adage that a disgruntled customer will tell 10 people what they think of you, while a happy customer might tell two. Your money is better spent retaining and serving happy customers than on damage control.

Remember, too, that you are always marketing, and people will recognize you both inside and outside of your business; maintaining a lifestyle of integrity and authenticity is actually an important part of your marketing. The main focus of your business should be to get customers; your second objective is to have those customers become repeat customers. Do that well and the rest will take care of itself.

V. Be Original

Have you ever noticed how repetitious animal behavior is? Dogs greet each other the same way every time they meet, salmon spawn in the same river that their ancestors used, birds migrate to the same winter location every year. They can't help it. It's instinctive. Human beings, on the other hand, have the capacity to make *choices* and *changes* in our behavior. That gives us the potential to learn from our mistakes and make course corrections as required. It also provides us the opportunity to fill our lives with possibility and surprise.

But we can't live full out to the edge of our business potential if we are following the crowd. Sure, there are some things that have been proven to work, and there is no advantage in reinventing the proverbial wheel. But there *is* a danger in mindlessly following the pack on every issue that comes along, and, in the process, stamping out the creative spark that makes us unique and fuels our individuality. Have you ever seen images of a Bald Eagle in flight? This beautiful, powerful, independent animal is majestic and predatory. It soars higher than the other birds, always in a class of its own. It is original, committed to results and focused—and it doesn't get distracted by rumours of scarcity. It is fearless. I've spent no small amount of time watching eagles in flight and I believe it is that spirit of independence that can spur our imaginations forward to create more business success.

So what's stopping you from being unique? What's preventing you from trusting your own judgement and stepping boldly into a world where your only limitation is your own willingness to be different? I think it's time to change the paradigm of how we have traditionally done business in this world. You don't serve anyone well by holding back the core part of you that makes you different and unique. And you can't build a business if you don't express the truth of who you are. Is marching to the beat of a different drummer a scary prospect at times? In the beginning, maybe so. But once you get in the habit of making independent choices, you'll love the results. Just be committed. Be focused. And be unique.

About James

Business mentor James Bennett helps entrepreneurs define and implement the brilliant distinctions that allow them to develop better processes, offer superior services and expand their customer base so they can generate more revenue and have more fun. He is insightful, analytical and passionate about the abundant opportunities for growth that he believes lie at the heart of almost every business. And he fluidly supports business owners to the discovery of avenues for growth they never knew existed.

An unconventional background helped James develop a system for identifying why many businesses don't expand their revenue base as quickly as they would like. And his years as a business mentor have allowed him to develop customized solutions that drive to the heart of what every business owner wants to hear: business is up this year!

Committed to excellence in all aspects of his work with clients, James has a knack for combining creativity and discipline in ways that shine a clear light on the path ahead. He helps his clients step up and step out of the paradigms that have limited their past results. And he can help you embrace the best of everything your business – and your life – can offer.

For more information on how James can help you unleash the masterful results you desire and deserve, please check out his website at: www.thesummiteffect.com. Or, if you are ready to put his vision to work for your business, you can email him directly at: James@thesummiteffect.com.

CHAPTER 19

HUNGRY FOR CHANGE

BY BINETA NGOM

*Man cannot discover new oceans unless he
has the courage to lose sight of the shore.*
~ Andre Gide

When I look back at my childhood in Bargny, Senegal, I recall the desire I had to transform people's lives, because mine was painful, lonely and fearful. My father passed away at the age of 34, leaving my mom with five children, I was four years old. My life was filled with pain, struggles and uncertainty. I was brilliant at school, but seeing my mother struggling made me stop going to school after some college to start working. My life was hard. My salary was not enough to support my family. Too many people around me were struggling. Too many children were in the street – orphans or just poor. I met a teenage girl who stopped school because of an untreated eye disease that led to blindness. I was devastated and sad, I wanted to be powerful enough to help all those people. I started dreaming of becoming someone who could alleviate the pain in women's and children's lives. Later on, after many years of confusion, my husband came to America and I was looking forward to coming and visiting.

After I got my visa to come to America, I realized that my dream would come true. My invitation to visit the USA could transform the lives of millions of women and children. I was excited, but at the same time, I was sad to leave my family.

My mom's only words the day I was leaving were, "Surrender to GOD and everything will be fine."

I came to America and was a total stranger. I was alone with my husband only at my side. Not knowing what to do next was a little bit irritating. My dreams were big, but I was stuck. I tried to avoid stress, so instead, I was relaxing, reading books and magazines, and cooking. Watching the Oprah show was my favorite. She inspired me. I loved what she was doing and wanted to do the same immediately. She's my hero as a woman who wants to help women.

I couldn't enjoy anything. My loneliness took all the fun away. Instead of enjoying my visit, I was sad and very quiet, I was homesick and at the same time I was thinking about the kids living in the street and how to help them. It was painful.

Joy lies in the fight, in the attempt, in the suffering involved, not in the victory itself.
~ Gandhi

Taking care of my family was my priority, that's how we are raised in Senegal, family is first and the women's job is to take care of the house, the men and the children. Now things are changing, women participate meaningfully in the economic development of the country. They are CEOs, business owners, and they are very much present in the work force.

So while I was thinking about school, I found out that I was pregnant. It was hard, for the whole nine months. I was alone. I couldn't go anywhere except for a doctor's visit. Three months after that, I got news from my nurse practitioner. My baby could have a chromosomal abnormality such as Down syndrome. That was it for me. I couldn't dream anymore, I was shut down completely. I never felt that much pain in my life up to that point. After they reviewed the size of the womb compared to the stage of the pregnancy, the baby was way too small. It was stressful. We were devastated. I physically changed completely, I was not sleeping well and my appetite was gone.

One morning, I woke up early and was meditating, and suddenly I thought about my mom's words, "Always surrender to God." I fell asleep and there was this vivid dream that was so clear that I thought somebody was really talking to me. The only words I could remember after I woke up was: "Why are you worried?"

Still to me it was only a dream, but few days later, I started believing in that voice and I started shifting my thoughts. That was an 'aha' moment, I changed my paradigms completely. I became positive, my optimism grew and I was ready to accept the situation no matter what. I drew the conclusion that was GOD's will, and I couldn't do anything about it. However, I had faith and I was strong. I surrendered and I prepared myself. It was unbelievable to see how my life changed by just changing my thoughts. The pain was replaced by excitement, suddenly I became happier.

They sent me to a local hospital to do an amniocentesis. At that moment, I didn't want to know anymore. I was just ready to move on and get ready to welcome my first daughter to the world, the pain was too much to deal with. I asked the doctor before signing any papers if this procedure would help my baby in any way. He said no. This was just to learn more about the situation, but it wouldn't do anything that could make it better. They just wanted to know if there was a disorder or any other problems.

I declined the test. Knowing about a problem and not being able to do something about it is another problem. I respectfully left the office with a smile. I was proud of myself, after I changed the way I looked at the situation, everything changed. I start visualizing a healthy baby, I was very excited again.

Three months after that we went to another appointment. As soon as the nurse entered the room, she started apologizing and said many things that I didn't even remember. The only words I could recall after her long conversation with my husband was that there was a mistake and I jumped out of the chair and start asking questions. She explained that they thought I gave them some wrong information. To make a long story short, I made a mistake on the date of my last menstrual cycle.

We were very happy to hear that. I was very relieved but still skeptical, I just couldn't wait any more for this pregnancy to end. It was hard, painful and long.

On my due date, things went fast and the baby came out very easily. After I heard her crying, with my eyes closed, I asked my husband about her condition with a face full of tears, fear and at the same time excitement. She was fine, healthy and beautiful. I then became emotional, it was like GOD was with me the whole time. I was thankful and grateful again. I was feeling the power of GOD in my whole body. The vibration was intense and I couldn't stop praising GOD again and again. It was a true blessing and a happy ending. This experience gave me more faith and made me stronger. Things happen for a reason and when they do, the only answer would be God. Take your mind off the problem and visualize the result you wanted. Take your experiences as your teachers.

Success is stumbling from failure to failure with no loss of enthusiasm.
~Winston Churchill

I refused to give up, I expected things to turn around and I had a strong belief that it would. I set my mind to victory knowing that I was in the biggest country in the world. I don't have a product to sell, but I can raise awareness through this book to transform the life of millions of women and children.

We can alleviate the pain in the lives of homeless women and children by building more affordable housing, creating more employment opportunities and by developing more programs for abuse, addiction, lack of skills and many more – to help women and children.

According to the U.S. Department of Housing and Urban Development, 1 out of 50 children or 1.5 million children in America will be homeless each year.

Most homeless families consist of a single mother and children. The number of homeless children reached a very high percentage in 2011-12 compared to 1983.

THE MIND BLOCKS...

Get rid of negative beliefs, they stop you from growing. Minimize stereotyping as much as possible. Just help. So many people miss the opportunity to make a difference in people's lives because of some false beliefs. How did that happen and why it happened is not the answer, the solution is to touch people's souls if you can – because there is nothing in life like an opportunity.

Stop stereotyping and be positive.

Set your mind at a higher level, keep it there and change your outlook. Change the way you look at things. When I ask people to help women in the street, most of the answers I got were that they have addictions, and no matter what you do, they still will feed their addictions and they don't even want to get help.

Why not do something to help them get out of the situation instead of blaming them? Why not give them a chance?

America is the country of hope and almost everybody in the world wants to come to visit this wonderful land. Being here means a lot to me, and I don't want to miss any opportunity that could open up doors for other women to get a better life.

After I had my fourth child, I became a housewife again, but this time it was different. I made a determined decision to do something that could make me happy. I would get up early in the morning and take my baby with me to the book store. I would spend three to four hours reading and searching. I knew at that moment that it was up to me to be successful and help people, I suffered too much in my life already; I have a mind and I want to use it wisely.

You can't suffer all of your life. You have to stop, think about your self-worth and take control of your life.

When I went to the book store, before reading or buying anything, I sat down and asked myself these questions:

- Who am I and why am I here?
- What makes me happy?
- What can I do to help women and children?
- How can I make a change?

My mind was working hard on those questions, I was visualizing many good things and at the same time I was thinking about mind blocks. I got up and started walking around the aisle of the leadership section. From that day on, the bookstore became my favorite place. Reading book after book increased my knowledge. I couldn't stop reading, it became my hobby.

From book to book, I learned some of the laws of the universe and knew that I'm the one and only person blocking my success by being negative, irresponsible in my actions and most importantly, not being clear about what I really want.

After a while, I started visualizing women's centers and safe places for children all over the world. I wanted to see that happening so badly that I created a non-profit organization.

THE FAMILY BRIDGE FOUNDATION

I'm looking for opportunities to help women overcome all kinds of addiction, help them take control of their life here, in Africa and the rest of the world. When women are happy, the world becomes a better place for everyone.

Calls to action:

- I call on everyone to make a difference in their community by donating.
- Be a mentor in your community.
- Donate money to organizations that help.
- Donate a building for shelter.
- Donate food or organize a food drive.
- Donate clothes, shoes, toys or school supplies.
- And most importantly, V-O-L-U-N-T-E-E-R and give back to America.
- Educate your children about the homeless, poverty and hunger and let them get involved in the cause of their choice. Teach them to appreciate and not to take what they have for granted. Making a difference starts with your family first.

This book is an opportunity for me to encourage everyone to fight for a better world and to raise awareness. Let's come together to find ways to give back and to transform the life of those in need.

GOD BLESS!!!

About Bineta

Bineta Ngom was born in 1964 in a small town called Bargny in Senegal, West Africa, and grew up without her father. She was raised by one of the strongest women on earth and a most giving woman – no matter how tough life was, her mom would always help others. Growing up was a struggle that molded her into a very strong person. She used to see women in her town living the life of hard knocks and she couldn't do much about it. She used to stay in her room alone for hours as a teenager just thinking of ways to help those mothers.

She came to America in 1994 to join her husband and she noticed opportunities all over the place. She feels really blessed to be here. She can see clearly now how much she can learn in America to change people's way of living. Her hobbies are reading and cooking. She likes to read books that improve her personal development, and in her spare time she likes to be creative in her kitchen. She is also blessed with four beautiful children who are growing up knowing that part of life is about serving others. She is proud of them.

No matter what type of work Bineta does, she doesn't feel happiness or any enthusiasm unless she's helping others, volunteering or working towards improving their situation – knowing that one day she will be able to reach out to many struggling families. From her teenage years, she knew who she wanted to be. She knew her passion was to have a career that involved helping others. Coming from a totally different world, she was lost during her first years in America. She was at the stumbling stage for a long time. It took quite a lot of time to figure out what to do to help people.

Bineta established the Family Bridge Foundation – a non-profit organization whose purpose is to help women and children's lives in any way possible. Her real journey starts with this opportunity to serve.

CHAPTER 20

MASTERING THE "FORMULA FOR LIFETIME WEALTH"

BY GARY CURRY

Have you ever asked yourself the question, "If America is so rich, why does everyone always seem so broke?"

Almost everyone wants to accumulate enough money to do the things in life that makes them happy. Despite this almost universal desire, many individuals are never able to reach this goal.

Ask yourself this question: What does enough money mean to me? In other words, how do I know if I will have the money to do what I want?

Does Enough Money® mean you can buy that fancy new car? Or that you can have money to buy and pay for your dream house? Does it mean one million dollars? Ten million dollars?

I don't know what your definition is, but my definition of Enough Money® is "when work is optional and retirement and leisure activities are affordable."

Most people agree with this definition. Do you?

I like it because it is very personal. What may be Enough Money® for you may differ considerably from what may be Enough Money® for someone else.

If we can agree on this definition, then the next question is, "Why don't people accumulate and enjoy Enough Money®?"

Could it be because they don't know the "Formula for Lifetime Wealth"?

If that is true, then the first step is to learn the Formula for Lifetime Wealth.

The "Formula for Lifetime Wealth" is:

- Regular Deposits
- Plus Diversification
- Plus Time
- Plus Compound Interest
- Minus the effects of Inflation and Taxes
- Equals Enough Money® and remember "when work is optional and retirement and leisure activities are affordable."

The Formula for Lifetime Wealth is simple and effective. It is a Formula that should be taught to all high school students. Unfortunately, it is a Formula that few Americans will ever learn and use.

To get you started on your way, let me explain how the five components of the Formula for Lifetime Wealth work. If you don't understand how the Formula elements can work FOR you—you may discover how the Formula can work AGAINST you.

REGULAR DEPOSITS

Many people often ask themselves, "Where does all of my money go?" It sometimes is something of a mystery, isn't it?

The first step in answering this question involves looking at your paycheck. What's the first thing you pay out of your paycheck? Taxes, which include Federal Income Withholding, Social Security, Medicare, state and local deductions.

After you contribute to the public good, you then pay for the necessities of life: food, clothing, housing, medical care and transportation. After you pay for the necessities, you use what's left to create your own lifestyle.

However, many of us tend to live beyond our means—much to our detriment—through the use of credit cards.

So, now what? After paying to keep our lights on, our families fed and bring a little fun and entertainment into our lives, we then save for the future. While this is a common practice, is it really wise or is it the best way to generate and grow wealth?

There is a right way to begin to accumulate Enough Money® and it involves paying yourself first. A portion of all of your earnings should be yours to keep. We should be paying ourselves first on a regular basis.

Yes, pay yourself first, ahead of your necessities, and especially ahead of your credit cards, and you will eventually be able to enjoy a stress-free lifestyle.

What is the amount we should be paying ourselves first? I believe you should consider saving at least 10 percent of your earnings.

Take a minute before you read on, and calculate how much you are paying yourself first.

DIVERSIFICATION

One of the most important rules of investing and money management is to diversify your assets. This will strengthen your protection against risk. It's important to remember that all asset categories –from Treasury bonds to mortgage-backed securities—all come with some inherent risk. The optimum balance for your assets will vary according to such factors as your time horizon and your tolerance for risk.

You, like most other people, have three asset categories available, which include:

1. Social Security or other government retirement plans;

2. Qualified plans, which may include Individual Retirement Accounts (IRAs), 401(k)s, 457s, Thrift Savings Plans (TSPs) or pensions; and

3. Personal Savings and Investments which may include cash, stocks, bonds, real estate, businesses or other revenue generating assets.

There are many differences among the three types of asset categories. Therefore, it is important to coordinate these three asset categories in order to make sound decisions regarding your strategy to accumulate and enjoy Enough Money®.

Further, it is advisable to research and implement the best Diversification strategy within the tax qualified plans and personal savings and investments categories.

It is of the utmost importance to understand how the various tax-qualified plans work and which saving and investment options you need to utilize to maximize the growth of your assets.

The total value of your assets, minus your debt equals your net worth. And I believe it is your net worth, not your income, that defines your wealth.

Although diversification and asset allocation cannot guarantee a profit or protect against loss in declining markets, diversifying among and inside the three asset categories—government retirement plans, tax qualified plans, and personal savings and investments—will help you guard against risk, and possibly accelerate the growth of your net worth.

Have you coordinated your three valuable asset categories?

TIME

As the saying goes, "time is money." If you understand the time value of money, then you know that Time is an investor's best friend.

Everyone wants to maximize the time they have, but almost everyone is guilty of procrastination.

You've probably heard more than a few people say, "After I pay for my big screen TV, new furniture, next vacation or whatever, that's when I'm going to start saving money."

Have you ever put off paying yourself first?

I will now illustrate the cost to putting off paying yourself first.

To do that, I want to tell you a story about a man named Larry Later. Larry is a planner and he plans on accumulating $250,000 by the age of 65.

Larry told himself, "If I can earn a 8 percent rate of return on my money and if I start when I'm age 30, all I have to do is save about $112 per month to have $250,000."

"This is simple," Larry said, feeling proud of himself.

But, do you remember Larry's last name? Later. As you may have guessed, Larry doesn't start paying himself first the day that he turns 30. Instead, he waits and allows time to go by. How much time? A decade.

He is now 40 years old, but still wants $250,000 at age 65. He calculates that if he can earn a 8 percent rate of return, he will need to save about $264 per month.

"I can handle this," Larry says to himself, a bit nervous, but still confident. "It may be tight but I can do this."

Again, what's Larry's last name? That's right, Later. Larry waits one last time until he is age 50. Now, at 8 percent rate of return, he has to save a whopping $711 per month to do what $112 per month would have done if he had just taken advantage of time.

Of course, this and my other hypothetical illustrations do not represent any specific investment, nor do they take into account that it is unlikely that any one rate of return will be sustained over time. All investments involve risk and you may have a profit or a loss and remember seeking higher rates of return involves higher risks. The scenario also doesn't take into consideration taxes, fees or charges associated with investing. But the lesson still stands.

Time is money. And as the infomercials state, "So act now!"

COMPOUND INTEREST

You may have learned about Compound Interest during a boring grade school math class, but I'd like to illustrate the power of this concept by explaining the "1% Difference."

Children and grandchildren are the most precious gifts in our lives. So let's assume you wanted to make a one-time $10,000 gift to your newly born grandchild.

Your goal is to let the $10,000 compound until your grandchild is age

65. At the same time you wonder if you should pursue a 7 percent rate of return or an 8 percent rate of return. Would a 1% rate of return increase really make a big difference? Let's see.

If your grandchild earns a 7 percent rate of return on the $10,000 single investment compounded annually until age 65, he or she will have $812,728.61. Wouldn't that be great?

However, if your grandchild earns 8 percent compounded annually on the same $10,000, at age 65 he or she will have $1,487,798.47. WOW! That's $675,000 more!

The "1 Percent Difference" compounded annually for 65 years almost doubles the return.

How can that be? The amazing power of Time plus Compounding Interest is the answer. Compounding interest is truly an astonishing power!

It is vitally important to understand and use the power of Compound Interest. Wouldn't you agree?

EFFECTS OF INFLATION

We have all read and heard about how inflation has eroded our purchasing power, but would you believe that thanks to inflation, a stamp that costs six cents in 1972, costs 49 cents in 2014? Think about the gas that you have to put in your car every week. The gallon of fuel that averaged 63 cents in 1978 now hovers between $3.50 and $4.00.

Housing prices have probably been affected the most by inflation. In 1978, in some areas a person could move into a high-quality home for $54,800. Today, the idea is almost laughable. Buyers today can expect to spend around $300,000 for the same high-quality home.

Who would have predicted these price jumps if we had asked them back then?

No one can accurately predict the future, and there are no foolproof methods for protecting against inflation. It is important, however, that when you do your planning, you should consider the impact of inflation. Are you?

EFFECTS OF TAXES

Taxes are a fact of life that you can't avoid. Everyone has to pay taxes—sales, property, income, and estate taxes—just to name a few. The good news is there are certain strategies that will let you choose when to pay your taxes and help you possibly reduce your tax liability.

The landmark Supreme Court ruling in the case of Gregory v. Helvering states, "The legal right of the taxpayer to decrease the amount of what would otherwise be his taxes, or altogether avoid them by means which the law permits, cannot be doubted."

An example of this legal reduction in tax liability is the mortgage interest deduction on your primary residence or the tax deductible gift to your favorite charity.

This isn't just good news, it's great news. The only problem is that the government, not surprisingly, does not provide us with an easy-to-use reference guide.

It is up to you to learn about things such as mortgage interest deductions, IRAs, Roth IRAs, College Education 529 Plans, Charitable Gifts, Non-modified endowment life insurance contracts and other tax-advantaged concepts.

Here's another question for you: "Are you required to make use any of these tax-advantaged concepts?" The answer is, of course, "no."

However, I'm sure you would agree that it is very important that your money enjoys the maximum tax protection allowed by law.

Have you checked to see if you are using the tax advantage concepts that will benefit you?

ENOUGH MONEY®

Have you thought about your finances lately? Really thought about them? Are they a mess?

If so, you may want to implement the "Formula for Lifetime Wealth" – which is: Regular Deposits, plus Diversification, plus Time, plus Compound Interest, minus the effects of Inflation and Taxes equals Enough Money®.

Remember, my concept of Enough Money® is defined as "when work is optional and retirement and leisure activities are affordable."

To reach this worthy goal, you must move beyond wishing.

Start implementing the first step of the "Formula for Lifetime Wealth today. And then implement each successive step.

When you do, you will *transform* your financial life.

ABOUT GARY

Financial Professionals come in all shapes and sizes – from seasoned veterans, thought leaders and innovators to successful entrepreneurs, superior performers, and client favorites.

Then there are the rare few who embody them all.

Gary Curry, who founded ORBA Financial Management in 1982 and Redtail Technology Inc. in 2003, has spent 50 years distinguishing himself as an award-winning financial advisor, business owner and consultant, and life insurance guru. Beginning in 1978, Curry built top-performing regions for insurance giants before co-founding and taking public an agent-owned life insurance company. He later joined Transamerica Financial Advisors Inc. Curry's branch office remained number one for 15 consecutive years.

Curry is also renowned for his visionary ideas. Over the years, he has developed new ways to educate clients and streamline financial solutions that have met with rave reviews and tremendous success.

As a widely sought resource in the financial services industry, Curry has been invited to speak at high-profile corporate events, industry roundtables, and educational seminars across the country. His desire to educate consumers led him to develop his trademark concept Enough MONEY®, which is defined as "When work is optional and retirement and leisure activities are affordable."

Curry also fills a largely unmet need: educating the public about how to make the most of their social security income benefits. Social Security Associates®, a firm he established in 2011, is dedicated to that cause.

"Above all," Curry says, "advisors must always put the client first."

Gary Curry is an Investment Advisor Representative with and Securities and Investment Advisory Services offered through Transamerica Financial Advisors, Inc. (TFA) member FINRA, SIPC and a Registered Investment Advisor. Non-Securities products and services are not offered through TFA. TFA is not affiliated with any other entities referenced.

You can connect with Gary at: gary@garycurry.com
www.facebook.com/thevirtualmentor

CHAPTER 21

ACHIEVING FINANCIAL SUCCESS THROUGH GREAT FINANCIAL PLANNING

BY LIM CHER HONG, ChFC®

In every aspect of life, have a game plan,
and then do your best to achieve it.
~ Alan Kulwicki

I'm deeply honoured to be invited to co-write a book with Brian Tracy. In this chapter, I will be showing you the secret to achieving financial success through a great financial plan for yourself. I will be highlighting the essence of creating a great financial plan. If you require the full details and framework for creating a great financial plan, please get a copy of my new book *Framework for Creating a Great Financial Plan*.

Many of my clients whom I have helped to create a financial plan, appreciated the effort that I put in for them to understand their current financial situation and implement solutions to meet their shortfall. Over the years, many of them saved tens of thousands of dollars by simply implementing the recommended solution. I even have clients who were bankrupt and eventually became debt-free and are now leading a comfortable lifestyle... and clients who aspired to be millionaires but didn't realise how easy it was to be one.

Don't get me wrong, this chapter is not about how to get rich fast, but merely to show you the way to create a basic financial plan for yourself. You are strongly advised to seek help from a professional such as a chartered financial consultant for a more comprehensive financial plan. Again my new book on "Framework for creating a great financial plan" will be able to give you a more holistic way to create a great financial plan.

The problem with today's world is not about not having information on how to achieve financial success, but on the contrary, we have too much information. For example, we can google from Internet for the result that we want or we can find a self-help book. Ironically, all of these created another obstacle for us to fully understand which is the best way of doing things. Sadly, there aren't any books out there that teach you how to create a financial plan for yourself. The mystery will be uncovered as you read along.

I personally have written a financial plan for myself. The greatest satisfaction that I get from my financial plan is a big overview of my financial situation – which allows me to make changes and implement solutions to cover my shortfall. Whenever my financial situation changes, I am able to better manage my finances to achieve overall financial success.

I wasn't born with a silver spoon in my mouth. When I was young, I used to stay in a small one-room rented flat with my mother and sister. My mum had to work long hours to support the family. Life was very tough for her, so I made a decision to study hard and hopefully get a well-paid job when I grew up so that I could give her a better life. I decided to go into the banking and insurance industry to provide wealth management advice as I fully appreciate and understand the importance of financial planning. When I was working in the bank and insurance company, I realised that I was merely selling what the company wants us to sell, even though they kept emphasizing to sell based on customer needs. There was something missing, so I decided to pursue a professional qualification and gained myself a Chartered Financial Consultant title. Now, you do not have to be like me to pursue a professional qualification to be able to create a great financial plan. You can do it yourself as well. All you have to do is to follow through my framework in this chapter to create a plan for yourself.

It's a myth to think that personal financial planning is only for the wealthy. Everyone needs to plan for their finances. Even if you are heavily in debt, this chapter will guide you how to get out of your debt burden. If you are rich, I will be able to guide you on protecting your wealth and grow it further. As I mentioned earlier, I have personally used some of these strategies for myself and achieved great financial success. You too can achieve this financial success.

Now this is what you have been waiting for. The framework for creating a great financial plan to achieve financial success emphasises four key steps.

THE FOUR STEPS FRAMEWORK

1) Preliminary assessment of your financial needs and goals

2) Developing a Financial Plan

THE EIGHT KEY AREAS

 i) Money Management

 ii) Credit Management

 iii) Risk Management & Insurance Planning

 iv) Education Planning

 v) Retirement Planning

 vi) Investment Planning

 vii) Tax Planning

 viii) Estate Planning

3) Implementation

4) Monitoring and reviewing

The most difficult part of financial planning is when you start to construct the plan. If you are serious about planning, go and get a pen and paper now to start constructing. Or simply get a laptop or even a smart phone and start typing. In the next paragraph, I will be going through details on the framework. This is where the work began.

Remember you need to take action in order to achieve financial success. By not taking any action, you are certainly not going to change your financial situation. I hope this chapter serves you and helps you achieve great financial success through creating a great financial plan for yourself.

STEP 1 - PRELIMINARY ASSESSMENT OF YOUR FINANCIAL NEEDS AND GOALS

First, you need to understand your own *risk tolerance*. Are you a risk-adverse or a risk-seeking person? A risk-adverse person is simply someone who avoids risks and does not mind lower returns to preserve capital. A risk-seeker is someone who is willing to take a higher risk for the potential for capital growth and does not need the capital for the long term. They are prepared to invest a bigger amount during a market downturn.

After conducting your preliminary assessment, you need to identify your *financial goals and concerns* for your family, yourself, your business and any other concerns which you may have. Make sure your goals and concerns are specific, measurable, achievable and time-framed. It should be quantified in today's dollar. Rank your financial goals and concerns in terms of importance and wants or according to short term, medium term or long term.

STEP 2 - DEVELOPING A FINANCIAL PLAN

During the whole planning process you will be making some personal and economic assumptions to facilitate your calculations. Note that any changes made to the assumptions may have drastic results. You are strongly advised to compare the results when you are making changes to the assumptions.

For *money management*, we will be looking at a cash flow and net worth statement. The objectives of creating a cash flow and net worth statement is to understand your current cash flow and your current net worth. It will give you an overview of your current financial situation.

To create a *cash flow statement*, you simply list all your cash inflow and subtract all your fixed and variable cash outflow on an annual basis. If the outcome of the net cash flow is surplus/positive, it means you have excess cash for your planning. However, if you have a deficit/negative net cash flow, it does not necessary means you are doomed. What is important is you must understand what are the contributing factors for the deficit. Be aware of the weaknesses and strengths of the current cash position. Do your own budgeting on each of the items.

To create a *net worth statement*, you simply list all your cash/near cash, investment assets and personal use assets less all of your current and long term liabilities to get the net worth. If the outcome is positive, it simply mean if you liquidate all your assets, it will be able to cover all your liabilities. If the outcome is negative, you should be worried. You need to work extra hard to generate more assets and pay off your liabilities, as much as possible in the shortest period of time. Find out whether you require insurance protection for your assets and liabilities. Also find out whether you need to diversify your investment. All these will be covered in greater detail in the next few paragraphs.

For *credit management*, list all your debts and liabilities in order of the highest to the lowest rate of interest. Find out whether there are any ways to reduce the interest or start paying off loans with the highest interest first. Are you able to refinance the loan with another institution or use another type of loan for the same purpose? Take into consideration whether you have any large upcoming expenditures such as buying a new house. You can also consider credit protection or mortgage-reducing term insurance to fulfil this need.

For *Risk Management* as a business owner, you need to analyse your business risk. Are there any better forms of business setup? Ensure you have a business succession plan, credit protection, and "golden handcuffs" to retain your key employee(s) where applicable.

For *Insurance Planning,* you need to provide adequate funds for living needs of love ones in the events of premature death, partial or total permanent disabilities, critical illness, hospitalisation (medical expenses) and long term care. Ensure you have sufficient funding for your children's education and pay off outstanding debts, taxes, etc. (whichever applies). Consider using term or whole life insurance for premature death, partial and total permanent disabilities. Use an appropriate standalone insurance plan for critical illness, hospitalisation and long term care. It can be a rider attached to the term or whole life plan as well.

For *Education Planning,* you need to know the current cost of education and how much would it cost in future when you need the funding. Taking into account tuition fee and living expenses. Consider using investment or insurance endowment plan to fulfil this need.

For *Retirement Planning,* you decide your own retirement goals such as desired life-style and retirement income. You can either use the replacement ratio or expense ratio method to calculate your retirement requirements.

Assuming replacement ratio method, the following are the calculation steps:

1) Your current annual income (pv)

2) Years to retirement (n)

3) Salary growth (i)

4) Desired 1st year income at retirement (fv, PMT)

5) Number of years to provide (N)

6) Inflation-adjusted investment return (I)

7) Lump sum required (PV)

Consider using an annuity plan or investment plan or any other retirement insurance vehicle to fund this need.

For *Investment Planning,* you need to know your current financial situation. What are your financial goals and objectives for investment? What is your risk profile and investment horizon? What is your desired rate of return and whether it is achievable? You need to have a good understanding of investment. If you are new to investment, you are strongly encouraged to engage a professional banker to provide you with the necessary advice. Ensure you have sufficient emergency funding before investing. What are the costs and risks in the investment? Avoid investing solely in any investment asset.

For *Tax Planning,* your objectives are minimising tax payable and maximising any deductions and/or reliefs. Check with your jurisdiction as to whether you are able to enjoy any tax exemption (for example, if you are self-employed, married with kids, etc.). Does your government offer any form of supplementary retirement scheme to enjoy deferment of income tax. You need to understand the advantages and disadvantages of doing so.

For *Estate Planning,* your objective is to find out the provision of liquidity for your personal and dependents financial needs should anything unfortunate happens during your lifetime and for your dependents upon your death. Estate consists of everything a person owned, or jointly owned with someone else, which includes both assets and liabilities.

Go write a Will if you have not done so. Make a nomination for any government provident funds. Ensure all your insurance policies beneficiaries are in line with your Will. Find out whether there is any estate duty payable for overseas assets. If so, plan for ways to fund it. You can also consider setting up a trust. If you have children, arrange guardianship. In the event of incapacitation, you may want to consider setting up a power of attorney.

STEP 3 - IMPLEMENTATION

Implementation is by far the most important part of the whole financial plan. Imagine you have the greatest plan in the world but you choose to sit on it and do nothing about it. Nothing will change and your life will still be the same.

This is where you need to consult a professional like a Chartered Financial Consultant to help you evaluate your wealth plan, a lawyer to help draft or vet your Will, a tax officer to further check on any other claimable amount or deductible, a regular doctor who has your medical history, a banker to advise you on investment or loans, etc. Do keep their contacts in your phone book or mobile phone for easy reach.

After seeking the advice from all the professional, it is important that you make your own decision whether to take their advice or seek a second opinion. Before you take any action, make sure you are fully aware of the features and benefits of the products. What are the risks inherent in the products? As well as the commitment period and whether it is by far the best when compared to other similar products. Best does not necessary mean the cheapest. More importantly is whether the product will meet your financial goals and objectives.

STEP 4 - MONITORING

Do not assume that all your plans will definite meet your financial goal. It is important to schedule time for reviewing. Recommended time frame is every three months. If you are reviewing with your advisor or banker, do evaluate your options properly before committing. Ironically, sometime doing nothing may be the best solution. Just make sure you are on track with what you have already planned.

You should also review your financial plan whenever there are changes in your financial situation. Example, you may be getting married or planning to have a child, etc. You have to decide what sort of changes need to be made to your plan. Consider whether you need to get another product or liquidate any investment.

CONCLUSION

Now that you know the way to achieve financial success through a great financial plan, I really hope you have already created one for yourself and started working on your shortfall to achieve your desired financial success.

If you want to create a more comprehensive financial plan, please get a copy of my new book *Framework for Creating a Great Financial Plan.*

I hope my chapter on achieving financial success through a great financial plan has served you and may your life be transformed with great financial success.

Lim Cher Hong, ChFC®

About Lim

Lim Cher Hong is a Chartered Financial Consultant. He has been in the banking and insurance industry for the last eleven years. He achieved many awards such as Million Dollar Round Table, which was attained by only the top 3% of Financial Advisors around the world; Top Performer Aviva Achievers Award; and POSB Top Insurance Team Sales Award. Lim Cher Hong has also received recognition as being titled AXA Top Rookie Advisor, which was featured in Straits Time Life Section. While working at Treasures Onshore as a Relationship Manager, he received the Onshore Award & Royal Gold Award.

Upon graduation at the University of London, he was acknowledged as the Top Business Graduate and was featured in the Today Papers *The First Degree*.

He is the author for the new book release *Framework for Creating a Great Financial Plan*.

Log on to: www.limcherhong.com to find out more. You will be able to access many valuable free resources.

You may connect with Lim Cher Hong at:
www.facebook.com/limcherhongchfc
www.twitter.com/limcherhongchfc
www.linkedin.com/in/limcherhongchfc
Email: limcherhong@limcherhong.com

CHAPTER 22

RAISE YOUR SALES: RAISED AWARENESS INCREASES SALES EXECUTION

BY KIRK MANZO

In the summer of 1982, I worked for the Southwestern Co. headquartered in Franklin, Tennessee. (Yes, I realize some readers weren't even born yet. Humor me— I'm the old guy). Southwestern had a simple, but effective sales formula.

If you lived in the south, you went to sell in the north, and vice versa. It sure pushed you out of your comfort zone. For a college kid who grew up in Hollywood, Florida, selling books door-to-door in Rockford, Illinois, felt like another world. Even ordering a Coke (known as a "soda' to me) required a different language, *"I'll have a 'Pop,' please, with my burger."* It also made you think twice about driving home back to South Florida after a tough sales day.

Our target customer was well-defined—families with children in school. Sure, we could knock on EVERYBODY'S door, but there are only so many selling hours in a day (13.5 to be exact—8a.m.-9:30p.m.), and we wanted to present our products to qualified people.

Going door-to-door was quite the adventure. You never really knew what to expect. Some folks were great. They would be polite, let you in and even offer to make you a peanut butter sandwich for lunch, if you asked. Others—well, let's just say they made you appreciate the nice ones.

One such person was obviously having a bad day. After she proceeded to slam the door in my face and hurl profanities instructing me to get off her porch, I thought, *Why not try one of the strategies they taught us in training class?*

I ran around to the back of the house and knocked on the kitchen door. When the woman answered the door, she looked at me with a stunned expression. Using my same friendly introduction, I explained about being the college kid from Florida talking to families about the importance of education. I then remarked that I simply wanted to verify if perhaps the person who lived in the BACK of the house was in a better mood than the one who answered the front door!

While this strategy did not always work to make a sale, it sure helped me keep a good attitude when dealing with difficult people.

My presentation of the *Webster's Student Handbooks* would focus primarily on the subjects that were most difficult for their children in school. These were identified during the rapport-building and interview questions with the family. Understanding the specific needs made it much easier to provide a relevant solution.

The beauty was that the two-volume set covered all the key areas. Unlike a full set of reference books (encyclopedias—yes, those did exist before the internet—like libraries), our books were more cost-effective, easier to use, and saved time.

The end of each sale was well-designed and orchestrated. The sale was finalized when the customer filled out the order pad and verified the address where they would like their notification mailed, prior to delivery at the end of the summer. A great percentage of people whom objected on price could be convinced through the comparison of the cost of education versus the cost of NOT having one. Thus the importance of knowing, "Who is your ideal customer?" BEFORE launching your sales campaign.

1 - *RECOGNIZE* YOUR IDEAL CLIENT AND *REDUCE* SALES *RESISTANCE*

Pareto's Principle is hard to ignore, since it applies to both the use of your time and to the type of customers you will encounter when offering your goods and services. For those who may have forgotten about Signore Pareto, he was an Italian mathematician and economist who identified the "80/20 Rule."

According to Pareto's Principle, 80 percent of your return comes from 20 percent of your efforts, and yes, therefore, 20 percent of your sales team and clients will produce 80 percent of your sales! Accepting this reality allows you to allocate your time and resources to solicit and attract your "Ideal Client."

Remember that, birds of a feather do indeed flock together. Identify your top accounts or clients, and then separate them by industry, size, or geography so you can target your audience more effectively. After all, there are a limited number of hours in a day. The problem you helped solve for your top client is not typically UNIQUE to that one company. If your product or service helped ABC Company, then why wouldn't it help others just like them?

Become the expert in your niche. When working as an Account Manager for U.S. Surgical, we were required to read medical journals and memorize sections of articles to increase our credibility with surgeons and hospital staff. It was one of the reasons that U.S. Surgical dominated the Florida market in the early '90s. At one point, they controlled a 90 percent market share of the surgical instruments they offered.

2- *ADAPT* TO YOUR PROSPECT AND *ACQUIRE* A CONNECTION

People buy from people they Like and Trust. So, how can you help yourself in this area? A couple of years ago, my wife, Sharon, and I decided to head up to Northwest Georgia on a Saturday morning in December to check out a community called Big Canoe. They were offering tours of a Christmas-themed showcase home and access to their private clubhouse and facilities. By the way, this is a classic application of the "Law of Reciprocity," which timeshares have used as an effective strategy for years. Why? Because it works! Provide something of value at no charge and the recipient feels obligated to return something in kind, like their willingness to hear about your products or services.

After touring a magnificent home and enjoying a terrific lunch in the clubhouse, our sales guide Marty offered to show us some of the new homes and lots available for sale. Before doing this, he very casually pulled out his Evidence Manual (a visual sales tool to build rapport with customers) to show us his home and family, including his grandkids visiting and using all the facilities. Swimming at the pool, playing tennis, sailing on the lake—you get the picture.

My wife, Sharon, later commented on the ride home, how nice it was that Marty took the time to share pictures of his home in Big Canoe and of his family and grandkids enjoying all that the community had to offer. While we were not in the market to purchase a property, it's a wonder we didn't buy a second home that weekend.

3 - *IDENTIFY* THE PAIN AND *INCREASE* THE ANXIETY

It is with rare exception that a person wakes up and decides, *today I am going to buy myself a new car!* Numerous studies confirm that the overwhelming majority of people are pushed into the market by an external force. Perhaps it is a new driver in the family who is heading off to college, a pregnancy that now requires a larger vehicle, a new job, a large repair bill, an accident, or theft.

With that in mind, how important would it be for the success of the salesperson at the dealership to fully understand, "Why are you looking to replace or add a vehicle to your household?"

Yet, so many salespeople want to start the conversation by prematurely talking about the price and what a great DEAL they can get for you!

Linda Richardson, in her book *Stop Telling, Start Selling,* does a masterful job of explaining how effective questioning skills differentiate between the average and the exceptional sales professional. Your questions must not only uncover the need or pain, but must also emphasize the extensive difficulties that can arise if the issue is left unaddressed, thus increasing anxiety and the need to take action NOW.

Developing a battery of thought-provoking and probing questions will ultimately separate you from your competitors, regardless of what you sell.

You may say, *Oh, but Kirk, I'm not a salesperson!* Really. Have you ever persuaded someone to go eat Chinese food when the original plan was to go out for Italian? We're all salespeople on some level.

4 - *SOLVE* THEIR PROBLEM AND *SIMPLIFY* THEIR LIVES

In 1985, my folks bought me a college ring for graduation from my alma mater Florida State University. I've never really been much for jewelry, so aside from my wedding band and a decent watch, this is the only jewelry item that I own.

Realizing that I would want the ring to last a long time, I purchased it in 10-Karat gold, since it is harder (and less expensive) than 14-Karat gold. Even still, over the years the ring has needed attention. The local jeweler would clean it up as best they could and round out its shape every few years, so it would easily slide on and off my finger.

About 15 years ago, the stone and my fraternity letters were damaged. I shipped the ring back to the manufacturer and, other than paying for the shipping cost, they repaired the damage free of charge.

Last year, my ring had once again become flattened at the base as it typically does from use, and needed to be rounded out again. Off to the local jeweler I went, but this time the unthinkable happened. Instead of using a soft mallet and a ring sizer as support, the young man behind the counter used a very different tool with an outward expanding flange and managed to crack the base of the ring. I was furious.

After contacting the manufacturer, they suggested I ship the ring to them for inspection. They informed me that the ring was damaged beyond repair, but they would gladly melt down the ring and recast it for just $215, essentially producing a new ring. A new ring would have been more than five times that cost! All I can say is that if you want to keep your customers, solve their problem and simplify their lives.

By the way, the only company you should ever purchase a class ring from, in my opinion, is ArtCarved, which is now owned by Balfour. Just sayin'…

5 - *EXPEDITE* THE NEGOTIATION AND *EXECUTE* THE SALE

After more than 12 years as an independent sales trainer and consultant, the most common request I get for content is, "Can you teach me some new closes?" Like training, selling is a process and not an event. You don't exercise and take care of yourself for years and then eat one piece of cheesecake and suddenly become overweight. Nor do you go to the gym for a week and look like the guy on the Bowflex commercial or the young beauties on Univision's Nuestra Belleza Latina!

Closing happens as a result of making a connection with your prospect to uncover a problem that your product or service effectively addresses.

Here are the last two elements that will always come into play: negotiating the terms of the sale, and closing out the order with a commitment to take action.

First, prepare for the negotiation by understanding that most prospects will request a lower price. Be prepared to concede something to close the business, but on your terms.

For example, if your paint and fabric protection only costs you $100 and the retail price is $500 then offer to sell it at cost. Sure you lose the $400 in profit, but you will retain the full asking price of your main product, while still providing a $400 concession to the customer!

To justify a reduction in unit price and close the sale, perhaps you can push back the delivery dates to reduce your costs or have the client agree to pay for shipping. Volume purchasing could also help justify a price concession. Selling in full pallet quantities means no labor loading the truck, only a forklift. Just remember, if you concede on pricing without the customer reciprocating a concession on some term or condition, you lose credibility for the pricing of your product or service.

It's ok to be creative when negotiating to come to an agreement. The important thing is to decide what you are willing to concede BEFORE the prospect asks you for a price concession.

Lastly, you must secure a commitment to take action. Begin by deciding the outcome you seek when engaging the customer. Ask yourself, *what is the desired outcome?* Sell her the product? Sure, in the end that will be the objective. However, there are often many steps to this journey and it likely begins with making contact with your prospect to set an appointment (either in person or via the phone/video) to discuss her situation in more detail.

More appointments will provide more quality conversations, creating the need for more presentations and proposals and, yes, in the end, will produce more sales. Learn to control what you can control—your activities. The sales will follow.

Write out the script for your close. This should consist of a series of five to seven questions that are structured in sequence to produce a predictable outcome. Be assumptive about the sale by explaining what the next steps will be in the process. Integrate either/or questions about quantity or delivery dates to keep the conversation moving forward. Sequential questioning assists your prospect in overcoming the natural tendency to procrastinate and put off their decision to do business together now!

Strategies to Raise Your Sales Results:

1. **Recognize** your Ideal Client and **Reduce** Sales **Resistance**

   - Apply Pareto's Principle to both account management and prioritizing your time
   - Birds of a feather flock together—Profile your top accounts and clone them
   - Become the expert in your niche

2. **Adapt** to your Prospect and **Acquire** a Connection

   - Apply the Law of Reciprocity—Obligation is your first step to a close
   - People buy from someone they Like and Trust—Use an evidence manual
   - Speak your customer's language—Understand their business

3. **Identify** the PAIN and **Increase** the Anxiety

   - Find facts—Uncover their need—Understand their PAIN

- Thought-provoking and probing questions separate YOU from the competition
- Create urgency to take action now by asking "What if?" questions

4. **S**olve Their Problem and **Simplify** Their Lives

- Make it easy for customers to do business with you
- Stand behind your work—Offer a money-back guarantee
- Look for solutions, not problems

5. **E**xpedite the Negotiation and **Execute** the Sale

- Like training, selling is a process, NOT an event
- Make a connection = Make a sale
- Be prepared to concede something, but on your terms

Implement the sales principles above to transform yourself into an exceptional selling professional. Raise your standards and awareness to execute your sales strategy more effectively and consistently. *Good luck and good selling, my friend!*

ABOUT KIRK

Kirk Manzo, CSP, is the Owner and Founder of The Manzo Group, a firm that specializes in working with automotive dealerships on Sales, Sales Management and F&I Management to increase profitability.

Sales success and leadership are about influence.

The ability to cooperate with others determines your success. In other words, *"How well do you play with the other children?"*

Performance-based occupations, like sales, often seduce us into believing that success is measured by our ability to "will" (code for "intimidate") a prospect or team member into cooperation. You can achieve greater influence with your team members through specific communication principles that pull people up, rather than push people around.

As a John Maxwell Certified Trainer and Coach, I can guide you and your team through Maxwell's programs on communication, self-growth and leadership. I have successfully trained and coached individuals and organizations to achieve their sales objectives in my more than 25 years of sales and marketing experience in various industries, including healthcare, building materials, and retail automotive.

Since becoming an independent trainer and consultant in '02, my straightforward and practical approach has produced immediate and lasting results for clients. My Spanish-speaking clients in Puerto Rico and Latin America find my bilingual skills invaluable. I am a member of the National Speakers Association and hold the professional designation of Certified Speaking Professional (CSP). Established in 1980, the CSP is the speaking industry's highest earned designation. Fewer than 10 percent of the more than 5,000 members of the Global Speakers Federation earn this certification. I am also a professional member of the American Society of Training and Development, and the Institute of Management Consultants (IMC USA).

By implementing Maxwell's leadership philosophies and communication strategies, you will help each member of your team grow to their full potential! I look forward to beginning our journey together.

I can be contacted at our offices at (770) 995-7808 or via email at:
Kirk@manzogroup.com

CHAPTER 23

LIVING TO LEAVE A LEGACY!

BY KIT MATTSON

What a spectacular morning it is today. The sky is an amazing bright blue and the clouds look like puffy, white marshmallows. As I sit on my terrace relaxing overlooking the city as I do most mornings rain or shine, drinking coffee and going over all the things in my life that I am grateful and thankful for, as well as all the favor and blessings that God has given me, will give me and is currently giving me. I think, wow I'm blessed. I am also thankful for the day, because it is another opportunity to outdo, overcome, beat, defeat all obstacles the day might hold, as well as what was left undone and on my plate from yesterday.

I have heard it said that great sailors are not made on smooth seas! Life wasn't always like this and won't always be like this I know, so when I have had turmoil in business or personal life, I use it as an opportunity to get better in every possible way.

It was the late '80s, oh yes, in Orange County...the O.C. were most everyone acts, walks, talks and looks like millionaires, but we know that's impossible – at least in my neighborhood. We lived in an upper middle class white-collar neighborhood, even though my father was a super high-paid, blue collar, hard-working saver, tight- to-the-last-penny man. I was almost 20 years of age washing my car out front of the house when I noticed the neighbors up and down the street getting red tags on their houses and their cars repossessed in broad daylight. In less than an hour, I saw four car repossessed and three houses tagged with red slips. It was the most action and movement I had seen in the neighborhood in two years. I asked my Father what was going on. He told me interest rates were skyrocketing, and people couldn't afford the variable loans they had taken out on their homes. So the banks were coming to collect property. I quickly panicked and started to worry. I asked if we had those same type of loans or problems. I asked if we were going to have to move as well or lose our cars. He put his hand on my shoulder and told me I had nothing to worry about, because he followed the Mattson legacy secrets his father told him.

He asked me to sit down and he began to tell me the secrets to his and my grandfather's success in life that I will now pass on to you. He told me of my grandfather in his 20's was serving our country in Hawaii, and was a champion boxer in the navy. Then in his 30's, he built a company. In his 40's he lost it all. In his 50's made it all back and then some. In his 60's, he was a business owner. He passed away in his 70's. All this was a culmination of his life. I said, I know all of this, but why are you telling me these things and what does it have to do with being successful in life? He then told me everyone is given seasons in life. My Grandfather was given 70 plus summers, 70 winters, 70 falls, 70 springs, 70 Christmases, Easters, Birthdays, New Years. He maximized each season to the best of his abilities in business and in personal life.

He then began to tell me that my grandfather sacrificed almost all his personal family time for business success. He said it was for him and his sisters and mother, so that they would never go without. My father said the Great Depression shaped my grandfather's thoughts and actions, and that in turn shaped my father's actions and thoughts as well. Wait. I do remember my father working all the time when I was growing up. Hardly ever home. I thought that this was a normal thing to only see my dad on weekends. Well, at least one day on the weekend.

He told me, "Son, anyone can achieve success, financial security, riches, dreams, anything in life, as long as they are willing to trade something really valuable for it." I thought…I have nothing of great value…I'm only 19! He told me why I had nothing to worry about. Like losing our things because he had traded a very valuable asset just like his father did before him for our family. Time!!! Time that he could never get back, 30 years of his life with family, with friends, or watching sports or TV like most normal people do in their daily life. All for his dream of success.

My Dad said normal isn't what he wanted for himself, my mother or their kids. He didn't want a mediocre life. He then told me, "Son, the effort you put into your future is the future you will get. You put in excellent effort, you will get excellent rewards. You put in mediocre effort and you will get mediocre rewards. You put in poor effort, and you will be poor!"

He asked me what kind and size of home I wanted to live in? I, of course ,said, "A big one with a great view! Just like yours."

He then asked what kind of car I wanted to drive? A Porsche or a Pinto? I quickly said, "Are you kidding, I want a Porsche and a Jaguar."

He said I could have all that and more, but I needed to trade something of great value for it, and the sooner I make the trade, the sooner I will get and earn my dreams. Just like my grandfather accomplished his dreams, and my father most of his by this point.

The last things he told me that afternoon were the most important he said. Always be grateful and thankful for all of your blessings you have been given, will be given and that you are enjoying now first from God, second from all the hard work and sacrifices your grandfather had made for me and now I make for you. We hugged, He told me he loved me. Then went to work.

Let's fast forward four or five years. Now I am happily married and we are thinking of starting a family. I remember as if it were yesterday. My company started as a hobby in my garage just to make a few dollars here and there till I found something better to do. The hobby fast became very big, too big to stay in my garage. I was at a turning point and so was the hobby. Then I recalled the lessons my father had told me and taught to me my whole life, but really emphasized on the sit down talk we had in the O.C. 5 years ago.

LESSON #1 - SEASONS!!!

That kept ringing in my head. Thankfully, I listened to the ringing and picked up that phone, metaphorically speaking of course. The lesson on seasons had to be implemented. Know your days know your ways and I will tell you your future. I didn't want to be a ship at sea without a rudder going nowhere. I want to be the master of my destiny and captain of my future! I sat down and looked at how I used my past seasons. All the holidays, days, weeks, months, years, winters, summers, springs and falls – where have they gotten me to this point in my life?

Sure, parties are fun when you're young, but my grandfather used to say work hard while you can, so you can party when you want. I then began to write a very basic road map to success in different stages in my life. Where I wanted to be money-wise in my 30's, 40's; what I wanted to have at 35, 45 years old. Like the Jaguar and the big house.

I had to decide right then and there that good enough just wasn't good enough. I made excellence my standard on all that I did. Nothing in the beginning was perfect, far from it, but my resolve was that of making excellence so that I could attain excellent rewards. Not so much detail, but a basic outline on goals, you know, the American Dream. When I sat down and planned a season outline, it became real and not just a dream. I could and did see myself in the future getting my dreams and goals accomplished. If you believe, you achieve. I heard that somewhere. All of this had to be done by the young age of 50 years old!

LESSON #2 - THE TRADE

Use time wisely! The funny thing with this is that I know my father was always working long hours and gone all the time. He would sleep, eat, and go back to work. He did this for 42 years. It was time he had given up for his success. I have heard eight hours is for survival and ten hours is for success. So I decided for the next 20 years of my life that I would outwork and outthink anyone in my industry. It was 12 to 15 hour days and sometimes longer. I'll sleep when I made it. I also would trade my time for my dreams, and my future seasons of success that I had planned and envisioned, I would attain. I made excellence my standard on all that I did daily. I pushed the limits and set new ones on what could be accomplished in my industry. I always found the best in other industries and asked why them? What do they do that sets them apart? What makes them the best in their industry?

How can I apply and implement the basic elements that they use: effort-integrity-outstanding service-fantastic product-belief-faith-efficiency-blind implementation-education—into my company? I went on a quest for knowledge. I learned all that I could as fast as I could about business, marketing, relationships, my industry, other industries.

So I would benefit from all of the best ideas and wisdom that I had gained by trading my time. If I was going to trade all of my time, I wanted it to payoff big, Real Big! The Bible says in Proverbs: Work brings profit but mere talk leads to poverty. So I trained and worked my mind, body and soul daily – focused always on the prizes in the future that were on my seasons list.

I never listened to the naysayers, who seem to be all mediocre and like to settle for second and third place. You know what Vince Lombardi said about Second place? Nothing! If you look at all of the winners in life, they have always given something up for success – time, money, energy, sleep, something. We have all seen the stories of the Olympic athletes that sacrificed all kinds of things just to get a chance to "Go For The Gold." *Sacrifice the Trade is the key.*

A choice must be made and that decision must be final, and the results must be attained no matter what. My focus for the last 20 plus years, and for years to come will be on defending myself and my family from mediocrity. It is now a habit. It has become second nature. The habits we train are habits we gain. My friend T.R. says that and it is the truth.

So now you know how to track, trade and make season goals.

Review these weekly, daily, they are your road maps for life's successes. You also now know what and how to trade for success! This is a must for any traveler on the highway of success, at least in the fast lane in the Porsche or Jaguar!

LESSON #3 - BEING GRATEFUL AND THANKFUL

This is really the key to it all! Why I say that is being in the state of gratefulness and thankfulness for your seasons successes is only in the daily reflection of the journey of the victories in the past and present. There are no victories without celebrations, and that's why you should go through all the things you are thankful and grateful for daily.

My son, brother, nephew and I all recently went to see the modern day Elisha, Joel Osteen speak at a packed convention center on Christianity. It was amazing on how he spoke of sacrifices Jesus made for us, and how in turn we should be grateful for this, and how we didn't have to earn any of it. He gave freely to us. Later we got to meet with him back stage and talk for a bit. I could see the joy, gratefulness and thankfulness coming from him like a glow. I know it sounds crazy but it's true. I know he is trying to live up to his father's legacy and leave one himself. I have been told I have a joy and gratefulness and thankfulness about me as well.

I hope I can glow half as much as Joel, but that is what Gratefulness and Thankfulness on a daily basis creates. Daily saying thank you for your favor and your blessing you have been given, will be given, and are receiving now!

Wow! Like I was thinking, what a fantastic day. The sky is truly amazing and my coffee is fantastic. I am very thankful for my family, my friends, my health, my mind, my business, my clients, my students, all my blessings! This is how you really feel Rich all your life!

I now entrust the Mattson Season Success Legacy to you. Your Choice! Live your Dreams, or as my father says, "Make it Happen, Captain!"

I need to get another cup of coffee.

About Kit

Kit Mattson is a Christian Faith-filled father, husband, son, brother. He is the youngest of five kids. He gives his father, brothers, and wife all the credit for giving him the drive he needed for life, as well as creating a sense of perpetual competition in him to strive to be the best in everything he attempts or puts his mind to, from checkers to business to sports of all types. He wants to leave a Godly legacy for his kids, family and friends.

At the young age of 16, Kit started his first business and caught the entrepreneur bug and never looked back. Kit has owned and operated highly successful businesses in fitness, marketing, real estate, martial arts, and business consulting for over two decades.

His business philosophy is to make the ordinary extraordinary! From sales to outstanding customer service, the goal is simple: make everyone you come in contact with feel important.

Kit has been a world-class championship athlete in football and martial arts. He has been in numerous action films, films, infomercials, T.V. shows, print media, and newspapers. Has been a high fashion runway and print model. He has met people from President George W. Bush to Paul McCartney to Pastor Joel Osteen and Greg Laurie. He is really a been-there-done-that worldwide man.

His laser focus and self-discipline as well as his Mattson Legacy Secrets he accredits to his ultimate success, will be shared with you.

You can connect with Kit at: Masterkm@att.net

CHAPTER 24

THE TRANSFORMATIVE MARKETING MACHINE THAT WORKS HARDER THAN YOU DO—SO YOU DON'T HAVE TO

BY GREG ROLLETT

You can't save souls in an empty church.
~ David Ogilvy

It occurred to me that entrepreneurs and business owners are under the assumption that the customers that walk into your door, find their way to your website or dial up your phones, is out of their control. That by random acts of marketing, they never know who is going to call or what they are going *to* want.

This is a crying shame.

It means that you are still trying to be everything to everyone. And that is a sure sign that your business is in trouble.

The truth is that you have the ability and the responsibility to be everything to the right type of customer or client, and actually repel those that you cannot, will not or have no desire to help.

Marketing gives you that ability. You can be polarizing and that is a good thing in marketing. And the first step is to determine who it is you want to do business with. Yes, tell yourself who it is you want to walk through your door, visit and interact with your website and pick up the phone and dial your office.

Start by going down the list:

Age

Male/Female

Married/Single

Kids/No kids

Location

Occupation/Industry

Then start to look at some of the intangibles:

Hobbies

Interests

Political affiliations

Religion

Personal beliefs

Life stages

When you put it together, you should have the description of an ideal client or customer that you genuinely want to and can help. It is the person that is most valuable to you and your business, not just the riff-raff that came waltzing off the street.

These should be your easy to manage, high profit and lowest headache clients and customers. The ones that get what you do, value it and value you.

When I first got started marketing my own products, I was selling information products to musicians, helping them to market their band and their music. I was not looking for any musician with a guitar and a song book. I was looking for a specific type of musician. I was specifically on the hunt for the singer-songwriter, in their mid to late 20's, who was working in hospitality, eating Ramen Noodles, playing cover songs at the bars on the weekends, wearing khaki shorts and rocking a backwards hat.

I knew his problem, his fears and desires. I also knew he didn't know how to promote or market his music. More than anything in the world, he wanted to quit his job and play music to pay the bills.

Did jazz musicians or wedding bands or hip-hop artists make their way into my customer base? Sure they did. But some were also turned off. And that's great, because I filled my pipeline with musicians that understood who I was and what I was able to do for them, the riff-raff never got into my machine.

Once you understand who it is that you want and desire to do business with, you need to determine who you want to be to that market. You must become their hero, their advocate, their trusted advisor.

DEVELOPING YOUR SUPER HERO POSITIONING

You develop hero-like or legendary positioning by telling your story and making a direct connection to your audience.

Your story is the most powerful and valuable weapon you have in your bag of tricks. And when you use it, you will be the heavy favorite in a Vegas title bout, playing in the heavy-weight division squaring off against weakling 100-lb, dripping-wet-from-the-ears business owners who are fighting to get business by lowering prices and succumbing to the opportunities at the bottom of the barrel. Superheroes are looking for the opportunity to save the world, make the headlines and get the girl. Let your competition direct traffic or give out parking tickets.

I want to put this into context for you. Let's say you are a financial advisor. And you know there are dozens upon dozens of other advisors in your market all going after the same ideal client - affluent, pre-retiree, conservative, married, kids in college or working and living in a certain part of town.

Every week this market gets invitations to seminars, workshops and dinners. They are being sold to on every corner. And they are being pitched, prodded, poked and invaded from people that have no connection to them whatsoever—just salesmen with a brochure hawking the latest products that promise to beat the market.

This is where you have the ability to be their hero…to rip off your suit and become the knight in shining armor…to be the admiration of your market. And you start by telling your story to this market from the get-go.

Much like every Batman or Superman movie starts with the telling and demonstration of their origin story, you too must do the same. You tell this story to reveal to them that you understand them, their situation and their desires. You do this to establish authority, positioning and credibility. It shows that you are not a scary monster like everyone else hunting in the marketplace.

When you write, develop and share your story, you get to decide who you get to be to this market by drawing on your past and your present. You get to design your costume and explain your superpowers.

You might begin a letter by sharing how you got involved with financial planning, starting when your grandparents needed help from your parents to make it through retirement and then explain your parents poor planning habits, which led to your own revelation that this type of thinking and investing had to stop for future generations.

What if you are a business coach or consultant? Maybe you share the story behind your first business that was failing miserably until you found a coach that helped you. Now you are paying that forward to help others with their businesses.

Or you might be someone who grew up in the community, played Little League here, went away to college and then came back to help the community grow and prosper.

These are all stories people can relate to. They are stories we recognize and plotlines that are familiar. And the underlying tone is that you understand what they are going through and can help them.

Once they make this connection, it's time to perform the most important part of any marketing system, the offer. You see, there is only one way that I know how to make money in a business. Send an offer. Make an attempt to exchange value for money. Heck, even McDonald's makes offers. What do you think their $1 Menu is? It's a sales letter. It's a flyer. It's a promotion designed to exchange money for value.

DEVELOPING AN OFFER MACHINE

Your profits are directly related to the frequency of value-added offers you make to your target market that we defined above.

Here is the biggie to get from this. The offer must solve a problem that your market has and it must resolve a core desire that they have. Note that I never said anything about cool features or even benefits. There is a time and a place for both, but right now you need to be a problem solver. You need to be seen as the trusted advisor that can move your prospect closer to their core desire.

What is a core desire? It's what we really want. It goes beyond the surface level wants that everyone else is selling to, and speaks to your market on an emotional level.

Many weight loss experts will tell you that their system will help you lose 20 pounds. So what? Everyone says that.

You are the person that gives them confidence to start a new life…to have the confidence to get out in the field and find true love…to make them look their best when delivering a presentation…that helps them to live long enough to see their grandkids graduate from high school.

You are the trainer who gets people the photos that make them look like a million bucks on their wedding day, or on the cruise with their in-laws.

Maybe you run a pool cleaning service. Think about selling desires, not benefits. You're not selling a blue, crystal clear pool. You are selling the place where you can host your kids' 5th birthday party or have the annual 4th of July party or even be the envy of your entire neighborhood.

You are even selling time - not having to wake up on Saturday morning to go and clean the pool, but to actually swim in and enjoy the pool.

That is what your market really wants. Having a blue, crystal clear pool helps us to get there and is the product that you sell, but you need to be much more than that. You need to be a hero, remember?

When someone thinks of you, get them thinking about how you impacted and affected their life, not just the job you performed.

Now you have to make an offer to fill this desire. Most business owners will try and go for the kill on the first attempt. You are going to be smarter. You know that consumers today need information. They need more than just a coupon, they need to know they are getting the best.

Remember we are only going after the perfect audience, not anyone searching for the low-price provider or who is running a special discount this month. We want the client that understands how you make their life better and sees you as the only person that can solve their problem and fills their desire.

Therefore you need to tell them about this transformation. And you do so through marketing. It is not evil to be a marketer. It is actually beneficial. When someone is made aware of what you do to satisfy their desires, they thank you for that by exchanging their money for your services. That's what it's all about, right?

The first goal of any marketing campaign is to generate leads. You want to activate a targeted portion of your overall market that has raised their hand to hear and learn more from you. At this stage of the game, you are not yet selling your products or services, simply building a pool of interested prospects who want to know more.

This group is volunteering to learn more. They have gone out of their way to call your office or recorded message, visit your website, fill out a form or stop in to your office and inquire more about what you do.

It does not mean they are ready to buy. It means they are ready to listen. It is your responsibility to give them something worth listening to.

And you must continue to work with them, educate them and inspire and motivate them for the long-haul.

DEVELOPING YOUR POWER POSITIONING

Through this brand of marketing, you want to be seen in a field of one... as the only logical choice your prospect can and will do business with. When they first raise their hand in the lead generation process and initiate contact, you want to be ready with a sequence that pre-frames them to know who you are, what you do and how you can help them.

This can be done through mailing out a Shock- And-Awe package, a big box of your best materials designed to shock and awe the prospect to all of the incredible things you are doing and the people you are helping. When a prospect opens it, they are completely blown away. They literally stop in their tracks, open your package and start to go through all of the assets, the materials, the testimonials, the videos and the pieces you have put together that will help steer them towards working with you.

But a Shock-And-Awe package alone is not enough. In order to win in business today, to transform the lives of your clients and customers as well as your own bank account, you must be seen everywhere your market turns.

You want to be famous to the people that raise their hands. You want to show up in their mailbox and their inbox. You want to be seen and heard. You want to be read. You want to take up a position in their social sphere where they are thinking about you on a regular basis. In essence, you want to be a celebrity in their eyes.

To do this, you must develop a marketing sequence that is sent out automatically, no matter if you, or your staff, are staying on top of your new leads and prospects.

Otherwise, it won't happen. I know because it happens to me. When I am left to remember to do these things myself, on my own time, other things get in the way. Using automated tools, and developing systems and sequences that are created and written at one time, and then leveraged with technology and fulfillment partners, ensure that you never miss a beat and your marketing machine runs in the background – spoon-feeding you new business that has been Shocked and Awe'd, seen your videos, heard you via audio or Podcasts, is getting mail pieces, emails and everything but the kitchen sink, in a sequential manner that advances the sale.

During this entire process, you never want to forget to inject yourself into the equation. You must continue to advance the sales process by inserting you into the marketing equation…sharing stories, not features and benefits…sharing resources and information to help them see you as a trusted advisor. You want them to see you for more than just what you do. You want them to do business with you because of who you are. Once you do this, you will have a customer or client for life. And your business will forever be transformed.

About Greg

Greg Rollett, @gregrollett, is a Best-Selling Author and Marketing Expert who works with experts, authors and entrepreneurs all over the world. He utilizes the power of new media, direct response and personality-driven marketing to attract more clients and to create more freedom in the businesses and lives of his clients.

After creating a successful string of his own educational products and businesses, Greg began helping others in the production and marketing of their own products and services. He now helps his clients through two distinct companies, Celebrity Expert Marketing and the ProductPros.

Greg has written for Mashable, Fast Company, Inc.com, the Huffington Post, AOL, AMEX's Open Forum and others, and continues to share his message helping experts and entrepreneurs grow their business through marketing.

Greg's client list includes Michael Gerber, Brian Tracy, Tom Hopkins, Coca-Cola, Miller Lite and Warner Brothers, along with thousands of entrepreneurs and small-business owners across the world. Greg's work has been featured on FOX News, ABC, NBC, CBS, CNN, *USA Today, Inc Magazine, The Wall Street Journal*, the *Daily Buzz* and more.

Greg loves to challenge the current business environment that constrains people to working 12-hour days during the best portions of their lives. By teaching them to leverage marketing and the power of information, Greg loves to help others create freedom in their businesses that allow them to generate income, make the world a better place, and live a radically-ambitious lifestyle in the process.

A former touring musician, Greg is highly sought after as a speaker, who has spoken all over the world on the subjects of marketing and business building.

If you would like to learn more about Greg and how he can help your business, please contact him directly at: greg@dnagency.com or by calling his office at 877.897.4611.

CHAPTER 25

50 WAYS TO DELIVER A FIVE-STAR EXPERIENCE IN A MEDICAL PRACTICE

BY DAVID J. WAGES, M.D.

INTRODUCTION

When was the last time you went to a physician's office and thought you were treated so special that you felt like you were the President or a member of the Royal Family? The experience was so memorable, that you just could not forget about it for days. You told all your friends. If you said "never," then it's more likely that you had an experience filled with frustration, lengthy waiting, and so unpleasant you just dreaded it. The good news is that it does not have to be that way. It can be transformed and you can begin it today.

What is a five-star patient experience in the medical practice and why is it important? Some people would say that five-star service is being treated like you were an important person or that you were special. Others may say it is having a positive emotional experience, a carefree event without problems or headaches. You should strive to make the patient feel so good that by just being in your office they feel better, even before they have seen the physician. The experience should be uplifting and memorable. When patients receive five-star customer service, it will transform your practice to one that patients will love.

It also leads to improved staff morale, and decreased liability. Your staff will need to transform their attitudes and interactions to be successful. Before your staff can deliver a unique experience to patients, they must develop a culture of treating each other special. Achieving a five-star experience is not simply a list of items to do. It is not just what you do or say but how you deliver it. It is a transformation of how you treat patients and staff. You must develop passion to do this. You will find that it will be well worth it.

I will be giving you examples of ways to get started on delivering a five-star experience for your practice. There is not one single item that is going to make a difference, but many little items that will impact the patient experience. During this process, you must keep in mind that everything matters, attention to detail is imperative. Some of these items are subliminal to the patient. You must get your office team on board with your mission. The staff must understand and be committed. Put your commitment on display for the patients and staff. "We are a five-star practice. We strive to go above and beyond any physician office you may have been in before. If things are not to your expectation, please let us know and we will be happy to improve your experience!" This generates accountability. I will describe a few areas to improve the patient experience including: the office environment, the staff interaction, the physician interaction, and some bonus ideas.

ENVIRONMENT

Start with having clear, accurate, and easy directions. Before a new patient shows up, they have made an appointment and need to find your office. Even with a GPS, directions can be confusing. You should have directions that are accurate and easily understood. Upon arriving to the parking lot, is the signage clearly visible? Is the parking lot clean and well-marked? Is the entrance obvious? If the patient has a difficult time finding your office or parking, this creates stress and anxiety. You are officially at a disadvantage for making a good first impression.

These are areas that can aggravate patients if they have a difficult time finding parking, and are feeling stressed about being lost because the directions to the office were inadequate or inaccurate. Find ways to make it easier for the patients by having clear directions and an obvious sign that says, "This is the place."

Upon entering the office, it should appeal to the senses. An office with warm, earth-tone colors is more appealing. Have aromatherapy throughout the practice to create a soothing environment. Attractive plants liven up an office. In place of radio, have soothing, relaxing background music. Cleanliness and neatness are of the utmost importance. Are the vents clean and dust free? Are the carpets old and worn out? In a medical practice, carpets that are older than five years should be replaced due to soiling, as well as wear and tear. Remove all clutter. Having too many old magazines that are worn and outdated is messy. Eliminate the gossip magazines. Consider limiting magazines to just a few higher quality ones. Having warm colors, having a fresh appearance, cleanliness and the elimination of clutter, sends a message that this office provides a different experience.

Go to the restrooms. Are there any special amenities? Consider having some mints, fragrances, and hand lotion for patients use. In the waiting area, do you offer refreshments? Having a refrigerator with bottled water and napkins is a nice touch, having a coffee maker and spa water dispenser with your lemon-flavored water is even more impressive.

STAFF INTERACTION

How long does a patient have to wait before the staff acknowledges them with eye contact? If it is more than five seconds then there is room for improvement. Having eye contact within the first two seconds should be the standard. The welcome should be warm and friendly, not a dry, bored or miserable grunt. A smile and a warm genuine voice is a good beginning.

How does one sound excited and energetic performing the welcome multiple times a day? Actors on Broadway do this multiple times a day and so can you. It is called work. It takes effort, but it is worth it. Use the patient's name. People love to hear their name. It makes people feel welcome and appreciated. Don't let a difficult pronunciation hinder you. People love that you tried. Instead of a simple "hello, how are you?" encourage your staff to compliment the patient on how they look. "Oh what a nice dress! Oh the shoes look great on you! Did you change your hair? Have you lost weight?" If you only ask the patient how they are, then it makes you susceptible to a grumpy patient downloading on your staff and stirring up negative emotions. However, when the patient comes in who may be in a grumpy mood and you compliment them on their appearance or express what a pleasure it is to see them again, you have created a different outcome.

Upgrade your name badges. Spice them up with an idea from Disney. Below the name of the person is a trait, such as: "I have a Pug" or "Red Sox fan" or a zodiac sign. This is an icebreaker for interaction between the patient and staff. Staff should be cheerful, friendly, big smiles and a helping nature. Staff should have well-rehearsed scripts and language regarding what they should say for the most common interactions. The Ritz Carlton uses "My pleasure", or "At your service." Remember, it is not just what you say but also how you say it.

Instead of pushing a clipboard in front of the patient to fill out necessary registration forms, try coming around the desk, welcoming the patient, giving them a handwritten welcome note to the practice on nice stationary in an envelope. Once the patient is ready to be seen, the staff would greet the patient using their name. Patients should hear their name five times from initial greeting to physician meeting. As they escort the patient to the exam room, give a brief tour of the office. Show them where the bathroom is, and where the exam room is, and as you pass different offices, introduce the staff. "Oh this is Colleen, she is in charge of billing, this to Suzy, she is in charge of patient accounts and this person is Brendan, who is our manager." This type of attention lets them know that they are being welcomed in to your family and your practice.

Have a scripted dialogue with the patient. Begin credentialing the office. These are things that you may take for granted that patients do not know. "You are going to love Dr. Patrick, he has been Board Certified for ten years, all of his patients enjoy his bedside manner, etc." Reinforce that you are grateful they came to see you. It is nice for them to hear that from staff. For new patients, once they arrive into the room, have a small welcome gift. This does not have to be an expensive gift. For a few dollars you can get a mug, water bottle, tote bag, or an umbrella. Have it personalized with a note letting them know that you appreciate their business. It's like inviting somebody into your home and sharing with them the things that are important.

PHYSICIAN INTERACTION

Once the patient is seated, the physician should be introduced in a professional manner. Professional introductions set the level of respect for the physician. Always introduce the most important person first then a brief handoff such as: "Dr. Patrick, this is Ms. Matthews. Ms. Matthews is here for a routine physical examination. This is her first visit and she comes from Lexington." The physician now begins the visit. Before diving in and focusing on the patient's chief complaint, pause and spend a couple of minutes visiting with the patient. Once you have done this if the patient needs to undress for an exam then step out of the room, let them change, then perform the exam. Having that extra couple of minutes of rapport with the patient to establish a relationship is important before performing a sensitive exam. Once the visit is over, the patient is handed off to an assistant who escorts them out and likewise hands them off in a professional manner to be checked out.

BONUS ITEMS

Who doesn't like to get an unexpected gift? This could be something as simple as a handwritten thank you note or a small gift. Patients are surprised and appreciative of little details that can make them feel special and important. Things you may want to consider would be an unexpected occasional gift such as roses on Valentine's Day. This could be done inexpensively when buying in bulk. Remember the presentation is just as important as the gift. Make it special. There is a difference between simply handing them a rose versus a rose that has been trimmed, wrapped with colored tissue paper, tied with a ribbon and a handwritten note saying: "Thank you, We appreciate you, You are valued." These are items that your staff will be happy to do once they see the smiles that are created. In addition to flowers, you could consider homemade cookies, small candies, thank you cards, birthday cards and thank you notes after visits.

SUMMARY

These were just a few items to get your creative juices flowing. Realize there are always going to be ways to do better. Once you get involved with the process you will find the more you study it, the more creative you become in providing benefits that improve the patient's experience. The more you implement these ideas, the more you will improve. This will help create an office that patients look forward to visiting. Your staff will be proud of their accomplishments. When your staff is on board with delivering the ultimate patient experience, all of these suggestions will easily fall into place and be executed. It takes diligence, attention to detail, planning and persistence to maintain the pursuit of perfection. The five-star service is not only what you do and say, but also how you execute it.

ACTION ITEM

Have a working brunch for your staff at a nice restaurant, such as The Four Seasons or The Ritz Carlton. Give each staff member the assignment to come up with a list of all the things that made their experience at the brunch special, things that made them feel important and appreciated. Ask them how they can implement these items. The person who has the list with the most useful information on it will then be the recipient of a gift prize. This will be a fun and learning experience for your entire team.

About Dr. David J. Wages

David J. Wages, M.D. is a board-certified plastic surgeon practicing in the Boston suburb of Peabody. He has been a physician since 1991. He specializes in delivering the "Mommy Makeover" procedures that help women reclaim their bodies after pregnancy. He spent time developing a turnkey practice with an on-site surgery center. His practice also offers a full spectrum of non-surgical as well as surgical treatments including personal fitness training, skin care, and lasers. He is passionate about changing the way physicians are perceived, and has developed a solution for delivering excellent health care wrapped in a five-star customer-centric environment. He receives frequent accolades for his customer service. He has been the recipient of the America's Top Doctor award for 11 consecutive years from 2003 to 2014 by Consumers Research Council of America. His ideas have been transformed and used in various practices from orthopedic surgery, cardiology, dermatology, plastic surgery, and internal medicine. His charity, Botox for the Cure, was founded in 2011, and raises money for breast cancer awareness through the sales of Botox. He is a member of a mastermind group that challenges members with new ideas to improve customer service in the medical field. He also mentors other physicians.

Dr. Wages is from Denton, Texas. He graduated from the University of North Texas, and went to medical school at University of Texas Medical Branch, Galveston, Texas. He did his training for general surgery and plastic surgery at Emory University in Atlanta, Georgia and then went on to an advanced Fellowship in Microsurgery and Hand surgery at Massachusetts General Hospital, where he held a teaching appointment with Harvard Medical School. Nowadays he enjoys making snowmen during the long Boston winters with his family of five. Other hobbies include magic, trick roping, hiking, and spending time with his family in Boxford, Massachusetts.

CHAPTER 26

ALIVE AND SUCCESSFUL!

BY DR. TAYO

So... I get admitted to medical school and a new phase of my life begins. Along with that are expectations - huge ones! This is a long five-year journey with no guarantees, but my (and a whole number of other people's) expectation is for me to become a certified and practicing physician at the end of it. I have my work cut out.

Will I actually get to graduate as a doctor? There is no doubt in my mother's mind that I will, but I am not so sure. This will take five years - a very long time in the life of a teenager, almost a third of my life so far. One thing I know for sure is that I have to settle down quickly; study and learn, if I am to get that medical degree at the other end. It is a giddy thought – I'm both excited and fearful, often at the same time.

The first challenge came up quickly - to pass the first set of exams: Biochemistry, Physiology and Anatomy. For me, that was a big hurdle. Our main recommended physiology textbook, Sampson Wright's Applied Physiology, was pretty tough going. At best, I would manage two pages a day, but some of my fellow students were able to read many more. One in particular would come into class and tell us he'd read 50 pages overnight! I couldn't understand how that was possible, but I tried hard to increase my reading speed. Comprehension did not follow.

I then decided to wake up to read at night. When that didn't work, I asked some friends to wake me up, but the next morning, I was still very much in bed - and had not gotten out of it! The next step was to make sure I got out of bed and to our reading room, where I would promptly put the book in my lap, my head on the table and go to sleep. Ahhh!

Something needed to happen, and fast! It soon dawned on me that following other people's habits and reading at night obviously did not work for me. When I analyzed my study habits, I did better when I attended lectures live, after which I would read to build on what I had read. So that's what I did and still do to this day.

What happened? At the physiology exams, I passed so well that I was one of only four students from my year and the only female (out of a class of 200 – including 20 females) who was offered the option to spend just one more year to earn a B.Sc. Physiology degree, a direct result of our high scores. One of the others was my 50 page per day friend! I decided to continue with my medical studies. Five years was already plenty - I did not want to make it six.

A few years later, I was at an interview, held a few weeks before taking the specialty certification exams. During the interview, it was made clear to me that the offer of a position was conditional on my passing those exams. I confidently replied that I would. I wasn't being arrogant - it was a knowing based on my application of the 5 key success steps I had defined and practiced. Even the interviewers could not understand why I was so confident.

This was the moment I realized it was *critical to share this information* to help as many people as possible. We face challenging and overwhelming situations every day. We could come through them, living happy and successful lives simply by following what I'd discovered.

It is my mission to spread the word that SUCCESS IS A CHOICE. That is the very start of any journey to success.

1. BE THE MASTER CREATOR OF YOUR LIFE!

What took me from feeling overwhelmed to being tuned in to success? The gateway, the most important aspect, is to take personal responsibility for your entire life. Your brain will be rewired to take the successful path. Once you are able to take responsibility for the not-so-good things that have happened in your life, you now have the power to turn things around and be THE creator, creating great things instead. Successful people don't have victim mentalities.

Be very firm about this and aware that opportunities will come your way when you focus on your goal. Have POSITIVE EXPECTANCY - expect whatever you set out to do to be successful, and be prepared to sort things out when obstacles appear.

Your subconscious directs your actions over 95% of the time, but you can influence your subconscious by choosing what you allow to influence it. Until you choose to do so, it'll be dominated by your fears and other negative thoughts and beliefs, affecting you physically, emotionally and mentally.

Make it YOUR choice whether to take an opportunity or not. Decide to say either no or yes, accepting full responsibility for either decision. Do not abdicate that choice. Procrastinating or being passive is worse than a "no" decision. Let's be clear about this: to take advantage of an opportunity, you need to put in effort. Work is required to turn that opportunity into the success it will be. Eliminate the word "try" from your vocabulary - that word is setting you up - for failure! Decide to either do or not do, making a firm decision either way. When you say you'll "try" to do anything, it weakens you. How you appear to the world is also weakened.

Now that you have got the mindset of the master creator of your life, it's time to focus on how to do it.

2. PURPOSE & CLARITY

Be purposeful about what you want, and the most important question here is WHY? That's because we all have a purpose, and the closer you come to aligning with your purpose, the more successful you will be. Your Purpose is a combination of what and why.

> *The two most important days in your life are the*
> *day you are born and the day you find out why.*
> ~ Mark Twain

The first thing in discovering your purpose is to recognize that it does not have to be this big thing, this world-changing story, movement or product. Your purpose may be important to one person, but to that person, it is life-changing. Your purpose may be to be a great mother, to teach kindergarten with passion, or to care for seniors in a home.

You can count on this: Your purpose will make you happy, and once you're happy, you'll be successful. This is not the time to buy into some other person's big dream for you. You have the freedom to design your life to your exact specifications.

Here are two simple exercises to help you out. The first one is a brainstorming session. Take out a blank sheet of paper and write down 100 things that you want to do, like doing or that enchant you. Let your mind open up – any dream is up for grabs. Leave out the how and the why, just write without censoring. Next, trim that list down to ten and look for any common ideas between them. Then, pick just one thing from that list. It will be something that gives you the most joy and probably has several other items on your list linked to it.

The second exercise is to dig deeper and is essential. For your top pick, keep asking why it's important, until you're left speechless or with a vast sense of peace and wonder, feeling like you just discovered the holy grail. One thing I can share with you - money is never the end of that sequence of Why's - it's nearer the top. Dig deep beyond that!

By the time you've been through both exercises, you'll have gained significant insights.

Once you've defined your purpose, it tends not to change. What may change, and frequently does, is your goal, which, for maximum effectiveness, is designed around your purpose.

Successful people make decisions quickly and change their minds slowly. That is because they are clear about what they are doing and why they are doing it.

Gaining clarity also gives you the ability to deal with the inevitable doubts and fears that will come along by asking - What kinds of things can go wrong? What are you afraid of? What's the very worst that can happen? Would that really be the end of the world? Can you lessen the risk sufficiently that it is not such a disaster that will stop you from moving forward?

3. GOALS

Now that you've discovered your purpose, it's time to develop goals to help things along. Knowing your purpose will drive your goal and defining your goal will feed your purpose. Of the various goal-setting processes I have used, the easiest and friendliest are a series of **W** questions.

You don't have to do them in any particular order, and it's easier to remember than most other goal-setting techniques.

The first, **Why**, has been taken care of when you did the exercises to unearth your purpose.

Who is going to help you? Who must you talk to? Who can be a coach or mentor to help speed things along? Who offers expert services in areas that you can't do yourself?

What do you want EXACTLY? No time for wishy-washy ideas here - you need to be definite. If you can't describe it easily in a sentence or two to someone else who then understands what you mean, go back to the drawing board and redo!

When to start? That's an easy one - its NOW!! How long will it take, and when is the target completion date?

Where will you be located? Is this a physical location, an online store, a book you are writing? Your intellectual property needs a home. Give it one.

A great goal will excite, stretch and scare you, all at the same time. You want to fulfill your purpose, so taking a few chances are worth it. You may have to break a big goal down into smaller ones. If so, do only one at a time, or confusion may follow pretty quickly.

The closer your goal takes you towards your purpose, the stronger will be your incentive to complete it. To set a strong goal, ask yourself how far it takes you along the road to fulfilling your purpose? If it takes you most or all the way, you'll probably persist a lot harder than if it was only a minor component.

Now that you've set great goals, time to figure out HOW to get them done!

4. ACTION PLAN AND ACTION

This is where you look at your goal and draw a map to help you get there. The more detailed the map, the better your chances of arriving at your destination. This part is also very important - not having a plan pretty much leaves your chances of your reaching your goal, as well as fulfilling your purpose, to chance - those odds are not good.

Have you chosen a safe goal? Probably. I can say that because, for most people, setting a more challenging goal evokes the fear of failure. It's time to toss that one out of the window and ascend to a higher level of potential and mastery!

Based on research, you are capable of at least four times the goal you set, but you decided to play it safe so you do not feel like a failure. Let's stretch this a bit (not too much) and double that goal. How do you feel? A bit anxious but excited? Here is something to consider. If you don't stretch yourself, you won't reach your full potential and will probably end up feeling dissatisfied. This is where you detach the results from your fears. ALL results are great! They have no other meaning!

Make a commitment to start RIGHT NOW. Start by doing something to immediately anchor it into your mind; or your great idea, plan or goal will get tossed aside then forgotten, along with all the other 60,000 thoughts that come and go through your mind each day.

Here is one thing I know for sure: if you commit to this, you WILL make it work!

5. MOMENTUM: SUSTAINING IT ALL

So how do you go about staying the course? Simple – by developing the discipline and habits necessary to sustain a successful life: building habits through daily practices. Think of it like training for a marathon or nurturing your plants. Piling on a months training (if that is possible) in one day will probably end up as a serious injury or illness, even if you are fit.

The road to success is consistent training in bite sizes.

Decide what habits you want to build and start doing them consistently. A great way to nurture a habit is to reward yourself when you've formed a habit that helps you towards your goal. Choose something meaningful, but not painful or vastly expensive and not something that will affect your progress; for example, you really don't want to reward a positive dietary change with food.

Of all the habits out there, the one I would encourage you to develop first is **GRATITUDE**. Don't underestimate how powerful this simple tool is. When you practice gratitude, your brain releases more of the neurotransmitter substance called dopamine, which stimulates the pleasure center of your brain, relieves stress, helps you sleep better, fights cravings and controls your appetite! This also strengthens your immune system, improving your health. You too can access all this for the cost of a cup or two of great quality coffee.

As soon as you can after reading this (I suggest within 5 days), buy yourself a really nice looking journal, one that is a reflection of the success you see in your life. I like journals with faint ruled lines. At the end of every day, just before you go to sleep, write in the date, then write down five things that you are grateful for on that particular day. This process allows you to reflect and feel as you write, making gratitude a stronger part of how you assess your day and your last thoughts before you go to sleep.

Since you have to write five things every day, you'll always be on the look out, which is why this is such a powerful habit. The changes that happen from this habit are life changing. I've been doing this for several years, and clients have reported how powerful it is.

You'll become more aware and appreciative of people, things and situations. That lifelong habit of gratitude in any situation is the true source of Happiness and Success.

I will also encourage you to make sure you enjoy the journey, including all the obstacles you encounter. The scenery can be stunning.

About Dr. Tayo

Dr. Tayo helps her clients gain clarity, purpose and passion, so that they can lead the successful life of their dreams. For many, success is a dream... meant for other people! With her proven and unique style, Dr. Tayo takes direct aim at busting this myth by using her vast knowledge and experience; distilling it into a process you can easily apply in your own life to achieve the results you desire. She is an authority in getting the best out of you.

Dr. Tayo was born in London, UK, and moved to Nigeria with her parents, where she grew up in several cities. She graduated from the prestigious University of Ibadan Medical School, following which she specialized in Radiology at the Welsh National School of Medicine, Cardiff.

With a medical degree, five specialty certifications and a sub-specialty fellowship under her belt, she has practiced in several countries around the world. In addition to a busy career as a radiologist, she is the Founder and CEO of ProRad, whose mission is to be the home of leading-edge radiology in emerging countries.

An avid traveller and life-long student, Dr. Tayo discovered and distilled a critical set of success principles she uses herself. They have been honed over several years of personal experience and research into a process you can apply easily in your own life.

Dr. Tayo is leaving no stone unturned in spreading her easy-to-apply system far and wide. Her clients trust her to get them results and have described their time with her as life-changing and transformational. She aims to cut your own success journey time as short as possible, and keeps the journey interesting, practical and relevant.

You can connect with Dr. Tayo here:
DoctorTayo.com
DrT@DoctorTayo.com
www.facebook.com/tayodeefanpage

CHAPTER 27

HOW YOU TURN YOUR WEAKNESSES INTO STRENGTHS

BY THOMAS FRIEBE

Have you ever given a speech? In front of a larger group of people? Say, in front of at least 30 people? No? Unfortunately, if you want to promote your business, your career or yourself, there is no way around it. Before you start turning pages now, take a deep breath. On the following pages you will learn how to shed your fear of public speaking and, if you already are a practiced speaker, even how to improve on that. Deal? Great, then let us begin.

A confident and convincing performance is the basis for every success. The ability to speak with enthusiasm belongs to the number one soft skills needed and is one of the most important career boosters there are. But unfortunately, the fear of speaking in front of other people is greater for some than the fear of death, or let's say, many a person would rather die than deliver a speech. I know this from experience, because my fear, too, was so great that I couldn't utter one proper syllable. That is a bad condition for a newscaster on the radio. Yes, you read that correctly. I was a newscaster and couldn't utter a word. Nothing. Nada. Nichts. Well, to be perfectly honest, I could speak a bit, although that would sound like: New, niew, Nnnneewww New YYYo Yooo, YYYYorkkkk. Uhm, uuuhh, uhm cough, hem, sorry, again, Nnnnnew Yokkk, ehhm York. I didn't quite reach the end of the first sentence, because the anchor sitting behind the window in the radio studio quickly pushed up the controller for the music. I had half a mind to flee the city, preferably with a crash helmet on my head so nobody would recognize me. But do you know the actually fascinating and hopeful part of this story? Today I'm a professional voice-over artist and have completed numerous live-broadcasts in front of an audience of millions. I love the work as a voice-over artist. Every time, I feel fascinated and delighted that I can provoke emotions, seduce and amaze people simply by the sound of my voice. My trauma became a dream. "How is that possible?" …you might ask yourself, and the answer is very simple and contains the title of this book: Through <u>Transform</u>ation.

I transformed my *fear* of speaking into a *joy* for speaking. How I accomplished that and how you can turn your weaknesses into strengths as well, I will tell you now in detail.

For a few years now, I've been coaching executives and entrepreneurs to help them achieve a confident and "coherent" appearance. For me, there is nothing more fulfilling than to watch my clients change for the better after they shed their fear of speaking. They grow more confident, their posture and attitude change, they begin to radiate and activate their true charisma, and they experience an inner joy that is contagious. And all the time they come closer and closer to their core, their vocation. I am convinced - and my experiences prove - that only after we overcome our fears, can we actually live out our true talents and passions. That should be an objective for all of us. That makes us happy. It is not the money, not the fame and prestige we enjoy (those are just side-effects), it is what we do with passion, full of joy and love, that fulfills us, and this always has to do with living out our talents. Fear keeps us from following our vocation and reaching our true goals.

How then do we overcome the fear? I have developed a simple 5-Step Plan that has helped me bring about the transformation. This guide can also help with every feeling or situation you seek to change.

1. Analyze it. What exactly is it that you fear? (For me back then it was the red light and the notion that once it turns on, every person "out there" would hear me). What is it that hinders you from unfolding your potential? Perhaps it's just an uncomfortable feeling and you have been avoiding it for years. Why? Write down WHAT that is.

2. Accept it. That might seem wrong at first. But to change something, you first have to accept the situation as it is, and stop pretending everything was alright. No longer will we run from our problem, but face the challenge – this uncomfortable feeling, this shirking and avoiding, our bad conscience. Say, and write down: "Yes, I am afraid. Yes, I have always shirked to speak. I accept that. That is what was - and now I will change it."

3. Audio-visualize it. This is a potent tool, the most potent to reach our goals. Imagine how you want the situation to be: In sound and visuals, like a living movie. Write down what your ideal situation would be, how you speak in front of a group of people, how you look them in the eyes, how they cheer for you excitedly. Let your imagination run wild, feel how you speak in front of others full of joy. What's important: Phrase it positively and in present tense, as if the situation was happening right now. That is the number one trick for overcoming the fear of speaking, but also to achieve your highest goals. With this exercise I managed to turn my red light panic into joy.

4. Activate it. Produce your movie. Become active and let your audio-visualization become reality. Deal with the basic rules for a successful performance. Look for like-minded people, join a speaker's club - I can recommend "Toastmasters International" - join a rhetoric course, let someone coach you, practice in front of the mirror. No matter what you do - Get into action and practice. When I did that, I shut myself in a training studio before going to work for weeks and simulated the emergency situation, until one day, I suddenly had "fun". Wow! That's a great feeling. You will experience that as well, so: Practice.

5. Archive it. Document your successes. Document them daily, and most importantly…in writing – both small and big improvements. That will give your self-confidence a boost, because you will realize what has improved and you will be an eyewitness to your own growth, your own transformation. We frequently mark on our walls how much our children have grown. It is always nice to see the surprise of the kids and how proud they are – when they see that they have grown several centimeters in only a few weeks.

If you keep to this 5-step-plan, you will soon be unstoppable, you will speak and give presentations that convince and inspire others. You will overcome your fear, reach your goals and fulfill your dreams.

I remember very well how I had just overcome my fear of speaking and of the microphone to become a really good newscaster, and how this improved my self-confidence drastically. It gave me the feeling of being unstoppable, and in a sense, I was. I finished my training as a radio editor and then worked as an editor-in-chief with a small TV station, later as a producer for bigger TV companies and as a creative director in my own production company. These things did fill my days, more often than not my nights as well, and they certainly filled my wallet. However, they did not "fulfill" me. I had the feeling that I wasn't utilizing my talents and abilities properly. As a result, I decided to resign my secure post as a creative director and swap it against the insecure occupation of a freelance voice-over artist. Especially at the beginning, I had some months in which I would spend more money on advanced education, further training, books and classes, than I actually made with my voice-over jobs. But I knew that it was the only way to really excel at it. It was an exhausting and difficult time of deprivation, without which I wouldn't be the person I am today and I would hate to have missed it.

I had prepared my exit quite well, increasing the marketing efforts for my voice-over services, acquiring studio equipment, and as a second mainstay founded a small video production company that was to deal only with content that was important to me. In the beginning I was off to a good start, but then came 9-11, the 11th September of 2001…the attack on the World Trade Center.

In addition to the emotional and political confusion created by this unprecedented act of violence, many might also still remember the economic effects. Companies and television broadcasters put their marketing budgets on the back burner, afraid to invest, and just waited for what would happen next. The area of advertising in particular experienced a massive drop-off. The income I would have with my voice-over jobs on the side had dropped to less than 50 percent in full-time. I had one or other smaller documentary projects with my production company, but even those yielded too little to live and too much to die. H-m-m-m – what was I to do? To bury my dreams was out of the question. Soon I realized that I would have to decide whether

I wanted to be a voice-over artist or a producer for Christian spiritual videos. I opted for voice-over work with everything I had. While many colleagues complained about the recession, I researched the addresses of all local and regional radio broadcasters in Germany, printed postcards that outlined my services and introduced myself as the "new and fresh voice for your radio spot" with my own studio and live-broadcasting equipment. I then sent those postcards to suitable radio stations. Within one week, I was in business. Initial inquiries and jobs poured in, the clients were happy - and so was I! Some of the radio stations and spot producers who worked with me back then have remained in my client base to this day. In the "Yellow Pages" (that sounds kind of cute in the era of the Internet, doesn't it?), I searched for recording studios and commercial productions in my area and sent CDs to them, containing convincing audio samples with a short introduction on the first track. Three days after sending them, I called to inquire whether or not the CD had been received and how they liked it. Trust me, every single phone call took an effort. Despite that, I held on to the golden rule: *"Whatever you do, do it with all your heart and undivided attention."* (By the way, that's a saying from my mother. Thanks Mom!)

I did not want to give up on my dream, despite having been about to do so sometimes. I don't know how many phone calls actually yielded how many voice-over jobs, but I know that the number of interviews, casting invitations, price or project inquiries and actual jobs was growing, and that I was growing more confident with each phone call. Because the income from my voice-over jobs didn't suffice and we were slowly using up the savings, I struck a "deal" with my wife Gesine in the meantime. The reason: We were expecting our first child, and in times of pregnancy and "nest-building", most women are not exactly willing to compromise - nature has arranged it that way, I think. The result of our discussion was: If I couldn't manage to feed the family on my freelance voice-over work within three months, I had to find a secure job.

Thus, I had to increase my efforts yet again. At 8.30 in the morning I went into my little office with the adjacent vocal booth (one and a half square meters). At about 6.00 PM I came out again. When I was not sitting in the vocal booth filling an order, or speaking with another studio, I would sit at my desk to make sure I would sit in the vocal booth or another studio again as soon as possible – by specific, planned-out, thought-through and consistent means. More often than not, it was very laborious.

At that time, I got my hands on a CD. It was a live recording of an event in Germany, on which an American was speaking. Clearly, directly, easy-to-understand and stirring. The words that this man was shouting to me through the headphones of my CD Walkman, and that were always repeated by the simultaneous translation into German, shook me to the core. The speech stirred a part of myself that fascinated and motivated me. I listened to this CD again and again, wrote down the key sentences and acted upon them. The speaker used simple and powerful phrases like: "Write down everything you wish for…in detail! Make a plan out of them. Implement one thing each day. Any successful person plans and implements." Who was that man who spoke to me? Brian Tracy! And I am glad and thankful today, at this moment to say, "Thank you, Brian Tracy, for this speech that has contributed so much to my success." And that I may now contribute a chapter to Brian Tracy's book *Transform* fills me with joy and gratitude.

The hard-earned money often went straight into acquisition again – among other things into an Internet performance with audio samples of various categories for download. But, a bit at a time, my efforts showed results. The jobs were pouring in and with them the income. I had to convince my wonderful wife to agree to extending our "deal's" deadline by another two months to actually reach a break-even point, but because our financial situation had already improved so much, a real discussion wasn't even required. The endurance had paid off – as it always does, by the way.

And someday, the "miracle" happened. A big movie production inquired to have me narrate a 12-part TV documentary. The production manager had found my audio samples and had simply forwarded them to the TV channel's editor. She liked the recordings and I had the job before I even knew what was happening. In the end, my efforts yielded results – and have done so to this day. This initial big television job spawned many more voice-over jobs in television.

Today, I run a professional recording studio with a permanently-employed sound engineer who records my voice for the various productions and who also runs the technical procedures for live broadcasts with studios all over the world. I also know that this success was not random, nor luck, but the result of hard work.

From my story, you can take six crucial points - which - as I've learned in several discussions with successful personalities - are quite universal. No matter what your occupation is, wherever you are standing right now. Whether you've been in your job for a long time, find yourself at a crossroads or are just starting out. These 6 points will help you to be successful, to unfold your talents and make your dreams come true with a passion.

1. Decide on ONE thing that is really important to you - Something you are incredibly interested in.

2. Set a clear goal for yourself and keep moving towards it with passion and endurance. (Don't worry. If your passion is great enough, the endurance will follow automatically.)

3. Never give up.

4. Experience the "miracle".

5. Be happy and grateful. And the last point that I haven't talked about yet:

6. Stay curious and keep learning each and every day.

You cannot fail.

I believe that at the end of our lives we will be asked what we have done with the talents that were given to us. Our answer shouldn't be: "I buried them" but "I nurtured and cherished them and let them unfold to their full potential!" What will YOU say?

About Thomas

Thomas Friebe is one of the most successful voice-over artists in Germany. Millions of people know and are familiar with his voice. Whether it is a show, a documentary, sports or commentaries - you can hear him every day throughout different genres on various TV stations. He is the German voice for the hero "Desmond Miles" from the blockbuster game series *Assassin's Creed*, the station voice for the national TV channels RTL Nitro and BibelTV, as well as the narrator for numerous audio books. His great success and his popularity stem from his distinctive, clear and sonorous voice and especially from his tremendous versatility and the precise attitude with which he breathes life into the texts and characters.

After his journalistic training in radio, he switched to television and was at that time, the youngest TV editor-in-chief in Germany at only 22 years of age. After that, Thomas Friebe worked as an on-air producer for national TV stations (RTL Television, RTL2, VOX) and was the first German employee for the American TV station Nickelodeon in Germany.

Together with his brother, he founded the TV production company "Tof Intermedia". As the creative director and executive producer he has been responsible for several TV shows, campaigns, events and industrial films for notable international clients - many of which were award-winning productions. Since 2001, Thomas Friebe works full-time as a voice-over artist. His freshly-founded production company "Media Productions To Free" successfully runs a recording studio and produces videos for mobile and social media.

Because Thomas Friebe suffered from fear of the microphone in the beginning of his career, he has been helping clients for a few years now to overcome their fear of speaking and to act with self-assurance. For this, he developed the digital program "In 5 Schritten zu einem sicheren Auftritt und mehr Selbstvertrauen" ("In 5 steps to a confident and self-assured appearance"), which has already helped many people.

As an expert on convincing performance, Thomas Friebe also coaches executives and entrepreneurs. In doing so, there is nothing more exciting to him than to ferret out the often hidden talents of his clients and uncover these together with them, and nothing more fulfilling than to observe and share in this positive change.

Thomas Friebe is convinced that a happy and fulfilled life can only be led by unfolding your own talents and using them to their fullest. To this message, he devotes all his energy and passion, in his family (his wife and four children), in his coachings, as a voice-over artist and as a keynote speaker.

Learn more about Thomas Friebe on the website: www.thomasfriebe.com

CHAPTER 28

TRANSFORMING YOUR BUSINESS INTO A BLOCKBUSTER

BY NICK NANTON AND JW DICKS

*The biggest thing is to let your voice
be heard, let your story be heard.*
~ Dwyane Wade

When you tell your story in the right way, you can achieve a level of success that's almost criminal.

Take Jordan Belfort for example. This super-salesman made $20,000 by hawking Italian Ice from Styrofoam coolers in summers down at the beach when he was in college – but his ambition was to be a dentist. However, he quit the Baltimore College of Tooth Surgery on his first day, after the dean told the new class that if they wanted to make a lot of money, they were in the wrong place.

Instead, Belfort became a notorious stock swindler who made millions bilking small investors – and at one point employed 1000 people to help him do it. The Feds finally ended up catching up with all his scams, and he ended up being sentenced to 22 months in jail. The government also sold off all his assets to pay back the victims.

End of story? No, actually just the beginning.

While in prison, Belfort met Tommy Chong, one-half of the hugely popular comedy duo Cheech and Chong. Chong was in jail for helping promote a business that sold drug paraphernalia over the Internet. When Belfort told Chong about all his insane adventures running his stock-swindling company, Chong advised him to write a book about them. That advice turned to be a critical turning point.

The finished book, *The Wolf of Wall Street,* became a huge bestseller. And you're also probably aware that it was made into a lavishly-produced movie hit directed by Hollywood legend, Martin Scorsese, with Leonardo DiCaprio playing the part of Belfort. The critically-acclaimed film was nominated for 5 Oscars.

More importantly for Belfort, the celebrity status he gained from having his story told through the book and movie fueled a business comeback as a motivational speaker. That's because, even though the book and film clearly showed his criminal activity, it also clearly showed his skill at sales, a skill many are willing to pay large sums of money to acquire.

And that's why Belfort now earns tens of thousands of dollars for each speech and seminar that he's hired to do – although he calls what he teaches: the art of "*ethically* persuading." And we certainly hope he's sticking to that "ethically" part.

STORIES: THE FOUNDATION OF SUCCESS

Belfort's experience illustrates the power of stories, which has been heavily researched and validated (and is discussed at length in our StorySelling™ book). To summarize a couple of important points here, studies show that our brains *love* stories because they help us make sense of the world. Stories actually hit the pleasure centers of our minds – which causes us to often disregard the facts if they get in the way of a narrative we want to believe. Finally, we actually *need* stories – without them, we might not be able to make sense of our lives and how to approach them. We have a basic need to connect the dots of our existence, and the way we do that is through *stories*.

That's why, as Belfort discovered, telling the right story in the right way in the right medium can take you to a level of business success you might ordinarily think is out of reach. That's the principle we've built our own business on – and we've practiced what we preach.

When we first opened the doors of our Celebrity Branding Agency®, one of the first things we knew we needed to do was write a book to explain who we were and what we did. That book became our very first best-seller, *Celebrity Branding You*™ - but it wasn't written for the purpose of being successful; it was written for the purpose of explaining what our Celebrity Branding techniques were all about and why they *worked*.

Result? That book got us a lot of business and really sent us on our way.

Back in 2012, we realized it was time to write *another* book that would amplify the importance of exactly what we're talking about in this chapter – telling your story in the most impactful way through movies, books and other media. That book, *StorySelling*™, happily became an even bigger success, rising to #4 on *The Wall Street Journal's* non-fiction list and to the #1 paid non-fiction book on the Amazon Kindle.

Result? More people understood what we did at a deeper level – and were ready to do business with us.

So – why a book? Couldn't we explain these things to potential clients in person? Or over the phone?

Well, yes, we could – but we still wouldn't be able to cover the hundreds of pages of content in our books. You can only communicate so much in a conversation before you get tired of talking - or the person on the other side gets tired of listening to you!

But there was another bigger reason to present our ideas this way. Because our information *was* in a best-selling book, it ended up having much more weight and credibility than if it was just conveyed in a sales pitch.

In a way, putting your message out through a book is really a big test: You have to really have something to say in order to pull one off, you just can't fake your way through one. And anyone who read our latest book would discover a mountain of verifiable facts, proven strategies and high profile case studies that support what our agency offered our clients.

What it comes down to is this: What you do for your customers and clients involves *your* area of expertise, not theirs. And they may not necessarily understand what makes your specific professional process both different and more effective than your competitors' – and why it will ultimately benefit them greatly to hire you or your company.

A book is a managed, prestigious way to help them understand: It allows you to tell *your* story and present your unique selling proposition in a clear and powerful way. When done correctly, you not only explain the key to *your* success – you also explain why it could be the key to *their* success, in terms of what the product or service you're selling can do for them.

But, as Jordan Belfort found out for himself, a book serves only as the foundation of your StorySelling™. To really attain a whole new level of success? You must build your business into a blockbuster.

GOING BEYOND BEING JUST ANOTHER BUSINESS

Here are a few book titles we're sure many of you have heard of (if not read):

The One Minute Manager

Who Moved My Cheese?

The Seven Habits of Highly Effective People

Eat that Frog!

The above were, of course, all highly influential business books that crystalized their authors' philosophies in an easy-to-grasp concept (and, by the way, the last one happened to be co-authored by Brian Tracy, the legend whose name you'll find on this book).

Now, because of the phenomenal success of these books, because of the way they resonated with their readers, the authors were able to build their personal consulting businesses into *blockbusters*.

But they didn't reach blockbuster status by simply publishing one book. No, they did it through media appearances, videos, in-person appearances and seminars, online marketing, and magazine and newspaper interviews. They continued the story laid out in their books into other media, just as Jordan Belfort continued his into a hit movie; they reinforced their essential narratives over and over and over until they *owned* a substantial segment of their audiences.

This, of course, is nothing new. Walt Disney started his incredible entertainment empire by producing a short black-and-white cartoon featuring a talking mouse. He continued to expand his core brand story, first into animated features like *Snow White and the Seven Dwarfs*, then into live-action movies like *Mary Poppins*, and finally into theme park game-changers like Disneyland.

But what if Uncle Walt had just continued to make cartoon shorts? Would he have ever been able to build the awesome multi-billion-dollar blockbuster business that still dominates the Hollywood arena today? Of course not.

Then consider Donald Trump, who not only has written many best-sellers, but has also had his own game show (*Trump Card*), reality show (*The Apprentice*) and has even hosted WrestleMania events! But even with all his different ventures, both in entertainment and business, he always preserves his basic story and persona – and carries it through in everything he does. You don't confuse Donald Trump with anybody else, ever!

Building on your story and finding new and different ways to tell it is what truly transforms your business from a successful one into a *legendary* one. When you continue to deliver the same narrative across a broad range of venues and media, people remember that narrative – and you. You become your own version of Starbucks, McDonald's or any other world-famous brand – and you become an instantly-recognized authority in your field, as well as the go-to person for your specialty.

What are the advantages of that? Well, there are at least three very big ones:

- **You can charge more money for what you do.**
  When you enter the rarified atmosphere of a business blockbuster, you achieve a name and reputation that people are willing to pay top dollar for in order to gain access. Moguls like Donald Trump and Richard Branson make millions just lending their names to other people's business ventures, just because everyone knows who they are and what they represent – and because it delivers a level of prestige that's unmistakable.

- **You will wield more influence.**
  When you achieve blockbuster status, people and organizations are more willing to listen to what you have to say, even if they've

never done business with you. The right word from you can have an enormous impact on others' dealings, which gives you more personal power out in the marketplace.

- **You can dominate your field.**
Apple is an obvious example of a blockbuster business. They've always had a consistent and dynamic sense of StorySelling that's created not just customers, but disciples! The pay-off for that long-term vision has been a company that not only completely dominates their particular slice of the computer market, but also music distribution through their iTunes platform, as well as the cellphone industry through their phenomenally popular iPhone. Because they told such an incredible brand story, consumers were willing to follow them into whatever field they decided to diversity into.

THE BUILDING BLOCKS OF A BLOCKBUSTER

As you can see, being a blockbuster business delivers some awesome rewards. So – are you ready to kick your business up to blockbuster status? Here are a few pointers from us on how to do just that:

Building Block #1: Drill Down on Your Story
Before you start StorySelling, make sure you've got a narrative that will not only attract the kind of clients you want to attract, but also accurately reflects who you are and what you do. Making sure you have the right story in place *before* you aggressively StorySell is THE most important step you have to take. If you're pretending to be something you're not, it will catch up to you; that's why, before you put a lot of time, effort and money into your StorySelling, you should make sure your story isn't going to blow up in your face down the line.

We can return to Jordan Belfort for a good example of that. As we noted, he's now selling himself as an ethical persuader – unfortunately, he's recently been accused of hiding the money he's making down under in Australia, so he doesn't have to pay back the people he originally swindled! If that's true, his new StorySelling attempts already have an unhappy ending.

Building Block #2: Be a Person
It's okay to show some of your warts in your StorySelling – as a matter of fact, it's preferable. The more you can show you're a human being,

flaws and all, the more relatable and the more memorable you are. Obviously, don't take this to extremes, although it does work out for some people!

Building Block #3: Be Unconventional

We quickly passed over an interesting item a little earlier in this chapter, so we're going to repeat it here – *Donald Trump hosted WrestleMania events*! Now, that might be the last place you'd expect to see The Donald, sandwiched between two mammoth wrestlers getting ready to break chairs over each other's heads - but the fact is, it does him some substantial good, from a StorySelling perspective. Think about it – his appearances at these matches (a) get Trump more attention, (b) expand his exposure to a whole different audience, and (c) actually kind of fits in with his aggressive brand!

The unconventional gets attention – and the more you do things that your competitors don't do, the more you stand out. As long as it fits in with your narrative and you're not doing something that will land you in jail, embrace the weird – and even post about it on Facebook and Twitter!

Building Block #4: Don't Be Camera-Shy

If you're like many people, you probably don't like to look in the mirror more than you have to – but, unless your brand story is that you're a recluse like Howard Hughes was, you're going to have to get over the impulse to hide whenever anyone snaps a photo with their iPhone. A vital part of StorySelling involves showing yourself as much as possible — in films, online videos, the above-mentioned social media platforms, even on the cover of your book, so again, people can bond with you on a human level. The more potential clients feel like they know you, the more they will trust you and the more willing they will be to do business with you.

Building Block #5: Keep Your Core Value Front and Center

Most blockbuster brand stories can be boiled down to a couple of words that really define what they're all about. Apple? Innovation. Disney? Family entertainment. Wal-Mart? Low prices.

The word or words you use to define what you and your business are all about represent your *core value*, the thing that, when all is said and done, represents you the best. This quality should be present in *everything* you do from a StorySelling standpoint – because it's what you want people to take away more than anything else.

The great thing about creating a blockbuster business brand is that, once in place, it continues to generate its own success; people recognize it and reward it, often just because it *is* a known quantity. Of course, not every business can achieve blockbuster status – that's why those who do are perceived as being incredibly special and unique.

You too can StorySell yourself to greatness if you take the steps to tell your tale in as many different high-profile media as possible. You may not become *The Wolf of Wall Street* – but you could become the Mogul of Main Street!

About Nick

A 3-Time Emmy Award Winning Director, Producer and Filmmaker, Nick Nanton, Esq., is known as the Top Agent to Celebrity Experts® around the world for his role in developing and marketing business and professional experts, through personal branding, media, marketing and PR.

Nick serves as the CEO of The Dicks + Nanton Celebrity Branding Agency, an international branding and media agency with more than 2200 clients in 33 countries. Nick has produced large scale events and television shows with the likes of Steve Forbes, Brian Tracy, Jack Canfield (Creator of the *Chicken Soup for the Soul* Series), Michael E. Gerber, Tom Hopkins, Dan Kennedy and many more.

Nick is recognized as one of the top thought-leaders in the business world speaking on major stages internationally and having co-authored 34 best-selling books, including *The Wall Street Journal* Best-Seller, *StorySelling™*.

Nick has been seen in *USA Today, The Wall Street Journal, Newsweek, BusinessWeek, Inc. Magazine, The New York Times, Entrepreneur® Magazine, Forbes,* FastCompany. com. and has appeared on ABC, NBC, CBS, and FOX television affiliates around the country, as well as E!, CNN, FOX News, CNBC, MSNBC and hosts his own series on the Bio! channel, Portraits of Success.

Nick is a member of the Florida Bar, a voting member of The National Academy of Recording Arts & Sciences (Home to The GRAMMYs), a member of The National Academy of Television Arts & Sciences (Home to the EMMYs), The National Academy of Best-Selling Authors, and spends his spare time working with Young Life, Downtown Credo Orlando, Entrepreneurs International and rooting for the Florida Gators with his wife Kristina and their three children, Brock, Bowen and Addison.

Learn more at http://www.NickNanton.com and http://www.CelebrityBrandingAgency. com

About JW

JW Dicks, Esq., is America's foremost authority on using personal branding for business development. He has created some of the most successful brand and marketing campaigns for business and professional clients to make them the credible celebrity experts in their field and build multi-million dollar businesses using their recognized status.

JW Dicks has started, bought, built, and sold a large number of businesses over his 39-year career and developed a loyal international following as a business attorney, author, speaker, consultant, and business experts' coach. He not only practices what he preaches by using his strategies to build his own businesses, he also applies those same concepts to help clients grow their business or professional practice the ways he does.

JW has been extensively quoted in such national media as *USA Today,* the *Wall Street Journal, Newsweek, Inc.*, Forbes.com, CNBC.com, and *Fortune Small Business*. His television appearances include ABC, NBC, CBS and FOX affiliate stations around the country. He is the resident branding expert for *Fast Company*'s internationally syndicated blog and is the publisher of *Celebrity Expert Insider*, a monthly newsletter targeting business and brand building strategies.

JW has written over 22 books, including numerous best-sellers, and has been inducted into the National Academy of Best-Selling Authors. JW is married to Linda, his wife of 39 years, and they have two daughters, two granddaughters and two Yorkies. JW is a 6th generation Floridian and splits his time between his home in Orlando and beach house on the Florida west coast.

CHAPTER 29

HOW TO TRANSFORM IN LIFE, BUSINESS AND HEALTH

BY DR. CARLO BIASUCCI

As is the case probably with most people in a health-related profession, I became a dentist because I wanted to help people. But I quickly discovered there was an incredible opportunity to do so much more in my field to impact the lives of others. Early in my career, I became heavily involved in studying cosmetic dentistry and offering these options to my patients. What I began to realize was that I was not just helping people, but I was literally a part of changing and transforming their lives. Seeing someone smile who previously hid their teeth and seeing the total personality change that ensues is very powerful. It seems to literally draw out their once hidden personality. It is a complete transformation in self-confidence, and it makes me feel very humble yet proud to be able to positively affect another person's life in this manner.

It is very apparent that the people who need the most dental work done are the same people that are absolutely terrified of dentistry. Recognizing this factor drove me to extensively study and offer to my patients conscious sedation, a process whereby the patient is awake but they really don't care what is going on and in most cases they don't remember much of the procedure. Conscious sedation has been a miracle for these people who were unable to have the treatment they needed due to their fear of dentistry, and now they beam with confidence from a beautiful, healthy smile.

The icing on the cake for me is that often these anxious and fearful patients – once the bulk of their treatment is done under sedation – will overcome their fear and be able to attend for regular visits and even have minor dental work done without anxiety or fear. In my 10 years of practice, I have seen this scenario hundreds of times and each time I am reminded that we all have the power to effect positive change in the world and in each other. Very honestly, the transformations I am able to bring about in people is what drives me to continue doing what I do.

Throughout the years I have also experienced transformation in my personal life and business. I have found that transformation is a process that brings about change. Change, just like creating a new, beautiful and healthy smile, can be influential in transforming multiple areas of our lives. It seems there is a systemic process that occurs in various facets of our lives almost simultaneously when transformation occurs. Based on my experience, there are certain contributing principles to transformation I would like to share with you. These principles have allowed me to create the personal and professional life that previously would have seemed out of reach.

A. Stay Positive

My core belief and strategy in life and business is staying positive and always looking for the positive in every situation. I think most people realize that in every situation you have a choice. You can find the negative or you can look for the positive. By looking at the positive, you will always find opportunities. I've used this concept as one of the main principles in my life to find opportunities to grow, and do a lot of things others are not doing or have tried doing only to give up. If you will reprogram your mindset to stay positive you will change your life. Positive people attract more positive people and the fire builds. On the other hand, negative people can quench that fire. If you are going to commit yourself to being positive, you will have to actively distance yourself from negative people who drain your energy. Your attitude and mindset will be an average of the people you associate with. This concept of staying positive will drastically impact your business and your health in a very productive way.

If you have a positive mindset and you're interpreting situations from that frame of mind, you will automatically lower your stress. If you distance yourself from negative people and remove any negativity from your workplace, you automatically create a healthier overall environment. It is much easier to function effectively in a low stress, positive environment.

A positive person will look for the opportunity in every adverse situation, and in business there will be many. I have often said, "When everyone is running for the hills, stop and think." Stop looking at and following what others are doing, unless you want to be like everyone else. If you want to do better or truly succeed, accept that the majority is wrong about their views, and move forward on the opportunity you have identified. Allow me to illustrate this point with my own experience building my dental practice.

When I first opened my current practice in 2009, the economy was not the best – to say the least. A lot of people told me what I was doing could not be done. Opening a large, state of the art office in a smaller community with the economy taking a downturn was viewed by many as bad business planning. However, instead of listening to that, I stuck to my vision, stayed positive and really succeeded. I also aligned myself with mentors with a similar mindset. The business grew even in a down economy because of the drive to realize my vision to create an amazing team of positive, motivated individuals who exceeded the expectations of our patients. Had I listened to others, I would have delayed the opening of my office and would have missed the successes we have experienced, or at minimum, delayed my success.

In my office, we (my entire staff) consistently portray a positive attitude and look at ourselves as friends helping friends. We strive to develop relationships and know each patient. Patients aren't just numbers in our office. They are part of our dental home. We actively and purposefully engage our patients in personal conversation. In fact, the first ten minutes of a new patient visit is usually talking about them, their family, their likes and dislikes, what they do for a living, etc. We take time to get to know them and make it a personal experience before we start talking about their teeth. Everyone in the office engages each patient in conversation and we call them by name. They are not just a number to us. Focusing on relationships is critical in any business, but also increases your enjoyment of work in a day, further fueling your positive mindset.

I built a state of the art practice because that was the opposite of what others were doing. I didn't want to do what every other dental office was doing and get the same results. I'm a firm believer in, "If you don't want the same results others are experiencing, then do not follow their lead." Figure out what they are doing and then decide what you think is right for you. If you have no role model or other successful business to emulate, at least start by not following the majority.

I also recommend getting unplugged from mass media and other time-thieves like your email, random web surfing, and your cell phone. I rarely watch the news or read the paper. For the most part these are a series of doom-and-gloom messages. I'm not suggesting you become oblivious to the world around you. You should however pay close attention to messages you let in, because they will affect you and ultimately your success. You would be far better off using the time you save by unplugging a little to read a book that inspires you to be more successful in your life.

B. Find a Mentor or Coach

I grew up in a business family in that almost everyone in my family runs a business. My father has operated a construction company my entire life. I grew up in that business, so I've seen firsthand his way of doing things, and he has been very successful. I also read a 'book a month' on leadership or something business related. I'm passionate about expanding my knowledge of business, customer service, and leadership as well as my chosen profession. I have found you can always learn something from anyone, whether it is from a conversation or a book, so keep an open mind.

Finding a coach or mentor is extremely important to succeeding in business. I've always had someone to bounce ideas off of. It can potentially be anyone, but ideally they should be someone who has achieved the level of success that you desire – for certain, not someone who is *status quo*. What that does is drive you to fulfill your vision, and also helps you learn from what others have done to be successful rather than learning from trial and error. There is no purpose in reinventing the wheel. It will take you much, much longer to get to the level of success you desire by going it alone.

I look to my father who has been in business for many, many years, other successful dentists, and mastermind groups to fulfill that role. A mentor is anyone that can intelligently discuss with you in a helpful fashion your ideas, offer direction and hold you accountable. I believe by listening to the right people, I have achieved in five years what may have taken twenty-five years if I did it on my own.

I have followed and studied successful people in various businesses, not just dentistry. I've pulled whatever I could from other industries that applied to my business in improving the patient experience, how I deliver services, how I market and how I can improve every aspect of my profession.

C. Keep Your Life Balanced

In the first three or four years after I opened my current practice, I really pushed into workaholic territory and didn't take time to reenergize. Even for a younger person, in a very short time your health can go south pretty fast if you neglect to take care of yourself. Fortunately, I recognized that lack of balance and began to make changes before I caused further damage to health and other aspects of my life.

In regard to overall health, many studies show the positive benefits of 30 minutes of daily exercise combined with at least 7 hours of sleep every night. Additionally, eating properly will add to the overall balance in your life. Cut out the junk food (fast food, processed food, etc.) and feed your body natural foods that are rich in the nutrients your body needs to function properly. All these are factors that will keep your brain sharp and maximize your productivity. There are many excellent resources in this area. My favorite book on the subject currently is Grain Brain by Dr. David Perlmutter.

Giving the proper attention to your family life is also crucial to maintaining the balance you need to transform to the level of success you desire. A neglected family is not a happy family. If you allow things to decline at home, it will have a negative effect on you personally and will likely carry over into your business. Many entrepreneurs get wrapped up in their business quickly and easily and it doesn't take long to lose focus. A balanced family life enables you to keep your stress level in check, and will make you a better person by keeping you focused on what really matters in life. It will also keep you focused on efficient uses of your time in your business so you can spend more time with family.

D. Keep True Friends

This goes back to my previous point about purposefully weeding out of your life individuals that bring negative energy into your life. True friends are individuals that will want the best for themselves as well as for you. They will be people that know how to maintain proper balance in their life and will share your positive perspective. Often these are also people that you will engage in conversation about your ideas and plans. True friends will be listeners, not just talkers. The bottom line is this, if someone does not have a positive impact on your life, they will likely hurt you in the long run. So choose your friends wisely.

E. Laugh Daily

I find in the evenings, no matter how hectic the day has been, my wife is always able to make me laugh. She has a great personality and has a unique way to help me calm my mind and refocus on what is important. You have to have those types of people in your life to keep you grounded. There are many studied health effects of laughter and positive attitude. One can easily see the connection between being positive and being able to laugh. They just go hand in hand.

Success in business or in any area of our lives requires transformation. I have found these principles of:

- Stay Positive
- Find a Mentor or Coach
- Keep Your Life Balanced
- Keep True Friends and
- Laugh Daily

...to be concepts that have literally transformed my life, my business and my health and I know they can do the same for you.

About Dr. Carlo

Dr. Carlo Biasucci, BSc., DDS, is the owner and CEO of Northern Dental Care in Sault Ste. Marie, Ontario, Canada, a state of the art dental facility focusing on family and cosmetic dentistry.

A graduate of the University of Western Ontario in London, Ontario, Dr. Biasucci helps patients achieve and maintain beautiful, healthy smiles and overcome their fears of dental treatment. With conscious sedation, he has been able to alleviate the anxiety for hundreds of individuals, which often prevents them from seeking out dental care.

Being the only family member in the dental profession, but fortunately brought up in a business-oriented family, Dr. Biasucci has had a great deal of skills and examples to draw from and to apply to his own practice. His dental practice is built on the philosophy of "friends helping friends" and delivering a unique dental experience for patients.

To further his education and expertise, Dr. Biasucci has completed the Core Curriculum at the Las Vegas Institute for Advanced Dental Studies – which focuses on Cosmetic Dentistry and the inter-relationship of the teeth, as well as numerous courses in Conscious Sedation, Implant Dentistry, and Orthodontics. He also was recently recognized with a Fellowship in the Academy of General Dentistry.

Dr. Biasucci is the author of over 100 articles and guest editorials on a variety of topics in dentistry and is an active member in multiple organizations in dentistry and healthcare.

Dr. Biasucci and his wife, Ashlee, are the very proud parents of their daughter, Allison. In their spare time, they both enjoy the outdoors and take full advantage of everything that living in Northern Ontario has to offer.

Additional information about Dr. Biasucci and Northern Dental Care can be found at: www.northerndentalcare.com or by calling their office at: 705-575-7572.

CHAPTER 30

TRANSFORM YOUR ONLINE STRATEGY —SOCIAL MEDIA MYTHS AND MUST-DOS

BY LINDSAY DICKS

The evolution of social media has presented a sort of "good news/bad news" scenario for small businesspeople and entrepreneurs around the world.

The good news is, Twitter, Facebook, LinkedIn and the rest have provided us with all of these new and exciting possibilities for connecting with customers, forming relationships and building our brands.

And the bad news?

Well, when it comes to actually using social media, most of us still don't exactly know what we're doing. Sure, anyone can post a Facebook status, but very few of us understand exactly what we *should* and *can* be doing with social media to accomplish our goals. And with new platforms popping up every few months (Pinterest, anyone?), whatever we do master is almost certain to change in the near future.

So how do we get the most out of the current social media trends, while developing a plan that will be easily adaptable to new platforms, new products and new audiences in the future?

Let's start by poking a few holes into conventional social media wisdom…

SOCIAL MEDIA MYTHS

Before you can fully grasp what *to* do with social media, it's also important you know what *not* to do. Because social media is so new and, at the same time, so pervasive, there is a lot of misinformation out there about who it's for, what it does and how it works. So let's take a few moments to tackle some of the misinformation that may be holding your social media strategy back—or just pointing you in the wrong direction.

Myth #1: Social media is FREE (or at least extremely cheap!).

It's true, membership in sites like Facebook and Twitter won't cost you a cent. But using them effectively takes time and expertise—time and expertise most of us just don't have. Bringing in a paid expert may not be free, but it may very well be the best way to insure your social media presence receives the time and guidance necessary to succeed.

Myth #2: Social media is EASY.

We all know mastering the basic tools and broadcasting information on social media isn't complicated–how else could all our grandmas be using it? However, the tools that may offer the most benefit to your business are a bit more complex than the ones granny uses–and more and more of them are appearing every day. Figuring out which of these tools will benefit your business *and how to use them the most effectively for your particular niche* takes time and patience you may not have, but a social media expert will get you going in no time flat.

Myth #3: Social media is just a fad.

Just like the Hula Hoop and Rubik's Cube, many believe social media is just another craze that will soon die down. Well, the fact is, while fads may happen *on* social media (like flash mobs on Twitter), the platform itself is not going anywhere.

The Internet gives individuals and companies a place to freely exchange ideas and information with people down the block and around the world. That's a complete paradigm shift just as newspapers, radio and television were in their time. Until something even more groundbreaking comes along that facilitates this in an even easier way, social media is here to stay and will only get bigger. Hang on to those antiquated beliefs that social media will simply run its course and you're asking to be left out of the most lucrative and growing market on the planet.

Myth #4: Social media is for kids.

If you've seen "The Social Network," you're no doubt aware that Facebook was launched by a college student. But are you aware that today, almost half of Facebook profiles belong to people aged 35 and up? Facebook is no longer just about "hanging out," it's about doing business–which is why adults with buying power are fast emerging as a powerful online target market.

Myth #5: Facebook Ads are the best way to use social media marketing.

Mot of us are marketed to from the moment we wake up to the moment we go to bed at night. So we become immune to much advertising. The beauty of social media is that it offers a chance to reach people in a *different* way, because social media channels are fundamentally all about communication. So start by listening. Contribute to some conversations, and eventually start some of your own. Take time to build relationships and establish trust, then those people who have gotten to know and like you won't view messages about your business as just another ad. And when you finally do advertise, keep it subtle and low-key.

Myth #6: Anyone can market successfully using social media.

As I've already pointed out, using social media in a business context is complicated and time consuming. To get the most out of it, you need to understand the tools available to you and your business, your target market, and what works and what doesn't work when it comes to reaching them. You may not have the time or expertise for that, but a professional social media specialist (or team of specialists) will. Social media experts are uniquely suited to bring your existing branding message into the social media world; they'll work closely with you or someone on your team to gain insight into your product or service offering, and combine that with their knowledge of the online landscape to give you and your company maximum online exposure.

Myth #7: Social media marketing success can't be measured.

Most people who worry that they can't measure their social media marketing efforts also don't know what to expect from social media marketing, so they don't start out with clearly defined objectives. If you set concrete goals (things like increased traffic, sign-ups for a newsletter or other measurable activities), systems can be set up to accurately measure your progress. Define what success means first, then set up systems to determine how close you are getting to that definition.

Myth #8: Social media is a world without rules.

Entering a new social media platform is like entering a new culture; as the various platforms have evolved and become more sophisticated, each has developed its own system of etiquette and its own set of rules. Some basic rules, like not over-promoting yourself or your business and not attacking other people or groups, are common to most platforms. However, the diversity and constant change associated with social media means that each platform's "unwritten rules" are different; they also tend to evolve and change. If you don't know what these rules are, your best bet may be to team up with someone who does, to guide you through the initial phases and possibly give you valuable ongoing advice.

Myth #9: The more "friends" you add, the more successful you are.

Boasting a long list of Twitter followers is not a guarantee of business success. You need to look more closely at *who those people actually are*. They need to be people who are interested in your product and in a position to support your brand, not necessarily your nine year-old niece who's posting a video of her piano recital on your wall!

Focus on connecting with people who care about what you have to offer and with whom you can also form a clear communication channel. The sheer numbers of random strangers, family members and people you went to school with may look impressive, but when it comes to increasing business, the *quality* of your connections counts. Seeking out and engaging with the right kind of people takes skill and knowledge of consumer behavior.

SOCIAL MEDIA SUCCESS SECRETS

Okay, now that we've talked about what *doesn't* work, let's move on to the positive and what you can start focusing on TODAY to start elevating your social media efforts. Here are eight surefire ways you can utilize your social media presence to establish yourself (and your brand) as the go-to guru within your market.

1. Tweet your analysis of breaking news in your field.

Keeping your audience updated with all the latest breaking news in your industry helps keep them apprised of what's going on. Providing your own thoughtful analysis of the story or event helps keep *you* at the top of your audience's minds as an expert in your field. For example, if you are a tax lawyer, don't just report that a new law is making its way through Congress...take the time to add your own, expert analysis of how the new law might affect your audience and what they can and/or should do about it.

2. Post pictures on Facebook and Twitter of yourself "in action."

Anyone on my Facebook friend list knows that I get around. One day I'm at the Grammys, the next filming on location in Washington, D.C., the next riding a scooter in beautiful Bermuda. However, I don't post those pictures simply because I like to share the fun of the places I get to see, but because, in most of those pictures, I'm also working hard helping my clients boost their celebrity status (I know, it's a tough job, but somebody's gotta do it!). Any opportunity you have to show yourself doing what you do makes your work seem that much more real and relatable to your clients and customers–so don't be shy...post those pics!

3. Post video tips on YouTube and then pin them on Pinterest.

Whatever you're an expert at, take a moment to share what you know via a YouTube video and then pin that video on Pinterest! Video tips are a great way to connect with your audience–people feel closer to you when they can see and hear you, rather than simply reading your status updates or Twitter posts. If you produce these videos well, they act like your own personal commercials. You'll be amazed at how much mileage you can get out of a collection of well-produced video tips. And you won't just reap the branding benefits; you'll also score with the search engines!

4. Share your blog entries and articles across Facebook, Twitter, Google+ and LinkedIn.

If you've been listening to me (and if not, why not?), you should be regularly publishing blog entries and articles. Now is your chance to let those blogs and articles do double-duty for you by posting them to your social media accounts. This not only drives traffic back to your website, it also reminds your audience of what an expert you are in your industry!

5. Answer questions your followers and connections may have.

One of the best aspects of social media platforms like Facebook and Twitter is the fact that they allow you to interact with your audience in real time. When you pay attention to the conversations going on in cyberspace, chances are you'll run across people who are asking questions or looking for advice. If they happen to be asking a question you know the answer to, chime in! You won't just help the person who asked the question, but also everyone else out there who might have a similar question. And at the same time, you'll be subtly demonstrating your expertise to your audience, reminding them that you are THE go-to person in your industry.

6. Get personal... but not TOO personal.

I like to think of the social media world as a giant cocktail party–a place to interact with interesting people, have fun, relax and tell jokes...all while networking and getting my brand out there. I firmly believe that social media doesn't have to be all business, all the time. By letting my audience know what I'm up to—traveling, eating, shopping or just hanging out with my friends–I get to share a little piece of myself they can connect with that actually helps me build my brand. So don't be afraid to be yourself and talk about your family, your pets, your hobbies and whatever makes you *you*. Just remember not to drop your guard *too* much when mixing business with pleasure (think classy cocktail party, not drunken fraternity bash)!

7. Share actionable tips for your customers and prospects.

There's nothing wrong with sharing information with your audience, but sharing advice on how to do something is even better. In the business realm, we call this *actionable content*, and it's incredibly powerful. Whether you're a real estate broker sharing inexpensive ways to add value to your home, or an accountant providing a checklist of things to take care of before tax time, providing your audience with actionable, easily digestible tips is an ideal way to show that you really know your stuff.

8. Post valuable content from authoritative sources... and add your commentary.

Have you ever seen a piece of content by a celebrity or fellow expert that struck you as something your audience might find valuable? Go ahead and share it. You don't want to promote the competition, but posting content from big names in your field or related industry shows your audience that you're "in the loop" and looking out for them. Add your own analysis and you'll definitely cement that expert status in their minds.

The endless possibilities offered by the social media universe can be confusing–especially when it comes to using it to promote your business. But at the end of the day, the most important thing is to be able to say "Yes" to the crucial question, "Am I providing value to my audience?"

If you aren't working to give your audience information they can use, they'll likely pass over your messages and focus on those that will make their lives easier. And even if you have a whole army of Twitter followers, it won't do you much good if none of them are listening or looking forward to what you have to say.

So remember, in the social media universe, it's *not* all about you. Your goal should be to bring something to the table—to make them smile, to help them out, to keep them up to date on the latest news in your industry, and/or to shed light on new developments they might find scary or confusing.

Act like the knowledgeable, helpful expert you are and your audience can't help but pay attention to each and every interaction—and to turn to *you* as the true celebrity expert in your field.

About Lindsay

Lindsay Dicks helps her clients tell their stories in the online world. Being brought up around a family of marketers, but a product of Generation Y, Lindsay naturally gravitated to the new world of on-line marketing. Lindsay began freelance writing in 2000 and soon after launched her own PR firm that thrived by offering an in-your-face "Guaranteed PR" that was one of the first of its type in the nation.

Lindsay's new media career is centered on her philosophy that "people buy people." Her goal is to help her clients build a relationship with their prospects and customers. Once that relationship is built and they learn to trust them as the expert in their field, then they will do business with them. Lindsay also built a proprietary process that utilizes social media marketing, content marketing and search engine optimization to create online "buzz" for her clients that helps them to convey their business and personal story. Lindsay's clientele span the entire business map and range from doctors and small business owners to Inc 500 CEOs.

Lindsay is a graduate of the University of Florida. She is the CEO of CelebritySites™, an online marketing company specializing in social media and online personal branding. Lindsay is recognized as one of the top online marketing experts in the world and has co-authored more than 25 best-selling books alongside authors such as Brian Tracy, Jack Canfield (creator of the "Chicken Soup for the Soul" series), Dan Kennedy, Robert Allen, Dr. Ivan Misner (founder of BNI), Jay Conrad Levinson (author of the "Guerilla Marketing" series), Leigh Steinberg and many others, including the breakthrough hit *Celebrity Branding You!*

She was also selected as one of America's PremierExperts™ and has been quoted in *Newsweek*, *The Wall Street Journal*, *USA Today*, and *Inc.* magazine as well as featured on NBC, ABC, and CBS television affiliates speaking on social media, search engine optimization and making more money online. Lindsay was also recently brought on FOX 35 News as their Online Marketing Expert.

Lindsay, a national speaker, has shared the stage with some of the top speakers in the world, such as Brian Tracy, Lee Milteer, Ron LeGrand, Arielle Ford, David Bullock, Brian Horn, Peter Shankman and many others. Lindsay was also a Producer on the Emmy-winning film Jacob's Turn.

You can connect with Lindsay at:
Lindsay@CelebritySites.com
www.twitter.com/LindsayMDicks
www.facebook.com/LindsayDicks

CHAPTER 31

STRATEGIC TRANSFORMATION

BY DR. DEAN BANKS
AND MARTY COATES

To go from where you are to where you want to be requires transformation. For some, it is a transformation of thoughts and ideas. For others, it can be a transformation of a company or organization to a new level of performance or accomplishment. For us, Dr. Dean Banks and Marty Coates, it was both.

We had no idea when our paths first crossed that we would find ourselves braving the corporate world together. In fact, our meeting was a chance encounter at a political function. We were both successful in our respective fields; Dean was a talented and business-savvy chiropractic physician, and Marty, a business consultant and professional speaker. Ours is a story of theory and practice colliding with opportunity and passion; of diverse experience engaging knowledge, attitude, and charisma.

The combination of the two of us (along with a team of talented employees) resulted in the successful transformation of FirstChoice Healthcare, P.C., a small medical practice operating two locations, into a multi-disciplined, multi-location medical company positioned to make a significant impact in the world. Here's the story.

When we met, Dr. Dean Banks had just built an impressive new facility, added a few physicians, and had gross sales of approximately $3 million annually. He planned to work hard and to make the business successful, so that over time he could work less, enjoy more time with his family, and enjoy the rewards of his success.

What was not clear was how to arrive at the desired end. So he asked Marty to work with him to develop a strategic plan. Dean was motivated to attain his goals. He possessed a positive attitude that served as fuel for overcoming the obstacles that were certain to arise. He knew what he wanted.

"If you are working on something really exciting, that you care about, you don't need to be pushed, your vision pulls you." ~ the late Steve Jobs, Founder and CEO of Apple. Dr. Banks did not necessarily need a push, but a guide, coach or chauffeur. He was convinced that together with Marty, he could accomplish his desired end-state. Marty knew that if he could help Dean strategically align his vision with the right people and the right plan, Dean would realize his goal.

Marty began the process of helping Dean to refine his mission, clarify his corporate vision and establish a set of organizational values. They then got his team involved in developing other key components of this plan.

At this point, the weight of the company and its future was sitting upon the shoulders of Dean and a few key staff members. He was handling much of the day-to-day operations and still treating a few of his own patients. The new building, as well as an under-performing remote clinic location was placing a strain on our financial position. The company was carrying a few hundred thousand dollars each month to cover operations. Investments continued to perform, but Dean was itching to grow the company. What he needed to do was back away from patient care and management functions, and focus on accomplishing his vision. In this new relationship with Marty, Dean's role could change. He could become more visionary, less involved in the day-to-day operations, and Marty could play a more pragmatic role, seeking to plan each move or at least pause to consider the steps. Dean's entrepreneurial spirit, his in-depth knowledge of medical operations and his openness to taking business risks were vital to making the transformation.

How would we merge the talents and strengths of each of us and devise a path forward? If we were to transform this small company to a medium-size corporation within a prescribed number of years, we would have to do so systematically. We began by analyzing every aspect of the company- its people, problems, processes, and priorities. Marty led the group through a stringent SWOT (Strengths, Weaknesses, Opportunities and Threats) Analysis. We surveyed our staff and customers, researched our markets and customer profiles, and reviewed the finances for immediate ways to cut costs to generate additional capital for growth. We renegotiated with our vendors for preferred rates and better terms. We bid out our banking operations, which resulted in us making a change in our banking relationship and significant savings.

Over the course of the next seven years, we transformed the company. Marty came on board as Chief Executive Officer (CEO), but continued to serve in a consulting role. We grew from two offices to seven, expanding into new disciplines discovering a couple of niche areas that became fundamental to the transformation. We made adjustments to services based on market shifts. This all happened during one of the worst economic recessions in modern history. While many medical professionals were going out of business or merging with larger companies, FirstChoice stayed on plan. Dramatic changes in government reimbursement for healthcare, followed by third party insurance companies reducing reimbursement, did not negatively impact our growth. Dean had the vision to expand ancillary services that complimented our basic services. We remained open and flexible to the opportunities as they appeared.

There were a number of principles that were central to our transformation. In every turn along our journey, Dean Banks made sure we practiced each of them.

We call them **Dean's Theories of Success.**

1) Be **disciplined** in your work and practices.

2) Hire **the right people**, train them, pay them well and expect them to perform. Ensure you have technically competent people. (Degrees are less important than what one knows.)

3) **Always be open to trying new things**. "Innovation is the mother of invention," someone once said.

4) **Be willing to make tough decisions**. The right decision is often times the most difficult one.

5) **Do not be afraid to take risks**. Grab opportunity, succeed or fail, but don't look back, your future is ahead of you.

> *A boat is safe in the harbor, but that is not what a boat is built for.*
> ~ Anonymous.

6) **Be confident and consistent** in your practices, actions and instructions.

7) **Give people room to explore their own capabilities**. Give directions and get out of the way. "Let me know how that works out for you," Dean would say when a team member proposed a new idea. In other words, you give it a try.

Here's an outline and diagram of our strategic process. Consider how you may apply this transformation effort in your organization, or similarly, in your life.

OUR STRATEGIC PROCESS

Dr. Stephen Covey, author of the book *Seven Habits of Highly Effective People* said, "Begin with the end in mind."

Vision — What is your picture of the organization at some point in the future (3, 5, 7 years)? This picture should be seen and stated as if you are already there. Visualize it this way. You are at Pinehurst Country Club, Course #2, standing on the tee box of Hole #1. From the tee box you can see the flag on the green in the distance. You know where you want to hit the ball onto the green. You have an end vision. See your company as you desire it.

Mission — What is your purpose? Why are you in the business you are in? When properly stated, a personal or organizational mission should define the "why" and the "what" but not the "where." Mission is foundational, usually answering a need or call, providing a product or service. Your corporate or personal mission does not propel you forward, instead it holds you up.

Key Business Drivers (KBD) — What key indicators will you use to gauge your progress toward your goals and vision? You should create a list of questions to be superimposed over the organizational activity at any time. For example, "Do we have the right people on the bus?" "Do we have enough money in the bank to cover our expenses?"

Critical Success Factors (CSF) — What issues, external to your organization and outside of your control, can you identify that might impact your ability to accomplish your vision? In most cases, we cannot stop these from happening, but we may be able to influence how they impact us. By attempting to identify CSF's and preparing contingency plans in the event they arise, we position our organization to weather most challenges. For example, we might identify governmental regulations as a CSF. How do you prepare? How will you respond?

Goals — What are your long-term objectives or targets, usually marked to be accomplished between 3 to 5 years, depending on the span of the vision. These are more specific and measureable than the vision, but less specific than the strategic objectives that follow. Goals must be developed by using what's called the SMART TEST. The variables of the test are listed below:

Smart Test —

- Specific
- Measurable
- Attainable
- Realistic
- Time-bound

Strategic Objectives — As you accomplish strategic objectives, the picture of your goals becomes clearer. These mid-range targets must be accomplished in order for you to reach your goals. In most cases, strategic objectives are targets about 1 to 3 years out.

Actions — These are near-term tasks that must be accomplished in order to reach your strategic objectives. Taking shortcuts here will cost you later. Normally, actions are required to be completed within 12 months.

Values — These are our right and left out-of-bound markers. They keep our actions in check. If we move too far right or too far left, our Values bring us back into alignment or help us to realize we have moved away from our core plan. Each organization should prepare its own list of core Values, which best describe its intended internal compass.

The diagram below is a visual representation of the way the strategic process that we followed should flow:

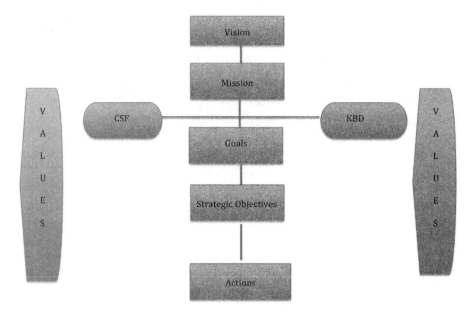

Figure 1.

The strategic process is critical and necessary in order to accomplish transformation. More plainly stated, there are nine key actions that an organization must take to accomplish its vision.

NINE KEYS TO STRATEGIC TRANSFORMATION

1. Clearly state your vision

2. Institutionalize your corporate mission

3. Set actionable goals, strategic objectives and near-term actions

4. Communicate clearly your corporate Values

5. Measure progress along the way

6. Hold your team accountable

7. Be flexible and adapt to changes in the plan

8. Revisit your plan periodically

9. Celebrate your accomplishments with the team

Oh yeah, what is the rest of this story? Well, Marty moved on about a year ago to make way for a transitional leader to help drive the final leg of the journey. Dean, with new leadership in place, went on to achieve everything he desired in the original strategic plan, and just a few months ago he sold his company for a sum greater than even he imagined. Is this story about the successful transformation of Dean's business or about making a lot of money? I think Tony Hsieh, CEO of Zappos, said it best when he said, "Chase the vision, not the money." The money will come if your motivation is right and your plan is aligned properly with the vision.

Today Marty and Dean continue working together on other projects through a corporation they formed many years ago, WayMaker Learning Corporation(WLC). Moving forward, their energies – through WLC – will be focused on helping other individuals and companies grow and accomplish their visions. Both are convinced that deliberately crafting a strategic plan was crucial to the move from a small player in an even smaller market to a large regional medical corporation including seven locations, a highly complex laboratory facility and nearly 100 employees. Dean also fulfilled his dream by working a bit less and now enjoys life at a higher level with his family.

You can accomplish this kind of transformation in your own life and/or business by applying the simple yet useful tools we have discussed in this chapter. What is critical now is one thing that Dean has maintained from the start...you have to START! Take action to team up with a coach, a mentor, a seasoned consultant or trusted friend, and design a strategic plan forward. Then start moving toward the vision you have for your life or organization.

The accomplishment of the transformation of FirstChoice Healthcare, P.C., was far more than a small company becoming larger. We transformed a marketplace and dispelled the notion that an organization's vision can't be accomplished. It can, and Dean Banks and FirstChoice Healthcare, P.C., headquartered in sleepy little South Carolina are proof.

About Dean

Dean Banks, D.C. is an entrepreneur, successful businessman, chiropractic physician, mentor and family man. He started his company, FirstChoice Healthcare, PC, in 1992 and since has built it into a multi-location, multi-disciplinary provider of world-class health services.

Dean served as President of FirstChoice Healthcare until May 2014 when he successfully sold his company. He has held numerous leadership positions in various organizations and has received numerous awards and citations. He most enjoys time with his family. Among many business ventures, he is co-founder of Waymaker Learning Corporation.

About Marty

Marty Coates is President and Senior Consultant of Coates and Associates, Inc., a consulting, training and speaking firm he started in 1992. He has presented keynote speeches and conference training to groups in many foreign countries and all across the United States. Marty has led a number of companies during his twenty-five year career, to include serving as CEO of FirstChoice Healthcare, PC.

He is co-founder of Waymaker Learning Corporation. Marty produces and writes his online blog, "The Coates Perspective," where he discusses current business and social issues.

Marty is a Best-Selling co-author of the book entitled, *Think and Grow Rich Today*. He has authored a number of other books to include, *The Waymaker Principles... Eight Principles to Living a Meaningful Life, Race to The Finish Line* and the national award-winning work entitled *Roadmap To Quality.*

You may contact Dean or Marty at:
Waymaker Learning Corp.
1082 Greenview Dr.
Florence, SC 29501
www.waymakerlearningcorp.com
(843) 229-3546

CHAPTER 32

ARE CEOS AND BUSINESS EXPERTS HELPING OR HURTING U.S. COMPANIES?

BY MACODOU N'DAW, CFA

Globalization, free trade agreements, and the advent of the Internet have created a world market with no boundaries. We now witness an easier movement of goods and services, a quick and instant transfer of funds, and a worldwide and better communication system. An easier gathering and quick dissemination of data has also greatly improved market intelligence.

Furthermore, country borders are becoming artificial because of the establishment of economic communities. We have, just to name a few, the European Union (EU), the Association of South East Nations (ASEAN), the Andean Community of Nations (CAN), and the Southern Africa Development Community (SADC).

This state of affairs has made access to any market quicker and easier, but also has made competition much stiffer. U.S. companies which must, but are reluctant to explore new markets, will see competition brought to their own local or national markets. Therefore, international expansion might be a smart way to protect one's own market. To repeat an old adage: *the best defense is offense.*

The old ways of doing business are no longer appropriate. Production parameters and particularly marketing strategies have drastically changed. This will continue to be so, and at a faster rate because when technology is a dominant part of the new economy, obsolescence and innovation become the norm. Change becomes the only constant. Those companies that embrace change and develop their business strategy accordingly will be ahead of the competition, and those that don't, will at best, survive, and at worst, disappear.

It should be common business sense to, at least, study the feasibility of expanding internationally when 96% of the world's consumers and almost 2/3 of the world's purchasing power live overseas.[1]

Therefore, shouldn't CEOs and business advisers be cognizant of these new developments? Unfortunately, many CEOs think they have a good product and that the U.S. market is safer and "if it ain't broken, don't fix it." I have also come across many business experts who are still providing advice based on antiquated business assumptions.

A NON-OPTIMAL USE OF BUSINESS MODELS

Many U.S. companies are not going overseas because the CEOs only see challenges, not opportunities. They are not aware of the many programs that provide assistance for going overseas.

Unfortunately, many of the business experts who advise them are also not aware of these programs. And because they are not familiar with these resources, their analyses and recommendations are still done as if we were still in the pre-globalization, pre-new economy environments.

To illustrate, let's look at the use of the SWOT[2] matrix. I could have used any other model but chose the SWOT model instead because it is favored by business analysts. Used properly, it can give you a lot of useful insights on the issues and challenges facing a company, and consequently, what recommendations to give. But, if the assumptions used do not take into consideration the new environment in which we live now, the conclusions reached will be faulty, and more importantly, can be harmful to the company.

For example "strengths" and "opportunities" can be grossly overestimated if the analysis fails to incorporate international competition. For the same reason, "weaknesses" and "threats" can be underestimated. Therefore, the SWOT analysis might show a strong company while more relevant

1. sba.gov
2. Strengths, Weaknesses, Opportunities, and Threats.

assumptions would have resulted in showing a much weaker company being advised.

THE CASE FOR INTERNATIONAL EXPANSION

It is no longer enough for a company to be cognizant of external trends in its industry. It should also be willing and able to integrate those trends in its corporate strategy. If a company is operating in a global industry and is not expanding outside of the U.S., chances are that a foreign company will be coming in to its backyard, likely erode its market share, and possibly put it out of business.

Six (6) of the ten (10) biggest Argentine agri-business companies went bankrupt in the 2000s when Chinese companies entered the Argentine market. They limited their competitive analyses to the national market, hence did not see the threats coming from China. Also, according to the Financial Times (FT), almost 50% of companies (238) listed in the FT500 in 1999 were no longer on the list in 2009.

Beyond survival, expanding internationally is also a good tool for recruiting high-caliber staff. Young professionals are now more interested to work for a company with an international presence because they can acquire greater skills and cross-cultural experiences. Going international also allows a company to have access to an international talent pool.

CHALLENGES IN INTERNATIONAL EXPANSION

Although expanding into a foreign market is no longer reserved for only big companies, it is not easy. Emerging markets have more differences than similarities. Neighboring countries in the same region are at a very different stage of development, face different economic challenges, and consequently are looking for different solutions. Many companies trying to expand overseas have made the mistake of analyzing two countries in the same way.

However, expanding internationally does present great opportunities when a company knows how to manage the risks and make use of programs especially designed to help enter foreign markets. Unfortunately, these programs discussed below are often unknown to many domestic CEOs and business experts.

Some of the main challenges usually faced by a company entering a foreign market are listed below.

A. Culture and Business Practices

Obtaining permits, licenses or customs clearances can be quite frustrating and time-consuming. Also, in many regions, especially Asia, deals are concluded mostly based on personal relationships and a congruent long-term vision. These two factors precede the potential benefits that might result from a deal. In many countries, "time is not of the essence" in forging business relationships, as opposed to the U.S., where people consider that "time is money."

Business practices also differ from country to country. For example, when we advised a U.S.-based cellular company, we had to readjust revenues because in many developing countries, the practice of billing for incoming calls is not accepted by customers—the rationale being they should not pay for a call they did not initiate.

Hiring local managers will help navigate through bureaucratic red tape. They can also advise on how to conduct business negotiations. Hiring U.S. trained professionals who fully understand the U.S. culture and have returned to their native countries is also an effective way of addressing these challenges.

B. Marketing

When I tell business owners that they are not in the telecommunication, or manufacturing, or mining business, but in the marketing business, they are startled. Many business owners are in love with their products and services and still think that "if you build it, they will come."

Customers must be able to find a company quickly, at home and abroad, when they search for its product or services category. It does not do a company any good if it has the best products or services but no one can find it.

Therefore, a good social media marketing strategy and a marketing website, not a static website, are required for good search engine optimization (SEO).

Also, the company should learn the marketing channels that are effective in a given country and not embark on a "one size fits all" marketing strategy.

C. Financial, Economic and Environmental Results

It is no longer sufficient for a project to be just financially viable. Economic viability and sustainability have also become integral parts of the decision-making process. Consequently, they are determining whether a project receives the green light from administrative authorities to proceed, or get funding from financial institutions.

Furthermore, consumers are increasingly demanding sustainable products and advocate groups are better organized and more vocal. They hurt a company's image when they demonstrate against its policies and production systems or wage a boycott campaign.

This is why many financial institutions have come to adopt what is called the "triple bottom line" requirement, i.e., projects have to meet the financial, economic, and environmental tests before they fund them.

EXPORTING AS A FIRST STEP

The U.S. lags behind other economic powers when it comes to exporting. According to the World Bank[3], U.S. exports in 2012 accounted for only 14% of gross domestic product (GDP), as compared to Germany (52%), Spain (33%), United Kingdom (32%), Italy (30%), and France and China (27%).

U.S. Companies that are lukewarm to expanding overseas can start the process by just selling their products and services. Thus, they can test the market, have a better understanding of the cultural challenges, and consequently decide whether to establish a physical presence or not.

Also, exporting to developing countries as a first step might be less challenging than trying to enter a developed market. Chinese companies have adopted this strategy in Africa, the Middle-East, and in Latin America. This can be done through strategic alliances or joint-ventures.

---

3. Worldbank.org/data

WHERE TO OBTAIN ASSISTANCE
TO ENTER FOREIGN MARKETS?

We discussed earlier some of the challenges in expanding overseas. The good news is that there are many programs whose sole purpose is to alleviate, if not eliminate, most of these challenges.

Below are some of the organizations and agencies that can make an entry to a foreign market a lot smoother:

US Agencies

The U.S. Commerce Department

Provides a program called Gold Key Services. "It offers customized market and industry briefings; timely and relevant market research; appointments with prospective trade partners; help with travel, accommodations, interpreter service, and clerical support."[4]

www.commerce.gov

The Small Business Administration

"Many small businesses think they are too small to compete in the world market. In fact, 97% of all exporters are small businesses. The federal government has loans, insurance and grant programs to help a company become an exporter or expand its exporting business."[5]

www.sba.gov

Business.USA.gov

Contains a wide range of resources to help small businesses begin and expand into exporting.

State Trade and Export Promotion (STEP)

This grant program is an export initiative to make matching-fund grants for states to assist "eligible small business concerns."[6]

STEP@sba.gov

The Export-Import Bank (EX-IM BANK)

"It is responsible for aiding the export of American goods and services through a variety of loans, guarantees, and insurance products. Its mission is to create and sustain U.S. jobs by financing sales of U.S. exports to international buyers."[7] One of its most popular programs is

---

4. commerce.gov
5. sba.gov
6. sba.gov
7. sba.gov

the Export Credit Insurance. The policy generally covers almost the entirety of the invoice at an insignificant cost.

www.exim.gov

The Overseas Private Investment Corporation (OPIC)

"It helps U.S. businesses gain footholds in emerging markets, catalyzing revenues, jobs and growth opportunities both at home and abroad. OPIC provides investors with financing, guarantees, and political risk insurance."[8]

www.opic.gov

Multi-lateral Organizations

They excel in what I have termed "The Growth Pyramid Paradigm"[9] (see diagram below). They can help a U.S. based company establish operations in an emerging or developing country by providing equity and/or loans, help understand the legal environment, provide political risk insurance, and ensure that the "triple bottom line" requirement is met.

The Asian Development Bank (ADB)

"Provides loans, grants, technical assistance and equity investments for projects located in the Asia and Pacific regions."[10]

www.adb.org

The Inter American Development Bank (IDB)

This agency "supports clients in the design of projects, and provides financing, technical assistance and knowledge services to support projects in Latin American and The Caribbean."[11]

www.iadb.org

The African Development Bank (AFDB)

"Its mission is to fight poverty and improve living conditions by promoting the investment of public and private capital in projects and programs that contribute to the economic and social development of the region."[12]

www.afdb.org

---

8. sba.gov
9. The "Growth Pyramid Paradigm" was discussed at great lengths in the book "Successonomics" that I
    co-authored with Steve Forbes and other experts.
10. sba.gov
11. iadb.org
12. Wikipedia

The International Finance Corporation (IFC)

IFC operates in all emerging and developing countries. "It helps mobilize financial resources for private enterprise, promoting accessible and competitive markets, supporting businesses and other private sector entities, and creating jobs."[13]

www.ifc.org

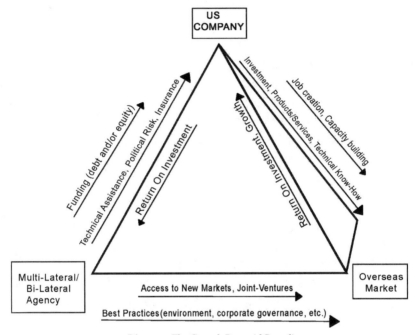

Diagram: *The Growth Pyramid Paradigm*

In conclusion, CEOs and business experts have not only to recognize the new world in which we live, but they have also to be visionary and not reactionary. They must cherish the new realities or perish. It's that simple!

For more information on the "The Growth Pyramid Paradigm", please visit: www.businessconsultingmasters.com

13. Wikipedia

About Mac

Macodou (Mac) N'Daw is the CEO and Chief Consulting Officer of Business Consulting Masters, LLC, a company that teaches aspiring as well as established consultants how to get engagements on a consistent basis and how to add great value to clients.

Mac, also known as the "Business Consultant's Consultant", has more than 33 years of experience in transnational investments (debt and equity), corporate finance and restructuring, strategic analysis, syndication, and joint-ventures. During his 27-year tenure at the International Finance Corporation (IFC), the private sector arm of the World Bank, Mac consulted, supervised and advised on projects located worldwide and in various sectors such as mining, telecoms, agribusiness, fisheries, aquaculture, etc. His last position at the IFC was Associate Director in charge of a world-wide portfolio of 105 projects totaling US$1.5 billion, with Argentina, Brazil, China, India and Ukraine holding the lion's share.

He has visited, conducted workshops, participated in seminars and delivered speeches and talks in 67 countries located in 4 continents (Africa, Asia, Europe, and America).

Mac is also the owner of a real estate company (www.imacrealty.com), which invests in single families residences and apartments buildings nationwide.

Mac has been a Chartered Financial Analyst (CFA) since 1993, holds a B.S. in Finance and Multinational Enterprise from The Wharton School (1979), a M.B.A and a M.A. in Agricultural Economics from Stanford University (1986), and attended The Harvard Business School Executive Development Program (1998).

CHAPTER 33

HOW TO AVOID THE DOUBLE-TAX TRAP AND RECEIVE TAX-FREE MONEY

BY STAN JACKSON

A few years ago, a sophisticated lady (let's call her Jane), sat in my office telling me how she had lost over $500,000 in the market within just a few months. Too many investors feel like Jane, as though they are at a Vegas roulette table. They possess a feeble hope that their investments will not lose money!

The majority of financial advisors offer products with risk. Why do most financial products have a prospectus? A prospectus describes risk. A safe, financial instrument with guarantees does not need a prospectus. The prospectus does not describe safety and guarantees, instead it reveals the uncertainty of the investment.

When clients are losing money in the market, most financial advisors chant the mantra, "In time your investment will come back!" If we look at history, the Japanese Nikkei 225 hit its all-time high on December 29, 1989, before closing at 38,915.87 having grown six fold during the decade. Subsequently, it lost nearly all these gains, closing at 7,054.98 on March 10, 2009—81.9% below its peak twenty years earlier. It has been over 24 years, and the Nikkei still has not returned to the heights of 1989.

Some financial skeptics might propose that the US market has always done better than overseas markets. How long did it take to recover from the market crash of 1929? The year of recovery was 1954, 25 years later.

One of the greatest fears of retirees is outliving their money. If they leave their money in the stock market, they face the risk of substantial losses. If they place their money in CD's, retirees risk losing their investment due to the effects of inflation and taxes. One of the key foundations for wealth preservation is to protect your investment. Never take a loss is the investment philosophy of the sage, investor Warren Buffett. He said, "The first secret is, don't ever lose."

Let's review three financial strategies that will help investors navigate through financial landmines.

FIRST, THERE ARE THE NON-TAXABLE INVESTMENT STRATEGIES.

The top tax rate in this country is 39.6% and the average top tax rate since 1913 is 69%. Most economists believe that we will see much higher taxes in the future. Given these facts, tax-free income strategies may be ideal for retirement planning.

Most investors diversify their investment portfolio, but often they fail to diversify into non-taxable accounts within their investments. We believe that an investor should enhance their portfolios with non-taxable accounts before and during retirement. This gives the investor more spendable money, as the monies that would have otherwise been submitted as tax, stays right where it belongs – with the investor.

The following are three non-taxable incomes strategies:

1. Roth IRAs/401(k)s

2. Municipal Bonds

3. Life Insurance

One possible solution for non-taxable money is to convert your IRAs/401(k)s to Roth IRAs or Roth 401(k)s. Roth IRAs/401(k)s greatest benefit are that the monies, if held properly, go to the client tax-free. However, a lot of clients don't qualify, because they make too much money. Roth IRA's also have limits on what you can contribute each year.

The conversion amount is taxable. The high cost of this conversion is usually too expensive for most taxpayers.

Municipal Bonds are exempted from federal taxes. In some cases they are exempted from state income taxes. However, they are becoming more and more risky due to the fiscal problems of many municipalities. They can also trigger taxation of your Social Security benefits.

Life insurance is an overlooked option. The story of Goldilocks and the Three Bears helps us understand the different types of permanent life insurance policies. The first porridge was too hot; the Variable Life offers growth, but is risky for retirees as there is typically no downside protection. The second porridge was too cold; the Fixed Universal Life and Whole Life products offer safety but normally have high cost structures and low growth potential. The last porridge was just right; the Indexed Universal Life product offers growth tied to market gains with lower costs of insurance, low fee structures and downside protection – safety – all tax-free, if designed properly.

If you could come up with the ideal investment product, what features would it have?

1. You can take money in your retirement tax-free.
2. You can receive market returns without the risk of principal losses.
3. You can access your money at any age.
4. You can continue making contributions, even if disabled.
5. You can provide a tax-free lump sum for your family, if you die prematurely.
6. You are protected from judgments and lawsuits in many states.
7. Does not create taxation of Social Security benefits.

Indexed Universal Life is an ideal financial instrument with the benefits described above. Many Social Security recipients are shocked to realize that up to 85% of benefits are taxed. If they take out more money from their traditional IRA, more of their Social Security benefits are taxed. You could have more money during your retirement, if you combine your Social Security benefits with an Index Universal Life insurance policy. "It's not how much income you have, but how much you have to spend." - Doug Warren

The following two examples demonstrate the tax-benefits of the Indexed Universal Life with Social Security planning:

Example #1

Example #2

If Income from Social Security is:	$70,000	If IRA/401(k) is reduced $20,000 & replaced with Indexed Universal Life	If Income from Social Security is:	$70,000
IRA/401(k) is $20,000:	$20,000		IRA/401(K) is:	$0
		Tax-free Income:		$20,000
	$90,000		Total	$90,000

Tax Treatment of Income

	$35,350	Total Taxable		$1,500
	$54,650	Non-Taxable		$88,500
	$90,000		Total	$90,000

Are you interested in having a tax-free income during your retirement as well as a financial plan for your loved ones after you pass way? Indexed universal life insurance is a vehicle with cash value that can earn interest based on a fixed, pre-determined interest rate. You can earn interest rates based on an equity or bond index, like the S&P 500, which historically has earned a higher interest over time. This coverage has benefits that you can use – tax-free – while you're alive. It has a death benefit that passes to your loved ones tax-free when you pass away.

In the event of a financial need, be it business or personal, the money in your tax-deferred cash value accumulation account can be accessed through the tax-free loans. Better yet, the value of the amount you have borrowed can continue to participate in the market gains that your cash value account accumulates with compound interest.

Your money is paid to you in the form of tax-free loans against your account value at retirement. This money could be a **lifetime** income stream with no risk of principal loss. In fact, most Indexed Universal Life Insurance products have minimum **guaranteed** returns!

THE SECOND FINANCIAL STRATEGY IS AN IRA RESCUE

Because taxes have not been paid on retirement account funds, this could be your **tax-time bomb**. IRA's or qualified plan funds that are unneeded to maintain your lifestyle can use the IRA Rescue Strategy to dramatically amplify the legacy that is passed on to loved ones. With 90 percent of IRA accounts being cashed in at the death of the second spouse, you run the risk of making the IRS one of your **prime beneficiaries.**

This model is to use a quality Indexed Universal Life policy that will provide tax-free income. The Index Universal Life Insurance concept is that the policy takes advantage of the IRS tax code section 7702 and 72(e). These sections state that the cash value inside a life insurance policy grows tax- deferred and can be withdrawn tax-free.

One of the biggest questions about this strategy is what happens, if the tax law changes? In the early 1980's, Single Premium Universal Life policies could take unlimited amount of money into these policies. These benefits were so good that the government changed the law. No longer can unrestricted dollars go into these policies.

I introduced my father and my mother to these tax-favored instruments, from which they reaped these benefits for about 25 years. Dad and Mom and all other policies holders still maintained all the original benefits, even after the law changed. The reason they kept the benefits is that the old law was grandfathered. When there are significant tax changes, the government normally grandfather's the old law.

The IRA Rescue strategy will allow you to take non-recourse loans from your policy to pay the tax. IRA/401(k) money cannot be transferred directly into life insurance products. The funds must first be withdrawn from the IRA/401(k), become subject to tax, then the life insurance policy can be purchased and tax deferred accumulation can begin. Any withdrawal from a qualified plan will be taxed, whereas most withdrawals from an Indexed Universal Life product can be taken tax-free.

In this plan, the taxes are due on each distribution. The amount needed to pay the taxes is borrowed from the policy. This will not disturb the earning power of the original principal. If properly structured, the money borrowed is from a side fund of the insurance company not the client's money. This loan will accrue with interest in the policy. It does not have to be repaid until you pass on. The insurance company will deduct the loan balance from your death benefit before they send your beneficiary the remaining tax-free death benefit.

Depending on your allocations, the cash value account in the policy can grow at a better than market rate and policy loans - even annual loans - used as income are tax-free. With this strategy you are converting your taxable IRA or 401(k) to a tax-free cash value life insurance policy with a tax-free death benefit. You then can borrow against the death benefit to offset the conversion tax. You can minimize the death benefit to keep the cost of insurance low and maximize the cash build up in the life insurance policy. Sound too good to be true? It's not, we are simply leveraging the tax-benefits of a life insurance policy for maximum tax-free income.

The cash value account in the policy grows at a better than market rate. The policy loans can be used as income and are tax-free. With this strategy you are converting your taxable IRA or 401(k) to a tax-free cash value life insurance policy with a tax-free death benefit. You then can borrowing against the death benefit to pay the conversion tax. You minimize the death benefit and maximize the cash build up in the life insurance policy. You are utilizing the tax-benefits of a life insurance policy for maximum tax-free income.

For example, a male, age 55, has an IRA valued at $500,000. His number one concern is safety from market losses. He wants his investment to earn a reasonable rate of return. He also wants to "lock in the gains" when credited, all on a tax-advantaged basis.

In this example, 15 years later, when he is 70, this client can receive a tax-free income in the amount of over $108,000 per year – all without raising his tax bracket! He also wants to "lock in the gains" when credited, all on a tax-advantaged basis of over $108,000 per year. That is a taxable equivalent yield of over $155,000 per year! This allows the client to receive an income for 20 years of $2,160,000, tax-free! In the 20th year, the death benefit is still $400,000.

THE THIRD FINANCIAL STRATEGY IS TO SOLVE THE DOUBLE-TAX TRAP

What is this double-tax trap? Some financial advisors have called it the 75% tax trap. Clients with large estates, who have money in IRAs and/ or qualified plans may qualify for these double-taxes. You can nearly always guarantee that such clients will have that money double-taxed at their death. Many people over the age of 60 have accumulated large sums in qualified retirement accounts or deferred annuities that may not be needed to fund their retirement. Their intent may well be to defer taxes and pass the account to their future generation. They end up passing most of their gains to their least favorite relative – Uncle Sam!

Take a client with a large estate and a $3 million IRA. The IRA may only be worth $690,150 after income and estate taxes, if he and his wife die in that year. This same client could have established a wealth replacement trust with more than $5.7 million going to his heirs, should he have allocated those IRA dollars to a Life Insurance policy.

Your Large IRA (or qualified money)	$3,000,000
Federal Estate Tax (50%)	$(1,500,000)
State Death Tax (7%)	$(210,000)
Balance Subject to Income Taxes	$1,290,000
Federal Income Taxes (39.6%)	$(510,840)
State Income Taxes (7%)	$(90,300)
Balance to your Heirs	$688,860 (i.e., 23%)

The client's heirs could lose 23% of the 3 million IRA. With proper planning, the double-tax is solved with a tax-advantaged wealth building Life Insurance policy.

Having your retirement money exposed to financial losses in the market is not an effective strategy to provide for your financial future. The insightful advice of the legendary fund manager from Fidelity, Peter Lynch is still practical: "The absolute golden rule about investing is – No matter how good the market looks, never invest money you can't afford to lose." Will Rogers made the following wise observation: "I'm more concerned with the return of my principal than the return on my principal."

We have reviewed only three of many financial strategies that can provide you peace of mind, knowing that your money is safe. First, there are non-taxable investment strategies. The second financial strategy is an IRA Rescue Strategy. The third financial strategy is to solve the **double-tax trap** sometimes called the 75% tax-trap. Indexed Universal Life insurance can provide a financial instrument capable of lowering your taxable income in an environment of increasing taxes.

The Indexed Universal Life has these many outstanding features: You can take money in your retirement tax-free, without principal risk, you have access to your money, continued premiums even if disabled, tax-free death benefit for your family and protected from judgments and lawsuits. They could also avoid the 85% taxing of Social Security benefits. Do you know of any other financial instrument that surpasses these benefits?

I have heard that Warren Buffett has encouraged other investors to utilize the "Age Investment Ratio" (AIR). An individual age 60 would have 60% of his investments in safety. One of the safest financial instruments available today is Indexed Universal Life.

"Right now, you are able to grow the cash value inside of your Universal Life policy tax-deferred, and then access this cash value tax-free, utilizing the Policy Loan Provision. **You might want to consider getting on this train before it leaves the station! Because once it leaves, it's likely gone."** The Retirement Miracle, Patrick Kelly

"The tax exemption for life insurance is the single biggest benefit in the tax code! Make it a part of your retirement savings plan and your estate plan. Now is the time to create a plan to rescue your retirement and move your money from accounts that are forever taxed to accounts that are never taxed." —Ed Slott, *CPA, America's IRA Expert, Best-Selling Author, Public Speaker, Educator*

About Stan

Stan Jackson is a Proactive Tax Planner. Stan uses tax-advantaged strategies to provide material solutions, lowering applicable taxes. His solutions can protect assets, estates and beneficiaries from tax-consequences. His goal is to use safe, suitable and compliant financial instruments to lower or eliminate taxes.

Stan has been working in financial services since 1979 helping clients grow and protect their assets. Incorporated with Executive Business Counselors, Inc. in 1990, his firm EBC, Inc. is a DBA of his corporation. He specializes in helping individuals increase their wealth, working exclusively for their benefit, focusing on safe investment vehicles.

Stan helps his clients utilize all viable financial instruments, identifying client's goals, risk tolerances and concerns. He provides recommendations to protect his clients' assets, estate, heirs and income. His mission is to help you Keep Your Wealth Safe. He utilizes strategies designed to protect original dollars, while adding safe and steady growth potential with zero risk of market loss. This steady growth and disciplined income strategy will protect money from the volatility of the market. No longer will you wrestle with the question of "How much gambling with risk of loss is worth it enough for me to potentially lose my original money?" Instead, you can have the one thing that risk cannot buy – peace of mind!

Stan was raised on a farm where he learned hard work and integrity; values which he brings to his practice. Stan graduated from Missouri State University and now lives in Hazelwood, Missouri with his wife, Cathy, and their German shepherd, Dori.

Here's what his clients have to say!

"Stan Jackson was able to solve a business problem for me, through insurance that saved me a good deal of money. No one else could come up with the right answer... just Stan."

- Bill Glastris, Business Owner

"I have been doing business with Stan Jackson for nearly 14 years. I've come to know and trust him to responsibly handle many of my financial affairs. He's one of the most professional brokers I have ever done business with."

- Benny Recht, Business Owner

311

Through his excellent ability to understand financial goals and means of reaching these goals, Mr. Jackson has, through his knowledge of available plans and his seemingly inexhaustible source of information, been able to greatly improve my portfolio."

— Robert R. Davis, Business Owner

"Stan Jackson has handled my financial services over the last ten years. I appreciate his honest, straightforward approach. I have a great deal of confidence in Stan's ability to always put the client's interest first."

— John Weigel, President -
National Association
of Business Leaders

Stan spoke to the Creve Coeur Lions Club. Ken Schimel, Past District Governor wrote, "We would highly recommend him as a speaker and the program itself as a presentation to other organizations. He certainly knows his stuff."

Stan Jackson
EBC, Inc.
Two CityPlace Drive
Suite 200
St. Louis, MO 63141
800-725-7283
314-291-1590
314-308-9988 cell
http://www.taxlater.com
mailto: ebc@taxlater.com

CHAPTER 34

PLUNGING TO SUCCESS

BY STEPHEN DEVLIN

I first met Brian Tracy in the spring of 2014 in New York City at the National Association of Experts, Writers & Speakers conference. Brian was there to receive a lifetime achievement award and I was there to receive a writer's award for a book I wrote in 2013. This was nearly 15 years after reading Brain's life-transforming written word.

It's 1999, and my job with a consumer goods company has fallen victim to downsizing. Thirty-three years old, already divorced for three, I had no savings. Armed with eight years sales management experience, I was at a complete loss as to what I was going to do. Despite a pretty good severance package, I was floundering.

Job loss can cause all sorts of weird things to your brain: depression, laziness, low self-worth, and the inability to see the positive. My severance package lasted me eight months after a half-hearted job search. A couple of weeks earlier the panic button went off while lying on a local beach. I had to stop feeling sorry for myself. I had to get out there and find something I would love to do. I turned to the Internet and ironically, at the time, found a sales position working for an online job site.

An innovative job in the dotcom industry, I headed up the BC office for an Ontario-based company. I had been an ice cream guy for eight years. Motivating kids and teenagers to sell frozen treats to folks who hated our repetitive vending music. This job was new territory for me, because this job required more than sales management. It required hard-core cold calling. I had to call on human resource executive officers, managers and assistants to pitch them on the benefits of posting their jobs on our website. I didn't know a thing about selling to businesses (B2B). And, I was on 100% commission! I was terrified but excited at the same time!

It was a lot of fun but I needed to learn how to sell strategically and to close more sales presentations. I decided to work on myself, investing in programs such as *The Pursuit of Excellence*, *The Wall*, and *The Advancement of Excellence*, amongst others. I gained a better understanding of myself and how to fight through my insecurities and life's obstacles. I am a big believer in learning from the expertise and experience of others.

During my self-improvement journey, I came across *The Great Big Book of Wisdom*; it was my first introduction to Brian Tracy. He shared his life experiences and advice through motivational quotes. It was one of those books that didn't become "shelf-help". I read it during my challenging days. It made me feel better, more capable. The cold calling was tiring and stressful. The beginning of each sales month gave me "world collapsing on top of me" moments. I don't think many people like cold calling. However, I learned great lessons about myself; especially how to react and live with rejection.

Brian's work enlightened me to opportunities to better myself, to find places in my life that were not comfortable but necessary to be stronger and happier, to be positive. I won several top sales awards and was consistently the number one sales rep in that company. That career was really the place I learned how to sell and how to help solve problems for people with solutions that worked. Unfortunately, the dotcom melt down ushered me into the unemployment line once again. I found myself shutting one door while another one opened.

I believe my entrepreneurial spirit really started after that last layoff. I didn't like relying on someone else's decisions on how they wanted to run their business. I wanted to be in control of my own destiny. To create a life that had more purpose and the ability to help more people. The opportunity came to me and my wife, Michele, back in 2003 when we bought the Canadian rights to a web-based realtor marketing program. It was an extremely successful venture for us for 4 years, but we had no control over development and could see that market changes where quickly whittling away at the company and exited that business. The learning experiences from those years were huge. We realized that working for ourselves was the best way for us to achieve our goals and dreams.

When you achieve a certain level of success you have a decision to either stay comfortable and stagnate or take more risk to grow. The fear can be so strong that it prevents new successes from happening. We knew what our goals were and we had the confidence to take more risk, so we bought a magazine-publishing franchise. We hired the best business coaches and lawyers to help us set-up this new venture. Unfortunately, we lost our shirts and went from having a significant net worth down to having a massive amount of debt. It was a humbling experience. The stress was monumental, but our tenacity to succeed and our dedication to each other made us stronger.

Debt was suffocating us, and I was a daily worrier. Despite an excellent credit rating, the banks turned their backs on us. It was a slap in the face after doing so much business with them during the good years. I can remember talking to one of my best buddies who was also in business for himself and going through similar challenges. He pointed out that we were still living well. We all owned houses, drove decent cars, went out for dinner and on vacations occasionally. He said to keep moving forward and not to put so much fear around it. Look at it as just numbers. This advice really helped us as we started to figure what we wanted to do next.

Transforming any part of your life is not an easy thing to do. When I was pouting and stressing out about the debt and lack of income at that time, Michele would always say, "You don't become successful without the plunges." I don't know what I would have done without her. She is my rock and the person I can rely on to help me get through some of the darkest days. She is the problem solver and has an incredible ability to quickly find solutions to our problems.

The falls in life teach us a lot about ourselves. I don't know you, but I have pretty good idea about what you stand for and want in life. You're reading these chapters from all these amazing people because you want hope and lessons which you can apply to your life and business – to be more successful. Probably one reason is to make more money, right? Heck, there is nothing wrong with wanting to be rich. But, there is no magic bill or silver bullet. Life is a series of challenges to help you grow. It's hard work. These challenges suck and feel awful at the time, but as you get through them you become stronger and have more skills to pick yourself up on the next fall. Don't brush them away because of fear of pain. Embrace them and know it's a learning experience.

I also believe in embracing my spirituality and building my relationship with God. It comes with serving others. Whether it's family, friends, clients, or strangers, helping people brings me great joy. I felt I needed to find my place in the world by making people's lives easier. It was something I had been searching for since I was a teenager. Funny how life works out because my calling was the exact thing that was stressing me out for most of my life; debt and how to manage money!

You learned earlier about my pain around debt and losing all our wealth to a bad business venture. There are lessons in my experiences I already talked about, but one of the largest transformations for me came in learning about the financial world. Now I need to pass that knowledge on to you. I actually could write an entire book about it but I'll have to do it in the 1,200 or so words I have left. A tall order for sure. Perhaps you're wondering why I spent so much time on my life. Well, the reason is because you need to feel some sort of connection with me. To know I've been there. The bottom line is that I can help you become financially set for life WITHOUT taking unnecessary risk. How? From my own experiences and what I did to put our financial house back in order. Begin having a life without financial stress.

When Michele and I were going through our own financial hell, we had many money worries and questions. So I ask you: Are you concerned about not having enough money for when you get older? Do you want to know your money is safe and guaranteed? Are you tired of losing money in the stock and real estate markets? Will you be able to support your family if you get sick, disabled, or die? Are you sick and tired of having to pay interest to banks and credit card companies? Discouraged in having to prove your worth to get money? We asked ourselves these things and more.

We knew there had to be a solution out there, but conventional financial wisdom and advice was, frankly, letting us down. That's when a dear friend in Florida introduced us to two books that had a huge impact on our lives and completely transformed our financial wows into financial freedom! These books were *Becoming Your Own Banker* by Nelson R. Nash and *Bank on Yourself* by Pamela Yellen. We were blown away by how simple the concepts were and how powerful it could be in our lives. It gave us the safety net we needed and the solution to never rely on a bank again; for not just our lifetime, but our son's and future generations. It gave us a strategy to eliminate all that debt we had and never go back into debt again. We certainly were skeptical and wondered why our financial advisor didn't tell us about this incredible concept. So, the lesson for you is to do what we did and read these books. Conduct your own due-diligence. Ask questions and be open to learning. If your financial life is a disaster like ours was, there is hope. You can transform it! The answers to your deep questions, worries and insecurities start with these books and my help. This is my passion and the reason I became a financial coach, advisor and author.

So before we part ways for now, you're probably wondering what this financial miracle could be; Right? Surprisingly, it is one of the most least-understood financial instruments out there. Yet, it has been around for more than 160 years in North America. Dividend- Paying (participating) Whole Life Insurance through a mutually-owned life insurance company! OK, I know. Not that exciting and kind of boring. Don't turn to the next chapter. Stay with me, because what seems boring on the surface is actually pretty interesting and exciting!

Not all whole life insurance is created equal. There are the boring and gloomy policies to cover your loved ones from financial losses in your demise. But what if you could own a policy to help you while you are living? One that gives you an asset greater than real estate! If designed right, these types of policies turn you into your own banker. I've been my own banker for several years now and you can too. You don't have to die to win!

We were able to get ahead because these policies gave us all the things we wanted our money to do. They'll do the same for you: contractual guaranteed growth, liquidly, tax deferred growth, guaranteed death benefit to transfer wealth tax-free to loved ones, creditor protection, access to money with no restrictions or credit checks, and much more!

But the most exciting aspect of these policies for me is you compound 100% of your money while borrowing up to 90% to finance your life's necessities. Pay off debt, finance cars, vacations, business equipment, education, or whatever and without a credit check! It's your money to do with what you want.

A participating whole life insurance contract will be the one of your greatest assets you will ever own in your lifetime. It takes patience and long-term vision, but the rewards are huge. The key is to use the equity in your policy while you are living. It gets more efficient each year and becomes a "cash storage facility" you can rely on – no matter what happens in the real estate and stock markets. It is NOT about rate of return. It's about reversing the flow of your money so you can stop paying interest to others and free yourself from banks and finance companies. There is no better feeling than to hear my clients talk about the freedom they now have. How relieved they are to now have a place for their money that really works to THEIR benefit. My clients are the reason I do what I do, and I am so grateful to have them in my life.

Life is precious and short! Michele had cancer last year at age 47 and we almost lost her. I can't tell you how scared I was for her, my son and myself. But I wasn't scared about our finances. Will you be if such a tragedy strikes? You don't have to be. To eliminate your financial stressors and transform your life takes a different way of looking at things. In this chapter I showed you my choices to persevere despite life challenges. They gave me the opportunity to learn, but most of all I realized I had to work. I couldn't just sit on a beach waiting for things to happen. Your finances can't wait either.

Thanks for reading and God bless!

About Stephen

Stephen Devlin, Licensed Life Insurance Broker, is a Canadian life insurance expert, a Bank on Yourself Authorized Advisor and Infinite Banking Concepts Authorized Practitioner. He is also an accomplished financial coach, specializing in cash flow management and wealth building strategies. He is the co-founder and president of the MacDev Financial Group Corp.; headquartered in Vancouver, British Columbia, with agents across Canada. Stephen is an agent and consultant for several major life insurance and alternative investment companies. He is a seasoned professional and entrepreneur with a wealth of experience in all aspects of the business life cycle. Besides his numerous successes in executive management of private and public corporations, Stephen has taken his own companies from a local presence to those of national acclamation, speaking to audiences from the very few to thousands.

Stephen landed a place as co-author in the best-selling book *The Secret to Lifetime Financial Security,* which was published September 19, 2013. The book reached best-seller status in seven Amazon.com categories - reaching as high as # 1 in the "Budget and Money Management" category. Stephen won a Quilly for this accomplishment, and earned membership in the National Academy of Best Selling Authors. He also won an EXPY award on April 4, 2014 from the National Association of Experts, Writers & Speakers. He has appeared in *USA TODAY, Forbes Magazine,* A & E and the Bio Channel's *Times Square Today* show.

Stephen is passionate about helping Canadian individuals, families, and corporations become financially self-empowered by teaching them the key principals to creating long-term security and controlling their financial futures. The Bank on Yourself and *Infinite Banking* proven concept allows clients to benefit from increased cash flow, resulting in the ability to finance endeavors such as the purchase of vehicles, real estate, beginning a business, or whatever life goal requires funding. Stephen greatly enjoys coaching others and witnessing the results as businesses and families flourish under his guidance. Because of his own hard-earned wisdom gained through personal difficulties and life experiences, it brings him great joy to share the security that financial stability brings.

Stephen lives on British Columbia's beautiful Sunshine Coast with his wife and business partner, Michele, and their young son. He loves spending quality time with his family and also enjoys traveling, cooking, golfing, hiking, kayaking, swimming, hockey, and coaching youth sports.

To contact Stephen Devlin and begin on the path to financial security, please call 877.534.7266 or email: stephen@macdevfinancial.com. You can also find him on the web at: www.macdevfinancial.com where you can also learn more about the many services offered by MacDev Financial Group Corp.

CHAPTER 35

THE GREATEST LIE MY DAD EVER TOLD ME AND HOW HIS DEATH REVEALED THE TRUTH

BY DR. PHILLIP YOO

My parents were hard-working immigrants from Korea. Many Americans take this great country for granted, growing up with a sense of entitlement. Quite the opposite is true with immigrants. They show up with nothing more than a suitcase and a strong work ethic. They only see the future; they don't have a past to blame. That's why so many immigrants achieve the "American Dream."

I grew up listening to my mom tell stories about when she and my dad first arrived in New York. They had to survive on my dad's meager salary he earned as a hospital resident. They lived in a tiny, cockroach-infested apartment and barely spoke any English.

Like all Korean-American kids, I was expected to excel academically. Truth be told, I was more interested in reading about my favorite comic book heroes. But my parents told me that if I study hard, get into a good college and become a doctor, I could then get a job that would provide financial security and a good lifestyle.

I grew up watching my dad do all the things he preached. He worked hard as a medical doctor. He was always on call, chained to a pager that would go off late at night and on the weekends.

He worked like that for decades.

Just two years away from retirement, my dad suffered a sudden brain stroke. It happened as he was driving through Tennessee on his way to Florida for some much needed relaxation. He got a severe headache and checked into a hotel to get some rest.

He never woke up.

The doctors in Tennessee couldn't save him. My mom had to pay $10,000 to have a plane fly him home. His "elite medical insurance" didn't cover this expense. At my dad's funeral, I remember thinking how the so called "best medical care in the world" had failed.

Here was my father—a Medical Doctor who specialized in brain and mental disorders—supposedly with access to the best medical providers and insurance coverage money could buy. Ironically, the very institution he worked in couldn't save him, let alone cover his medical bills.

So, the greatest lie my dad ever told me was the same lie he'd been told: That being a doctor would provide financial security and freedom, and that the medical profession would take care of me and my health.

The day my father passed away, I vowed to NEVER become a slave to my work. Instead, I'd work on my terms and dedicate my life to transforming the way medicine is practiced in America. This would mean taking the power away from the bureaucratic hospital, pharmaceutical and insurance companies, and giving it back to the doctor where it belongs. Imagine ... patients would actually receive the care they need—not what the hospital administrators and insurance companies approve or deny, based on their cost containment policies.

Life moved on ...

After completing pre-medicine studies at Michigan State University, I went on to get my Doctorate in Chiropractic Medicine. Upon graduation,

I chose to give back to the world before starting my own practice. So, I devoted one year of my life doing voluntary medical missions in Central America—despite being carjacked at gunpoint the day I arrived and surviving Hurricane Mitch. During my mission there was a shortage of primary care physicians, so the local medical doctors trained me how to prescribe common drugs, deliver injections and assist in minor surgeries.

After my sojourn to Central America, I moved to Korea and opened up two chiropractic practices.

After working long hours running my clinics for 10 years, I was burnt out. I had become a prisoner of my business, which was the very thing I had set out not to do. It was a job I couldn't quit. As the sole proprietor, I had taken on a business that wouldn't run without my presence. On the home front, my wife was complaining that I was never around—and when I was, all I did was sleep. It got so bad that we were on the brink of divorce.

To save our marriage I knew that I had to make a big transformation. I left the two practices in the hands of my associate doctors and moved to California to get help with our marriage from the minister who married us.

Going back to Korea was not an option. I had to find a way to run the practices without being there!

After much research, trial and error, I discovered that a professional practice, or any business can be run without physically working "in the business." There are four primary roles the owner must fill that can be universally applied to any business. They are:

1) The Manual Laborer

2) The Macromanager

3) The Mighty CEO

4) The Marketer

If these four roles are not in balance, business burnout is likely on the horizon.

In my SuperHero Coaching Program, I teach 40 "Super Powered Skills" in those four specific areas. Because you're reading this book you're about to discover a few nuggets in these areas that you can IMMEDIATELY implement in your practice or business to make more money and to spend more time with your loved ones.

The first role is the "manual laborer," where you find yourself performing the hands-on, hourly-wage type of work. In the chiropractic profession that typically means treatments and office work. When I started my first practice, I did much more than treat patients. I did bookkeeping, answered phones, emptied trash, etc. Excessive manual labor may be necessary in the beginning when hiring staff is too costly. The irony is that business growth will be restricted unless you replace yourself by hiring employees to do the $10/hour type of work.

Once you've hired employees to perform "manual labor," you'll have to manage them. **Manager is another role that doctors get trapped into doing. They're terrible at it because they're multi-tasking as doctor, manager and manual laborer.** Many business owners not only make the mistake of doing too much manual labor, but they also think that they have to manage the employees by themselves. They end up getting in their own way—which is inefficient, unproductive and leads to frustration.

In my case, I also made the mistake of being in the office micromanaging the staff. Although I took myself out of the manual labor role, I created another full-time "job" acting as the business macromanager. I solved this by hiring a clinic manager to oversee the staff and run the internal operations. This freed me up to use my time where it's most valuable, which takes us to the third role ...

The CEO is not just the company's figurehead, but a Super Hero who can effectively envision, innovate, strategize and lead his team to implement the company's goals. The CEO should always be looking to the future of the business through research and innovation— and effectively communicating the big vision to the staff.

Furthermore, being CEO doesn't mean you have to sit in a big lonely office all day. Your physical presence may be necessary a few hours a week to keep a pulse on what's happening in the office and to maintain employee morale. But, you'll find that your best business ideas and breakthroughs occur when you're disconnected from the office. There's an old saying, **"A successful Entrepreneur CEO spends most of his**

time working ON the business, not IN the business."

In my industry, most practice owners are in their offices all day grinding away with patient treatments, writing patient notes, billing insurance and micromanaging staff. After all that, there's not much time left to be CEO and plan for the future. That's how most doctors, or any business owner, will eventually burn out. Being in the business all day and trying to do everything yourself is unsustainable. No wonder 80% of businesses fail within 5 years.

As CEO, it's imperative to create reproducible systems for your business and hire quality people to run those systems. Theoretically, if you were to open your practice or business in any city in the U.S., you should be able to operate successfully and smoothly because you have reproducible, documented systems and you can hire replaceable employees to drive those systems.

However, be forewarned that systems can fail if they're not constantly improved. For example, disaster struck my business when I discovered that the associate doctors I had entrusted with my Korean clinics had started their own practices without my knowledge, swiping my patient records and recruiting my patients and staff.

This brings us to the next *Super Powered Skill:* always be looking for and recruiting super staff to run your Super Powered Systems. Don't expect employees to last forever, even the stars. **Eventually those who work for you will either wake up one day with an "entrepreneurial urge," taking what they learned from you to start their own business, or they'll go lame and quit or have to be fired.**

Pay close attention to who you hire, and always be on the lookout for your next ex-star employee. Create a "virtual bench" so you won't find yourself in a bind when a position needs to be filled.

After miraculously selling off my practices in Korea, I figured I could start a practice in California and implement the systems which I learned and developed. So, I bought another doctor's practice. Long story short, the seller didn't stick around for a smooth transition, didn't introduce me to his patients, nor did he show me the ropes on insurance billing. The few patients that remained had insurance plans that discontinued coverage.

Adding insult to injury, I severely injured my back during this time and developed excruciating sciatic leg pains. Life as I knew it changed in an instant. I couldn't play sports. I couldn't concentrate. I couldn't even lift up my kids. I was to the point where I could either shut my doors because I was headed to the brink of bankruptcy, or I could fight to salvage my practice like I did in Korea.

Well, I'm a Spartan. In Spartan law, it's illegal to surrender or retreat in battle. So I decided to fight on.

This brings us to another *Super Powered Skill:* although business systems are necessary, they're not evergreen. Eventually they'll become obsolete and need to be changed through innovation.

Transformation is a never-ending process.

I knew I couldn't totally rely on the systems I created in Korea, nor could I rely on billing insurance. I needed a game changer to transform my practice into one that would thrive. One thing was for certain: I knew I had to find a way to charge cash, up front, for services.

But, before I could take action, I needed to eliminate the debilitating sciatic pain. Ironically, all the treatments that I provided as a chiropractor did not help! Instead of taking drugs, or getting injections or surgery, I discovered hi-powered laser therapy. After only a few treatments my pain disappeared. **This was a blessing in disguise; it was the exact game changer I needed. I integrated hi-powered laser therapy into my practice. This not only set me apart from other chiropractors, but gave me an "unfair advantage" as the only one using hi-powered super laser technology.**

This brings us to the next *Super Powered Skill*: To avoid commoditizing your business, you must position it to stand out in the marketplace as the only one doing what you do, or selling what you sell—then do it extraordinarily well. In my case, I had discovered this super powered laser which no other doctor had, and developed unique treatment protocols.

Despite my new "Super Power," I needed to find a way to effectively promote it to the public.

After countless hours of research, I discovered direct response marketing and started implementing some of the principles. Lo and behold, they actually worked!

This brings us to the fourth, and arguably the most important practitioner or business owner role: being a marketer of your business. Your real profession is not what you do, it's not the degree you earned, nor is it the industry you're in.

If someone asks me what I do for a living, my natural response is: "I'm a chiropractic doctor." Although that may technically be what I do in the business, the real answer is: "I'm the marketer of my chiropractic practice."

If you're a medical specialist, you're really a marketer of your medical practice. If you're a podiatrist, you're a marketer of your podiatry business. Whatever industry you're in, if you don't look at your primary role in business as being the marketer, then you'll quickly find yourself without a business. It's marketing that brings in new paying patients, clients and customers. You can be the greatest doctor, or have the greatest skill in your industry, but if you're not out marketing and promoting, your phone won't ring.

Turns out, I'm my own best case study. Back in 2010, before I started viewing myself as the marketer of my chiropractic practice, my gross income was about $30,000. After implementing my Super Powered Business Principles I collected $695,000 in 2013, nearly 23 times what I did in 2010. In 2014, I'm on track to collect approximately $1.2 million in revenue, a whopping 40-fold increase. This is unheard of in my industry especially considering that I'm the only doctor working part-time, three to four hours a day Monday through Thursday. My full, three-day weekends are devoted to recovery, recreation and relationships.

This brings us to the final *Super Power Skill:* you must design your practice to serve your lifestyle, instead of being enslaved to serving the practice or business.

In order to do this you must sit down and identify the most important things in your life. You must write down a set of priorities and vow to never compromise them.

Here are mine:

1. "QT" (Quiet Time), which is my personal time with God, every morning.

2. Always take the kids to school.

3. Exercise six times per week and when the weather is nice, perform my workouts outdoors.

4. Spend no more than 4 hours per day, 4 days per week at the clinic (Monday-Thursday).

5. Have a full 3-day weekend to devote more time to my faith, family, friends and fitness.

6. Until my kids are out of the house, I will spend as much time as possible with them. Thus, I will not do any business travel more than necessary.

7. I never work or even attend seminars on Sundays, as that is church and family time.

No matter what, these seven priorities take precedence over my business, in order to maintain my liberated lifestyle by design.

I've been fortunate to fulfill my mission of achieving a liberated lifestyle, while helping to transform the practice of medicine. Now, my new mission is to help other doctors and those in the health care industry or any business achieve the same.

About Dr. Phillip Yoo

New York-born Dr. Phillip Yoo is the best-selling author of *21ˢᵗ Century Pain Relief*, a world-renowned speaker, and an in-demand healthcare, fitness and wellness expert who is sought after by many professional athletes, Hollywood celebrities and entertainers. Dr. Yoo has been a provider for the 2008 Beijing Olympic Games, Beyoncé Tour Korea, U.S. Military Special Forces Units and Ambassadors from every continent. He has also done voluntary medical mission trips to Central America.

Dr. Yoo has over 17 years of experience and has traveled the world researching and developing the most 'state of the art' pain management techniques. Dr. Yoo stays on the forefront of medicine through his never-ending postgraduate studies which include Harvard Medical School's continuing education programs in the fields of pain management, sports medicine, neurology and functional medicine.

Dr. Yoo has received citations from U.S. Deputy Commander Army and Air Force 4-star generals. He is a graduate of Michigan State University's Human Performance & Wellness Program and earned his Doctorate of Chiropractic at the National University of Health Sciences in Chicago. Furthermore, Dr. Yoo earned his International Chiropractic Sports Science Diploma in Europe. He is also the founder *of Create Wellness Centers Worldwide, O.C. Laser Spine & Disc Center* and the *21ˢᵗ Century Pain Institute* in Newport Beach, California, where he lectures and trains doctors from around the world on his proprietary 'state of the art' treatment protocols.

Dr. Yoo only uses the world's most advanced and powerful Laser and Pulsed Electromagnetic Field (PEMF) medical technologies, etc. to treat the most challenging chronic pain syndromes such as those caused from sports injuries, spine disorders, degenerative arthritis, peripheral neuropathy (nerve disorders), fibromyalgia and other severe pain syndromes that have not responded to all other forms of treatments, such as drugs, injections, surgeries or other alternative medical modalities. All procedures are FDA-cleared, safe, are scientifically proven effective and non-invasive. Dr. Yoo is a true Spartan, and will not give up when it comes to winning the war on chronic pain and degenerative diseases.

When he's not out saving the world from pain, he enjoys doing Crossfit workouts, spending time with his family and volunteering at his church. Dr. Yoo's mission is to help people live more active, healthier, happier, and pain-free lives and do this in the safest, fastest and most comprehensive and natural manner.

Dr. Yoo is also the founder of "The Concierge Clinic"—where he consults and coaches chiropractic, podiatric, and pain management medical doctors, and other specialists on how to run an innovative, successful, patient-centered concierge clinical practice. The program enables doctors to deliver high quality health care without the hassles of dealing with the Medicare mayhem or the profit-driven private insurance industry.

The Concierge Clinic empowers doctors to deliver superior healthcare, without being overworked and underpaid, and not having to deal with the politics of working at a hospital, while actually getting paid what they're worth up front.

You can contact Dr. Yoo at:
Dryoo@lasermedinstitute.com
www.theconciergeclinic.com
www.twitter.com/chirosportdoc
www.facebook.com/drphillipyoo

CHAPTER 36

THE RELATIONSHIP TRANSFORMATION... TAKING RELATIONSHIPS FROM TERMINAL TO TRANSFORMED

BY SANDY LAWSON

Was there ever a time in your life when you looked back and thought, I'd give anything for a do over? When I looked back on the absolute worst time in my life, I pondered that very question and came to the conclusion that I wouldn't trade the life lessons I learned during that dark time for anything.

My wonderful husband, Kip and I have been married for over 45 years. We have 3 amazing grown kids, and 8 fabulous grandkids. Today, we are best friends, and more in love than ever. We get to serve together as Care Pastors at one of the fastest growing churches in America, which just happens to be pastored by our oldest son.

It wasn't always that way…

Our marriage in every rational sense was doomed from the start. After a whirlwind romance of three months, we ran away and got married in Mexico when I was 17 and he was 18. The fact that everyone said we'd never make it was often the only glue that held us together. Our life was a roller coaster ride at best, until we became Christians when our first-born son was about 5. The next few years seemed stable to the untrained eye, but under the surface issues that had never been resolved simmered at a slow boil.

About the time our oldest faced the challenge of middle school, what had been simmering below the surface erupted, and my husband and I went through three years of pure hell dragging our poor kids in tow. Counselors told us that they had never seen a marriage in worse condition in their 25 years of counseling experience. They told us it was hopeless. Divorce seemed the only sane option, and so my husband filed. Throughout the whole ordeal, we were only a signature away from a final decree, neither of us quite got around to signing on the dotted line.

I came to my senses first, and began the journey back to sanity. I can only describe it like waking from a bad dream, I remember thinking, "I did that?" I thought that? It was a bit surreal, but despite the trail of destruction in our life, and the fact my emotions were numbed from all the abuse, I knew in my heart that God was not done with Kip and Sandy yet. I refused to believe the naysayers, even though they were supposed to be the experts. I chose to forgive myself, and my husband for all the horrendous things we'd done to ourselves, each other, and to our poor kids during that time. I decided to make my stand, no nagging, just living a changed life. It took a year, but my husband decided the right thing to do was to come home.

Let me make it clear, we both felt little for each other, but realized forgiveness was a choice not a feeling. The first thing we did was call a family meeting and ask our kids forgiveness for all we'd put them through. We vowed that we were committed to building our family and there was no turning back.

That was over 30 years ago and we could not be happier about the pivotal decisions we made at that time. Would I want to relive those three years, absolutely not, but the person I've become on the other side of the pain makes it worth the struggle. It's my hope that our story will help others to change their story as well.

In our 21st century global society, I believe we tend to overcomplicate things. We can take the simple and make it complex. Perhaps it makes us feel safe to hide behind convoluted mysterious rhetoric, because it does not require us to change. As for me, I've decided that life is not that complicated. It can be boiled down to some simple principles, that when applied, optimize your chances for joy, peace, and health in every relationship in your life. Here are 7 keys to transforming your relationships.

1. EVERYTHING STARTS WITH A THOUGHT

Every great invention, noble deed, personal breakthrough, and conversely every act of adultery, divorce, and all mayhem started with just one thought. When that thought was held for more than a moment, it led to another, and another, until it became an attitude that expressed itself in words and actions. Amazingly, for the average person, 80% of the thoughts they think are the same thoughts they had yesterday, and the day before, and the day before that. I think you can agree that we need to stop and think about what we are thinking about. We really do have the power to choose our thoughts.

2. OUR WORDS HAVE CREATIVE POWER

Back when man came into being, the Creator taught the created how to create. He said, "Adam, name the animals." And, whatever Adam named them, that's what they would be called. Today, our words hold the same power, what we name things is what they become.

Here's an example: a young man, we'll call him Fred, is offered an opportunity. What does Fred call it? "That's impossible, it is way too hard. I could never do that!" Another young man, we'll call him Bob, is offered the exact same opportunity. What does Bob call it? "This is the opportunity I've been looking for all my life. I must be the luckiest guy on the planet! I can do this!"

Now let's take this "Name It Principle" into our personal lives, what are you naming your relationships?

Are your kids, "Can't you ever do anything right?" "How many times do I have to tell you?" "Do you have anything between those ears?" "You'll never amount to anything." Or do you name them, "You have amazing potential." "I can't believe how bright you are!" "There's an amazing plan for your life that's better than anything you can imagine or dream."

How about your marriage, your job, your finances, what are you naming them? How about this, what do you name yourself? Be careful what you say, you are creating something. Make sure it is what you want.

3. 90/10 PRINCIPLE

In our close relationships, it's easy to focus on the 10% others do wrong instead of focusing on the 90% that they do right. Unfortunately, what you focus on tends to get bigger. I believe that a common reason people fall into the trap of focusing on the 10% deficiency is because that person is making them look bad. This is especially common in the parent child relationship. The parent feels their child's actions are a direct reflection on them.

On the flip side, think of your own life, when someone, a parent, a spouse, a boss, tends to focus on what you do wrong and never or rarely praises for what you do right, what happens? Do you feel defeated, or does it make you angry? Or worst of all, does it make you want to give up?

I'm not advocating overlooking positive correction, but I'm recommending in all your relationships you focus far more of your energy on encouraging others in what they do right. There are already enough sources telling them everything they do wrong. The really great thing is when we focus on the 90% right, the 10% usually self corrects. So make a choice to affirm what others do right daily and tell them.

4. KEEP SHORT ACCOUNTS

Be quick to forgive. Unforgiveness is a personal prison you sentence yourself to. This was one of the biggest keys to harmony and peace in our family. We called it keeping "short accounts."

Forgiveness has nothing to do with how we feel, it is a choice we make. It's not an emotional decision, it's a heart choice. Sometimes we have to make it, and make it, and make it, as many times as it takes until it sticks. Your choice will bring you the life-changing freedom that only true forgiveness can bring, if you stay consistent in making good choices in the thoughts you keep and the ones you discard.

We taught our kids that when they realized they did something unkind to one another, they needed to immediately go to the person involved and ask their forgiveness. We taught them to say, "I was wrong for

_____, will you forgive me?" And hopefully the response would come back, "I forgive you." Remember, there is creative power in our words. Important: once we forgave, we never brought it up again.

We all lived by, when you blow it, man up and own it. Ask forgiveness quickly so bitterness and unforgiveness never have the opportunity to take root. "I was wrong, **but** you . . . " just didn't get it. That was blaming not owning in our household. Any time you put a "but" in a sentence, you can forget anything that came before.

Are you in a self-imposed prison of unforgiveness? Now you have the key, use it and set yourself free.

5. PUT OTHERS FIRST

It's not all about you. In our take care of number one culture, this goes cross grain with our logic. Humans by nature tend toward self-centeredness. We can have such a fear of loss that if we aren't careful, we can get swallowed in a vortex of selfishness. Then, we lose sight of the simple fact that true joy comes from giving not from getting. When we decide to put others needs before our own, something almost magical happens, our soul feels truly fulfilled. Over the holidays we experience a microcosm of this truth as we exchange gifts, or when we hand out Christmas dinners at a homeless shelter. Giving just makes us feel great. The truth is, at the very core of our being we were designed to find our life when we give it away.

6. KEEP FIRST THINGS FIRST

The most important thing in life is knowing
the most important things in life.
~ David Jakeilo

Sometimes life controls us instead of us controlling our life. It is vital to periodically stop and take an accounting of our priorities lest we fall prey to the tyranny of the urgent. Your priorities will be determined by your value system. However, I would encourage anyone to think long and hard before they put their career at the top of their priority list. Life passes all too quickly and you know the old saying, "You never see a hearse towing a Uhaul." The "stuff" stays behind. Our real legacy remains behind in the lives of those we impacted along the way.

For me, my priorities are my faith, my marriage, my kids and grandkids, then my career. It seems when I keep things in that order, my life is really great. When my priorities shift, my life can go into a tailspin in nothing flat. When I see the very first tell tale sign that I've gotten myself out of sync, I stop and do a quick self evaluation and invariably I find that my priorities have gotten misplaced.

Keeping your priorities in order is like a pilot keeping his eye on the Altitude Indicator to make sure that the plane is flying level. Remember to do regular "Priority Checks."

7. NEVER STOP DREAMING

Children are dreamers, they see themselves doing great and noble things. "When I grow up, I'm going to be . . . a firefighter, a policeman, a nurse." Yet, as the realities of life sink in around us, it is all too easy to give up on dreaming.

Is it because dreams involve risk? I don't know, but I do know that I sit and counsel with way too many people who have quit dreaming. Without dreams we do not live, we exist. Without dreams there is no passion. Without dreams there is no vision and as it is written, "Without a vision the people perish." Don't let the comfortable and the convenient rob you of your destiny. You were created for greatness, but before greatness comes dreaming. Chose big humongous impossible dreams that challenge you. Take the risk, dare to dream again.

If you apply these seven keys faithfully to your life, I promise you'll experience personal freedom like never before, and a new level of joy, peace, and health in all your relationships.

About Sandy

Sandra (Sandy) Lawson serves as a Care Pastor at Element Church, in Wentzville Missouri, one of the fastest growing churches America. She has over 30 years of experience partnering with her husband, Kip, in family ministry and outreach.

Sandy's had the privilege of serving on staff at three mega churches prior to Element Church. In addition, she and her husband also had the honor of building the bus ministry of the Oneighty Youth Group at Church on the Move in Tulsa, Oklahoma from 400 riders weekly to nearly 1,500 riders each week.

Her biggest joy is coaching people in their personal relationships and helping them reach their God-given potential. She and her husband have helped hundreds of couples turn failing marriages into happily-ever-afters, as well as assisting parents in their quest to create healthy thriving families. In their career, Sandy and her husband have been a major influence in the lives of thousands of children, teens, and adults around the world.

Sandy is the mother of three, and the grandmother of eight wonderful grandkids. She and her husband have been married over 45 years. She was educated at Santa Rosa Junior College and Sonoma State University in California.

Sandy Lawson is the author of a parenting book, *Parenting Through the Mirror* which explores the concept that great parenting must begin with personal transformation. She is also the author and illustrator of a children's geology book, *Iggy and the Volcano* that teaches kids the cycle of igneous rocks. Sandy is a freelance writer, speaker, blogger @ scourtneylawson.com, and was a major contributor to an internationally distributed children's curriculum.

You can connect with Sandy at:
www.twitter.com/sandralawson
scourtneylawson.com
www.facebook.com/scourtneylawson

CHAPTER 37

MODERN DAY PROJECT MANAGEMENT:
WHAT YOU NEED TO KNOW
TO BE SUCCESSFUL
IN TODAY'S CHALLENGING
ENVIRONMENT

BY ANDREW CLINE

I hate project management and what it has become. It has been analyzed and dissected so much that it's on its way to becoming a commodity. It seems that everyone wants to dive into the nitty-gritty, and if you subscribe to any of the PM groups that have discussions, most of the chatter is about what is the single biggest risk your project faces, or what certification is better to have, or what is the one sign that a project is failing.

It is a shame that a skill set that has been the cornerstone of productive society since the Greeks and Romans is being reduced to quick 140 character blurbs that seemingly can save your failing project. There is so much more to project management success. The current day conversations are like discussing exercise without mentioning diet. It is tough to build a better body while eating Pop Tarts and drinking diet cola.

So, why the defense of a topic that I rarely talk about to people outside of work? Because I would not have achieved the success I have had in both my professional and personal life if it were not for project management.

I used to joke that when I was managing a project, there was part science and part art involved. The ratios changed based upon what the circumstances called for, but the two parts where always involved. After all, the goal of project management is to deliver a "successful" outcome, on-time and on-budget, right?

But what I realize now is that project management was one component of a three-part success formula that every successful project manager I have known utilizes. The other two components that worked with **project management** were **relationship management** and **subject matter** expertise. Each of these three components plays a key role. No one is more important that the other, and they rely heavily on each other to deliver successful outcomes. The best project plan with linked dependencies, validated with a Monte Carlo Analysis, supported by a robust resource management plan won't deliver success if the stockholders are not engaged to the right level, or if you have no idea how to identify and mitigate the major risks if you cannot understand what the project team members are saying to you.

PROJECT MANAGEMENT

There are five major things that successful project managers focus on. There are dozens of smaller items that you need to pay attention to, but the most successful project managers focus on Timing, Budget, Resources, Communication, and Process.

The first three items, timing, budget, and resources should be straightforward. If you wonder why a project manager needs to be concerned about the project timeline, how much money has been spent, how much is committed, and how much is left or who is doing the work, and who is needed to complete the outstanding work, then I would not go any further in this article. Please find a basic project management guide and start at chapter one.

- **Communication:** I once found myself in charge of the technical team tasked with saving a $1.3 billion, 10-year project. The prime contractor was fired after three years of negative progress. The first thing I did every morning for the first four months was participate on a call with the other team leads and key stakeholders for 30 minutes. The agenda was simple and clear: What did you accomplish yesterday, what are you accomplishing today, and what do you need help with? This simple communication process helped set the team up for success in the roughest part of the project. I took that lesson and applied it within my own team, and I have used it many times, especially when dealing with difficult decisions. How predictable and capable are the communication methods you have in place? Can you get to the information you need when you need it? Is there a lot of wasted effort gathering and compiling information that no one will review? Begin with the end in mind. Determine what information you need to be an effective leader and then design the process to get that information as easily and consistently as you need it.

- **Process:** When I worked for Deloitte and Oracle Consulting, the one item that was repeated most often was that following the established project delivery process would lead to project success. I have carried that with me throughout my career. When I am managing a large multi-million-dollar project I know that I need to establish and maintain key processes for information to flow and for the work to be done at a high level of quality. I know that a repeatable process leads to a predictable outcome. I would have regular meetings—weekly/monthly/quarterly—that were arranged so that information could be rolled up and then back out in a logical fashion, so the work and decision-making could continue unabated. Other key processes established include those related to to requirements, testing, risk mitigation, and resource management. Successful project management peers of mine also have a set of key processes that work for them and can be applied to a variety of projects with minimal adjustments.

RELATIONSHIP MANAGEMENT

Relationship management is a term that encompasses a lot of territory. For brevity's sake I will define it as how you deal with other people, and how you let them deal with you. I have identified five keys to better relationship management that are exhibited by successful project managers. The five are Diplomacy, Accountability, Engagement, Consistency, and Motivation.

- **Diplomacy:** You need to seek out the win-win around 80 percent of the time. There are times that call for unpopular decisions, but you cannot rule like a dictator and be successful in the long term. Additionally, you need to learn how to manage up as well as down. This includes learning how to share information so that there are no surprises, and so you can avoid the catastrophic scenario of over-promising and under-delivering.

- **Accountability:** This is a two-way street where you must practice what you preach. In order for team members to be held accountable, you need to set the example and hold yourself accountable to at least the same standard if not a higher one. If you need people to work full weeks to hit project milestones, don't run out the door every Friday afternoon at 3 PM to avoid the traffic.

- **Engagement:** It is key to actively seek out and nurture engagement at all levels of individuals involved in your projects, from the executive level, to the front line worker. Engagement breeds trust, information sharing, and lasting relationships. Motivation is a key component of engagement, especially on long-term projects. You need to be sure to celebrate milestones and remind people that what they are working on will have a major impact on the project and the organization as a whole.

- **Consistency:** I once had a manager that was the typical Dr. Jekyll and Mrs. Hyde. When you brought an issue to her attention, you never knew if you would be prized for being proactive or chastised for obviously missing the warning signs. It made everyone around very uneasy and it became a huge barrier to the free flow of information. Be measured and consistent in how you deal with people, information, and situations. People will appreciate knowing what they are walking into and this will result in the better exchange of information.

- **Motivation:** When you make people feel valuable and appreciated, they give you their best. Not when you send them 15 emails on Monday morning before lunch telling them to get their status reports in and update their timeline estimates. You need to seek to build relationships that last. My trick for this is to try to remember everyone has a sign above their head that reads "make me feel special." This will not happen every day or every week. But listen to people, look at them in the eyes when you talk to them, and recognize a job well done. You will be amazed at how much this makes a difference.

SUBJECT MATTER EXPERTISE

Subject matter expertise is knowing enough about the topic involved in the project/discussion to be able to do three things well. First you need to be able to ask intelligent questions to satisfy yourself that what you are being told is accurate and complete. Second, you need to know enough to call bullshit when someone is trying to snow you over. Finally, you need to know enough to make decisions and be right about 80 percent of the time. A leader leads, and usually this means making a decision. If you are not the ultimate authority, then you need to know enough to decide what and how you will present the options and which one you endorse.

How do you gain subject matter expertise? The same way you eat an elephant, one bite at a time. Deconstruct the larger set of material into smaller portions and repeat again if necessary. Then you need to determine what the 80-20 allocation of material is and focus. That is to say, what is the 20 percent of the information that will allow you to understand 80 percent of what goes on. I know there are always the one-off, contingency items that occur once every 10 years, but when you are learning something new, focus on the main components first.

To me the best way to get a sense of how a process works is to see it/ do it—observe it. I learned the flow of materials in an electronics and appliance repair depot by following repair technicians around for a couple of days; watching them strip out the components of big screen TV's and cleaning out bird nests from dryer vents. I saw how they did their paperwork, where the spare parts came from, and how much they could accomplish in one day.

My mind works in a linear, logical method. I have found it helpful to create process flow charts for the main activities you need to learn.

Additionally, you can find a guide that will coach and advise you when you are getting going. Find the person that has been there, done that, and has the T-shirt to prove it. They will save you a dozen times in your initial time on the project. Seek their counsel on an ongoing basis to ensure you remain on the right track. This is especially true when they are not involved in the day to day of the project. They will have an easier time seeing the forest for the trees.

I was involved in a project for a small city in the Midwest and was assigned to the water and sewer department as part of my responsibility. My interactions with public water and sewer departments at that time was limited to paying my water bills. When I showed up, I was quickly told that I was the third consultant that was assigned to help them; the other two had failed or left, and they did not want to invest the time to train me. So they loaded me up with SOP's and wished me luck in discovering how they worked. Without really having anywhere else to turn for info I fell back on my skills of deconstructing, developing processes and observing. Within a week I had learned enough to ask intelligent questions that neither of my predecessors had asked. I was able to win over my three main contacts at the department and we were able to successfully implement the new system ahead of schedule due to their desire to work with me. We worked so well together that when I left I received a retired, but freshly painted fire hydrant as a reminder of how well we worked together. I still have the hydrant. It is the heaviest trophy I have ever been given.

Finally, ask stakeholders and key participants what success looks like? Where should the project be at the end? As you ask an increasing number of involved people, you will start to see overlap in the answers. You could develop a Venn diagram to see the overlap, but I am hoping that you are astute enough to see the commonality in the responses and the know-how to weigh an executive's answer more than a random interaction in the lunchroom.

This three-part formula has worked for me over and over during my rise from IT project manager in a Fortune 500 company to becoming the Chief Information Officer for a $9 billion enterprise with a project portfolio of $500 million. Your success will not happen overnight. My climb took 12 years. But this is not academic theory; success happens to other project managers as soon as they implement the formula and grow their skill sets. These three components give you the power to be successful. The question is, will you take the next step to becoming a more successful project manager take action?

About Andrew

As a certified information geek, Andrew Cline finds fulfillment in each new task he is presented...finding great gratification in the intense process of becoming engrossed in knowledge. He has essentially evolved into a human compass in his coaching work at The CIO Coach, guiding his clients into new and exciting business territory. But his supportive talents also aptly compliment these trailblazer qualities, because Andrew is a self-described confidant and insightful companion for those who need help discovering their voice.

Andrew's goals are to not only help others achieve at work, but he also ventures to help others overcome personal issues they may be facing—lending anyone who needs a helping hand the opportunity to work through whatever issues that may be ailing him or her. This problem-solving attitude has assisted his teams in several instances overcome obstacles and work together as a like-minded and undistracted group. He is an all-around team player with the greater goals in mind.

Furthermore, his ability to logically connect points of confusion and translate them into new and thoughtfully-cultivated solutions makes him the best at what he does. And his organizational techniques allow him to build lasting relationships based on trust and delivery...leading to nearly all of his customers seeking his assistance in additional work endeavors. Andrew has never done the same job twice. And he adapts to each new situation with enthusiasm and interest—allowing the results to speak for themselves—refusing to get hung up on the application of fixed methodologies. He brings value to every business growth effort, and his visionary attitude places him in a invaluable position.

And when Andrew isn't being the superhero for his clients, he can be found lending his volunteer spirit to raising money for those in need and at-risk individuals—which provides quick responses to those who need support while assisting them in finding long-term help through existing social services.

He hopes to always leave things better than he found them.

More information about Andrew can be found at: www.rouguemgt.com.

CHAPTER 38

CONTINUOUS TRANSFORMATION: A LIFELONG PROCESS

BY WES JACKSON

I was born into a loving family, being the third of four children. My father worked outside the home while my mother was a "stay-at-home mom." Unfortunately, our happy home was disrupted when I was just five years old with my father diagnosed as being terminally ill. He died slowly over the next seven years and his slow death devastated me and my family emotionally, and drained us financially.

As my father was dying, during his last days, I lived with my grandparents. They lived simple, yet very consistent lives. Often my grandmother would gently tap my face and say "Wes, stay sweet for Jesus, don't let this world make you hard." She would also say "God loves you and he has big plans for you." These words went a long way to build my self-worth, heal my hurt, relieve my pain and bring hope to a preteen who was experiencing life as it shouldn't be. People in your life that provide you hope and encouragement are a true gift!

Grandmother also showed me the power of being positive. It seemed she could always make something out of next to nothing and this gift made her a positive person. She expected things to work out and they did. She believed there was always a way and there was.

347

My grandfather and grandmother also imparted to me the concept of giving and encouraging. Ministering to others by giving and encouraging was their call, their duty, and their lifestyle. As I watched their selfless love for others, I got hooked.

Even as a small boy, giving was a part of me. I collected bottles and cans to recycle for money. Much of the time I would use the money to buy little glass figurines at the Ben Franklin store for my mother. I wanted to make her life a little more bearable as my father was dying. But, I did always try to keep at least a little for myself to buy candy.

Over the years I found that giving has chipped away at my hurt, pain and negativity, cultivated seeds of hope and made me feel better about myself. Little did I realize that by making a willful choice to perform this positive action, healing and a positive attitude would be the result. I also learned through giving, that I could be a victor instead of a victim.

After my father died, my mother remarried a nice man – at least when he was sober. You see, my step-father was an alcoholic and that made things go from bad to worse. The moral upbringing I once knew didn't seem to matter, and as a result, doubts, fears and insecurities grew within me.

At 15 years of age, I knew I needed to leave home. Moving out of state to live with other family gave me respite and the opportunity for me to work on me. This was the start of my personal transformation. I was able to find comfort and new direction. From this experience I learned where you live, what you do and who you hang around with dramatically affects where you go and where you end up.

As I entered adulthood, I was attracted to the financial services industry by an ad in the newspaper that indicated I could make a lot of money by helping people with their finances. And, there was no limit to the amount of money I could earn! I knew how to work hard and I thrived on helping others. This was a natural fit!

At the time, I had a good paying job and was up for a promotion with the possibility of even obtaining a company car. The majority of those around me told me not to leave this security, but I'm glad I didn't listen to them. I refused to allow these people to crush my dreams. I took the risk. Interestingly, as time has passed, these same people have either worked for me or borrowed money from me. I learned from this experience not to let others negatively influence my high ideals or my dreams. I will listen to them, respect them, love them, but I will not compromise that which I believe to be my destiny.

With high ideals and big dreams, I studied to pass my insurance and investment licenses. Even though I passed, I still didn't know what to do or how to do it. I needed good mentors. I have found that positive mentorship is a priceless gift that people of all walks of life vitally need. A true mentor is someone who can meet you where you are, teach you what you need to know and take you where you want to go. I've heard it said that experience is a good teacher. However, I quickly discovered a better teacher is learning as much as possible from the experiences of others. I found that if you get all the help you can get from others that are doing what you want to do, you avoid their mistakes and enhance the chances of your achievement!

Zig Ziglar, now a mentor of mine, gave me two guiding principles that have influenced me greatly over the years. First, he emphasized positive self-talk. Secondly, he said that you can have everything you want in life if you just help enough people get what they want in life. I remember how these thoughts inspired me, gave me hope and resonated in my heart. To this day, I practice these principles on a daily basis. It's a great thing when we can plant seeds of hope in others by sharing positive words of encouragement.

As a young financial services professional, I was extremely hungry to learn. I went through sales training and product training and my district manager made me enroll in the Life Underwriter Training Council. This preparation gave me the foundational knowledge I needed. I eventually joined NALU, now the National Association of Insurance and Financial Advisors (NAIFA). This gave me access to the experienced professionals in my area that I wished to be like and they became mentors and examples for me to follow. These great professionals kept me focused, encouraged me and held me accountable.

Drawing from my years with my grandparents, and my respect and appreciation for their age group, I was moved to specialize in working with seniors and pre-retirees. Amazing things began to happen because many of them wanted to meet during the day (which I liked), they were concerned about financial planning, they often had money and needed my help.

Interestingly, the tragedy from my past that sent me to my grandparents actually prepared me for my future. I had familiarity and a connection with this generation that may not have happened any other way. This and many other experiences have taught me to look for opportunity in the obstacles that come my way both personally and in business. It takes courage and optimism to do this and to face adversity head on. I believe courage is the ability to push aside fear in order to do what is right – regardless if it is uncomfortable or risky.

Adversity gives us the opportunity to practice seemingly irrational tenacity and focus on what makes winning possible. I know my tenacity and focus has been instrumental in greatly increasing the odds of my success. Frankly, without it my success would not have been possible. Many times I have used the negatives that others have aimed at me as fuel that has energized me in my quest for my goal. In fact, their comments have often helped me reach my goals.

I purposefully surrounded myself with people who were like what I wanted to be and I often had to ask them for help. I have discovered that the process of asking for help actually opens you up as well as others around you, enabling the natural goodness in people to come out, and allows them to fulfill their desire to help. Before the availability of a GPS, I often had to stop and ask for directions. Inevitably, two or three people would stand around me wanting to help! People I did not even know, using their valuable time, stopped to help me with no strings attached. I find that most people like being asked to help.

As I mentioned previously, early in my career, I found my niche in helping retirees and pre-retirees. I also discovered that you can't help people if you are not familiar with what is important to them. So, I purposed to become an expert on the needs of retirees. This positioned me for my next opportunity. A local national insurance brokerage firm wanted me to help them develop their retiree and pre-retiree market. So, I went for it. Within a couple of years I was able to develop, build and lead this new department in becoming a strong and prominent national market leader.

The formula "focus + boundaries + direction = desired results" became my guiding principle. I had to stay focused and maintain boundaries which kept me from diversions while I kept moving in one direction. I found my niche based on my interest, knowledge, strength, integrity and personal commitment. This proved to give me crazy success!

What did this success look like? I started getting contacted by financial service trade publications for interviews. I began winning trips all around the world. I was making considerably more money than ever before. In time, I was asked by home offices of insurance companies to help develop and market new products to those in the niche I defined for myself years before.

In business, you have to find ways to stay fresh and informed within the industry and to continue to excel in your niche. I found one of the best ways to learn the business was to teach it. Taking my understanding of my specialty, I wrote a training manual on senior market issues. I became an approved continuing education instructor, teaching insurance agents and providing continuing education credits.

Using my personal experience, today I am working with organizations to define their niche and empower them to develop their market and possess it. As their vision comes into focus and is defined, a wonderful thing happens. They find freedom to dream again because they are freed from distractions. When you have a clear vision, you are able to make your best decisions personally or corporately, because you will know what will be best for you or your business based on your vision.

In 1993, I had the opportunity to start working with financial institutions. As I started working with advisors, licensed branch employees and program managers sharing financial planning principles, they began to teach me how things work within a financial institution. It has been interesting to observe the principle of reciprocity at work in business. As I have given to my clients I have always received more than I have given.

These people have given birth to my new-favorite niche – working with financial institutions. Interestingly, the story of many financial institutions mirrors my personal story. Out of the struggle of the Great Depression many strong institutions arose.

Recently, I have become a certified Zig Ziglar trainer and speaker, in order to provide hope and encouragement to the organizations with which we work. We are helping reinvigorate their organizations with a needs-based culture, empowering them to reach their potential. My strong business relationships in my defined niche have made it possible for me to discover what is important to my clients and to uncover their unspoken needs. They, like most organizations and most people, lose their passion and need to be reminded of their greatness. These institutions need to hear again and again what makes them great and how they achieved the success they enjoy.

After I earn my clients trust and they earn mine, I like to ask my financial institution clients:

- How do you plan on positioning your financial institution for the future?
- What enhanced services do you plan to provide that truly add value to your clients?
- What niche will you focus on to become more relevant in your communities?

These are the questions senior management wrestles with continually. I know helping my clients contemplate where they want to be would be useless if it weren't for the gift life has given me to help and encourage them to make their vision a reality. When you finally commit to a worthy goal, you will get a vision. One of the best ways to commit to a vision is to begin with the end in mind and establish objectives that will help you reach your anticipated destination. Once your vision, along with your objectives and desired outcome, is in place, it becomes a valuable tool to guide and direct your focus.

I have been told by counselors that I had a substantially high risk of becoming a dysfunctional alcoholic because of the abuse I experienced as a child. I am certain I could be stuck in an emotional prison today with a victim mentality. Fortunately, these potential atrocities have been avoided because of the goodness of others in my life giving me hope and encouragement. They have empowered me to give. Receiving help at every level in life and business equips you with the confidence and personal passion to give to others! Tragically, some will not ask for help or accept any help and they are doomed to be less than what they conceive because we all need the help of others. I have found when you develop a healthy habit of giving, you expand your capacity to receive all the goodness that life has to offer – enabling you to truly enjoy your career and life.

From birth to now, I have been in the process of continuous transformation. I would like to summarize the specific principles of transformation woven throughout the content of this chapter that have influenced me that I hope will also be beneficial to you:

- Be A Giver
- Provide Hope And Encouragement To Others
- Practice Positive Self Talk
- Help Others Get What They Want In Life
- Don't Allow Others To Crush Your Dreams
- Always Look For Opportunities In Obstacles
- Don't Be Afraid To Ask For Help
- Find Your Niche
- Develop A Vision

Receive this message of hope from me and be encouraged. The negatives of life have hidden treasure and opportunity. Find them and take advantage of them. As you receive, give. I am giving because I have been given. I am a receiver who is continuing to grow and to be transformed. As my mentor Zig Ziglar would say…"And I will see you over the top!"

About Wes

Wes Jackson helps to empower financial institutions by assisting them in identifying, developing and implementing new strategies within their organizations to truly meet the needs and make a difference in the lives of their co-workers and clients.

Wes draws on his experience of working with financial institutions for more than 20 years, sharing time-tested systems, coaching and consulting to empower financial institutions to experience new levels of success.

Wes is passionate about helping financial institutions refine their vision, connecting that vision with the personal goals of their co-workers. This connection inevitably births new passion within their organizations. It is this passion that taps and expands any organization's capacity for new, sustainable levels of growth.

Wes entered the financial planning business as an advisor in direct sales in 1987. Within a couple years, he was asked to start a senior benefits division for a national brokerage firm. He led this newly-developed department into becoming a prominent market leader.

Wes Jackson has had the privilege of being the guest speaker for many national and regional groups regarding financial issues. He serves on various professional industry boards and insurance company advisory committees. Wes has written and developed various curricula for sales and continuing education classes, successfully teaching industry Best Practices since 1993.

His mentor Zig Ziglar taught him: *You can have everything you want in life by just helping enough other people get what they want.*

Wes is a certified trainer for Zig Ziglar's Legacy training curriculum of Ziglar, Inc.

You can connect with Wes at:
www.facebook.com/CoachingOnPurpose
www.WesJackson.net
www.coachingonpurpose.biz

CHAPTER 39

NEMESIS CONQUERED, GOAL ACCOMPLISHED AND TRANSFORMATION IN PROGRESS!

BY TONY SIDIO

I am going places I have never been.
Places that I have only dreamed about!
~ Tony Sidio

Your life can and should be an adventure! If not, begin the **Transformation** of your life as I have.

On January 27, 2013, I finally acknowledged the little voice that had been prompting me for several years to make major changes in my life. It was time to decide what I really wanted to do, have and be. It was time to **Transform** my life. For more than 19 years, I have earned my living in Information Technology—initially as an employee, then as a business owner.

Transformation is a process, not a destination. Why should you invest the time and effort into Transforming your life? If you want more than you have now, you must become more. You become more through Transformation.

Here are 3 recent scenes from my ongoing Transformation that may help you understand what can be accomplished. Later, I will tell you how I accomplished this so you can Transform your life, too.

Scene 1
I am at the Hard Rock Cafe in New York City. I just rode the Shuttle (Subway) from Grand Central Station to Times Square, in my Tuxedo. It is a rainy Friday afternoon and I knew that getting a cab would be a challenge. So, my best friend, Ken, and I opted for the Shuttle. Armed with red umbrellas borrowed from The Grand Hyatt, we quickly and easily made our way from the subway station to The Hard Rock Cafe. Soon, my name will be called to receive an award on stage followed by a Red Carpet Interview.

Scene 2
I am at the historic Roosevelt Hotel in Hollywood, California. We have been in great seminars for two days, and it is now time for a quick change into my tux. I then make my way to the very room that hosted the first Academy Awards. Soon, I will have dinner with many great new friends. My name will be called to receive an award on stage followed by a Red Carpet Interview. Do you see a pattern developing here?

Scene 3
It is January 8, 2014 as I cruise north along the beautiful California Coast between San Diego and LA on Amtrak's Pacific Surfliner. As I settle in for the ride, the announcer says "It is 80 degrees in LA" and several things occur to me.

I have been on an especially beautiful ride for the past 9 months. I co-authored a Best-Selling hardcover book, *Against the Grain* with the legendary Brian Tracy. It launched on Amazon.com on September 5, 2013. It was an immediate best-seller in 5 categories. I earned the right to permanently precede my name with: "Best-Selling Author" Tony Sidio. It gets better...

I received The Quilly® Award from the National Academy of Best-Selling Authors® in Hollywood. Think "Oscar." Think "Emmy." Think "Grammy" for Best-Selling Authors. The Quilly® is a 14-inch commemorative gold statue that has been crafted by the same artisans who sculpt the Oscars and Emmy Awards. Quilly® in hand, I immediately proceeded to my Red Carpet Video Interview. This Black Tie affair included a Party and an After Party.

I met Jack Canfield, Best-Selling Author of *Chicken Soup for the Soul* renown, *The Success Principles* and many others. I had inadvertently left my sport coat in my cousin's car and I was embarrassed to be at the photo shoot without it. As I briefly relayed the story to Jack, he looked at me, smiled and said, "You look great just as you are." He is a class act!

There were about 150 Best-Selling Authors in attendance, and I am amazed at the quality, character and depth of those authors. Many of them are now new friends all over the world.

I received a Writer's Expy® Award at the National Association of Experts, Writers and Speakers™ First Annual Expy® Awards in New York City on April 4, 2014. The Expy® Awards were founded to honor experts around the world for their contribution to education, enlightenment and the advancement of business and life. The Writer's Expy®, like The Quilly®, is handmade by the same artisans who make the Oscars. Brian Tracy was inducted into the Speakers Hall of Fame at this Black Tie Golden Gala. Of course, we had our Red Carpet interviews, too!

Have you ever had lunch with a Rockstar? I did. I had a great lunch in NYC with Steve McCarty and his lovely wife, Trish. Steve is a legendary recording artist/singer/songwriter/guitararist who co-wrote "Fly Like an Eagle" with Steve Miller. Trish is CEO and founder of Starshine Academy in Phoenix, Arizona. Starshine Academy is a special school for Barrio kids, which has grown into a community where the parents and even grandparents can live, too. (Trish has also written Chapter 68 in this book!)

Many of my Best-Selling Author friends from Hollywood were also at the EXPYs, as well as many new friends from around the globe.

Now, I don't know about you, but, as you can see above, I am having a fantastic time traveling around the country, meeting great people who are changing the world. My transformed life may not be the life you would choose for yourself. However, I believe that you can transform your life into whatever it is that you would really enjoy doing, just as I have. What would your transformed life look like?

If you want something you've never had, you must
be willing to do something you've never done.
~ Thomas Jefferson

Do not misunderstand. I love technology. I love my clients and fellow Chamber Members. I have been very involved in my local Chamber of Commerce (my story begins on page 377, *Against the Grain*, my Best-Selling Book with Brian Tracy). My life has been rewarding and fun, but the little voice inside me kept demanding more. "You have served the business community here well for many years. You helped implement the changes you believed needed to be made. Now trust that others will keep things moving in the proper direction. You must seek new challenges, new opportunities to serve. It is time to do more and be more. It is time to take inspired action and become what you were always meant to be. To make a bigger impact and help more people, you need to perform on a national stage."

You should also know that I have maintained a secret identity for many years. I am well known as an IT company business owner. However, since my college days, I have studied, practiced and taught personal development. I have also been on a personal quest to learn how to break through the barriers that keep many people stuck and prevent them from achieving their goals. I have learned many ways to help people get unstuck (break through their barriers to success) through traditional coaching techniques and the latest in neuroscience. I have used this knowledge to Transform my life. I can help you transform your life too.

So on January 27, 2013, I committed to becoming a Best-Selling Author, Professional Speaker and Coach. I had no idea how I would become a Best-Selling Author, but I was committed to do it in 2013.

One of the things I learned many years ago is that nothing happens with a goal until you make a commitment. You must write down the goal, be very clear and specific about what you want to accomplish. Establish a definite time limit to accomplish it. Then you must commit to accomplish the goal.

Are you committed or are you interested? One of my friends and mentors, John Assaraf, two times a New York Times Best-Selling Author, asks that question. The difference he explains is, if you are interested, you will only do what is convenient in working toward that goal. If you are committed, you will do whatever it takes. When you are committed to an outcome, there will be no excuses, no stories, and no reasons not to accomplish it. You will achieve your goal!

What happens next? Frequently, all hell breaks loose. Yes, every possible thing that can happen to delay or derail you working toward your goal happens. Another mentor, Tony Robbins, describes it as "your nemesis shows up" like in a novel. You are the hero; your nemesis is the villain who stands in your way at every turn. He is usually a very powerful nemesis, not some weakling you can handily defeat. The bigger the goal, the bigger your nemesis. Yes, you will have to work smart and hard to defeat him and accomplish your goal! What you may not realize, and probably will not appreciate in the heat of the battle, is that your nemesis is necessary. He makes you stronger. He makes you earn that goal. He makes the adventure more challenging, yes, but also more interesting!

The other thing that happens simultaneously, and you had better be paying close attention, is that while you are frantically battling your nemesis, everything you need to accomplish your goal begins to show up. The people you need, the resources you need, the money you need, everything you need starts showing up. Bob Proctor from *The Secret* might say that you are attracting all of this to you through the "Law of Attraction." Tony Robins might say that all of these things have been there all along, but you did not notice them before you set your goal. Once you focus your thoughts, you activate your "Reticular Activating System." Your "Reticular Activating System" (RAS) directs your attention to specific tools, resources, people etc. that will help you accomplish your goal.

Law of Attraction? RAS? How it works may not be as important as the fact that it does work! Just be sure to pay close attention, because the resources you need may appear in unusual or innovative ways. If you can step back, and briefly look at your situation objectively, from a distance, in the heat of the battle, you may learn to appreciate and even enjoy the whole process of accomplishing your big goal! I have.

March 19, 2013, was one of the best days of my life and also one of the most difficult days. It was difficult because that morning we had to say our final goodbyes to our beautiful Bijou. She was 12 years old, half Boxer and half Coon Hound. She never knew that she was a dog.

She thought she was a princess, and we let her believe that. In fact, we encouraged it. She had not been able to eat for 5 days, and the vet said her time with us was up. I still get tears in my eyes when I think of her. We miss you very much, Bijou!

That afternoon I signed a deal with my new agency to co-author a hardcover book, *Against the Grain,* with the legendary Brian Tracy and other leading experts. The book launched on September 5, 2013, and was an immediate Best-Seller in 5 Categories. **Nemesis Conquered, Goal Accomplished & Transformation In Progress!**

Earlier I mentioned neuroscience, which is the study of the nervous system. I follow neuroscientific research that focuses on understanding the human brain and how it regulates the body and behavior. Neuroscience is teaching us better, faster ways to train our brains and break through our barriers.

It is only through the study of neuroscience and the contacts and relationships I developed that I finally found effective ways to help people change their internal self-image. Why is that important? Our self-image is a primary reason that we all get stuck. For example, the only way to double, triple or ten times your income is to change your self-image.

I combine time-tested coaching with neuroscience in my **Transformational Coaching**. I currently help business owners, high-performing entrepreneurs, executives, leaders, professionals and sales professionals double, triple or even ten times their business revenues while reducing the number of hours they work. I also help individuals who are stuck at certain levels, get unstuck, double or triple their income and reimagine their lives.

Tony's website is: www.tonysidio.com
His email is: tony@tonysidio.com

About Tony

Tony is a Best-Selling Author, Speaker and Transformational Coach. He is excited to co-author this second book with the legendary Brian Tracy. Here, Tony tells his story of "Transformation" from IT Consulting Business Owner to Best-Selling Author. He gives the reader a glimpse into his "Transformed" life and explains how he accomplished it. He believes that everyone, with help, has the capability to "Transform" their lives as well.

Tony grew up an "Army Brat." He lived in Japan and France as well as eight states in the U.S.A. The lessons he learned traveling the world and constantly meeting new people have proven invaluable to him. He developed a passion for people.

In the fourth grade, Tony was introduced to science fiction and technology when he read Robert A. Heinlein's *The Star Beast*. He went on to read virtually every book Heinlein wrote, and, of course, many other authors as well. He developed a passion for technology.

He was an avid athlete and graduated in the top ten in his high school class. He attended Purdue University where he majored in science, psychology and math.

He was introduced to the concept of personal growth while working part time in college. Earl Nightingale's *Lead the Field* audio series taught Tony valuable lessons which helped him become one of the Top 10 College Dealers in the U.S. for Wear Ever Aluminum, Inc. He was hooked. He developed a lifelong passion for personal growth and development.

Tony has worked for Fortune 500 companies, medium-sized companies, and small companies, He is a serial entrepreneur. He has succeeded in multiple industries including direct sales and marketing, radio and television, and information technology. He has worked in New York City, Chicago, Philadelphia, Indianapolis, Fort Wayne and other cities.

Tony combines time-tested coaching with neuroscience in his Transformational Coaching. He helps business owners, high-performing entrepreneurs, executives, leaders, professionals and sales professionals double, triple or even ten times their business revenues while reducing the number of hours they work. He also helps individuals who are stuck at certain levels, get unstuck, double or triple their income and reimagine their lives.

Tony is fulfilling his passion for helping people become all that they were meant to be.

Tony and his family live in the Chicago area.

You can reach him at: tony@tonysidio.com
Visit his website: www.tonysidio.com

CHAPTER 40

BE YOUR OWN DOG

BY LINDA WORRELL

When our daughter was young and struggling with the typical "growing up" angst, her father would advise her to "be your own dog." He told her not to live her life as others would have her live it, but to determine what she wanted and why. He told her not to believe what others believed but to be true to what she thought and felt. He told her not to worry about what others thought of her, and that it was a blessing not to have to please other people.

He was a Renaissance man before that idea was mainstream. He did not believe in the traditional ways of living and working. He did not define success as others in our social group did. Neither did he care. He did not want important titles, fancy cars and expensive clothes. He was happy being alone and communing with nature. Although he was a numbers man by trade, he was a poet and musician in his heart. The advice he gave our daughter was spot on—I only wish that I had followed that advice also. I would have saved myself a lot of time and disappointment.

He always encouraged us not to settle for what other people expected of us but to spread our wings and fly listening only to that voice inside. That is a hard thing to do. It is human nature for the people we love and trust to share their ideas on how to live a successful life. However, more often than not, they define success differently than we do. But to challenge "group think" takes courage. It also requires that we really know what we want and why. For one to live a bit differently, to want more or different opportunities requires a willingness to walk alone at least part of the time. It requires a commitment to be all that one can be on one's own timetable and for reasons that are important only to the one involved. Living like that takes a commitment of time and energy and a willingness to do the work to stay on track to what is true for oneself.

When I was a younger woman, I spent far more time planning a two-week vacation to California and Hawaii than I spent planning my life! I was not willing to take the time and to do the work to determine what I wanted my life to stand for and why. I set goals and I made plans, but I did not prepare a life map or a life plan so that at the end of my life I would be reaching a certain destination. Apparently, I was going nowhere!

Without developing and following a plan, life tends to take you first in one direction and then in another. Pretty soon, you feel a bit like a lightly tethered boat riding on the movement of the tides. Like the boat, you are only going to move so far in any one direction, but the constant movement does tend to take one off course. The next new idea, the next great opportunity or the next "have to" that someone proclaims uses up your valuable energy and time.

Constantly shifting focus and direction is not sustainable over the long term without creating stress and other negative emotions. It ultimately does damage to one's self-confidence. We can maintain someone else's idea of what is good, what is right and what is successful for only so long. Ultimately, one begins to feel out of sorts, a bit depressed or just plain blue for no apparent reason.

Fortunately, when we act in ways that are inconsistent with what we want and need, our body and mind provide us the insight that we need to get back into alignment.

I found that to be true in my life. Here is an example. I would accept a job or a responsibility that did not support my mission in life. Even though I was not yet clear on the terms of my mission, I knew that the job or project I had just committed to did not feel all that great. But because I was not truly listening to the warning signals, I would try to reframe it so that it would fit but inevitably there was always a disconnect. I would try to sell myself on the advantages of taking on the project but it still didn't feel good. I would start to get discouraged, upset and dissatisfied.

I did not have the joy, the energy or the passion that I had when I was doing something that really was consistent with my purpose in life. So in effect, I had helped move someone else forward, and my own soul received little or nothing in return.

WHY ARE YOU HERE?

To live the kind of life we were meant to live, we need to figure out why we are here and what we are supposed to do. Have you ever asked yourself those questions? Have you ever wondered what your talents and gifts are?

I would venture to say that most of us have asked ourselves those questions and that many of us are struggling with some of them right now. It has nothing to do with education, race, age or intelligence. It has to do with awareness and focus—awareness of who we are and what we want, and the ability to focus on achieving it.

We are born knowing exactly what we want and what we don't want. We know when we are hungry and want food, when we are sleepy and want rest and when we are frightened and want to be held and loved. Pretty straightforward, isn't it? However, we soon learn we are not necessarily going to get what we want, and sometimes we will get what we do *not* want. We learn quickly which battles to fight and which not to fight. We also learn to keep some of our thoughts to ourselves and are taught to listen to our elders because they have more experience and know more than we do.

There is some truth to that, but really nobody knows us as well as we know ourselves, even when we are struggling to figure out who we are. Fortunately, we have an internal positioning system, an IPS, very similar to a GPS in an automobile, and when we get off track our IPS alerts us. If we are overwhelmed or moving too quickly without thinking or feeling, we may not automatically pick up on the message, but ultimately we figure it out. Sometimes it takes a major crisis to stop us in our tracks, but we usually realize something is not quite right. We are not as successful at work, we are constantly at odds with the people in our life or we are always worried about making the car payment or the mortgage on time. Those are some of the alerts that we receive telling us it is time to reposition and make some different choices.

DO YOUR CHOICES MESH?

Even though we may know what we want to do, we oftentimes make choices that are inconsistent with our needs and desires. We do that because we want to be liked, we want to fit in or we think it is what we have to do to be successful. We also do those things because other people tell us to grow up and accept our responsibilities. We are told that what we want to do would be a great hobby but not a job and it won't pay the bills. Fearful people tell us that we need to get a good job with a good company and keep our nose to the grindstone until retirement. We think we can't possibly do what we want because that is not the way the world works and that is not what happens when you are an adult. Adults are supposed to get jobs, raise families and stay out of trouble.

Well, what if that premise is not quite right? What if we are supposed to do what we want to do because it is consistent with our gifts and talents? What if we are not all supposed to have 2.3 children, work for one employer for at least 10 years, wear certain clothes, belong to certain clubs and like certain people?

We come into this world with very specific gifts and talents that are unlike anyone else's gifts and talents. We have not earned them and we have not asked for them—we simply were given them. They are like fingerprints and no two are alike.

Because we were born with them and did not have to struggle to realize them, sometimes we take them for granted. We do not even realize what a gift they are, not only to us, but also to the rest of the world. What if we are provided the opportunity to use our gifts and talents in unique and wonderful ways to bring value and joy to others? What if, in doing so, we lived a life of energy, excitement and pure bliss?

WHAT IF?

What if you could spend the rest of your life doing work you love? What if you could live joyfully? There is always a way to get what you need. We oftentimes do not consider the possibility that we have options to work and live in ways that soothe our soul and bring us joy. We think that we are too old to make the change, not capable of doing anything differently, or that our families and friends will not support our dream.

If I told you that you *do* have options and that you could live a better life, would you be willing to try? It is not impossible but neither is it easy. It does require some work to dig deep and understand who you really are and what you really want. It is not about your family, your friends, your associates or your dog. IT IS ALL ABOUT YOU!!

So, are you ready to get started?

DETERMINE WHO YOU ARE AND WHAT YOU WANT

Take a minute to prepare your mind. Sit in a quiet room alone. Give thanks for your life and the opportunity that this journey will provide. Open up your mind to what you want and need. Shut out all of the other voices and distractions that are sending less than supportive messages.

Grab a paper and pencil and consider the following questions. Take the time to contemplate each question individually, completely, before moving on to the next one:

- Who am I and what do I like, dislike and need in my life? Why?
- When am I at my best?
- When am I the most excited, energetic and joyful?
- What do my friends depend upon me for?
- At the end of my life, what do I want to have accomplished? Why?
- What do I like about myself and want to share with others?
- What does my dream life look like? What am I doing? How am I living? What am I wearing? Describe in detail, as the details tell a story.
- What are my strengths?
- What about me is unique?
- Who do I admire and why?
- What does success look like?
- What does significance look like?

The answers to these questions will guide you in determining what you want to do and how you want to live. Continue pondering the answers and rank what the most important things are to you. If you need more input, there are some wonderful assessments on the market to help you further clarify your passion.

DETERMINE NEXT STEPS

Once you have determined what it is you want to do, write down five action steps that you must take immediately to move forward. Do not worry about developing a full plan at this point. You can do that later. Go to the next step NOW.

TAKE ACTION

Take action, right now!! It is important to take action so the dream takes on a life of its own. Do one thing on your list and then follow it up with the next item on the list. If you do not take action immediately, your dream will fade into the "Someday I will . . ." category – where dreams go to die. It is important to get energy behind the dream to move it forward. Completing one step—no matter how small—validates your ability to follow through on your plan.

RELAX

Now, relax and let the magic begin. Once you put your dream out there, determine your next steps and take action, the magic starts. The universe conspires to help you. You just need to believe and remove all barriers from your mind. Keep thinking about doing that activity that brings such joy. See yourself in your mind performing the task, feeling good about your achievement and being grateful for the opportunities. You will see it is quite possible to be your own dog! I am excited for you and hope to hear about you and your success.

About Linda

Linda Worrell, CEO of Worrell Management Group, is a consultant, speaker, writer and seminar leader. She helps her clients identify strengths, brilliant ideas, unique positions, best groups to collaborate with and develops a plan to support the outcomes desired. She has written training plans, strategic plans, economic development plans, operational plans and public policy positions. During her career, she has worked with state governments, universities, colleges, Fortune 500 companies, regional health care systems, small businesses and non-profit organizations.

She has been a real estate developer and has worked on legislation to protect personal property rights. She has drafted legislation that was passed into law to protect consumers and developers.

She has a history of involvement in state and local organizations including the Virginia State Chamber of Commerce, the Virginia United Way, the Community Foundation of the Rappahannock Region, the Fredericksburg Regional Chamber of Commerce, the Rappahannock United Way and the Fredericksburg Regional Alliance, which she helped found.

Linda is the recipient of the Patricia Lacey Metzger Distinguished Achievement Award and the Women of Distinction Award for the National Girl Scouts.

Linda is in the process of launching a new company, Kizmet, which focuses on personal development. During her years as a corporate consultant, she realized that the people who were really successful and leading joyous lives were the people who knew who they were and what they needed in order to live a fulfilled life. The people who were unhappy and unfulfilled were those that did not know themselves well and were controlled by the demands placed on them by others. They gave their life to others, without thoughts, and never realized their potential or enjoyed the benefits of living their life their way.

She decided to dedicate the balance of her life to helping individuals and not just organizations. Organizations are people. However in consulting with organizations the focus is on the process, more than the people. In this new focus, Linda is sharing different ideas and perspectives with individuals. In doing so, Linda believes that she can ultimately impact more individuals, as well as their families, businesses and communities.

You can connect with Linda at:
linda@worrellmanagementgroup.com

CHAPTER 41

VOYAGE OF AN ENTREPRENEUR —ACHIEVING YOUR DREAMS AND LIVING YOUR PURPOSE

BY JULIO ZELAYA, PhD

What is your greatest dream in life? If you had the opportunity to focus on the one thing you love doing in life, what would that be?

At first glance, they might seem like two simple questions, but upon closer observation – according to global statistics – we find a surprising reality. Sixty percent of all people are depressed in their jobs, feeling trapped, doing things day in and day out that they don't enjoy. So what is it that keeps us engaging in the purpose God has entrusted us with? How do we make our business and our jobs something we are passionate about? These are vital questions we need to answer.

During the last World Business Forum I attended in NY, I was surprised to see that the only speech receiving a standing ovation was the one by Nando Parrado, survivor of the 1972 Andes airplane accident. His conclusion was, "We must have a purpose in life that goes beyond just making money." In addition, I also recall reading an article in the

Harvard Business Review titled, "How will you measure your life?" The conclusion was clear: We are living in a world where external abundance is keeping us from living a life full of purpose. We are immersed in a culture full of 'having' but not of 'becoming'. We spend little to no time meditating on our priorities in life. And to make things worse, we spend time criticizing others instead of answering the question of who we really are and what our purpose really is. Rarely do we ask ourselves, "What can I do to improve my quality of life?" ...and, "What am I doing to have a positive impact on the lives of others?"

On more than one occasion, I've asked people what their priority is in life, mostly getting either God or family as a response. However upon inquiring about how much time they invest into each of these, never if ever do I get an answer different from "very little" or the ever-famous, "...don't have time because of work." So then what can our priorities really be if our answers aren't as congruous as we thought? We state one thing but tend to do another, myself included. I'd be lying to say that I always make strategically correct decisions for my life. Yet acknowledging this disconnect, facing up to it and doing something about it, is the change that could set us once again on the path towards reaching our dreams.

A second strategically-foundational premise is that your product is a direct result of your ability to measure things. It's vital to set key performance indicators (KPI's) and formal accountability systems in one's life. If we constantly measure our business' EBITDA, sales and turnover rate to determine our company's performance level, then why not employ similar measuring techniques for our lives? I was amazed by something Clayton Christiansen wrote in his article: *How will you measure your life?* – "God is going to measure my life not by the amount of dollars I make, but by how many lives I touch." It's really not about prominence, status or achievements, but rather about helping others develop better lives. How is God going to measure my life, my family, my friends, my colleagues and society as a whole? By the life-strategy I choose to live by to help make this world and those around me better.

As I meditate upon this whole life strategy to help reach our dreams, I can't help but remember a few experiences from my own life. I was about eight when I mixed a number of ingredients in a jar and labeled it "Mediopetril." Needless to say it was a foul-tasting concoction made up of: Vaseline, colorants, play-dough, water and other items I found around the house. I remember telling my parents, "I've invented a cure-it-all for everything." Back then my Dad worked for a pharmaceutical company and I asked him for an appointment at his company to present my idea. He asked me about performance testing and I answered, "I tried it on my turtles and they all died, but that's just because it's not designed for animals. Can I have a meeting at your company to explain it to them?" Just picture the scene - it was a critical point in my life. Without a second thought my Father assured me, "You can count on that meeting but you'll need to be better prepared." My Mom showed her support as well.

Days went by and every time my Dad came home I'd ask him about the meeting. Then a few weeks later it came, my Dad says, "tomorrow's the day; I got you a meeting with the general managers." With all the excitement an eight-year-old can muster, I put my suit on, readied my dreadful concoction, gathered some drawings I had made and went with my Dad to work. And just like he said, there was a group of managers waiting for me in the board room. I went through my presentation without a single one of them chiding or looking down on me. No doubt my Dad had prepped them ahead of time. By the end of the presentation, one of them took their watch off and handed it to me together with a book he had gotten from his briefcase. And I'll never forget the words he said for they forever marked my life, "I'm giving you this watch as an initial capital investment. Follow your dream and read this book *The Greatest Salesman in the World,* and don't stop preparing yourself." They were basically saying that I was headed in the right direction; but that everything was a matter of perfecting the product and if I was consistent there was no doubt I would reach my goal. Because of this assessment, failure never crossed my mind. Later on that day, we celebrated that important business meeting with my parents.

Sometime later when I was ten, in my home city of Guatemala, I was blessed with being chosen to be—"Mayor for a Day." It was a competition where children would qualify due to their grades and merits. In my case, thanks to my teachers and parents submitting me as a candidate—I WON!! After the experience, I thought to myself, "I'd like to dedicate my life to teaching and repaying all the good they've sown into me." I recall that as the first thought connected to my life's dream of impacting the lives of many. But I didn't just leave it at the declaration phase, because even at that young age, I started developing a long-term plan that included preparation time and goal achievement.

I'm sure everyone can bring to mind events that marked their lives, because they either allowed you to believe in your abilities or to doubt them. Why don't you reminisce on them once again and measure how they've affected your outcome so far. Understanding those events that have molded us greatly affects our outlook on the world, and on what we believe we can achieve. My goal here is to restore your ability to dream once again, and break any limits keeping you from achieving whatever you set your mind to.

Now, how do we recover our ability to dream? Here are five key steps to get you started:

1. **Stockdale's Paradox.** Bear in mind there must be a balance between faith and discipline. It's vital to believe in a better future and cultivate our spirit for it; but at the same time it's also imperative to face the facts and work hard right now. Success isn't a chance event but a direct result of preparation and opportunity. Now ask yourself: Do you really have faith in your dreams? Are you really doing all you can to prepare and work hard for them?

2. **View opportunities where others see problems.** Everything in life can be seen in two ways: as a problem or an opportunity. We must learn to develop an optimistic and positive approach to make the most out of every moment. Is traffic horrible this morning? Then view it as a wonderful opportunity to grow and develop through teachings and audio-books. Remember everything in life is always a new opportunity.

3. **Dreams are personal.** What works for some people probably won't work for others. Beware of destroying other people's dreams. Learn to ask and give advice that builds and motivates, rather than simply giving excuses to conform and settle for the way things are.

4. **Children believe everything.** Refresh your way of seeing life. Become like a child to dream once again, all the while being a grown-up that works hard to achieve what you set your heart to do. This is the best combination.

5. **A model is worth more than a thousand words.** Meditate on how to become a better role model for young lives to imitate. We have the responsibility of being dream builders. Meditate on this: How do you talk to your children? As the line from a famous Latin American song goes, "Lord I want to be more like you, because my children want to be more like me."

No matter if it was a past experience or you're just recently discovering it, but all of us can experience a moment in life when we discover something that impassions us. In my case, it was a personal epiphany that revealed my teaching vocation. Others discover their passion for singing, for writing, for researching, for working in politics. The possibilities are endless. The truth of the matter is that many times we discover what our passion in life is, but we don't take the necessary steps to make that entrepreneurship a reality.

By entrepreneurship I'm not necessarily referring to opening up your own business, but about adopting a lifestyle focused on making the most of opportunities that come your way. It's about developing your potential and adding value to your family and community. All of us are entrepreneurs to a certain degree, and we have an unlimited potential to create and bring to life ideas from the abstract to the concrete.

How do we go about developing an entrepreneurial lifestyle?

1. **Discover your purpose.** What do you believe is your goal in life? What do you consider is the mission you alone can bring to fruition in this world? There are no simple answers to these questions, but by taking into account other factors you'll probably notice certain significant experiences designed to lead you into your purpose. Here are some additional questions to reflect on: What is something you would like to change in the world? What social issues greatly unsettle you? What types of news bother you? What would you like to improve in the world? What would you like to accomplish before passing away? What would you do in life if you were guaranteed success? There are no limits. You can be successful in whatever undertaking you choose. What do you want your legacy to be in this world? This last question is pivotal because it sets you apart from the rest. Stop trying to reach someone else's purpose and start seeking to fulfill your own.

2. Discover your passion. What do you enjoy doing more than anything else? What challenges do you like to take on regardless of the hurdles they might include? When do you feel most enthused and fulfilled? What do you lament in society? Does poverty make you upset? Does corruption or negativity get on your nerves?

3. Discover your talent. What areas are you uniquely skilled for? Where do you have a personal competitive advantage? Everyone has something they're better at than others. What is that special talent in you? Upon discovering it you'll notice that it goes hand-in-hand with your passion as well. If you like music, then you'll probably have a talent along those lines—be it in song or some other implicit area such as being a talent agent.

4. Discover how to make your purpose, passion and talent profitable. Every entrepreneurial undertaking must be profitable. And I'm not solely referring to money or profits but about making it sustainable.

5. Act on it. The last step in this entrepreneurship model is the most important of all. Many times people discover their purpose, their passion, their talents, and may even have an idea of how to make it profitable, yet still leave it at the planning stage. This is usually the stage where all your fears start manifesting. We start asking ourselves questions such as: "Am I really ready? Is it really worth the risk? Do I really have what it takes?" Now, I'm not saying that you need to get up tomorrow morning, quit your job and focus solely on what you enjoy doing; but what I am saying is that you need to gradually act on it to make it a reality.

In order to encourage you to take the first step, allow me to share a practical, real-life scenario:

When I turned thirty I got the best gift I could have ever received – I got involved as a volunteer with a group of adults that had lost their sight later in life. When sharing with them about this entrepreneurial lifestyle and reaching for their dreams, they gave me a lesson I won't soon forget!

The majority of them were new to the business community, offering their services in mesotherapy and reflexology. When going about the exercise of reexamining what they really had to offer as a business and the essence of their services, I was blown away by the depth of their answers. One of them said, "I sell peace of mind." Another continued, "I sell love." Others would smile and say, "I sell them the opportunity to get to know God." I finished that workshop with this sense of faith exploding within me and saying to them, "Thank you for giving me one of the greatest lessons in life. For true vision isn't in the eyes, but in the mind and in the heart."

What are you really doing to make your life meaningful today? How do you view your job? As a business, what are you really selling? Entrepreneurship is about focusing on personal change and seeing life through the lens of possibility, not imitation. We must first set our mind on BECOMING, then on DOING and lastly on HAVING! Investing into our own purpose and personal development will provoke us to stop seeing things with our natural eyes and start seeing them through the eyes of faith.

If we just start envisioning in our hearts and minds all that we could actually accomplish for others, for our family, at our jobs and for our country, we will be the likes of those anonymous heroes restoring the dreams of our fellow men.

What are you doing today to make your dreams a reality?

About Julio

Julio Zelaya believes in a world filled with great and noble dreams and the people who will reach them.

He is Founder and President of the Learning Group (www. thelearningroup.com), a leading Latin American corporation focused on development and implementation of corporate universities, executive education and specialized Entrepreneurship programs.

Julio holds a Post-Doctoral Degree in Management and Marketing from Tulane University, a PhD in Psychology from Universidad Mariano Gálvez, an MBA from INCAE Business School, and has various certificates in entrepreneurship and management from MIT, Harvard, Babson, Cornell University and ASTD. He is a Professor of several MBA and PhD courses in Latin America.

Julio Zelaya is a bilingual, international speaker (Spanish/English) (www.juliozelaya. com) whose charismatic and inspiring style has led him to share the stage as a keynote speaker with some of the best in the world, including Dave Ulrich and Sir Ken Robinson. He's been involved in the training and formation of over 250,000 people in the continental U.S. as well as other countries in Latin America and the Caribbean, sharing on how to live with purpose and entrepreneurship as a lifestyle. He was a conference speaker at TEDx Guatemala City – sharing on "The Gift of Dreaming."

Author of twelve books, including *La Travesia del Emprendimiento* (The Entrepreneurship Voyage), and *Sólo por ser usted* (Just because it's you), both written in Spanish, his articles are commonly published in prestigious magazines of Central America such as *Business and Strategy*. He co-authored the book *SuccessOnomics* in English with Steve Forbes (available in October 2014). He's currently working on his next book on how to live a life full of purpose (available in English and Spanish in November 2014). Among his clients we find: Novartis, Kellogg's, Abbott, Wal-Mart, Exxon Mobil, PepsiCo, Philip Morris, Henkel, World Bank, Chevron, World Vision, Save the Children, USAID, Merck, and others.

He has taught at conferences at Penn State University, Tulane University as well as at a number of entrepreneurial summits.

He was selected as one of America's PremierExperts™ and has been featured on NBC, ABC, FOX and CBS television affiliates speaking on entrepreneurship and leading a life with purpose.

You can connect with Julio at:
julio@juliozelaya.com
www.juliozelaya.com
FB: Julio Zelaya
Twitter: zelaya_julio

CHAPTER 42

THE FUTURE OF MEDICINE:
MODERN DAY HOUSE CALLS®
A SOLUTION TO
MAJOR PROBLEMS IN
HEALTHCARE DELIVERY
"THE FUTURE OF MEDICINE PRACTICED HERE
TODAY AT A.P.P.L.E. MEDICAL HOMEHEALTH"

BY KENNETH ALBRECHT, M.D.

Please let me introduce myself. I am Kenneth E. Albrecht. M.D. I am an internal medicine physician with 13 years of training. I am proud to say I obtained my Internal Medicine degree at one of the top 10 medical schools in the country, The University of Michigan, Ann Arbor.

I am amazed at the fact that I am a doctor who actually makes house calls; let alone making house calls back in my home town, Crystal Lake, Illinois. I actually started my medical career in this town as a hospital orderly during my junior year of high school. That was over 30 years ago.

Through all my years as a physician, my colleagues have always referred to me as being "futuristic and ahead of the pack." I have always been referred to as a forward thinker and doer. Ultimately, I was known to be the guy to "make things happen." I was known as the most efficient and the most organized guy in helping to make things happen in medicine and get things done.

My personal goal has always been to find ways to make healthcare as personable and as cost-effective as possible. This was never so true than in the development of A.P.P.L.E. Medical Homehealth, otherwise known as Modern Day House Calls® (MDHC), a homehealth system of community-based healthcare delivery. A.P.P.L.E. stands for Associated Professionals for Personal Life Enhancement. In this chapter, I am going to reintroduce the concept of doctors making house calls.

My challenge was to see if house calls could be a viable personalized, high-quality cost-effective form of healthcare delivery in America. I have found that Modern Day House Calls is a solution to many of the problems that exist in today's healthcare system. Plus, I wanted to see if I could create a reproducible form of healthcare delivery known as Modern Day House Calls® throughout America.

WHAT MAKES A.P.P.L.E. HOMEHEALTH SO SPECIAL?

The answer is found when you see what we do and how we do it and the results we have achieved.

We at A.P.P.L.E. Medical have developed a process of delivering home healthcare as a solution to many of the problems that currently exist in America. Our mission is to bring A.P.P.L.E.'s state of the art healthcare to patients in their individual homes as well as in community environments, such as independent, supportive or assisted, or even the corporate workplace.

WHAT IS THE IMPACT ON PATIENTS AND HEALTHCARE PROVIDERS ALIKE?

Everyone is searching for that healthcare solution that will bring a more positive and cost-effective outcome than what currently exists in the healthcare system. The goal, according to A.P.P.L.E. philosophy, is to help each patient become as fully functional and alive as possible. This, of course, depends upon on each patient's desire, their personality, and in most cases consistent wishes of that patient's family.

We found that our level of care has a tremendous impact on the whole life spectrum of patients and their families. It is profound, even to me as a healthcare provider. For example, patients and families tell us that, unlike many other doctors, we at A.P.P.L.E. always present all diagnostic and treatment options to patients and their families. We educate and help patients pick and choose what is appropriate for them, once again based on patient personality. I have found that patient personality can be one of the greatest limiting factors in healthcare.

This is why I say to each patient and family when we are together on location, "You never need to do what I say, but I always have to recommend what is best." That is what is expected of me. However, I always present multiple options and help patients pick and choose what they think is best of all the options possible. The way we do this is drastically different than most doctors. I only say this because patients tell me so. It's the "A.P.P.L.E. difference," and they like it!

Here is another example of the A.P.P.L.E. difference. You can be an average doc and deliver regular medical care, which can have average impact on a person's life. However, we at A.P.P.L.E. have learned the ways to deliver a fantastic level of healthcare that has a fantastic impact on a patient's whole life spectrum, level of human existence, general feeling of well being, and performance both mentally and physically.

The question is, how do you bring all these kinds of issues together and make healthcare happen in a patient's home, let alone on location in the community? This personalized approach, as you might imagine, is a system design that required a tremendous amount of development.

It is a protocol at A.P.P.L.E. that I developed through a process that we call, "organized flexibility." This is the key to what we do and how we do it that makes A.P.P.L.E. so special to our patients and families.

WHAT IS THE DIFFERENCE BETWEEN OFFICE-BASED MEDICINE VS. MODERN DAY HOUSE CALLS®?

First you have to ask yourself, to what extent am I qualified to answer the above questions. I have been an office-based physician for many years; however, in the last 12 years, I have probably done more house calls than any other physician in America. So, based on my experience and what we have accomplished in A.P.P.L.E. to date, let alone having seen what seems like nearly a million patients in my career, I can tell you with certainty that there is a big difference between office-based medical care versus A.P.P.L.E.'s Modern Day House Calls®.

For you to fully appreciate the difference, let me tell you my story as an A.P.P.L.E. Medical Modern Day House Call Doctor®. You will see the contrast of how things are being done currently in medicine versus how we practice medicine in A.P.P.L.E. as a future benchmark model for the healthcare industry.

WHAT IS THE FUTURE OF HEALTHCARE?

A.P.P.L.E. was built to leave a legacy. A.P.P.L.E. was built as a futuristic model of personalized healthcare delivery for America. Ask yourself this: Where do you think the future of health care "should go"? In contrast, "where do you think the future of healthcare is going? What do you think the government is wanting to see happen? What do you think insurance companies and Medicare would like to see happen?

The stakeholders in medicine, those who make money in medicine, absolutely want to shift the increase in healthcare cost to your pocket book. Stakeholders want you to pay for the inefficiency in medicine. They want to shift the increasing cost to the consumer and pay all providers alike less money for the healthcare they provide.

That being said, if you are going to stay in the game of healthcare and plan on winning, the following needs to happen. Healthcare providers have to deliver the most efficient, cost-effective impacting healthcare possible. Baby boomer patients, as the consumers of healthcare, do and will increasingly demand and expect the same.

Having been an advocate of the above during my entire 30-plus years, I feel we at A.P.P.L.E. have discovered innovative ways everyone can win in this healthcare game. We have developed a system, a benchmark model of healthcare delivery that is most unique, and we have already proven that it works!

Here is an example of what I mean: When people ask me what kind of a doctor I am, I always take a little pause to get their attention and then say, "I am the kind of doctor most patients would like to have." I then wait to see what they think of my response. Invariably they say, "Why is that?" My response is always the same, "I help patients become healthy, wealthy and happy through a personalized approach to healthcare." In particular I say, "I am an A.P.P.L.E Medical Modern Day House Call Doctor®.

Not only are they surprised by the fact that we do house calls, they are very surprised by the high-quality personalized kind of care they receive while we are on location. And it's not just me, I always have a fantastic nurse, who helps "to help make things happen." What is interesting about the A.P.P.L.E. solution is that it does not require anyone from the government, insurance companies or other stakeholders to do anything different than they are currently doing. We are working within the system as it is currently structured, while doing our twist on things to get it right. Getting it right means cost-effective delivery and a satisfied patient. At days end, our design leaves both providers and patients alike with a great sense of satisfaction of having done a job well done with an impact on a patient's and family's life that goes beyond expectation.

A.P.P.L.E. is a community-based, workplace-based model of Modern Day House Calls®. This is a transformation that many patients are going to need. Patients and stakeholders are expecting this, but I believe few people know how to make it actually happen.

You might say why is this? My answer, is again based on my experience in the healthcare industry. The fact is that the current system is so caught up in trying to survive the chaos of what is currently going on that they find themselves with no time think or enough energy and resources to bring about change. In my opinion the industry lacks the insight, the talent and the leadership to transform the healthcare industry forward.

Our A.P.P.L.E. system of Modern Day House Calls® is a solution to a lot of problems that currently exist in the healthcare system:

- Inappropriate admissions to the hospital that could have been managed in the home environment.

- Inappropriate discharges from the ER that perhaps should have been admitted to the hospital.

- Appropriate discharges from the ER, yet a patient that is still too sick to go home or survive the long wait in some doctor's office for hours on end.

- The ever growing concern of the "prematurely discharged patients" who all too frequently end up back in the ER and in the hospital in less than 30 days.

The future of medicine, the transformation of medicine, is going to be community based, workplace based and home based as in the form of Modern Day House Calls®. This is the transformation that we have already done in A.P.P.L.E. Our services have been well received by patients and families alike including all stakeholders who benefit from this transformed level of care.

As one sees all the logical benefits that Modern Day House Calls® has to offer, one can logically assume this level of care will simply become expected by patients and stakeholders alike. The reason why this is true is because A.P.P.L.E. has proven that Modern Day House Calls® is the answer to what patients want and need, personalized high-quality cost-effective healthcare.

Modern Day House Calls® is the answer to inappropriate hospital admissions, early discharges, and early returns back to the hospital. Add to this a big problem in America known as the "overmedicated patient" as expressed in my previous best-selling book with Brian Tracy titled *Against the Grain.* You will see the problem of the overmedicated patient is all too often "the side effect of office-based medicine." My chapter explains why A.P.P.L.E.'s Modern Day House Calls® is the solution to the overmedicated patient because medication reduction is best dealt with in a home based environment. A.P.P.L.E. is networked with homehealth services and is connected through continuity in care with specialists and primary care office-based physicians.

Modern Day House Calls® is a solution to an ever-increasing problem of patients simply not being able to come to a doctor's office because of the fact that they are sick and in essence homebound. Modern Day House Calls is a tremendous benefit to family members who are frequently overburdened with difficulty getting their loved ones to the doctor.

HOW DO YOU MAKE THE TRANSITION FROM OFFICE-BASED MEDICINE TO HOME-BASED MEDICINE?

We at A.P.P.L.E. have already done this transformation in anticipation of the need for a model of how healthcare should be delivered in America. The details of how to actually go about the transformation is beyond the scope of this chapter.

In summary, I have presented the opportunity for patients and physicians and stakeholders alike to....realize that house calls and homehealth medicine is a real high-quality cost-effective solution to many of the problems that plague the current healthcare system in America. In building a legacy, a benchmark model of healthcare delivery, we have done it alone in a limited way, but we cannot do it alone in a big way.

We are interested in consulting and developing partnerships with parties who believe in our mission and wish to replicate what we have done and perhaps going beyond to what further could still be done. There will always be room for continued improvement.

It does not require anyone, patients or providers alike, to do anything different than they are currently doing. A.P.P.L.E. has simply created a system of healthcare delivery within the current system of healthcare in America.

In order to really make a difference in healthcare throughout America, my chapter in this book is a call to action, an invitation, to patients, physicians and other healthcare providers, including other stakeholders throughout the country, to join our network and our mission to support A.P.P.L.E. Medical Homehealth as the benchmark of how healthcare should be delivered in America today.

Finally, and most importantly, I know patients and families are very satisfied with the healthcare that we provide in A.P.P.L.E. Many of our patients feel so fortunate that A.P.P.L.E. as Modern Day House Calls® actually exists.

"I think, when it all comes down to it, what patients most want is quality time with their doctor."

Kenneth E. Albrecht, M.D.

About Dr. Ken

Kenneth E. Albrecht, M.D. is an internal medicine physician. He received his training from the University of Michigan, Ann Arbor.

He is the founder of A.P.P.L.E. Medical Network U.S.A. (Associated Professionals for Personal Life Enhancement). Dr. Albrecht has dedicated his entire medical career to the development of personalized cost-effective systems of healthcare delivery.

His focus has always been on helping individuals become healthy, wealthy and happy. This has been accomplished through creative personalized systems of networked healthcare delivery that helps patients become both mentally and physically fully functional and fully alive.

A.P.P.L.E. Medical Network has been established as a benchmark of how healthcare should be delivered in America today. This system is office-based, community-based and also a system of home health delivery.

Dr. Albrecht, as an innovator in medicine, is one who wrote the software that drives this system of effective healthcare delivery. Throughout his career, he has been highly aware of what he refers to as the "plight of both the provider and the patient." He has created system designs to address the frustrations of both patients and providers.

He is an avid lecturer on topics that address the above issues. Three of his outstanding presentations include:

1) How to Talk to Your Doctor—So Your Doctor Will Talk to You.

2) How to Live Your Best Life on the Least Amount of Medicine.

3) The Challenges of Healthcare Delivery.

Dr. Albrecht is married to Lizbeth, has four children and lives in the Chicago-land area. His personal interests include music and the entertainment industry. Since the age of five he has had a strong interest in music and has become an accomplished front drummer. He created a new form of musical entertainment for musicians and singers alike through the development of The CD's Come Alive Band. The band is a fusion of both live and CD sound.

He is entrepreneurial in both the medical and entertainment industry. He is inventive with four inventions. He has written five screenplays for production and is a consultant to the movie industry. He is a licensed pyrotechician, author of two books and a software developer. Outdoor interests include fishing, skiing and astronomy. He also is a safe rider of Harley Davidson motorcycles.

www.AppleMedicalNetworkUSA.com
email: DrKen@AppleMedicalNetworkUSA.com, (630) 204-0164

CHAPTER 43

COLLEGE SUCCESS *FOR A LOT LESS!* — 3 STEPS TO EDUCATE ALL YOUR KIDS WITHOUT "SETTLING" OR BANKRUPTING YOUR RETIREMENT

BY KEVIN ANDERSON

The parent names are all different—Ed and Rae, Bill and Lisa, Sharon, William, and others—but the concerns of the families I meet all center around a few common themes:

- I have some college savings but I am not sure it's enough.

- We are behind saving for retirement and college. But college is key, so we may never retire.

- How can we pay for college and not saddle the family or the kids with a ton of debt?

- I don't think we can afford the private school Holly wants to attend, so she is looking at State School U.

- Because of our income we won't get financial aid, but we want the best for our kids. We want them to get into the best schools, but also want to minimize the pain of paying for it.

Families are being severely challenged by college costs, which continue to increase by 6-7% annually. To combat this, I believe that every family should have the information, insight, and help to make better decisions about college. With this support, they can attain the "College Success for a Lot Less" they seek…getting their kids into a chosen school - even their dream school—at a price affordable for the family. Affordable so that they can comfortably send all their kids to school…with little to no lingering debt…without sacrificing retirement.

In the pages to come, I will share 3 Steps families can take. These steps are part and parcel of our proven college financial planning approach…. an approach that is different than college planning advice dispensed by traditional financial advisors. What does the typical college planning solution look like?

THE ROAD HEAVILY TRAVELLED LEADS TO A DEAD END FOR MOST

It is a road down which I have ventured. Nearly a decade ago, my son entered Georgetown University. Being a financial industry professional, I knew the traditional college planning process first-hand.

We identified income and assets to fund college, bought the Princeton Review, researched schools on-line, bought ACT prep materials, and much more. Then we made a decision on a school. But we were playing with only half a deck of cards.

That's because the college planning world is very complex. Without lots of *the right kind* of research or connection to a college funding professional with a holistic view, many parents operate without full knowledge of the college funding process, or how financial aid works and how to maximize it.

That's where I was too – I thought I had a good handle on the process, but there were myths and lack of knowledge that sub-optimized our result….we ended up over-paying for my son's college education. I discovered this after I did lots of research, and got connected to a leading college financial planning organization where I received extensive, specific training to better advise clients.

With intensive training and my subsequent experience in helping families, I began to see the heavily travelled road as a dead-end for many families. What is that heavily travelled road? It is this common advice:

- Retirement funding is your first priority.

- Once retirement contributions are proper, contribute to your college savings fund of choice (primarily the 529 Plan, or a Coverdell Savings Account or UGMA/UTMA Account).

- Money can be borrowed for college but not for retirement, so leverage student loans to pay for college.

What's the problem with this advice? For many families, it essentially means the kids are on their own! For most families I meet—even high income families—their retirement accounts aren't fully funded and they are w-a-a-y behind in their college savings.

Yet, all these families are absolutely committed to get their kids to college. And they are frustrated to no end because they can't see a way out. And what began as a frustration for me evolved into a passion to advocate for parents and their families. The "road most travelled" advice was not helping most families solve their college funding challenge... it was a dead-end where parents needed help getting on the right track.

Case Study: Case in point, the Goode's are a hard-working family with income around $70K/year, and two kids they want to send to college. They were following conventional advice, contributing as much as they could into their 401(k) plan (though still only half of goal).

They could only free up $60/month for college savings when we first met, as they were saddled with $15K in debt that they were paying off at $600/month We estimated their out-of-pocket college cost over the next 10 years would be $60K...their savings would be woefully short. They had little hope but decided to pay us a visit after attending one of our frequent free community workshops for parents.

After working collaboratively with the Goode's on a customized college funding plan, we landed on a plan they excitedly decided to implement. In a nutshell, we leveraged several strategies and showed the Goode's how they could pay off their debt, and redirect the monthly debt payment to their college fund.

In the end, we showed the Goode's how they could generate $90K in savings over the next 10 years. This was enough to not only cover their $60K out-of-pocket college costs, but also a $10K car for the kids, and some extra for "life happening." Importantly, this plan had no impact on their retirement funding, and may even enhance it since the freed-up savings can be redirected to the retirement account once college is funded!

The good news is that there is a better way…a way for many families to not to have to choose between funding "Retirement or College" but instead, to be able to fund "Retirement and College." A way for families to not face the terrible situation of having funded college for the first child, but not being able to fund the other children because they have already maxed out the loans the family can afford.

THE BRAVE NEW ROAD TO TRAVEL:
3 STEPS TO COLLEGE SUCCESS

As I coach families along the road to success, there are three stops we make along the way: 1) student readiness, 2) college selection/financial aid maximization, and 3) the college funding plan. Here's the roadmap:

Step 1: Student Readiness—You Can't Afford Slackers (Literally)
Student preparation is crucial for getting your child into a school of their choice *and* minimizing out-of-pocket costs. It encompasses engaging in activities to:

1) maximize the GPA.

2) maximize ACT/SAT test scores (test prep courses).

3) execute an impactful application, essay and interview, if required.

4) get as much clarity on the major and career of the student as possible.

Below is a list, though not comprehensive, of some key actions you can take. Warning: Your kid being a slacker in any area can cost big bucks!

- One of the highest-leverage opportunities is focusing on ACT/SAT test prep activities to increase scores to targeted levels where the financial aid award will increase. Spending several hundred dollars or more on test prep *that your kid actually engages* can potentially result in thousands of additional financial aid.

- Private schools will often cost families less than the local state school…that's right. Because of large endowments and more funding sources (alumni and private donations), many private schools can provide more financial aid/scholarships. Make sure you identify some private schools for your kids and at a minimum, explore them as stretch schools (a school that is a stretch for admittance based on your child's GPA and ACT/SAT scores).

- The biggest cost lever in this area is helping your child get a high level of clarity on their major and career. Primarily due to this lack of clarity, the average school length is 5.8 years. Based on the 2013/14 average cost at a state college of $22,846, families would have to account for an additional $41,123 in college costs.

But the real kick in the gut is the opportunity cost of the kids being nearly two years late getting into the workforce…at a 2013 average starting salary of $45,000 (National Association of Colleges and Employers), that's $81,000 in lost income. Ouch! Kids often will discount parent counsel (translated nagging to them), so if necessary, involve someone who can coach, counsel, and cajole them to a place of clarity.

Step 2: College Selection/Financial Aid Maximization —Look Before You Leap

When selecting a college, families look at fit and cost. But the wrong cost is targeted, the sticker price, specifically the total **Cost of Attendance** (tuition, room and board, books, fees, travel, etc.). Case in point, I recently worked with a family where they were looking at a local college because its sticker price was $40,000 less than their dream school, Vanderbilt. In actuality, the student had the academic chops to get into school anywhere, and we found the family's net cost would be $6,000 less at Vanderbilt than the state school!

Instead of looking at sticker price, families need to get to the net cost. At the risk of over-simplification, apply this formula to each school being considered so your family has a true sense of out-of-pocket costs per year:

Cost of Attendance – Need-Based Aid – Merit-Based Aid
– Private Scholarships – Your College Savings
= The Family Projected Annual Out-of-Pocket Costs

a. **Need-Based Aid (NBA)** is the Cost of Attendance minus the Expected Family Contribution (EFC). The EFC indicates what Uncle Sam expects your family to pay for college…could be $5,000/year or it could be $50,000 or more a year. It's calculated by U.S. Dept. of Education and looks at over 100 financial factors like the income and assets of parents and students, parent ages, and number of kids. Every family is eligible but not all will qualify.

However, what you must know is that not every school will give you 100% of the aid calculated by the formula. Some only typically give 30% or 50% of that aid. Also, of the NBA they will give, not all is in free cash…some will be in loans and some will be in the form of college work study. You've got to sort this out upfront.

Another opportunity is to lower your EFC. Similar to income tax reduction, there are strategies to legally and ethically lower your EFC based on understanding the Financial Aid laws and regulations. This can be big…a $10,000/year EFC reduction means a family saves $40,000 over the four years of college. Just make sure you check with college-funding professionals who understand this area, to see if you have opportunities worth pursuing.

b. **Merit-Based Aid (MBA)** are grants/scholarships awarded based on high academic achievement (GPA, ACT/SAT). A key strategy is to target schools where the student will be in the top 25% of the class based on ACT/SAT scores and a qualifying GPA (target 3.5 or better). This upper quartile is where MBA is awarded.

c. **Private Scholarships** provide "free money" you apply for on your own. If you have a duck-calling skill, there is a scholarship for you! Most families should limit time searching for these, as they make up only about 2% to 3% of total financial aid awarded. Instead, go to fastweb.com, set-up a student profile, then just apply for the scholarships of interest that are matched to your profile.

Once you have researched financial aid/scholarships (whew), you'll have the data to figure out your bottom line at each school. You can do much of this work yourself with a lot of time and diligence. Like many, you may instead prefer to use a special niche firm like ours, a college funding advisor with access to proprietary software that can do this analysis for you.

Step 3: The College Funding Plan—Cash is King

For college funding success, there is no way around it....cash is king. For most families, using significant amounts of debt to fund college ends up being a long nightmare.

Most parents will need to pay some out-of-pocket costs. Only .3% of all college students (less than 20,000) will get a "free ride" and even those parents find there will be some level of costs—travel, miscellaneous— not covered. So, here's the blueprint for your college funding plan:

- Assume the school each of your kids will attend and use the formula from Step 2 to calculate a total projected cost to send all of your kids to college.

- From your total projected cost to send all your kids to college, subtract out your future projected savings to calculate your college funding gap.

- Now figure out where you can free-up money or increase income to fund as much of the gap as possible. Like in the example of the Goode's, there is often not an obvious solution. That's when you need to seek coaching from an advisor with experience in financial aid, cash flow, tax planning, and general financial planning strategies.

- Once the funding source(s) have been identified, savings vehicles (529 Plans, etc.) need to be evaluated to house the funds. Some of the key factors to consider: Will your contributions be limited? Will the savings in the vehicle count against your financial aid? How much, if any, of the funds should be in the market vs. a principal-protected account? Do you want tax-deferral and tax-free use of the funds?

My philosophy is to create a "Firm Plan" vs. a "Probable (market-based) Plan" for college planning. Money in the plan needs to grow to protect against inflation but it's more critical for all the money to be there when needed for college. In the end, build a plan that you can stick with over the 6 to 15 years most families—that I see—will fund college.

WHAT ARE YOU GOING TO DO WITH THIS?

You just experienced nearly the entire college funding process crammed into a short chapter, insights very similar to what I share in monthly workshops with parents in St. Louis, Louisville, and beyond. Parents exposed to this body of knowledge do one of three things....one group proceeds and implements all the steps themselves. Another group seeks out the help of a professional to implement some or all of the steps. A final group ends up doing nothing. Oh, they think about it a lot, saying they will do something soon....but soon turns into a week, then a month, then "we'll figure it out somehow."

But I hope you are in Group 1 or 2....that you will resolve to solve your college funding challenge today while you can make the most of it, not in a few months or years right before college starts. And what's the payoff? Getting all of your kids to a school of choice, with little to no debt for you or them, at rock-bottom costs for college, with retirement unscathed. Stress-free college for the kids (at least from debt!)... and peace-of-mind for you, the parents! May College Success for a Lot Less be yours, I am pulling for you!

About Kevin

Kevin Anderson helps families comfortably put every one of their children through college. Kevin came to the financial planning industry after 25 years in management and executive roles – primarily in Fortune 500 companies. Now specializing in college financial planning, Kevin has over 10 years of financial industry experience spanning the areas of financial planning, retirement planning, life insurance and investments.

Frustrated by his own college planning experience with his children and the limited strategies available in traditional financial planning to help his clients, Kevin founded Exodus College Planning several years ago. Kevin's mission is to reach as many families as he can, to help them overcome the college cost juggernaut creating challenges for so many families struggling to pay for college. Exodus College Planning is a growing company. With the recent expansion from Louisville to St. Louis where he now resides, Kevin seeks to add to the hundreds of families already impacted by the community workshops and the services he provides to clients.

Kevin is in partnership with the largest and most reputable college admissions & financial aid service network in the United States, an organization in its second decade of existence. With this partnership and his college financial planning expertise, Kevin is able to squeeze money out of every area of the college process so his clients don't over-pay or over-borrow. From admission counselors to financial aid specialists to award appeal specialists, Kevin's team has all the expertise needed to provide holistic solutions to minimize college cost.

Kevin's college planning approach is built on the philosophy that "college requires ready cash." His goal is to help his clients "crack the code" for how their family can amass the cash needed for college upfront. With ample savings, parents are not only positioned to fund college with little to no debt, but they also have the funds to pay for extra tutoring or other student preparation activities to better position their children for acceptance into their targeted schools with maximum financial aid.

Kevin graduated from Florida A&M University, and has an MBA from the Wharton School of Business. He is a member of the Advisory Board at the Ulmer Career Management Center at the University of Louisville's School of Business. He is also an advisor to the Louisville Urban League's Urban Alliance Seminar Leader Development Program. In addition to being a member of the College Planning Network, Kevin is also a member of the National Association of College Funding Advisors.

Kevin's outside interests include active involvement in his church and volunteering to increase financial literacy through workshops and mentoring. In his leisure, Kevin enjoys reading and Bikram yoga. Kevin has been married over 28 years to his wife Phyllis, a healthcare marketing executive. Together they cherish time with friends and travelling, particularly to visit their "college-educated" children.

Connect at:
Kevin@ExodusCollegePlanning.com
www.facebook.com/KevinOAnderson200
www.twitter.com/KevinOAnderson

Investment Advisory services offered through Regal Investment Advisors, LLC., an SEC Registered Investment Advisor. Kevin Anderson is independent of Regal Investment Advisors, LLC.

CHAPTER 44

FITNESS TRAINING GOES HOLISTIC — HOW A RENOWNED STRENGTH AND CONDITIONING PROGRAM CAN IMPACT EVERY AREA OF YOUR LIFE

BY JOSH FELBER

People who know me as this serial entrepreneur always wonder where the seeds for my career were planted. My dad is a computer technician, which may explain why I started my first business as a computer dealer at 14. But it all really started when I read two books that influenced me just like millions of others: Napoleon Hill's *Think and Grow Rich* and Tony Robbins' *Unlimited Power*. It's definitely been an interesting journey towards success in various industries, starting with my founding of Merchant Financial Services and later including ventures into satellite dish installation, "nutraceuticals" (Lifemax) and green energy solutions.

I'm grateful for all the lessons I have learned about myself and building a business through these various ventures, but all of those experiences were a prelude to my current role as Founder and President of the Akron,

Ohio-based Functional Fitness Labs, LLC, originally called CrossFit Akron. Since we opened in October 2010, each year the operation has experienced a substantial increase in gross revenue, which led me to move into a 7,000 square foot facility and also open a second location. I've always found that success has a way of multiplying itself, and our facility has attracted the interest of potential partners to open additional locations, starting with a third site later in 2014, and starting to franchise in 2015.

TURNING MY PASSION INTO A BUSINESS OPPORTUNITY

The reason I'm probably more excited about this business, its impact on thousands of people in my region and its unlimited growth potential is simple: it grew organically out of personal passion for CrossFit, which I discovered in 2003. For the uninitiated, CrossFit is a fitness company and exercise philosophy created by Greg Glassman in 1974 and became popular in 2000. It's a strength and conditioning program with the aim of improving, among other things, muscular strength, cardio-respiratory endurance and flexibility via routines that incorporate high intensity interval training, Olympic weightlifting, plyometric, powerlifting, gymnastics, calisthenics, strongman exercises and other functional movements.

I've always been athletic and enjoyed running marathons. When I was in my mid 20's, I got back into it. Aaron, a close friend and exercise science major at that time, was interested in enlisting in the Navy SEALs and he inspired me to sign up with him. However, the only program we could enlist in was a delayed entry program in which we would ship out a year from the time we signed up. We were guaranteed a spot to go to BUDS SEAL Training in California – but we had to wait. Focusing on ways to get in better shape for when the time came, we discovered the CrossFit website. It struck us as different in that it combined functional movements of the things we normally do in life – squatting, pressing, lifting things – with barbells, kettlebells and Olympic lifting. We started pulling workouts from the site as well as designing our own based on the methodology.

Later I blew out my knee water skiing, so I couldn't follow through with the SEALs, but I used CrossFit for my rehabilitation. The feeling I got from CrossFit reminded me of the "runner's high" I would get running

15-20 miles on training runs, only I would also be discovering muscles I never knew I had. The challenging regimen fit perfectly into my desire to always try to do things out of my comfort zone. Because so many people were posting about their progress on the site, my competitive juices were stirred, which made me accomplish more. I was able to cut my running back because CrossFit gave me a complete full-body workout.

Long story short, around the end of 2009, I was building a company focused on Green Wireless energy products, but I was tired of sitting behind a desk. I wanted to get into some sort of environment where I could engage and help people directly – and CrossFit seemed to be an awesome way to do that. As I had in the past with other businesses, I did extensive research and began consulting with others who had launched CrossFit facilities across the country. In June 2010, I got my CrossFit certification and by October, we were open. You never know how things will turn out, but I was disheartened when I learned that most people who open these facilities have zero CrossFit or entrepreneurial experience. I was fortunate to have both.

The new venture quickly became the fastest growing of five in the NE Ohio region, and within the first year we had 120 clients, while the others had from 40-80 after being in business for three years. We delivered the most powerful training and excellence in coaching…and our attention to customer service and strong social media and marketing efforts paid off. While our average demographic is people in their 30s who were onetime athletes who wanted to get back into shape, we help everyone from kids to seniors, and about 60 percent of our clients are women.

I think one of the keys to achieving success in business and life in general is finding that passion that keeps you up late and fills you with energy on an everyday basis – something that keeps you moving forward and drives you to break through the challenges that come up. Once you identify that, then it's a matter of seeking the right opportunity.

OVERCOMING THE BARRIERS OF LIMITED BELIEFS

Not surprisingly considering the impact our beliefs about ourselves have on every aspect of our lives, I have found that the barriers that keep people from achieving their fitness goals are the same ones that hold us back in other key aspects of our lives. Two of the greatest benefits of CrossFit training are its ability to help people overcome the limited beliefs that create roadblocks to success and the importance of accountability. If someone is going to work out by him or herself, or work one-on-one with a trainer, that person will likely reach a certain plateau and not go further. CrossFit allows people to be coached in groups of 4-10 people who are peers in whatever age and experience level they are at.

They're not only being pushed by a coach to challenge themselves to achieve breakthroughs, but they are subconsciously motivated by the progress that athletes around them are making. Human beings are competitive and seeing others just like us succeed helps inspire us to 'up' our game. Just as I became more successful in my CrossFit training because of the athletes' postings on the website years ago, our clients will think things like, "She's doing all this and she's a lot older than I am. So I can do it too."

Often our beliefs are limited because the scope of our goals contradicts the conservative mindset we were raised with as far as the risks we could take and what we could achieve. Maybe you grew up thinking 'money was the root of all evil,' but that now goes against your goals of pursuing a business opportunity that could help you put your kids through college. So you must find a way to reconcile these things. Align your beliefs with your goals, and then once you have those in alignment, start creating through massive action.

PERSONAL DEVELOPMENT COACHING

At Functional Fitness Labs, we're here to help people achieve their fitness and weight-loss goals – but that's just the start. Our goal is to help clients succeed in all other areas of their lives too - the whole body, mind and spirit thing. So for those who want it, we offer personal development coaching. It's wonderful to watch people transform physically over the course of weeks or months, but even more exciting is hearing the way our holistic regimen has impacted their families, relationships and careers. How we train and coach here helps empower people who may have been timid in their lives outside the facility. They may have been timid about asking their bosses for a promotion or finding the energy and mental acuity to get a difficult task done. Some clients are entrepreneurial like I am, but have just never had the courage to break the chains of 9 to 5 and take what I call a "calculated risk." The confidence we instill in one area can take root in others.

When clients start their CrossFit training, we give them an interesting apparatus to lift. It's a white plastic PVC pipe, about seven feet long, which we use to help them learn different lifting movement patterns. It's lighter than a barbell but simulates one. The goal is to help them develop "muscle memory" and get the movement patterns ingrained in them. We had one client, Kristen, in her late 20s or early 30s, who was very timid and started group sessions with the pipe in the back of the room. Our coach Jason noticed her hesitation and started pushing her, engaging her to produce better results. We're always trying to gauge such things. She wasn't overweight, she had just come here to feel better and get rid of stress in her life.

Over time, with Jason's personal challenges to her and those challenges that came from being in an environment with her peers, we started seeing not only progressing strength, but also more personal confidence. She slowly came out of her shell – and now is that take charge person standing in front of the group during workouts and participating in some of our extracurricular events. While all this was going on, we were helping her with personal development. She told us of her outside life goals, and one was to progress in her career in the marketing and advertising field.

Our goal was to help her correlate the self-confidence and beliefs she had gained about herself in the gym with what she does in her job. She had come in with those limited belief shackles, thinking she wasn't good enough in a lot of areas of her life. But the fact that she had come here told us she wanted to change that – she just needed encouragement. In our personal development sessions, we taught her how to utilize all of the breakthroughs she was achieving – the pushing through fear and pain, her ultimate resolve to go after her goals – and bring it full force into the corporate environment.

Something finally clicked, and maybe a week after one of our sessions, she came in very excited. She told us that she had talked to her bosses and they had promoted her to the position she wanted. She wanted to give us credit, but we said we were just there to help her understand that what she did at the gym applied to her whole life. Many fitness facilities are impersonal places where people just come in, do their thing and leave. But we want our clients to come here and use what they do with us to change their whole lives. Of course, one of the drawbacks for us is that clients who have gotten these kinds of promotions often take them in other cities – so they leave Akron. But what's personally sad for us is ultimately great for them, and for that reason, we couldn't be happier.

Whether you're working out in a gym or a top athlete on a sports team, it's amazing what can be achieved through proper coaching. The same applies to success in business or any other endeavor. Having a coach who understands your goals and can help you achieve them can be a crucial element to your success.

THE MARATHON RUNNER

Which brings us to Raun, who joined us not long after we opened our doors. He weighed 350 lbs. and was very concerned because heart disease ran in his family and he was at high risk. During our free intro and consultation, he stated his goals simply: he wanted to lose weight and feel healthy again. We promised him that if he stuck with our program diligently, nine or ten months later, he would be running the Akron Half Marathon. He scoffed, saying he could barely walk around his house. But we inspired him, and he in turn inspired us with his dedication. Sure enough, he dropped 80 pounds in that time and was strong, toned up and had the stamina enough to run it. Now he's down to 222 pounds. Despite his weight gain, he had what most would consider a successful life. He was married and was an entrepreneur. But we were able to give him that extra confidence that came with all he was achieving here.

As much as we love to see bodies become stronger and healthier, these lifestyle transformation and success stories are the driving force behind what we do here.

Raun dedicated himself to a powerful transformation based on unwavering focus, discipline and determination – all qualities that can be applied to being successful in any area of a person's life.

BODY AND MIND CONNECTIONS

One thing is clear to me from working these past few years in the fitness realm. Regimens like CrossFit give people that extra edge to push themselves in business, while increasing the stamina and energy necessary to become more efficient in the business world and increase one's focus on success. When you work out, your brain releases hormones and chemicals that affect the body's wellness and well-being. Sometimes, this can create a true healing power, as in the gentleman named Bob who came to us when he had cancer. He had tried out an experimental hormone blocker, but he says that combined with the CrossFit training, the course of his cancer has reversed. And just as fitness can lead the body to heal itself, it can also heal a broken mindset in a different way. We have been able to train several thousand people over the past few years, and most of our best stories, like the ones I have written about in this chapter, come from breaking through those so called "belief barriers" and conquering one's fear of the unknown.

We don't work miracles here. CrossFit takes great commitment and hard work. But if the people who come for us seeking transformation in their physical lives can take away even a single nugget of wisdom - or just a little bit of the practical information they have learned - and then utilize that to dramatically change their personal, professional and psychological life, we feel like we have served our purpose.

About Josh

Josh Felber is focused on challenging himself and those around him to consistent excellence. Blessed with the heart of an athlete, mind of a leader and an entrepreneurial spirit, he is not only effective in his approach to business, but also extremely gifted in motivating people to achieve their own goals. His intense drive and dedication to succeed has laid the foundation for his innovative approach to leadership.

Josh is the President and CEO of JF Ventures, LLC, Functional Fitness Labs, LLC (CrossFit Akron), F2 Nutrition, LLC and Primal Chiropractic, LLC, all based in Akron, Ohio. Since beginning his first business as a computer dealer at the age of 14, the seed of entrepreneurship was planted and long-term success was destined to follow. While still in his teens, Josh started Merchant Financial Services, which became one of the largest entities in that industry. He led the company to generate annual transactions of over $5 Billion.

Other businesses in Josh's career have included ventures in satellite dish installation, nutraceuticals and green energy solutions. In each of these opportunities, he led the companies to be national leaders within their business vertical. As a Partner and Vice President of Lifemax, a nutraceutical company, he helped build the company from the ground floor, and under his sales leadership the company reached millions in sales within four years, and their products were on the shelves of 40,000 retail outlets in 30 different countries.

His most recent endeavor includes the opening and operation of multiple functional-fitness facilities, currently located in the North East Ohio area. As an avid health and wellness advocate, Josh has been a long-time runner and CrossFit proponent. He has received numerous awards for various competitions including multiple marathons and half-marathons. He has now taken his passion for health and wellness to a new level through the creation of Functional Fitness Labs, LLC (CrossFit Akron) in 2010. Each year of business has demonstrated significant growth.

Josh has also incorporated a chiropractic and rehab center with the gym facility for the benefit of his clientele. This model has proven to be very successful and will be used in future locations. Additionally, he will be launching a functional nutritional company to design, make and sell his own supplement lines.

Josh has been recognized multiple times in the National Who's Who of Entrepreneurs, was a National Winner of the *ATT* and *USA Today Investment Challenge,* and has been featured on radio and television in the greater Akron area. He is an EXPY Award recipient for Media and Communications and recently appeared as a guest on America's Premier Experts® presentation of Health and Wellness Today, a television program seen on various ABC, CBS, NBC and Fox affiliates throughout the country. He also holds numerous certificates in CrossFit, Sports Performance, Nutrition and is an Eagle Scout.

Josh and his wife Trina, an entrepreneur as well, reside in Akron, Ohio with their daughter, Mia, and twin sons, Cash and Roman. Additional information about Josh Felber and his companies can be found at: www.joshfelber.com

CHAPTER 45

THE SECRET TO TRUE HEALTH AND WELLNESS AND FIVE SIMPLE STEPS TO ACHIEVE IT

BY DR. JOSE AGUILAR

The doctor of the future will give no medicine,
but will interest his patients in the cause of the human frame,
in diet, and in the cause and prevention of disease.
~ Thomas Edison.

This quote shows just how far ahead of his time this forward thinker was. He understood that in order for our future doctors to understand health they would need to understand the importance of the human frame, our diet and most importantly, the cause and prevention of disease. So let's start off by defining what health is, first of all. I pose this question to all of my patients and some of the most common answers I hear include: feeling good, not feeling any pain, not feeling sick, or I don't have any symptoms. Based on these answers it shows me how most people treat their own health. In other words they wait for something to happen before they take any kind of action. But let me ask this, can a person not be healthy even though they feel good, or don't feel any pain or aren't feeling sick? Of course they can! In fact the top 2 killer diseases in the

U.S., Heart Disease and Cancer, are known as *SILENT KILLERS!* In the U.S, 1 in 2 people will die of some type of heart-related condition and 1 in 3 will die of some type of cancer-related disease. Many times a person is completely unaware of their prognosis until it's too late. As you can see now, health shouldn't be based on how a person feels.

So what is true health? In order to determine what true health is, let's start at the very beginning. The power of conception turns just two cells into a human being consisting trillions of cells nine months later. These two original cells go through numerous processes to multiply/divide into other cells. About eight weeks after conception we begin to form our very first organ. Do you know what it is? Is it our heart? Our lungs? No, it is our brain and from there we also start forming our spinal cord. Then we begin to see the nerves branch out and at the end of these nerves comes every cell, tissue and organ in the body. Why aren't the heart or lungs or any other organ the first? Simply put, because the brain controls everything; without the brain and spinal cord, the heart doesn't know how or when to beat, the lungs don't know how to breathe. Nothing can function without the brain communicating and controlling all of the information. No wonder our Central Nervous System has been referred to as the Master Control System for our bodies.

Your brain controls every single function of the body. How? Different people call this different things; some call it Mother Nature, some call it Chi and some call it Spirit or Soul. The Medical and Chiropractic professions call it Innate Intelligence. Innate simply means something we are born with, and intelligence is just that, intelligence. Innate intelligence is something within all of us throughout our entire lives. This is the power that allows us to breathe, digest, heal cuts, etc. You don't have to think about it. It is the power that controls everything. So we can say that 100% expression of this Innate Intelligence allows every organ, muscle, and tissue to function as it should be functioning, all of the time. When everything functions at 100%, that is when we are expressing 100% True Health and Wellness.

It is when we are no longer expressing 100% function that we are no longer Healthy and Well. What causes this decrease from 100%? Stress! What is stress? Stress is difficult to define because it is a highly-subjective phenomenon that differs for each of us. Things that are distressful for some might be pleasurable for others. For example, for those of you who are neat freaks, you'd probably agree that having ten people staying in your house for a long weekend could be incredibly stressful; however, if you are someone who doesn't mind chaos and clutter, then let the fun begin! Similarly, if you thrive on to-do lists and deadlines, a week with absolutely nothing to do and nowhere to go could make you crazy, whereas another person might feel rejuvenated and refreshed.

We each respond differently to stress, as it can have a wide range of effects on people's emotions, mood and behavior. The easiest way to understand stress is to view it as the source of any change in YOUR world that evokes some reaction from you. The most important thing to remember about stress is that it's a normal part of life. The problem is not with stress itself. Rather, the problem lies with how much stress, how often we feel stressed and what tools we have to deal with stress.

The fight-or-flight response is what enabled our ancestors to deal with a more hostile, physically-demanding world of hunting, fighting, and surviving. It's the body's innate response to a perceived threat. The stress response is optimally designed to protect us from direct, identifiable and short-term danger, such as running from a tiger in the wilderness. In modern life, however, most of the time the source of our stress is not as direct but rather indirect, as in the daily hassles of a commute; and not short-term but instead continuing for days, weeks or even months. When stress hormones are continually released and your body is continually in fight-or-flight mode, and yet you have no physical release for these surges of energy and hormones, then damage can occur.

Although the emergency measure of this stress response is undoubtedly both vital and valuable, it can also be disruptive and damaging. Most humans rarely encounter emergencies that require physical effort, yet our biology still provides for them. Thus, we may find our stress response activated in situations where physical action is unnecessary. This activation takes a toll on both our bodies and our minds. Diarrhea, constipation, and difficulty maintaining sexual arousal are typical examples. And when this response continues unchecked during times of chronic stress, the harmful effects inhibit digestion, reproduction, growth, tissue repair, and the responses of your immune and inflammatory systems. In other words, some very important functions that keep your body healthy begin to shut down. When this occurs for a prolonged period of time, our body breaks down at its weakest link in the form of symptoms such as a headache or a stress-related disorder. In this manner, stress can literally become a killer. We all know that stress can have wide ranging effects on emotions, mood and behavior. Equally important but often less discussed are effects on various systems, organs and tissues all over the body.

There are numerous emotional and physical disorders that have been linked to stress including depression, anxiety, heart attacks, stroke, hypertension and immune system disturbances that increase susceptibility to infections. We know that almost every system in your body can be damaged by stress. In fact, it's hard to think of any disease in which stress cannot play an aggravating role or any part of the body that is not adversely affected by stress.

Now understand that what I am saying is not that we need to eliminate stress from our lives, because quite frankly that would be extremely difficult since we are surrounded by some form of stress from the moment we are born until the moment we die. What I am saying is that we need to train our bodies to cope with stress in a better fashion. There are five steps that everyone needs to take to be better able to handle the stress we come face-to-face with on a regular basis – so that our bodies are more capable of staying in that 100% functional model we discussed earlier.

Positive Mental Attitude: Let's begin with number 1, a positive mental attitude. Staying positive can be difficult at times and that's ok, but the more we can stay on the happier side of things, the better off our body and our health will be. How many times have you seen someone who is really sick and happy about it? Not very often. Do things in your life that you like to do and which make you happy – such as spending time with your family and friends, reading a good book, watching your favorite TV show, etc. Promote positive things in your life. Thoughts of fear, anger and worry all lead to negative emotional states, which actually cause our bodies to secrete substances that promote aging and ill health. Positive thoughts cause our bodies to secrete chemicals that slow down the aging process and can actually bring about healing in our bodies.

Sleep: Second is sleep. A majority of American adults (63%) do not get the recommended eight hours of sleep needed for good health and optimum performance. An average of less than five hours of sleep a day nearly doubles your chance of suffering a heart attack, or dying from one, compared to those who get more regular sleep.

Sleep deprivation impairs mental performance almost as much as being intoxicated. A study found that one night's sleep loss is the equivalent to working or driving with a blood-alcohol level of .05 percent (to put it in perspective, the legal blood alcohol level in the US is .08 percent). If your body isn't getting the chance to rest and repair, then you are simply forcing your body to feel stressed and depriving your body of operating at its fullest capacity.

Nutrition: Third includes proper nutrition. Feeling stressed can cause acidic conditions in your body, and conversely, an acidic body will make you feel stressed and irritable. A major contributor to raising your acid levels is the food you eat. An excess of acid in your body fluids creates joint pain, weak bones, promotes weight gain, as well as makes you feel sluggish, tired or irritable. As you get older, your body becomes less efficient in getting rid of acid. For optimal health, it is suggested that approximately 70% of your food should be alkaline-forming foods and approximately 30% of your food should be acid-forming foods.

Problems occur when you consume more acid-forming foods than alkaline-forming foods. A study comparing the behavior of boys in a juvenile detention center with the type of food they ate found that when they ate more refined and processed foods, the violence rates increased. When the food was changed to fresh and less-processed food, the violence rates dropped dramatically.

The base of a healthy diet should be fresh fruits and vegetables. They hold many vitamins and minerals needed for optimal health, but they also hold a plentiful supply of phytochemicals. All three of these elements protect your body from illness and supply your body with an endless amount of energy. The main concept of a high nutrient diet is whole, unprocessed foods with lots of fruits and vegetables, whole grains, healthy fats and lean sources of proteins.

Exercise: Exercise is step 4. You don't have to "workout" or "lift weights" to get exercise. Everyone needs exercise, from babies to the elderly. Exercise includes physical activities such as walking, running, jumping, playing, etc. It also includes Mental Activities such as reading, writing, drawing, and other activities that stimulate your brain. Exercise improves your brain activity, improves your body's ability to heal, and generally makes us feel good. There's an old saying that goes, "If you don't use it you lose it." So make sure you get at least 30 minutes of exercise on a daily basis.

Fully Functioning Nervous System: The fifth step to 100% Optimal Health is a fully-functioning nervous system. This just so happens to be my area of expertise. As a chiropractor I have seen many different cases where people have come in to my office with some kind of condition – whether it be pain, illness or some other debilitating problem – looking for a sense of hope. They've tried pretty much everything else and can't seem to get better. In fact, it was seeing this same kind of reaction I saw growing up. You see, my mother suffered from migraines when I was a child. Sometimes these migraines were so bad that she would have to lock herself up in her bedroom with lights down and no other noise throughout the house. But as a child of only 10 years old at the time and with 2 other siblings, there was no way we were able to stay put for longer than 5 minutes. The ruckus we would cause led to our mother storming out her room, yelling at us, almost on the verge of tears at times, saying that we were causing things to get much worse for her. Hearing this come from my mother made me feel very afraid, so much that I started to change how I was interacting with other people. I was becoming more introverted and keeping to myself more and more.

Luckily for us, our neighbor saw these changes in me and asked what was going on. I explained to him about my mother's migraines and how I didn't want to hurt her anymore. Hearing this, he asked to sit with my family and talk to us. I didn't know it, but that is when my life changed. What I heard coming from his mouth was what I just shared with you above. And my 10-year-old brain just gobbled it up! It all made perfect sense. The brain controls everything. Check. Stress is how we react to something and our body has to react as well. Check. And the kicker, true health and wellness comes from our bodies being able to function 100% from the inside out, not by treating the symptoms on the outside.

My mind was blown away, and it was then that I decided that I was going to be a chiropractor and help my mom. When my mother began chiropractic care we saw a change occur within the first week. Her migraines went from lasting 2-3 days down to 20 minutes. Over time they were completely resolved. So not only was her health restored, but I also received a great gift as well. It's what I call the gift of having a normal childhood. I was now able to have fun and get rambunctious without thinking in the back of my mind, "Am I hurting my mom again?"

It is because of this that I devoted my life to chiropractic and the great healing capabilities the body is able to accomplish when expressing its fullest potential. The ability to transform one's health comes from within, and it is always a miracle to me when I get to see it happening on a daily basis in my office.

About Dr. Jose

After watching his mother go from debilitating migraines – that severely affected her ability to care for her family – to having them completely resolved due to chiropractic care, he found his calling. Born and raised in the Quad Cities, Dr. Jose Aguilar earned his Doctorate of Chiropractic from Palmer College of Chiropractic after earning two degrees in Health Sciences and Liberal Studies from Black Hawk College. During his time at Palmer, he and 25 others spent three weeks on a missionary trip to Fiji providing chiropractic care to underserved communities. After graduating, Dr. Aguilar also earned his Certification as a Strength and Conditioning Specialist and in MOTUS Therapeutic Taping. His passion is to provide everyone the opportunity to develop extraordinary health and wellness through Chiropractic care, and to reach an underserved Spanish-speaking population who otherwise would not be able to receive care.

Dr. Aguilar has also done various lectures with numerous organizations, speaking on various topics including Stress, Nutrition, Peak Performance, Proper Posture, Injury Prevention, Whiplash and more. He is available for speaking engagements. Dr. Aguilar frequently attends post-graduate seminars at some of the most prestigious venues such as Harvard School of Medicine and the Spine Research Institute of San Diego among others, to stay on top of a wide variety of topics, and he implements the most up-to-date information available in order to help his patients succeed in optimizing and reaching their specific health goals. He was also recognized as a Top Recommended Professional as a Chiropractor, and has been quoted on NBC, CBS, ABC and FOX.

He states, "Research shows that 80% of the population suffers from back pain, and numerous studies show how safe and effective chiropractic treatment is in resolving this sometimes debilitating condition. I have been blessed to have helped many people get relief, and in some cases their lives back, since 2004."

Dr. Aguilar's future goals include traveling to areas in a service capacity and providing chiropractic and health support to underprivileged communities. A devoted father to his children, Isabel and Orlando, Dr. Aguilar also enjoys working out and playing sports during his leisure hours. To learn about Dr. Jose Aguilar and his practice, visit his website: www.helpinghandsmassageandchiropractic.com or contact him via email at: doctor@helpinghandsmassageandchiropractic.com.

CHAPTER 46

FIVE INNOVATIVE STEPS TO ACCELERATE THE GROWTH POTENTIAL OF YOUR BUSINESS

BY JOSEPH INFANTE

Dreaming carries no risks. The dangerous thing is
trying to transform your dreams into reality.
~ Paolo Coelho

Creative genius. That's what you really are. Beneath all of your negativity, fears and concerns lies a very powerful being waiting to be unleashed. And the journey of becoming an effective creator of value in the marketplace is an important process of transformation that all entrepreneurs endure. It involves changing the way you think about yourself, your business, your role in it, your market, and ultimately your results. The fact is most of us run away from the challenge of having to think, and, indeed, learning how to think better. This requires dissolving some of our social and personal conditioning by going deep into the subconscious; but it also involves a grounding assessment of why you want to transform in a certain direction in the first place.

Why does all of this self-examination even matter? Because the realization of any goal and its speed of execution (whether it be building a business, becoming a better parent, finding your soulmate, or even losing weight), is dictated by achievable goals, rather than delusional fantasies.

Before diving into some of the details (at least in summary form), let me share a quick story about myself in order to highlight how our subconscious can stifle progress.

My divorce represented a major turning point in my life. It marked a period of incredible lows, but also became my greatest blessing. For the first time, I had to re-examine everything up to that point that I had been taught or I had come to know: my children, my career, my finances, my childhood, my family, my skills, and every personal relationship past, present, and future. For more than three years, I went on a journey of self-discovery, trying to learn where and why my movie had taken such a sharp curve in the wrong direction on so many levels, and how difficult moving forward was proving to be. All I did know is that I had three children who needed a father, and I wanted to be able to have the most flexible schedule possible to adequately assume that role. Working again on Wall Street seemed less viable, and I had no desire to find a traditional 9-to-5 corporate job. Time was running out.

I quickly turned my attention to the Internet and worked day and night trying to figure it all out. Living hand-to-mouth, there was only a deep desire and boiling ambition sustaining me. And it had become increasingly obvious to me that it wasn't because of a lack of effort that I was not achieving my desired results, I simply had too much unresolved emotional baggage at the subconscious level to *truly* move forward. All of this subconscious clutter was keeping me from manifesting a new life. Fortunately, I met Suzanne Biddiscombe of the Source for Change in Florida. Through her innovative Authentic Release Healing method, she cleared and released all of those mental imprints, going as far back as my early childhood, that were keeping me from tapping my full potential. This emotional cleansing of sorts dramatically improved every area of my life: my Internet marketing and lead generation business grew exponentially (including being recognized and featured as a leading Internet marketer in the book - *Internet Masters: Top Techniques, Tactics, and Tips From Online Marketing Experts*); my personal relationships were healed; and I learned to fully embrace my power. I would encourage you to learn more about Suzanne Biddiscombe at: TheSourceForChange.com.

I understand that you may find yourself in a similar place right now - not understanding why you are expending so much energy with such limited results. Indeed, the drag and friction of your clutter can certainly drain your power, and render you a weaker creator. So being able to identify and remove it (in all of its forms - emotional, physical, and relationship-related) is essential, particularly for those of you starting or trying to grow a business.

At the same time, there is also a tendency to be a scattered thinker, and not mastering the necessary skills to effectively execute your transformation. It is important to recognize that the brain has different stages of learning, which reflects, in large part, the extent to which the subconscious has recorded the new behavior. Essentially, the highest form of learning is where the conscience is allowed to focus on other matters, while the subconscious is practically operating on auto-pilot. Just think about how you drive today vs. when you first drove a car. You don't think anymore. You simply drive. Your objective is to reach this higher state of learning – unconscious competence – in relation to those new activities which you are uniquely qualified to perform for your chosen path.

Set out below are the broad stages of learning, from lowest to highest:

1. Unconscious incompetence: You don't know what you don't know

2. Conscious incompetence: You know what you don't know (e.g., a first-time driver)

3. Conscious competence: You are aware of what is required, but need to be consciously engaged to perform a given task (e.g., parallel parking)

4. Unconscious competence: You know and perform a task without effort (e.g., a seasoned driver)

Here's the problem: few people spend the appropriate time to evolve towards that higher stage of learning (unconscious competence), where they have, in essence, overlearned and subconsciously absorbed the critical things required to achieve massive results. Instead, they jump from one tactic to another, one shiny object to the next, one big idea to some other, while never mastering the skills and processes that can catapult their transformation. Ultimately, frustration, disappointment, and unrealized potential rule the day.

So what are five key steps that you can take to avoid some of the common pitfalls that prevent you from realizing the objectives desired in your business specifically, and life in general?

Step 1. Establish Achievable Goals. Not all goals are worthwhile pursuing. And, in certain cases, some goals are not congruent with who you are. While you may have very lofty goals, you probably have not considered what these goals imply in terms of time and resources required, the potential impact on other areas of your life, as well as their benefits and costs. In short, BIG goals imply BIG costs. Goal setting is not a list of dreams. Rather they need to be determined within the scope of what's desirable and believable. For your goals to be desirable, the benefits must outweigh the price you are willing to pay in terms of time and resources. And for them to be *really* believable, your belief system has to be congruent with the beliefs required to manifest them. Transforming into your new self can become very challenging if your beliefs about yourself are things such as, "I'm not good enough," "I don't have the capacity," "I am powerless," or "only rich people get ahead," just to a name a few. The point is that goals are irrelevant if the beliefs held by the goal setter are incongruent.

Step 2. Limit The Number Of Goals. There is a common misperception that humans are good at multi-tasking. This is the farthest thing from the truth. Humans are extraordinarily good at focusing on one task at a time, and our effectiveness declines as more and more tasks are added to the mix. As such, setting too many goals, even if they are "achievable" on an individual basis, may dramatically dilute your results. You also need to provide the necessary focus and total commitment to each goal you set, powering through with raw tenacity and persistence. A useful resource to understand the dynamics of living a high performing life is the book written by Jim Loehr and Tony Schwartz, *The Power of Full Engagement: Managing Energy, Not Time, Is the Key to High Performance and Personal Renewal.*

Step 3. Enact Daily Rituals To Reprogram Your Subconscious. Here's the good news – your brain can be re-wired to create a new version of yourself. Neuroplasticity is certainly a very large topic, sufficient to take up this whole chapter and the entirety of this book. Indeed, much of the inner workings of the brain remain an unresolved mystery. However, we do know this: you can start changing the circuitry of your brain, and your experiences, by deliberately changing your daily routines on a regular basis. These may include how you get to work, interacting with a different person every day, or getting ready in a different way each morning. If you are hoping for different results in your life, then you must start changing the way you engage with it. Having said this, there are other daily rituals that can allow you to accelerate the brain's re-wiring process.

Self-talk is one daily ritual that has been instrumental in helping me do just that. In the book, *What To Say When You Talk To Yourself*, Dr. Shad Helmstetter discusses in great detail how most self-talk is mired with negativity, and accounts for the lion-share of our actual conversations. By pro-actively managing this internal dialogue, you can reshape how you view yourself internally at a subconscious level, and thus produce very different results in your external world. With this in mind, I have programmed my phone, so that every morning at 8 am, it automatically launches a recorded audio of me describing in detail my ideal, average day in the present tense. Now I purposely have used the words: "ideal, average day." This is NOT an exercise in fantasy talk, where you are drinking coffee at a café in Paris, while millions of dollars are pouring into your bank. This is about crafting a story that is both achievable based on your current set of circumstances and can be experienced on an average day. This can help you to deliberately frame your thoughts each day, and to quiet competing thoughts that may be distracting you from your ultimate objectives.

Step 4. Use Obstacles as Objectives Rather Than Excuses. All of us have struggled with obstacles. And it is both reasonable and highly probable that you will face obstacles along the way. But rather than using obstacles as potential excuses for either falling short of your goals or not moving forward at all, plan for your obstacles ahead of time. By listing the obstacles that you are likely to encounter in advance, these same obstacles can be easily converted into intermediate objectives that need to be addressed as part of reaching the overall goal. In some cases, you may identify ways of avoiding certain obstacles altogether. In essence, the obstacles are turned upside down, and used for your benefit rather than a deterrent. At the same time, it's important to address the constraints that may limit your ability to address some of these obstacles. To do so, you need to have a clear understanding of your own limitations or constraints, and how they may possibly inhibit your progress in realizing your "grand scheme." By developing the scope of your potential obstacles, you are better equipped to identify these constraints and the necessary measures to remove them.

Step 5. Learn To Provide Instant Value. In this era of unlimited access to information, *free* has become the new norm. This can be a challenge to those of you looking to start and build a business. Consumers are less trusting today than years past. As such, you have to identify ways of providing instant value, long before a transaction has ever taken place. You may have experienced this model with software companies. They typically provide free 30-day trials before the first payment is collected. In other cases, this comes in the form of educating your target audience or by delivering actual results before they ever become a client. In my own Internet marketing and lead generation business, I send leads to potential clients before they become paying customers. This model has allowed me to build trust quickly and avoid any possible objections to my services, which would otherwise require attention in a traditional prospecting scenario. If this step is appropriately executed it can make a significant impact on the authority of your business and how it is positioned relative to the competition.

In conclusion, the path of transformation is multi-faceted. The steps described above should not be construed as a formula; they are guidelines that can serve to make the journey more enjoyable and fulfilling. I can certainly say that these very steps allowed me to become a better man and a more effective entrepreneur, and, most importantly, a more present and loving father. For you, it ultimately begins with who you believe you can be.

About Joseph

Joseph Infante is an Internet marketing and lead generation expert as well as a speaker on business growth-related topics. He is the founder of The IMS Firm, a leading Internet marketing company headquartered in Miami, Florida. Through its various divisions and portfolio of hundreds of web properties, The IMS Firm offers lead generation services in a number of targeted industries. Mr. Infante is also the Chief Technology Officer of Real Estate Long Tail, a lead generation platform catering to top realtors in the United States.

Mr. Infante's Internet marketing expertise, coupled with his strategic advisory background, have made him a unique asset to a number of businesses in a variety of niches. Prior to The IMS Firm, Mr. Infante was a Vice President of The Bank Street Group, a middle market investment bank primarily focused on telecommunications, media and technology companies. Prior to joining Bank Street, Mr. Infante was Vice President of Lazard's Telecommunications, Media and Technology Group in New York. He was also actively involved in Lazard's financial sponsor coverage effort and was one of the founding members of Lazard Capital Markets, where has was based in London and Paris. During his tenure at Lazard, Mr. Infante was involved in a number of notable transactions totaling in excess of $25 billion. Prior to Lazard, Mr. Infante was a financial analyst at Bear Stearns in New York and Madrid, Spain. He is a graduate of Dartmouth College and attended St. Catherine's College at Oxford University in the United Kingdom. He is also fluent in French and Spanish.

CHAPTER 47

THE BEST INVESTMENT OPPORTUNITY AVAILABLE TODAY —THAT THRIVES IN BOTH GOOD AND BAD ECONOMIC TIMES

BY MIKE CONLON

In the late 1990's, I owned a successful financial planning firm. If you remember that time, the stock market was in a big boom phase and everyone was scrambling to invest as much as they could in it. I had over $100 million in investable assets under management and nearly 400 clients. However, the client that I remember most was one of my smallest clients. He worked at the local paper mill and never made more than $50,000 in any one year. He had a small IRA with me, but I knew he had more money to invest because he was a saver, pretty frugal, and hardworking. I had a couple meetings with him, but couldn't convince him to invest more in the stock market. I asked him what he was doing with his extra money. He told me he was 50 years old and in the 10th year of his 15-year plan. His plan was buying an older, single-family house each year for around $50,000. He bought each house at a 15-20% discount from the market value because it needed work, which he was able to do himself and with a little help from some of his friends. He said he could rent it for $500/month, which was a little below the market rent, and keep it rented because "in good times or bad times, there is always a need for affordable housing in this country." His plan also included using all his profits to pay off his mortgage as soon as possible. Being young and naïve at the time, I thought he was crazy to invest in boring affordable housing because the stock market was averaging over 20% returns each year.

I didn't see that client again for five years. During that five-year period, the stock market lost nearly 40% of its value, with those invested in technology stocks losing much more. When I saw him, I asked the client how life was treating him. He said he had just put in his retirement papers at the mill because he now had 12 of the houses paid off and his net income, after all expenses were paid, was over $60,000/year, more than he ever made at the mill. More important, his net worth was now over $1 million. After hearing this, I thought to myself – why would you ever invest in the stock market when you could invest in affordable housing?

So I spent a couple months researching the real estate industry. My research more than validated my old client's thesis that "affordable housing investments perform well in good and bad economic times." So I did what at least 95% of the other investors won't ever do – I took action! I sold my financial planning practice and started to invest in affordable housing. My research led me to buying multi-family investments, i.e., apartments or mobile home communities, because all your tenants are in one place, making it much easier to manage. For the first four years, I bought affordable apartment complexes in Orlando, FL with the intention of holding them for the long-term. However, prices soared so I sold all seven of my complexes by mid 2006 because I had received unsolicited offers that were way more than I had paid a couple years prior. Once I sold, I wanted to reinvest, but Florida prices were too high, so I looked around, and with strong input from one of my commercial brokers, I decided to invest in North Carolina. But instead of buying more apartment complexes, I started buying mobile home communities (MHC's). I had no idea what MHC's were in 2005, though I had probably driven by many through the years. However, I found some information in the internet that indicated MHC's were better investments than apartments because, if they were well operated, they had much less turnover (i.e. residents moving in and out) and thus much less maintenance and repair expenses. So again I took action and bought an MHC and I did find it was much easier to manage than an apartment complex. So I kept buying them, mostly ones in distress from banks in 2011 and 2012. I now own 25 communities with almost 3,000 spaces in five states with annual rent exceeding $7 million. I have also done 16 full-cycle deals (buy, rehab, and sell) with sales proceeds in excess of $65 million. And best of all, I still work out of my house and rarely work more than 25 hours per week.

How have affordable housing investments treated other investors? A man who sold me a 175-space mobile home community in Raleigh, NC never graduated from high school and actually lived in the community for 28 years. That community paid for his three kids' college educations and he walked away from the sale with over $2 million (after tax) in his pocket. All from one community! Another guy I knew invested in three communities in California in the early 1970's. He sold one community for over $30 million and the other community, which has no debt on it, generates a check for over $100,000...per month! to him and his family. Finally, I visited I guy I know who lives in Buffalo who started buying affordable apartment complexes in the early 1990's. He now has over 60 apartment complexes throughout the East Coast. When I visited him last, he showed me his car collection, which had grown to 86 collector cars – Ferrari's, Aston Martin's, old Mustang's, etc. – pretty impressive.

Investing in affordable housing is not a get-rich-quick scheme. It is a great investment for long-term wealth, and one of the best for generating current passive income. The beauty of investing in affordable housing is that you don't need thousands of units. If you want to make $100k per year, all you need are 130-150 apartment units, 90-100 MHC spaces, or 35-40 single-family homes. This can be accomplished with one property or a couple properties. To obtain this type of cash flow from a property, you need to follow three important steps:

1. **You make your money at the purchase.** This phrase means you must understand your local market and find a property to buy that is trading below market prices.

2. **Cash Flow is king.** You never buy a property that isn't cash flowing day one. I can show you several ways to increase cash flow, but you never want the pressure of having to "feed" a negative cash flow property.

3. **Location.** If possible, you need to buy properties within 20 minutes of a major (200,000 people +) metro area, as that's where the jobs are. The key to a successful affordable housing property is that your tenants have easy access to lots of jobs.

Remember what my financial planning client said, that affordable housing does well in "good and bad times." Since the economic meltdown of 2008-2009, the demand for affordable housing has gone through the roof as millions of people have been forced to downsize. At the same time, the supply of affordable housing is at an all-time low as there has been very little affordable housing built in this country over the last 20 years because the land and infrastructure costs are too expensive. This is an Economics 101 perfect storm: big demand with limited supply means prices are going up and occupancy levels are at all time highs, whether it be in affordable single-family houses, affordable apartment complexes, or manufactured home communities. And I don't see any let up in this scenario as more and more middle class Americans fall into the lower class due to lower paying jobs and higher costs for everyday necessities like gas, groceries, education, health care, etc. Fortunately for my business, and unfortunately for the country (in my opinion), the gap between the rich and the poor continues to grow wider, which increases the demand for affordable housing. More than 50% of the country is now in a household that makes less than $44,000/year, which means they can only afford $500-$700/month in total housing expenses. Recent statistics show that nine out of the ten most prevalent jobs needed in this country over the next 5-10 years will pay between $8-$12/hr. As one of my friends in the industry who, who used to be a Wall Street guy and quit to own affordable properties full-time, said recently, "I love waking up every day knowing the demand for my product is only getting stronger."

The greatest thing about investing in affordable housing is that you can be part of the solution as well. We provide our residents with safe, affordable housing in clean and well-kept communities. We make a strong effort to get residents involved with each other by sponsoring activities at all the major holidays, putting in new playgrounds and soccer fields, planting a community garden, and coordinating with local organizations, such as the Boys and Girls clubs and local food trucks, to provide services to our community. The biggest mistake you can make with affordable housing is not reinvesting in the complex or community.

Re-paving the parking lots and/or community streets or rehabbing older apartments and/or homes every few years is a must. Slumlords are driven out of business quickly. Owners who treat their residents with respect (our policy is "firm, but fair") and reinvest in their complexes or communities will be the ones that thrive.

So how do you get started in affordable housing investments? Six steps:

1. **Get educated.** Any good business requires hard work and basic principles you need to understand so you don't make a big mistake on your first investment. You need to invest in education materials that provide a step-by-step process on how to invest in affordable housing.

2. **Find a mentor.** You need someone with experience in the business who can guide you through your first couple investments.

3. **Select a geographic area where you want to invest.** I like the Southeast and Midwest U.S., as they are more affordable.

4. **Choose your affordable housing investment type.** What do you feel more comfortable with – single-family homes (the easiest to get started with), apartment complexes (the easiest to get financed), or mobile home communities (the easiest to manage)?

5. **Put together a team.** You will need to find good local brokers, a local banker to finance your properties, a good CPA to handle your taxes, and a good property manager to oversee them.

6. **Put together a plan.** You will need a 1-year, 3-year, and 5-year plan that includes how many units you will buy, how much money it will take to acquire the units, how will you manage the units, etc. I have always found that written, measureable goals provide great accountability and are a great help to reaching your goals.

About Mike

Mike Conlon is President and CEO of Affordable Communities Group, LLC (acgmhc.com) based in Cary, NC through which he does his own affordable housing investments. He currently owns 25 mobile home communities with approximately 3,000 spaces in five states. He is also President and CEO of Affordable Housing Investment Specialists (ahis.guru or affordablehousingspsecialists.com) where he provides unique education materials and mentor programs for qualified investors looking to own their own affordable housing investments.

Mike is originally from Green Bay, WI (go Pack!). He received his law degree from the University of Minnesota in 1990. He was active in the financial planning business from 1990 through 2002 where he owned a financial planning broker-dealer that he grew from $1.6 million in revenue to over $40 million in five years and then sold to a large national insurance company. He also owned a large, full-service financial planning firm that had over $100 million in client investments, which he sold in late 2002.

From 2002 until today, Mike has been an active investor in affordable multi-family investments, first in Orlando, FL and now in Cary, NC. He has done 16 full cycle deals (buy, rehab, sell) in the last 12 years with sale proceeds exceeding $65 million.

Mike can be reached via his websites or at: mconlon1@gmail.com.

CHAPTER 48

8 WAYS TO TRANSFORM YOUR "JUNK-DRAWER FINANCIAL" INTO A BALANCED PLAN

BY JOHN HUTCHINSON, CHFC®, CLU®, EA

1. BALANCING YOUR EARNING EFFORTS WITH YOUR PLANNING EFFORTS

We've all seen sports teams that bought and recruited all the best talent in the world, but just can't seem to capitalize on it? On paper they should be crushing the competition, but the team constantly finds themselves falling short.

The same is true with many of the financial situations I come across. High-income earners who have all the visible symptoms of success, but when you look inside their financial locker room, there's a team divided and they're well short of making a run at the post-season. Like the sports franchise they've assembled a flashy roster, but lacked the leadership to provide a cohesive game plan.

Now I understand we're all busy at our job or business, and when we leave all we really want is to spend time with our family and friends. That's the way it should be. That's why team owners hire tactical specialty coaches and a head coach who has a fluent grip on the various facets of the game to coordinate the efforts of the team as a whole.

433

Take Dave, the owner of a thriving construction company. Dave spent more time last year trying to save an extra couple hundred dollars on his vacations than he did with the tens and hundreds of thousands of profits that passed through his fingers each month. He loved planning his family trips, which felt much more tangible than pursuing solutions to distant financial goals that all seemed so confusing. The few financial planners he spoke to didn't make sense to him, and he was sure they were just trying to sell him something.

It doesn't have to be that way. There are planners out there who can explain things in a way that makes sense, using analogies from your own business. They can start with near term efficiencies to better handle cash management and major capital expenditures like equipment and materials. Tying that into medium and long-term strategies could help Dave fully enjoy the present moment with the confidence of knowing there's a sustainable path to all his future moments that will someday be his now.

2. TRANSFORMING FRAGMENTED JUNK-DRAWER STRATEGIES INTO A COORDINATED BALANCED PLAN

The world makes way for the man who knows where he is going.
~ Ralph Waldo Emerson

We find that over time clients have adopted several different isolated strategies for different reasons, something we refer to as "junk drawer financial planning." All may have started with good intentions, but after years of neglect and auto-pilot they usually start working against each another, especially as life changes outside the junk drawer. Do all your different financial strategies still play nicely with each other? Did they ever? Or was each initiated in reaction to a situation or an emotional urge?

Take Brian and Karen, a realtor and a controller for a medical device company. As new parents, they started aggressively pumping money into a tax-sheltered college savings plan, which on its own merits seemed wise. After two years they had to make some home repairs and took on consumer debt because they didn't have sufficient liquid reserves to fund them. Sure their college accounts were growing tax-free, but if they took out any money they'd not only pay taxes, but penalties too. I look at these two fragmented financial decisions like having one foot on the gas and another on the brakes…not to mention the couple's own retirement goals were drastically underfunded. If necessary their kids could borrow for college, but there's no way Brian and Karen could borrow for their own retirement.

Find a planner who's fit to give balanced advice and who can make sure all the dials of your different instruments are calibrated and facing due North. Adjustments will someday be necessary, so it's paramount to find someone who is ethical and won't undo whatever quality work that's already in place.

3. GROUNDING COMMON OPINIONS WITH RELEVANT ADVICE

Have you ever heard a raving movie review from a friend or the media, only to be completely disappointed upon seeing it? Movies aren't inherently good or bad. They're just 90 minutes of imagery and dialogue. Our varying backgrounds, attitudes, hopes, and dreams shape whether or not the movie resonates with us.

Similarly some acquaintance or talking head can rave about certain financial strategies and slam others. Blanket opinions, however, are meaningless without the context of a particular situation. What are *you* trying to accomplish? How long can you allow for each strategy to blossom? What level of volatility are you comfortable with? Does this jive with what's already in place?

Also, when it comes to mass media and "financial entertainers," they aren't compensated by helping you build the optimal plan. They are paid to capture your attention while their commercial sponsors attempt to influence the masses.. The higher your income is, the less relevant that common advice from the media or the Internet will likely be. Did you know that according to data compiled by www.taxfoundation.org in 2010, households who made over $161,579 were in the top 5% of all income earners in the United States? This elite group paid over 59% of the total federal taxes paid. Households making over $116,623 in 2010 were in the top 10% of all income earners and paid over 70% of all federal taxes. Although you may not feel like one of the elite, your income is uncommon. The amount of tax you pay is uncommon. Therefore you may require customized advice, not just noisy opinions from media designed to captivate the masses.

Top % of Earners	Amount of Household AGI	% of Federal Taxes Paid
Top 5 %	$161,579	59.1%
Top 10%	$116,623	70.6%

4. IMPLEMENTING UNIQUE STRATEGIES VS. DIVERSIFYING SIMILAR PRODUCTS

Everyone's heard not to put all their eggs in one basket, but if keeping our eggs safe is the goal, maybe consider containers other than baskets.

Most advisors would describe diversification as investing in multiple companies of different sizes in different industries from different parts of the world. Doing so should protect a portfolio from big losses and violent swings.

How did that work out in 2008? How about the early 2000's? You see diversifying in this manner may have been effective in decades past, but with the rise of technology and globalization the world has become a much smaller place. When there's turmoil somewhere in the world, we feel the economic tremors everywhere.

In 2008, there was no place to hide. Everything was down: stocks, bonds, real estate, commodities, even the safe-haven of money markets was threatened momentarily. Traditional portfolios were chopped by 30%-50% within 12 months, and that is by no means a record with all the financial damage that occurred.

We tell our clients to "Diversify by Strategy." What does that mean? For your investments in the market, instead of owning ten different funds that trend on a similar path, we recommend using different institutional managers with different methodologies. Some managers have a track record of regularly outperforming the market while others are adept at avoiding large losses. For instance, there are a couple different managers we use that each lost less than 1% in 2008, yet still had very favorable returns in the years before and after that.

Another way to diversify by strategy is to layer in some products that offer contractual guarantees for either principal protection, a baseline growth rate, a future income stream, or possibly even all three. Having multiple unique strategies allows you to stick to your plan with confidence unlike having all your money floating in the exact same global risk pool. If the sky starts falling again like it did twice last decade, you won't get shaken out of your investments and miss the rise of the Phoenix.

5. BALANCING YOUR TAXATION ALLOCATION FOR A DISTRIBUTION-FRIENDLY RETIREMENT

It's not how much you make, but how much you can keep that matters.

For all the talk about diversification, the one area I find it completely MIA is in my clients' tax strategies. Since taxes can wipe out somewhere between one quarter to one half of your wealth building efforts, doesn't this deserve equally as much attention as the growth strategies themselves?

So how does one balance the taxation allocation? We're all for accounts that reduce our current tax liability, especially for higher-income earners. However, if the only places you're investing are inside accounts that defer taxes until the future, this can be a recipe for disaster.

Take Craig, a partner at a mid-sized accounting firm. He'd been told his entire life to maximize his 401(k) at work since he would be at a lower tax bracket in retirement, like it was a given. He also encouraged his other partners to layer in an additional defined benefit plan where his company could avoid paying tax on annual profits by aggressively socking away this money for retirement on a pretax basis. One of the junior partners will soon be buying out Craig over the first 5 years of his retirement.

Craig was very responsible deferring income into the 401(k) plan, plus the company defined benefit contributions. Both of these plans avoided tax during the working years, but will be fully taxable upon distribution. The buyout money will be taxable as well as his income from rental property he owns. Because of his success, 85% of his Social Security checks will also be taxable.

Not only that, but Craig will be losing some key tax deductions in retirement that he's been enjoying during his working years. His kids are grown up, the mortgage will be paid off, and certain fringe benefits he ran through the business won't be deductible anymore. So even though

Craig may be planning to live off say 75% of his final year's income, Craig might very well find himself heading right back up to those higher tax brackets he diligently planned to avoid during his working years.

Had he diverted some of his saving and investing efforts to tax advantaged accounts like a Roth IRA/Roth 401(k), certain municipal bonds, or Cash Value Life Insurance Contracts, Craig could have better controlled his tax situation in retirement. You see, those three vehicles mentioned above all can produce growth and distributions that are sheltered from taxation.* If they're in place, you can toggle and control your annual tax liability by balancing taxable distributions from retirement accounts with a layer of tax-free distributions. If taxes go up, this balancing effect becomes even more powerful.

6. SUPPORTING GROWTH WITH PROTECTION

*In business, I look for economic castles
protected by unbreachable 'moats.'*
~ Warren Buffet

When so much time and energy is spent growing wealth, it's absolutely vital to incorporate defensive strategies to protect it. Since the divide between the haves and the have-nots keeps widening, and we are by far the most litigious society on the planet, the concept of asset protection is essential. That could mean very intricate trust planning strategies, or it could simply mean choosing certain account types that have inherent creditor protection afforded to them by state and federal governments. How do you think OJ was able to be golfing in Florida despite the multi-million dollar judgment against him? The level of protection will vary depending on the state and the account type, but this is one aspect to consider when balancing your wealth building.

Another defensive facet to consider is contingency planning. Often times our clients have a strong steady income and a growing asset-base where, so long as nothing catastrophic happens, they'll have the game won. Layering in certain insurance products that protect against the loss of a major breadwinner's income and/or the inflated expense of long-term nursing care can be a prudent financial decision.

---

*Roths, Muni Bonds, and Permanent Life Insurance all have certain stipulations that need to be followed in order to retain their tax-exempt status. All three have unique risks to be aware of, so be sure to consult an advisor that can offer educated insights on each to determine the best mix for you.

When viewed as a hedge to carve off say 5% of one's wealth building efforts to protect the other 95%, clients can usually find some balance of wealth building and hedging they're comfortable with.

7. BALANCING NOW AND LATER

Forever is composed of nows.
~ Emily Dickinson

Let's just be clear that we are big proponents of living a fulfilling life in the present. That said, all of us will have to slow down at some point as our skills in the marketplace become less valuable. That's why we save and invest for retirement. Ideally, someday our money at work can replace us at work. Anytime we tap into our retirement accounts or delay contributing to them, we are borrowing from our future. This is where we work with clients to create some balance, and it doesn't need to be an either/or question.

Despite the fact that all the great advertising agencies of the world lead us to believe we need a myriad of products to attain happiness, we know that's not true. Our clients have found that laying out a monthly budget of their true needs, adding in some wants, and even building in a little extra cushion can be quite an eye-opening exercise.

I want to show you how powerful budgeting can be using a simple example:

Let's just say that somebody earns $100,000 a year, and saves $10,000 or 10% of their income. Now suppose this same individual is a very savvy investor and earns a 10% rate of return (net of fees, trading costs, and taxes due on the gains) earning them $1000 on that $10,000 saved. What if the same individual found a way through budgeting and efficiency to save even just an extra 2% of their gross annual income without compromising their quality of life? That would equal $2000, 2% of $100,000. Notice that through efficiency, our saver managed to effectively increase the rate of growth on their initial savings by 20% ($10,000 x 20% = $2,000).

Gross Income	$100,000	
10% Annual Growth	$10,000	
10% ROR	$1,000	
Saving an Extra 2% of Gross Income	$2,000	= 20% of Initial Annual Savings

That's double the somewhat optimistic investment rate of return, and obviously budgeting requires significantly less risk than trying to earn consistent double-digit growth rates on a consistent basis.

8. MAINTAINING THE BALANCE. KEEPING IT ALL TOGETHER

Life is what happens while you are busy making other plans.
~ John Lennon

It's important to find a financial planner that's more like a pilot than a ticket agent. A ticket agent sells you a ticket, you get on that plane, and they're gone. The pilot on the other hand stays in communication with the passengers and constantly adjusts in real time for the ever-shifting currents. The originally plotted course is never adhered to after the onset of the journey (just like those static financial plans).

Has life changed much since you last bought your last ticket?

About John

John "Hutch" Hutchinson ChFC, CLU, EA is President of Balanced Plan Financial. He specializes in helping entrepreneurs and high-income earners make deliberate financial choices considering the impact to their holistic situation. John takes a very educational approach with clients, boiling down complex financial strategies to simple concepts, stories, and sketches they can easily understand.

John's family situation gave him a special affinity for empowering business owners in the realm of financial planning and stewardship of capital. He was called to this niche of planning having watched his father's life's work as a successful entrepreneur come unraveled due to a premature death and a lack of proper planning. With his father in mind, John decided to join the financial services industry with the intention of building a more client-friendly model. He was given the opportunity to work as part of a major financial company's advanced planning team. Not wanting bias to taint his advice, John eventually left that opportunity to create his own boutique-planning firm not aligned with any particular financial institution.

John understands that a business owner's best rate of return will almost always come from within their business where they have more access, knowledge, and control. That said, he works with clients to grow their assets being mindful of principal protection, tax efficiency, and layers of asset protection. He often uses strategies employed by major corporate institutions, but rarely found in the small business arena. Strategies implemented today are designed with the client's endgame in mind by positioning for favorable distribution of assets and disposition of their businesses.

John lives in San Clemente, California with his wife of 11 years, whom he met in elementary school, and they have three daughters together. When not servicing clients, John enjoys biking and going on travel adventures with his family as well as playing tennis, golf, and stand-up paddle boarding.

CHAPTER 49

LEADERSHIP TRANSFORMATION

BY LARRY SZELIGA

As a manager, have you ever found yourself in a position where you felt overwhelmed? Where you were working harder than ever before and still were not generating the results that were expected of you? Where you were putting in more and more hours at work and having less and less time for family, friends, and personal enjoyment? Where your frustration level was so high that you hated your job and was dissatisfied with life in general?

Not long ago this was exactly my state of mind. My situation was amplified by the fact that in the various management positions I have held over the years, from First-line Production Supervisor to Chief Executive Officer, I was "golden," so to speak. I have worked in large publicly-traded companies, family-owned businesses, and small entrepreneurial enterprises. The companies I worked for included: DataRam, Inc., General Motors, DICO, Inc., Titan Wheel International, Inc., and OTR Wheel Engineering, Inc. It seemed that no matter what initiative I undertook, I was always successful. I appeared to have the proverbial Midas touch.

Since 1974, when I was first promoted into the ranks of management, the subject of leadership has been on my radar. I was infatuated with the importance of being able to influence and inspire others to achieve a common goal. In addition to the practical knowledge I gained as a manager, I had the privilege of being mentored by Professor of Leadership and author of Clear Leadership, Gervase Bushe, PhD. I also earned a Master's Degree in Organizational and Human Resource Development from American University which provided an academic dimension to my philosophical position that a leader's success was directly proportional to their ability to help those they are leading succeed in achieving their goals.

In 1986, I put this academic and practical knowledge to work as an independent consultant, and founded IQSS, LLC. My clients included, but were not limited to: General Motors, Ford Motor Company, Chrysler, Saturn, GE Medical, Shasta Beverages, Westinghouse Oceanic and Colgate-Palmolive. Helping others implement my philosophies toward leadership always generated positive results.

After 40 years of management experience, I could tell you a host of success stories that would be very impressive in any chapter about leadership. However, the real story I want to tell is a personal one, because about ten years ago, my golden streak of successes began to fade. I found myself struggling to achieve my objectives. I wasn't producing the same level of success I had previously experienced. Something had changed. It felt like I was losing more battles than I was winning. That was a new and unsettling dynamic for me. I wasn't exactly sure how or why it happened. My professional life had become one of confusion and frustration rather than success and fulfillment.

As time wore on, I felt as if I were caught in a downward spiral of being disheartened and exasperated. I was ill-tempered and moody. I blamed my lack of success on the incompetence of my people and an overwhelming workload. Needless to say, I was not pleasant to be around. In my mind, everyone was responsible for my less-than-stellar-performance, my diminishing success rate, and my extended hours. I was shocked and disgusted by the apparent level of incompetence that surrounded me.

Being naturally competitive and driven to succeed, I could not accept this. I found myself working harder and longer hours than ever before. I still met most of my objectives, but I did so through personal determination and individual contribution. The feedback I received from my peers made it clear that I was not meeting the overall needs of the organization or the expectations of the owner. The reality was that I had lost sight of the fact that my personal contribution could not be the winning factor for a team's long-term success.

I began entertaining thoughts of leaving the company. After all, I knew I could find someplace worthy of my talents. I needed a company where I could again thrive and where my proven abilities would once again be appreciated. In fact, the more I thought about leaving, the better I liked the idea. So I started trying to define the ideal company that would fit my needs. As I worked through this exercise, I began to notice that the characteristics of the company I was currently working for were a pretty close match to the ideal company I was trying to define.

That's when it dawned on me that it wasn't the company I was working for, its strategic plan, or the employees that were at fault. The reality was that I was already working for a good company and with some very good people. Through my pursuit of wanting to run to a better place, I came to the very uncomfortable realization that I was the root cause of my own ineffectiveness.

This pain of failure and frustration was a catalyst for starting an introspective journey that would change my life. I wanted to understand what had changed in the time lapse between my history of abundant successes and my current success drought. No matter how I approached this pertinent question, the answer was always the same. It was *ME!* I had changed and it wasn't for the better. This awareness was one of the most important awakenings I have ever experienced. It was also the beginning of some very penetrating, painful, and beneficial self-analysis that would eventually lead to a personal and professional transformation.

I turned to people I trusted and who would give me honest feedback and responses to my questions about my attitudes and behaviors toward leadership. Their answers were straight up, objective, relevant, and non-judgemental. I started to bounce thoughts, ideas, questions and experiences off my wife, Stephanie, who never failed to give me her unadulterated feedback; two of my closest cohorts: Andie Huberty and Tom Pitman; my very first mentor, Gervase Bushe; and my Life Coach, Jackie Bsharah. In addition to giving me straight up feedback, they frequently asked me questions about how I felt, how I interpreted some of my recent experiences, and how I reacted to those experiences. Their questions, challenges, and insights helped me to pull everything together into an integrated approach to leadership that not only made sense, but also worked with amazing speed, consistency, and most importantly, with long-lasting results time and time again. I was transformed!

What happened as a result was amazing! Everything began to fall into place and started making sense. I found myself riding a wave of successes that was unprecedented in my work experience. I was witnessing rapid and continuous improvement in every initiative I launched. I was working fewer hours and experiencing more successes. I found that I was happier and I had more balance in my life.

"So, what changed?" The answer is: a whole host of things – beliefs, attitudes, behaviors and methods. But, one of the most significant things was that I was finally understanding the leadership process and learning more about it every day. I realized that I had been pushing my people for results rather than inspiring, intriguing, and enabling them to succeed.

I realized that leadership is about helping those you are leading succeed in achieving their goals and objectives. It is not about the contribution or achievement of the leader. It is about the success their people have in the attainment of a common goal. Inevitably, their successes lead to the leader's success. This insight helped me realize that it was my responsibility to help my people generate results and meet their goals … *to succeed!*

As I applied my new insights on effective leadership, I found that people I had previously thought to be of questionable ability were suddenly becoming superstars. Others who previously tended to avoid me as their boss were seeking me out and asking for my involvement. Suggestions for improvement were forthcoming from multiple avenues. The organization seemed alive with excitement, positive feedback and employee engagement. And, I was actually having fun.

While I could write an entire book on my experience and what I have learned, I would like to focus on three principles that are Key to effective leadership: Establish a Foundation for Trust, Set a Compelling Goal, and Create a Supportive Environment.

ESTABLISH A FOUNDATION FOR TRUST

There is a significant difference between managing people (making sure they do what they were hired to do) and leading people (influencing people to achieve specific outcomes). Being an effective leader begins with knowing yourself. I found this out the hard way. I had lost sight of the fact that my previous successes were the direct result of my ability to help the people I was leading to succeed. Instead, I was focused on and enamored with my own success. I had lost track of who I was and what was important to me; my values, beliefs, needs, and wants.

Furthermore, I had lost track of what was important to my people, or maybe it would be more accurate to say that I stopped caring. To correct this, I made a conscious effort to be attentive to the values, beliefs, needs and wants of the people in my work world. I got to know them and establish communications at a level that was deeper than a casual, "Hello, how are you?" As a result, we developed a mutual trust. Without trust and deep communications it would be very difficult (if not impossible) to intrigue, inspire, and influence people to achieve the outcomes required by the organization.

Additionally, the leader must recognize that attending to the needs, wants, and expectations of those they are leading, means making sure that the people get credit for their achievements; are fairly compensated; and are adequately rewarded with positive affirmation for their contributions to the achievement of the common goals.

Once the deep communications and trust are established, it is time to introduce them to a Compelling Goal.

SET A COMPELLING GOAL

The second Key to effective leadership is having a Compelling Goal (mission, objective, or task), that is: an intended outcome that attracts strong interest and attention. During my self-evaluation, I discovered that I held my people accountable for the fulfillment of their job responsibilities and daily duties, but I failed to set a Compelling Goal that was important to the success of the organization. As a result, my people functioned as if they were on autopilot. Their Goal had become one of *"surviving the day."*

In order to create a Compelling Goal, the leader must make sure that the Goal is clear and achievable, and the people charged with achieving it must think and feel that it is legitimate, personally relevant, and that they have the discretion to determine how they will accomplish it.

This is also one area where the Leader's personal values, needs, and wants come in to play. I mentioned previously that the leader must be authentic and congruent, i.e. the leader's actions should match their words. I realized that I had repeatedly violated this responsibility. In one instance, for example, I clearly stated my value: "that we would operate our business with a "quality first" attitude." Then a situation arose where the product available to ship was not in compliance with the customer's specifications. It was the last day of the month, revenues were below target and I knew that the customer would probably not even notice that the product was not completely to print. I said, "Let's take the chance and ship the product." I hit my sales target, but I also sent a very clear message to my people that quality was not first. I was neither authentic nor congruent. My actions did not match my words. Inauthenticity and incongruence betrays the trust of the people the manager is leading,

Beyond Setting a Compelling Goal, the effective leader must demonstrate an unwavering commitment to its attainment. There may be times where difficult, unpopular decisions will have to be made. It is imperative that the leader demonstrates the resolve to make these decisions and take actions necessary to assure the successful completion of the Compelling Goal.

CREATE A SUPPORTIVE ENVIRONMENT

I define all of the external factors influencing the life, work, and activities of people as the Environment. The third Key to effective leadership is Creating a Supportive Environment, where others in the organization feel the Goal is legitimate to the wellbeing of the organization, will respond to the needs of those involved in achieving the Goal, and reward them appropriately.

An effective leader will create an environment that supports the efforts of their people, where they do not feel they are at risk if they try something new, where they are able to get the resources they need, and where they are expected to succeed. This requires the leader to network with others who control vital information and necessary resources—listen to the needs of their people, reward their efforts and progress, and identify and remove roadblocks.

Yes, there will be roadblocks. That's just part of the real world. Effective leaders do whatever it takes to assure the success of their people. That means that if there is something impeding the ability of the people to achieve their goal, it is the leader's responsibility to remove whatever it is that is inhibiting their progress. In the words of the great NBA standout, Michael Jordan, "If you're trying to achieve, there will be roadblocks. I've had them; everybody has had them. But obstacles don't have to stop you. If you run into a wall, don't turn around and give up. Figure out how to climb it, go through it, or work around it."

CONCLUSION

Leaders can significantly increase their potential to succeed if they realize that their success is directly proportional to the success of their people. Therefore, the more a leader can do to increase the opportunities for their people to achieve their Goals, the more success the leader will experience. Leaders who want to escalate the success potential of their people will "Establish a Foundation for Trust." They will "Set Compelling Goals." They will "Create a Supportive Environment." These leaders will do whatever it takes to assure the success of their people in the attainment of their Goals, and those who do will experience new levels of rapid and ongoing success. In fact, they will create a *Culture of Success.*

About Larry

Larry Szeliga is a Business Consultant and Leadership Coach with over 4 decades of management and consulting experience. As a manager, he has had a remarkable career progressing from first-line production supervisor to CEO, working in a variety of privately-owned and publicly-traded companies. He most recently helped grow a small privately-owned, $10 million Company into a $150 million dollar, worldwide organization.

Szeliga's consulting clients have comprised some of the world's largest organizations including: General Motors, Ford, Chrysler, Westinghouse Oceanic, Graybar Electric, GE Medical, and Colgate-Palmolive, to name a few.

Szeliga's experience as a manager and a consultant, supplemented by his Master's Degree in Organizational/Human Resource Development from American University, have helped him create ideas and techniques which have proven effective for newly-appointed managers, as well as senior executives. Larry has presented his concepts at hundreds of career-centric and corporate events. He is a sought-after speaker and a regular contributor to print and online publications.

As co-author of *Transform*, with best-selling author, motivational speaker, and consultant Brian Tracy, Szeliga shares his proven strategies, concepts and techniques.

Larry lives and works in Fresno, OH with his wife Stephanie, but travels the world meeting with business owners, managers, and other experts in the field of Leadership. He is the founder and president of Results Oriented Coaching/Consulting and can be reached at: larry.szeliga@rocoaching.com, at his office: 740-202-8000, or www. rocoaching.com

CHAPTER 50

BYSTANDERS AND INTEGRITY —MY TRANSFORMATION

BY JOHN DEWEY

*There I stood, frozen and not moving, sixty feet up, on top of a narrow
rock wall. The next few moments changed my life forever.*
~ John Dewey

When I was seventeen years old, I participated in a twenty-one day
backpacking trip in the Beartooth Mountain range of Montana. The trip
was organized by a Wisconsin-based summer camp. The group consisted
of eight seventeen-year-old males and two adult leaders.

One of the leaders was a former camper and college student. This was
typical as students and teachers had summers off to lead trips like this.
The other leader was not typical at all. I knew it the moment I laid eyes
on him. He was the most physically fit human being I had ever met in
my life. His name was Kermit and he was a former Green Beret in the
United States Army who had spent the past four years leading an elite
rescue team in the Alps. He was acutely aware of what led to success or
failure in the mountains and he did not waste any time conveying the
very basics to the group. Kermit's demeanor was calm, self-assured, and
not at all what I would have imagined of an elite soldier.

At that time, I was a high school athlete but I was not prepared for his
improvised boot camp. Early in the morning, he led us on nine-mile
runs, did push-ups, sit-ups, and stretching. Wisconsin summers can be

quite humid and this was one of the most humid summers on record. The humidity brought bugs and they were out in full force. Moments without a mosquito buzzing in my ear were few and far between. We whined and complained a bit in the beginning, but quickly started feeling the pride of being part of a budding and cohesive team.

We had five days in base camp to organize ourselves before our four-day drive to Montana. Those days were filled with navigation exercises, basic weather reading, organizing meals, and checking tents, backpacks and route planning. We also learned some basic rock climbing skills using some of the equipment. I must admit that I was not focused and struggled to pay attention at times. I also had a tendency to "wing it" at that age and worried more about looking good than actually asking questions and really understanding what was going on.

We headed west five days later on Interstate 80. On the second day, we arrived in the Black Hills of South Dakota, the site of Mt. Rushmore. After we hiked around the monument and took pictures, it was time to find a campsite and do some rock climbing. Local guides pointed us to a favorite area for climbing and we set up camp. Next we found a good spot to do some climbing.

Rock climbing requires certain pieces of equipment for safety. The first piece is a harness, which each leg goes through and secures around the waist. A figure eight loop secures the rope to the harness. The rope passes through climbing protection, which is either permanently or temporarily attached to the rocks. There is another person involved who is the belayer. The belayer is the security person on the rope who keeps the climber safe. The belayer has a belay device, which allows them to adjust the amount of friction in the rope. If necessary, they can stop the climber from falling.

We used a top belay, which means that the safety person was on top of the rock that the person was climbing. There I was, sixty feet up a rock wall. I was belaying for our leader, Kermit. There were two other people near me doing their own belays. Things were going fine for a while. When he was about fifteen feet from the top, I got mixed up in the ropes. I panicked. I started pulling the wrong end of the rope so there was a pile of slack in the rope and he was attached to the downside of that slack. I didn't know what to do and I froze. Kermit kept climbing and, moments later, he got to the top and saw the pile of slack in the rope. He said, "What is that?" I didn't know what to say except that I was sorry and I hadn't known what to do. His piercing green eyes focused on mine and he calmly and clearly said "Next time, you need to stop the climber, make sure that they are secure on the rock face, and get the rope straightened out...You can't ever let that happen again, do you understand?" He did not yell at me or shame me. The reality was that, if he had fallen, he most likely would have died. I had stood by, in that moment, and it could have killed him. My fear of looking stupid or not looking good got in the way of doing the right thing. I secretly hoped that someone else might have figured out my mistake and saved the situation. I was a bystander and I had never been so scared in all of my life.

I slept very little that night. I kept reliving my mistake over and over in my head. At first, I just beat up on myself for making such a stupid mistake. After I tired of my self-abuse, I got around to asking myself what I was going to do differently in my life.

Five days later, one of my fellow campers slipped and broke his ankle. He was in a great deal of pain and I was right behind him when it happened. I immediately called for help, pulled his pack off and got him comfortable. We camped right there for the night while the leaders formulated a plan to get him out. The next day we were down to one leader and seven campers.

Near the end of the trip we did a twenty-four hour solo experience. We each left the group at noon and returned 24 hours later. We were given coordinates on where we needed to go so as not to find our friends and cheat the solo experience. This also allowed Kermit to know precisely where we were in case of an emergency.

Right before I departed, I was confronted again with that sinking feeling of not knowing something. This time it was a lack of confidence in my navigation skills. Rather than sweeping it under the rug, avoiding it, or winging it, yet again, I told Kermit that I was not comfortable and I wanted to go over his navigation instructions again. I said this in front of everyone else. I believed, in that moment, that I was the only one who didn't know what he was doing. I felt stupid and inadequate but this time my feelings of inadequacy did not get the best of me. I stepped up and asked him for help. He started to explain it again and, almost immediately, three of my fellow campers joined in to watch and listen. The next evening, one of my fellow campers told me how grateful he was that I had stepped up and asked for instruction again, because he was not comfortable with his own navigation skills either. He said that he was too afraid to ask again because he thought that it had been covered enough, and he didn't want to look stupid. I told him that Kermit was not that way, and that it was more important to him that we know and understand what we were doing.

I left on my solo feeling much more confident with my navigation skills and knowing that I had done the right thing. Kermit taught me about integrity and that facing my fears, regardless of the situation, was the right thing to do.

Years later, while I was in graduate school, I was reminded of Kermit and my experience in the mountains after reading about Kitty Genovese. On March 13, 1964, something happened that drew a great deal of attention from social psychologists; in separate attacks spread over a 30-minute period, 29-year-old Kitty Genovese was stabbed, robbed, raped and ultimately murdered on a residential street in Queens, New York. Many neighbors and onlookers watched and listened as these attacks took place, taking no action whatsoever. Although her story was an urban legend magnified by a New York newspaper, it inspired social psychologists Bibb Latané and John Darley to develop the term "bystander effect" – wherein both diffusion of responsibility and social influence affect the way people do or don't act when others are in danger.

Diffusion of responsibility happens when onlookers fail to act if there are a number of other people around . . . after all, with plenty of other people who can step in, why should they? This could also be called the "well, don't look at me" effect. And social influence can be summarized as the "what's everybody else doing?" effect. If no one else is making a move, then you're sure not going to risk putting your own butt out there. Right?

I do my best not to be a bystander anymore but it is always challenging. In my work with wealthy families, individuals and their advisors no one is in danger of being stabbed, except possibly in the back. But maybe someone, something, or some tradition is actually at risk and if someone doesn't step up, individuals, the family, or the business will suffer. It could be that the CEO, otherwise known as Grandpa Toby, is making strange decisions or your brother, the CFO, seems oblivious to the downward turn in revenue. You could inform the board of directors, but you hold off, waiting for someone else to do it, especially since there is a good chance that the board, made up of more relatives, is more likely to blame you, the one who steps forward, for their own discomfort, and not Grandpa Toby. So, mentally, you avert your eyes; emotionally, you tune out. What's holding you back from acting? Is it that you are a coward, or could this be the bystander effect?

The truth is that if you huddle in silence, within the relative safety of the group, you're not doing the focus of your concern any favors. However, if you are afraid to open your mouth on your own, you could take advantage of the group and speak with one voice. After all, mobs enjoy a certain amount of anonymity. Get together, discuss what is on all of your minds and formulate a plan. Now, unless you intend to form a collective voice - a Greek chorus of sorts – then certainly one person will have to do the talking. But at least that person will have back up. And perhaps Grandpa Toby or brother Bart will be grateful; they may have been holding their breath, waiting for the axe to fall. You never can tell and if you remain silent you never will. I had Kermit to mentor me and he taught me how to step up and do the right thing.

About John

John states: *Trillions of dollars will pass from generation to generation over the next forty years; I've seen first-hand what happens when a lack of wealth planning issues are either ignored or only glimpsed, without thorough thought. Families can be torn apart, divorce becomes more prevalent, children lose communication with parents and grandparents. Siblings might stop speaking to each other. Most, if not all, of this family discord can be avoided.*

John Dewey offers both personal and professional insight into the world of high net worth multigenerational families, especially those with family businesses. He is one of several third generation heirs of a successful construction company and has experienced the psychological challenges that wealth and family business often causes.

After a painful meltdown of relationships in his own family and the successful intervention of a family wealth coach more than twenty years ago, John dedicated his life to helping others in his somewhat unique position. He holds a master's degree in psychology and his doctoral dissertation addressed the benefits and challenges of privilege.

John and Maureen have been married for twenty years and have four children. Together they have experienced many challenges in determining how to encourage their children to grow and develop in an environment where assets are plentiful.

The Dewey family lives in rural Minnesota in a renovated barn; they are active in their church and Boy Scouts and they value their community. John advocates, educates and coaches high net worth families, heirs, and their advisors.

John is passionate about breaking the self-imposed silence that plagues many families. He works to strengthen family members, as individuals and participants with a unique heritage, allowing them to prosper from generation to generation through his unique Prosperitage process. For more information, go to JohnDewey.com or call 866-945-9950.

CHAPTER 51

CHANGE YOUR OUTLOOK, CHANGE YOUR LIFE! NOW IS YOUR TIME TO LIVE HAPPY!

BY EVAN KLASSEN

Trans-form:

- *change something dramatically: to change somebody or something completely*

- *undergo total change: to change completely for the better*

- *convert something to different energy: to convert one form of energy to another*

> *Insanity is doing the same thing over and*
> *over again, and expecting a different result.*
> ~ Albert Einstein

We all know it, we've all heard it, and yet, so many of us are still stuck. We WANT something different. We WANT to be healthier. We WANT to be more secure. We WANT a better relationship... In short, we WANT to be happier, but we keep doing the same things over and over again, living and reliving the same mistakes, frustrated, unhealthy and unhappy, somehow expecting a different result.

How do I know? I was there. Actually, I was born there!

I was born as one of nine children in Dushanbe, Tajikistan, the poorest country in Central Asia to a German father and a Ukrainian mother. At that time, Tajikistan was a country torn by civil war, poverty, communism and racial strife.

Since I was five, I remember feeling not welcome in the world I lived in. Everything around me was telling me I was a second class citizen, and I bought into it, even at that young age. I began cultivating a strategy to survive: I became Nice. Not just nice, but Nice with a capital 'N'. I began spending my energy on finding something special in every person I met. Even with my enemies, I found some nice points, and this became my coping mechanism to avoid hatred and persecution. It was my secret weapon.

In this way, I was able to navigate a slippery path through my challenging childhood until our eventual escape and emigration to Germany. Along the way, some of the people – even one-time enemies – became friends. In these small victories, I found a happiness that became my escape from low self-esteem.

In 1992, I took the mandatory German school entrance exam and was downgraded a grade. Suddenly, in one of the clearest ways possible for a scared, immigrant eight-year old kid, I was told I wasn't smart enough to be with my friends my age. Talk about a confirmation of one's lack of self-worth!

I fell back on my old strategy of finding the good in others in my school; if I could turn them in to my friends, no matter that the friendship was primarily one-sided, I could fit in.

Over the next few years, I became good at finding something special about every person I met, and when I did, that was when I was my happiest. I had friends of all shapes, colors and creeds, despite our obvious and glaring differences. I was able to find a common ground and we were able to ignore the other details like our religions, traditions, families, etc… you know, the small things. The truth was I had many acquaintances but no real childhood friends. No one was close to me as I was afraid to let them get close enough to see the real me, the unworthy Evan inside, as I was ashamed of who I was.

I started working at age 11, in part to help support my family, but also, in a way, to run away and continue to hide from my pain. By the age of 14, I was working three jobs along with my schooling. I would leave home before sunrise, and some nights, I wouldn't return until after midnight. I was running from my challenges.

Despite the shallow friendships and the minor business successes I was having, inside, I was still stuck in my battle against my own low self-esteem. It became part of my daily prayer, asking God that if He loved me, why had He made me so worthless.

I also became a very good actor. I was able to hide my feelings and needs behind a façade of social skills so even my family was not aware of my fears. I was the social one, the happy one, but it was all a coping mechanism. I mastered what I called the "Seven minute friendship:" I would meet someone, and within five to seven minutes, try to make them a friend before moving on. I felt that if I spent more than seven minutes with them, they would start to find out I wasn't smart, that I wasn't really as confident as I let on. I spent the first 21 years of my life in secret shame of who I was.

Then, as so often happens, the world caught up to me. I was completely controlled by what others thought of me. My self-esteem—or lack of it—dictated everything in my life. I was burning the candle at both ends, and would have lit a third one if I could have. Even as I continued to put on my social face, I slowly began to slip further into major depression, until at my lowest point, I wanted to end my life, as I couldn't see the light at the end of the tunnel.

God answers prayers in three ways: 1) Yes, 2) No, and 3) Not yet; and when I was at my lowest, when I had been broken down to nothing, He finally started to answer my prayers. A college friend invited me to a business event, and I said "yes." It was as if the lights came on and the gates were opened!

Not only had I discovered personal development, that night I also found entrepreneurship, and my life had a new course. One of the mentors I met that night gave me a copy of two audio books that literally started to transform my life, one day at a time. The first was Napoleon Hill's *Think and Grow Rich*, and the second was Brian Tracy's *21 Secrets to Success*. They started me on an amazing new journey, and suddenly, instead of shame, the world was filled with endless possibilities.

At this point in my life, I had never heard of personal development or entrepreneurship, and the idea that there were books and audio books and seminars on how to grow personally was a foreign and awesome revelation.

It has been said many times that when the student is ready, the teacher will appear, and my friends, this student must have been ready!

I came across the startling and amazing idea that what **we** think, rather than what others think can influence our lives, and that it's our opportunity **and responsibility** to think positively about ourselves. In short, what others think is not the metric that defines my self-worth.

The books allowed me to look at my life differently. I was able to look at life through the eyes of people who had created and lived success, rather than just through my own, which were full of my perceived failures, and colored by my low self-esteem. These authors and leaders became my silent mentors.

I was able to compound a few small victories and these books and events helped me shift my philosophy and beliefs. It definitely wasn't overnight, and there were certainly setbacks, but little by little I was able to look at situations differently.

I discovered that life is much like looking at the world through a camera: you can focus intently on certain things, whether good or bad, and that if you don't take a step back, that narrow focus robs us of the entire experience, and can influence the meaning we give to it. The other side of the camera analogy is that we have control over what we focus on: for example, if you only focus on people being sad, or your own unhappiness, or, conversely, if you focus on joy and happiness, your outlook – your attitude – is influenced.

It wasn't until the age of 29, when I was co-authoring my first book "Think and Grow Rich Today" that I discovered that my skill of finding something special in every person I met, which had once been my protection mechanism, but now became a huge asset in connecting to the hearts of people. However, instead of doing it to assuage my own lack of self-worth, I was now using it to help others to discover the good about themselves. I became so intent on helping others be happy, regardless of their situation, that it has become my life's mission!

It turns out that God had spent 25 years developing my networking skills and teaching me how to touch people positively. Now I live to "empower people to live happy," by helping them find something great within themselves, and loving them from the heart. Now, instead of making a friend in seven minutes and moving on, I started to focus on transformational friendships.

I began to live life to the fullest. I gained a purpose and began to understand my life and who I was.

My life has come full circle, as I have now had the opportunity to contribute to both of the amazing authors who started my life on this new journey. A year ago, I was blessed beyond belief by being asked to co-author the new *Think and Grow Rich Today*, featuring Napoleon Hill. As I was working on my writing, I started looking at my past and was able to give a new, empowering meaning to the difficult events that happened. We can't change our past, but we can certainly change what this past means to us.

One of the keys is to start looking at our roadblocks and using them as building blocks, rather than excuses.

I am not saying this as some nice sounding platitude. Literally, when we change how we look at things, the things we look at change! Starting to ask the right questions for your life and meaning is your way out—the circumstances themselves can either empower us or kill us. Make our life or destroy it, much of the difference is how we choose to look at it. The circumstances themselves seldom change.

The world doesn't owe us a living. It doesn't owe us happiness. Warning: You are responsible for your own life and your own happiness. We were not promised happiness, just the opportunity to try to find it!

One of my favorite stories is the German shoemaker who sent two of his researchers to Africa to explore if there would be market for their products. One came back frustrated, saying that there is no market because everyone went around barefoot all day. The second man came back and told the boss to ramp up production because everyone was barefoot and needed shoes!

Do we find the problem in every opportunity or can we change our thinking to see the opportunity in every problem? The way we do that is to internally change the question and the meaning we give to things that happen to us. This is the basis of true happiness. Many studies have shown that people in poor countries are often happier than those in richer countries, and this happiness is very internal – happiness comes before success – we can't wait for success to be happy – we have to be happy for the success to come!

From the bottom of your heart, you have to have a desire to change and transform.

Now at 30, I look back at the darkest point in my life, where I hated everything, rejected my family and everything around me, and now I see that it was how God broke me down enough to make me look beyond my own suffering, and opened up a world where I could be my real self. Now I aspire to help people, but instead of doing it out of fear, it is my calling. I find the common good and find bridges that connect us as humans instead of the things that separate.

Until we give meaning to things, the things don't have any meaning.

Example? When it rains, a billion people wring their hands, another billion don't care, and another billion thank God.

If we are going to transform, we have to deal with what happens *in* us, not what happens *to* us. A dear friend had a heart attack, but rather than bemoaning his bad luck, he was able to change his eating, his health, his relationship with his family and more. Now he celebrates life like never before.

Events are going to happen to us in our life, and there will be our response (the meaning to us), and then the outcome, and of the three things, the only one we can control is our response – our outlook, which influences the outcome, which drives us to the top of our life, or the bottom, or keeps us where we are. Either way, it's in our hands! When we take 100% responsibility for giving our life events the right empowering meaning, we start creating a happier life!

Life is very much like a jigsaw puzzle. If you just look at one piece, it's tough to tell what it is, but as you put them together, you start to see the beautiful picture. Life is a collection of experiences that with the right meaning – putting the pieces together properly (not forced – that creates the wrong picture) – is revealed over time. The little decisions we make empower us, in both victory and defeat. Each piece of the puzzle, whether good or bad, is part of the picture, and can't be left out. Eventually, the entire picture will be clear, but for now, we have to take each piece and see what we can learn and take from it.

Some people are so full of fear, they hope tomorrow never comes. Others ask the right questions, and can't wait for tomorrow to come!

These questions are what reveal the true beauty of life.

I would like to leave you with the empowering question that guides my life everyday:

"How can I live my best life today?"

In short, what can I do spiritually, emotionally, financially, physically and health-wise to make this my best day ever?

Take the time to answer it and give it conscious energy and direction: write your answers down! **"Ink 'em and think 'em!"** This will help you create the clear path to where you want your life to go. This will not happen overnight, and yes, you will fail sometimes, or, like me, many times, but as Thomas Edison said, "you're not a failure until you give up!"

Challenges will come up, you may lose temporary "success" (I did for sure!), but learn, move forward, and you will end up growing richer, healthier and happier than you would have ever thought possible.

My friend and author David Adlard says, "Happiness depends on ourselves." Choose to live happy, my friends!

Special Acknowledgement from Evan Klassen:
To my beautiful girl Ella Klassen, my parents Johann and Tanya Klassen, my little brother Serge Klassen, my 7 sisters and family, as well as my mentors, John C Maxwell, Anthony Robbins, Brian Tracy, Darren Hardy, Jeff Olson, Art Jonak, David Byrd, Ron Forrester,

Leslie Hocker, Sven Goebel, Opher Brayer, Garrett and Sylvia McGrath, Eric Worre, Mark & Tammy Smith, Josephine Gross, Dennis Windsor, Ron Mathis, Dave Rothfeld, The Amazing Production Team at CelebrityPress™ and David Adlard and many others who have inspired me to grow.

I love and appreciate you all. Live Happy!!!

About Evan

Evan Klassen is a Best-Selling Author, Speaker, and Entrepreneur whose "rags-to-riches" story, from extreme poverty in war-torn Central Asia to becoming an American entrepreneur, inspires all who meet him. You might have also seen Evan as host of the show "Immigrant 2 Millionaire," which was created to bring to light incredible stories of success. Currently, Evan is leading the creation of a revolutionary organization with the purpose of empowering people to live happy and help them reach their maximum potential in life through entrepreneurship and personal development.

Evan was born in the mid 1980s into a life of war and poverty where getting food and clean water was considered a "good day." Being one of nine children in a blue-collar working family taught him to work hard for everything in life. After moving to Germany as a child, Evan began working for himself at age 11 and began developing his skills in entrepreneurship and music. At age 21, he was introduced to personal growth. To date, Evan has invested well over $120K into books, seminars, events, audio trainings and personal coaching. He believes that the best investment you can make is an investment in yourself.

In 2006, he moved to the United States, where, a year later he started a real estate business. Through many struggles and persistence he grew his business from 0 to over $22 million in revenue in a period of 4.5 years. His passion for music and business gave Evan the opportunity to travel to over 20 different countries and has allowed him to touch tens of thousands of lives.

His excitement and love for people brought him into the network marketing profession in mid 2008. Since then he has built sales organizations with over 20,000 distributors in 23 countries, and over $10 million in revenue, as well as a combined income, as an Entrepreneur between 2007 - 2012, in excess of 1 million dollars.

Evan Klassen is a true star in the field of personal development, having battled with depression and suicide at one point, and coming out victorious to share his story of failure and success to inspire people all over the world. Evan gives glory to his creator for all of his achievements.

Click here: www.EvanKlassen.com
Follow Evan at: Facebook.com/EvanKlassenVIP
twitter.com/EvanKlassenVIP
For his TV Show, go to: www.Immigrant2Millionaire.com

CHAPTER 52

TAKE A RISK! CHANGE YOUR LIFE!

BY ERICA WEST

Cold winds blew, snow piled. Then the rains came. Seven weekends in a row. My nose went from blue to running. I desperately wanted to escape from Massachusetts and my life. But to where? And how? For a shy, introverted school teacher and a consumer electronics salesman with two-teenage boys, just scraping by, the options were limited. But there are always options and we get to make a choice. As Yogi Berra pointed out, "When you come to a fork in the road, take it."

It came in a dream. My husband dreamt about the Grand Canyon, which he had never seen. He awoke with the thought, "Let's visit Phoenix."

That July the boys went to 4H camp and we flew to Phoenix for a look-around. We were awestruck by the bright sunlight, openness, cleanliness and July heat. Upon weighing the options we agreed that we would rather starve in the heat than in the cold.

We drove around Phoenix and Scottsdale getting a feel for the desert and the lifestyle. So opposite from the gray, closed-in northeast. A hotel concierge suggested we visit the tallest fountain in the world just east of Scottsdale in appropriately named Fountain Hills. Acting on his advice was a pivotal point in our lives.

The views made us gasp. The scenery was breathtaking. Mountains wrapped around this tiny desert community of 3000 people on three sides while the south opened to reservation land and the city of Mesa where a carpet of lights sparkled in the night. Watching the Fountain as the water cascaded from skyscraper height into the small lake was a Zen moment.

Here is where we wanted to be, this baby desert community. It never occurred to us that we couldn't do it. We didn't have a clue how, but confidently believed that we could succeed. We were in our early 40's, healthy, strong and willing to do what we had to. We had already survived a devastating time when the only way we could pay for the baby's medicine was to return the empty milk bottles.

We moved forward on blind faith. We took the risk. It changed our lives.

There is a difference between gambling and taking a risk. You have no control of the outcome when you gamble. You win by chance. But when you take a risk the odds are in your favor because you have some control of the outcome by the choices that you make. Whether you act on an idea or not you are making a choice.

The little equity we would receive from the sale of the house would be our nest egg until we got jobs. Back in Massachusetts we started the moving process. We put our house up for sale. Like most sellers we wanted more than it was worth because we needed it. I didn't learn until afterwards that I had inadvertently chosen a really good real estate agent. It wasn't until later that I discovered that there is a difference. So we threw the kids (aged 14 and 16) and the cats into the covered wagon and went west. Well, not exactly. Not without some drama.

The universe needed to test us first. On the second day, traveling along Interstate 71 east of Columbus, Ohio with my brother who was driving out with me, we hit a wall of snow, a whiteout. Blinded. Within seconds, 36 cars, semis, and a Greyhound bus carrying the elderly bounced off of each other – creating a ½ mile of mangled steel, and bone chilling sounds. Screams, sirens, helicopters. Snow continued to fall sometimes almost obliterating the scene.

Four hours later in the back of a police car, the promise of a warm motel room and my image of the vodka martini I was going to order (as soon as we took the ice and broken glass out of our splintered Samsonite luggage that we had retrieved from the accordion that had once been my car), lessened the trauma I was feeling.

The motel turned out to be an old wooden, somewhat rickety structure almost in the middle of nowhere. When I asked the receptionist where the bar was I got raised eyebrows. "This is a dry county, mam. You cannot buy liquor in this town." Huh? The heat was almost non-existent in the room. I warmed it by stuffing towels around the door and window and running the hot shower to create steam to fill the tiny room.

Okay, so my car got smashed, my luggage and most of its contents destroyed; I was freezing; I still needed a way to get to Phoenix and adding insult to injury I couldn't get a glass of wine. My brother and I took stock of our situation. This was all small stuff. We had survived and without a scratch or bump. Big stuff.

We started to laugh. Attitude is a choice.

I must have passed the test, because a week later I was in Fountain Hills signing a one-year lease for a house on top of a hill on 2 acres with 360-degree views. I had wandered into a real estate office on the unlikely chance of finding an affordable rental in this amazing environment. To my surprise and delight, they had one, the only one available! Huh!

The house was an early home in this desert community started in 1973. The owner built it himself. Its construction was rather dubious so no one wanted to buy it. While I waited for the rest of the family to arrive 5 weeks later, I explored the area. It was so different. Sometimes I felt as if I had landed on the moon, other times it appeared to me as the land of milk and honey.

Open houses were everywhere. The Valley of the Sun was beginning to grow. As a pastime I drove around Phoenix and Scottsdale looking at houses, talking to agents, asking questions. Little pink houses were springing up almost overnight. Something intrigued me. By chance an agent suggested I get a license to sell real estate. Who me?

Somewhere in the recesses of my mind I heard the words of a principal I had worked for, "Selling is teaching. If you are a good teacher you can be successful in sales." I had no idea what I wanted to do in this new life. I just knew that I didn't want to teach school. I chose to follow her suggestion.

My life was transformed. A whole new world opened up to me. Opportunity comes in many disguises. But you can recognize it because it always comes hand in hand with choice. In the meantime my husband, who had done some networking of his own before we moved, received an offer for a job.

Fountain Hills was, at the time, a small community in a county island. It was governed by the county. The land was owned by the master developer whose sole purpose at that time was to sell the lots to individual buyers to build their future dream home. Low on self-confidence, and completely out of my comfort zone, I began my career *selling* the lots for the developer. I learned all I could about the land, its structural and architectural possibilities. Blind faith led me to what I was meant to do, the place I was meant to be.

I watched the top producers in our office, listened to what they said and how they said it. Whenever real estate trainers came to the Valley. I paid to see to them. I traveled to hear them. They taught those who were willing to invest in themselves and learn that being a real estate agent is a business. They emphasized goals and clear vision, opening our eyes to the possibilities. Each trainer had something else to offer. The networking and sharing of ideas was priceless. The agents who attended these events were tops in the field. Real estate trainers like Tom Ferry, Monica Reynolds and the late Howard Brinton are greatly responsible for the professionalism of the real estate industry today.

They taught us how to run a business and what it meant to be a good agent. Good real estate agents are full-time career agents who market themselves, market your property and know the economics of pricing a home so it sells for the highest price the market will bear.

I began listening to self-development gurus. Brian Tracy, Jim Rohn and Tony Robbins became my companions. I listened everywhere. Goal-setting was not in the curriculum when I went to school. I started setting goals and writing them down, following my mentor's instructions.

My third year as an agent I was recognized as the top producer in the office. Just at that time the savings and loan debacle started and my husband lost his job. Banks were closing and homes were going into foreclosure. Chicken Little was yelling the sky is falling. Depression fell. Doom and gloom paralyzed everyone.

We had a choice; we could stay in the dismal atmosphere and eventually get sucked into it or we could find a way out.

By chance, an advertisement in an industry magazine caught my eye. A new real estate company with a different business model was selling franchises. It was targeted to top producing agents who wouldn't let themselves be influenced by outside circumstances that they couldn't control.

We saw an opportunity to grow and to be in business for ourselves. We made the choice to risk it and bought a franchise. Of course we were now seriously in debt. The country was in a full-blown recession and our credit cards were maxed out. But we moved ahead with blind faith and the confidence we had gained from success.

In those moments when we felt fear we remembered Brian Tracy's advice. "Think about the worst thing that can happen. If you are prepared to deal with it, take the risk." Our teachers had taught us well.

Lessons from history show us that life is cyclical. But I see the cycle more like a Ferris wheel, forever turning. You get on and it starts to move upward, swinging with the rhythm of the wind, taking you up and then down as it rotates. Sometimes it even gets stuck in a spot and you find yourself dangling. It is your attitude and your choices that can carry you back up.

 So after 10 years of success beyond our wildest dreams, we made a poor choice by selling our franchise to the wrong person. My husband and I found ourselves at the bottom of the wheel once more. It was a painful time. The old self-development tapes came out of the closet, the teachers reminding us to have a "can do" attitude. We took another chance and started over again opening a new independent real estate agency under my name. We took the ride back up to the top.

If you are one of the thousands of people who have a fear of heights you stay low, overcome by the fear that you will fall. Well, so what if you fall? Get up! The bumps and the bruises are small stuff. You are alive. That's big stuff. You can reach heights you never dreamed of if you take a risk. Hidden behind the veil of risk lies opportunity. Remember risk involves choice, but the odds are in your favor when you make these 7 choices:

1. Let go of fear.

2. Have an attitude of faith and belief in yourself.

3. Know the difference between the big stuff and the small stuff.

4. Set goals and write them down.

5. Take action. Stay in action.

6. Invest in yourself by investing in your education. Learn all you can in your chosen field. Become an expert.

7. Listen to self-development mentors' CDs, read their books and do the exercises. They will help you through #1 and #2

Be brave. Enjoy the ride.

About Erica

Erica has been a residential real estate agent since 1984, following an 18-year career as an educator. Migrating from Massachusetts to Arizona, Erica, her husband and two sons settled in Fountain Hills where she rode a path to amazing success – becoming one of the top 100 ReMax Real Estate Agents Nationally. Erica's approach to her clients is influenced by her background in education. "People move because they want a better lifestyle. Before they make a decision regarding the largest investment they will ever make, they need to understand the value of the house. They need to know what to expect, where the pitfalls lie and how to avoid them."

Working with a team, Erica provides services beyond the scope of selling, offering staging consultations and helping people prepare their homes for sale, even if it includes updating. She educates her clients by offering Equity-Building Consultations and Equity-Checkups, showing consumers how to build up equity and encouraging them to keep track of their equity. Erica is determined to see her clients succeed. When a homeowner called dismayed about what to do with the neglected home he inherited, Erica took charge of a complete remodeling project before getting the house sold.

Erica and her husband purchased a ReMax franchise in 1989. They sold it in 2000 and subsequently opened Erica West and Company, which they sold in 2005.

Erica's marketing is designed to educate. She has appeared on CBS affiliate TV live news program as a real estate expert answering consumer's questions. Erica is licensed by the State of Arizona to teach marketing to other agents. Her marketing ideas have been included in two books by real estate coaches, Bernice Ross and Mike Ferry.

Erica writes a weekly "Let's Talk Real Estate" column in the local newspaper and a weekly blog on her website. Consistently recognized for her expertise and production, Erica is a recipient of the ReMax Lifetime Achievement Award and a member of the ReMax Hall of Fame. Erica has been a speaker at many real estate events and has shared the stage with past President Gerald Ford and UCLA Coach John Wooden and some of the top real estate agents in the country. As a skilled Certified Negotiator and a Seller Specialist Representative, Erica has sold more than 2000 homes.

Erica believes in giving back to the community. She has served as a director and president of the Fountain Hills Community Foundation and secretary of the board of the Golden Eagle Education Foundation. Erica is a past member of Rotary and has been involved in a variety of local charitable events. Erica and her team currently work at the same ReMax franchise they used to own.

Erica can be reached at:
Erica West
Re/Max Sun Properties
Tel: 480-650-7002
Erica@ericawesthomes.com
www.EricaWestHomes.com

CHAPTER 53

BUILDING BLACK BELT CHILDREN

BY HILARY J. SANDOVAL III

"Its easier to build strong children than to repair broken men."
~ Frederick Douglass

In the martial arts the symbol of success, excellence, and achievement is the black belt. Please know that this chapter is not about martial arts for your children, its about using the character building skills that are inherent in the martial arts to help your child develop the skills to become a black belt in life. I have been in the martial arts business for over 30 years, however when I am asked what I do for a living my answer is that I help children build the foundation necessary for achievement and success.

Before I share some of the motivational teaching strategies that are used in the martial arts, I would like to share my own personal story how the positive thinking martial arts develops changed my life. Martial arts saved my life. No, I didn't find myself in the middle of a life-threatening self-defense situation requiring me to fight for my very existence. Instead, it was the leadership skills, the character values I learned, the confidence I gained, and the sense of self-worth I developed as a student that saved me from a path of certain self-destruction. It was the challenge to both my mind and body that transformed me from a life of potential misery and regret to an entrepreneur dedicated and passionate about helping children reach their full potential in life.

My spiral of descent began with the death of my father when I was a 15-year-old teenager. My father, put quite simply, was my hero. I knew he couldn't leap tall buildings in a single bound, however, I thought he had the powers necessary to defeat brain cancer. June 11th, 1973 was the day I realized that my father was mortal, the same as the rest of us. Three days later, only hours before my father was to be laid to rest my mother received a call from the doctor informing her that I had a brain tumor as well.

During my father's courageous and valiant fight for his life, I was losing weight, suffering terribly from headaches, and had no energy at all. The doctors assumed that I was merely suffering from the stress of witnessing my father's health deteriorate daily. Following my diagnosis, I was in and out of hospitals for the better part of a year.

After months of unsuccessful radiation treatment (it is a wonder I don't glow in the dark) brain surgery was required. I'm not writing about the non-invasive surgery of today where laser beams are used through the nose or mouth; I'm speaking about old fashion saw your skull in half, pulling your skin off your skull, and drilling-holes-in-your-head surgery. (I hope you're not squeamish.) The scar that runs from ear to ear across the top of my head serves as a reminder of this dark period of my life.

I write dark period, because at the time I grew very bitter and resentful. Bitter about the loss of my father and resentful about my health. Depression ruled my life, so much so that I was apathetic about the situation, not caring whether I survived the surgery or not. I watched my father suffer greatly from two painful unsuccessful brain surgeries himself. In my young and still immature mind, I had somehow formulated the idea that if the surgeries were unsuccessful for my father why would it work for me? Thankfully the surgery was successful. However, rather than being grateful, I continued to cling on to my anger, resentment, and bitterness.

My poor attitude led me to some very self-destructive behavior. I regularly challenged my mother's authority. Even after missing an entire year of school due to my health, I was regularly truant not thinking about how my actions would affect my future. I was making the wrong kind of friends, drinking heavily and was definitely heading down a path of self-destruction. At the young age of 16 I felt lost, hopeless, and completely empty inside.

Several months earlier my doctor had suggested martial arts as a means to get back in physical shape. The doctor informed me that the martial arts are based on individual achievement. He said I would start to feel better about myself, regain my physical strength and develop self-discipline. I'm embarrassed to admit that my reasons for enrolling in the martial arts were far less noble. Quite frankly, I wanted to take out my pain, anger, and frustration on anyone who dared crossed me. This is the opposite of what martial arts is about.

I quickly discovered that martial arts are not about hurting others. It's about developing yourself. It's about becoming the best you can be. In time, my depression was replaced with hope. My hope grew to passion. My emptiness was filled with a burning desire to earn my black belt and becoming a professional kickboxing promoter.

I achieved my goal of becoming a professional kickboxing promoter at the age of 18, becoming the youngest promoter in the United States to promote a professional world championship at the age of twenty-one. I also promoted the very first nationally-televised kickboxing match in the state of Texas. During my time as a promoter I had the good fortune to work with 23 world champions, including legendary film star Chuck Norris. After retiring from promoting I soon opened my academy.

The reason I share this story is because I truly believe if it weren't for the positive mental aspects of the martial arts – I wouldn't be here today. It was those empowering principles that I learned that gave my life direction and hope.

So how does the above story relate to helping your child build the confidence, discipline, and self-esteem to live a happy, productive, and successful life? … Because the qualities and character traits it takes to earn a black belt or become a champion are the very same life-skills it takes to lead a happy, productive, and successful life.

In our martial arts academies we have discovered that there are four key areas that are needed to build black belts:

1. A 'Yes I Can' Attitude
2. Black Belt Confidence

3. Black Belt Challenges

4. Black Belt Self-Esteem

A 'YES I CAN' ATTITUDE

Our school motto is Black Belt 'Yes I Can.' Every time students bow in our academy, they say 'Yes I Can.' Over my 40 plus years of experience in the martial arts I have learned that the most important key to earning a black belt is believing you can earn a black belt.

The greatest barrier for a child to earn his black belt is not a lack of self-discipline or desire. In our years of experience we have discovered the greatest reason some students fall short of earning their black belts is the lack of belief in their abilities. Without self-belief, it is nearly impossible for your child to reach his dreams and goals.

To illustrate the power of belief and demonstrate the limitations of fear and doubt, I'll use our white belt test as an example. For students to pass their white belt examination they must break a wooden pine board with their bare hands.

It's easy to explain the science and physics that cause a board to break from a karate blow. The velocity of the strike, plus the force, backed by mass will cause the board to break. However there is a very important mental aspect as well. For the board to break the student must fully commit his technique. Often times children fear they will hurt their hands when they hit the board and as a consequence they tentatively hit the board not fully extending their technique. As a result they hit at the board, rather than punching through the board. Fear prevented them from giving their best effort. Doubt prevented them from success.

Ironically, it hurts more when the board doesn't break than when a student successfully breaks a board. In most cases it was not improper technique that caused the student to fail to succeed, it was their own fear that held them back.

This is the perfect metaphor for life. As children, and later as adults, we hold ourselves back from what we are truly capable of because of our fears and doubts. Ask yourself if you have ever hit at the board, rather than punching through the board during a challenge or while striving for a worthwhile goal. Early on in your child's life, start programming them with a 'Yes I Can' attitude. Praise and recognize their efforts. Show your belief in them. Explain to them how important having a 'Yes I Can' attitude is.

BLACK BELT CONFIDENCE

Developing a 'Yes I Can' attitude and learning to control their fears and doubts is the first step to your children developing black belt confidence. People who have a healthy level of self-esteem and confidence are strong, secure and high achievers. Their self-confidence is evident in all areas of their lives; their education, career and personal relationships. During my time as a kickboxing promoter, I can say each of the world champions I had the good fortune to work with were all supremely confident. Often times the only difference between a contender and a champion was confidence.

Former world heavyweight boxing champion Muhammad Ali was perhaps the most famous athlete of all time. His fame transcended the sport of boxing. Arguably he is regarded as the best heavyweight boxer of all time. He was not only a master inside the boxing ring, he was a master of positive self-talk. He programmed his mind for success by repeating over-and-over again, " I'm the greatest!" in fact when people speak of him today many refer to him as simply the greatest. How successful would he have been, how memorable would his career have been if he merely, stated, " I'm pretty good." He was so bold and confident that early in his career he would accurately predict what round he would win in.

Of course I'm not suggesting that your child should walk down the hallways at school boasting "I'm the greatest." What I am suggesting is that you start programming your child's mind with a 'Yes I Can' attitude early and often.

The next step to building black belt confidence is to provide your child with meaningful goals. This is the key to how martial arts training help children become high achievers in life. Goals give our lives direction, focus, and meaning. In most martial arts academies the main goal is to earn a black belt. To earn a black belt in most styles of the martial arts takes three to four years. That is a long time for a child and most adults as well. What martial arts has done so well is to break down long-term goals like earning a black belt into smaller, more tangible, and achievable goals with the different colored belts that students wear on their uniforms.

Each time a child earns a new belt it is a personal victory for the student. The awarding of a new belt fosters a feeling of achievement, and a sense of accomplishment. This sense of achievement builds the child's confidence and self-worth. With each belt a child earns, the feeling of confidence and self-esteem grow.

Whatever goal you and your child decide on, it is vitally important to remember to break down the goal into challenging yet achievable steps. In the sports of kickboxing and boxing the same process is used. When a promoter discovers a prospect that he believes has the potential to become a champion, he will carefully match his prospect with suitable opponents – opponents who will challenge his prospect and yet at the same time, he will have complete confidence that his protégé will prevail.

It is extremely important that the prospect experiences a series of victories before moving on to more challenging competition. He must learn how to win and internalize each victory to create a feeling of confidence and esteem. The confidence the prospect earns will increase his belief in himself. The greater his self-belief is, the greater his skills will be. The higher skill level in turn creates even greater confidence, building a positive cycle of increased skill level and self-belief.

This beginning matchmaking process is extremely important to the ultimate success or failure of a potential champion. Over-matching a prospect too soon in his career can literally ruin a fighter. Conversely, not providing a prospect with enough challenge will leave the prospect ill-prepared for a big opportunity.

It is the very same process for children. If your child is currently struggling to pass a particular class in school do not expect him or her to earn an A+ on the next grading cycle. Instead break down the goal of an A+ in to achievable steps. If your child is a C- student, set a goal for a B- for the next report card. Should your child achieve that goal then raise the bar a little higher. With each achievement or goal your child accomplishes, always provide your child with a new more challenging goal.

BLACK BELT CHALLENGES

The reason goals are so vitally important for your child to become a black belt in life is because they provide challenges for your child. Challenges makes us grow, motivate us to learn, develop perseverance, and self-discipline. Challenges will stretch your children and provide them with the courage to leave their comfort zones. Challenges create new experiences, new opportunities, and provide your child with a sense of confidence for overcoming some of their fears.

Conversely, the unchallenged child will not learn how to handle the difficulties that are an inescapable part of life. Children who are not challenged will grow bored, often seeking diversion in less than healthy ways. Overeating, too much television, and perhaps later succumb to the lure of drugs.

Again the best way for you to challenge your child is to find something she enjoys and help her set meaningful goals within that activity.

BLACK BELT SELF-ESTEEM

Thus far we have discussed developing a 'Yes I Can' attitude in your child, building black belt confidence, and providing your child with black belt challenges. If all three of the aforementioned steps are successfully implemented your child will have a healthy self-esteem. Self-esteem is how we value ourselves. It is how we feel about ourselves. If your child has a positive 'Yes I Can' attitude, confidence and belief in his/her abilities and is provided with a challenge that will stretch her limits and help her grow as a person, self-esteem is a natural by-product.

Building all of these qualities in your child will play big dividends for the health and welfare of your child. A child with a 'Yes I Can' attitude, unstoppable confidence, who is unafraid of challenge, and who has self-worth and self-esteem, will indeed become a black belt in life.

About Hilary

Hilary J. Sandoval III just months out of high school promoted his first professional kickboxing event at the age of 18, along with his brother and business partner Tony Sandoval, age 12.

Special guest at his events have included Chuck Norris, martial arts film stars Ernie Reyes Jr. and Cynthia Rothrock, the Dallas Cowboy Cheerleaders, Randall "Tex" Cobb, and Rudy Ruettiger the subject of the hit movie "Rudy."

In 1980 he promoter the first nationally televised World Kickboxing Championship in the state of Texas. With El Paso, Texas as his home base he also co-promoted events in Phoenix, Arizona, Dallas, Midland, and Houston, Texas. He personally worked with or promoted 21 world champions. Along with Strike Force founder Scott Coker and several other prominent promoters he was one of the original founders of the ISKA (International Sport Karate Association). He opened his first martial arts academy in 1988.

CHAPTER 54

THE RAY OF CREATION

BY HERB G. BENNETT

The universe, Life and Man are interactive dynamic processes with powerful correspondences of all consciousness that's above and below. There is a ray of light connecting us to all of creation. Our inspirations, thoughts, ideas are 'above' and are transformed into reality 'below'. We are the 'mediators', travelling along 'THE RAY OF CREATION' using our imagination, creativity and resources creating life support systems to satisfy our physical, mental and spiritual needs. We also use this ray to elevate our consciousness to tap into the sources of inspiration and stimuli that transform into sense data, thoughts, concepts and ideas to design our lives and worlds.

The human mind reflects the universal Mind and connects to the ALL of ALL. Natural creative principles reveal structural logic, myths and mysteries to us creating value systems enabling us to synthesize knowledge within thought form frameworks and paradigms that are constantly changing. Physical expressions use symmetry principles that obey natural laws. The fundamental law is the *Law of Three* (3). Every thought, idea, expression or being is a corresponding vibration with flavors defining its form. Mind, Body and Spirit form a 'triad' of 'flavors' composed of subtle (above) and gross (below) expressions that are synthesized using the laws and symmetry principles that distribute flavors, qualities and gauges of matter into reality.

Abstraction is essential to 'transformative thinking' for clarity and true understanding. Using concepts like 'suchness' and 'muchness' instead of names help creative thoughts, feelings and emotions flow. Understanding correspondences with Body, Mind and Spirit; 'above and below' transforms electrical stimuli into sense data mentally. 'Mentalism' is being true to form. All things are mental. The 'ray of creation' leads to pure principles. Pure extension is Space. Pure duration is Time and pure thought is Spirit. All consciousness and its expressions of reality are governed by 'three principles' – physiology, psychology and spirituality. The word 'spirituality' used here means creative spirit or work-energy. The finest fuel of all we know is thought. All expressions of nature are made of three basic elements. The universal codes are physiology, psychology and spirituality. These are the instructions that created us with our qualitative and quantitative, gauges, behaviors and strength. They work with every Body, Mind and Spirit vibrational level we think of as reality. This is creation's code. We use it to create our worlds.

Space, time and energy correlate with all qualitative (suchness) definitions and quantitative (muchness) descriptions of natural phenomena and "thought forms." Stimuli are transformed into ideas based on natural phenomena encoding functions and behaviors. They are reduced to concepts that follow the fundamental *Law of Three* (3) becoming all regenerative symmetry principles for physical, psychological and spiritual expressions. Principles are laws or facts of nature encoded into thoughts, artificial devices and creative expressions adhering to discrete symmetrical rules with unique identities.

This symmetry is dynamic. It is not the mirror reflections we know, but "the behaviors of parts that make things work holistically." Geometric expressions have unique identities and symmetries. When rules and behaviors are understood, identities can be transformed. In addition to standard symmetry, with enantiomorphism or handedness, there are Rotational, Glide, Polygonal and Spiral symmetries. This Triad applies to periodicities of expressions in nature as light, orientation, matter, color and numbers. When the three fundamental elements are reduced and distributed they form expanded expressions of flavors and 'phyla' of natural and artificial phenomena. When symmetries and triads are aligned, creativity is harmonized and consciousness is transformed into reality. We see the *Law of Three* (3) as being fundamental to artificial and natural processes. Are there other number laws working in nature? Could living in a three dimensional reality be one reason? Does this relate to the three developmental stages of the human brain?

Transformations are created and experienced by tapping into the sub, the tangible and super consciousness. Our tangible consciousness is enriched when the sub (below) and super (above) dimensions support our normal 'RAM' minds. Attributes of the Body, Mind, Spirit (BMS) or Triad, are tuned to higher thoughts and correspondences. We use threefold symmetries to transform ourselves intuitively and unknowingly. We have mastered the materialistic expressions, leaving the psychological and spiritual components less developed. When we internalize this knowledge our actions become clear and lives are transformed. We stop rolling dies to begin living lives in total harmony.

What are the factors involved in developing our psychological, spiritual or electrical lives? Yes my friends, life is electric and magnetic like the cosmos with the 'ALL of consciousness' we mirror. Rene Descartes' definition of 'Man'; the 'plumbing model of circulation' is replaced by Man; the complex bio, magnetic, electrical, plasmic being. Transformation is about becoming our highest and best self-image, knowing who we are to develop a 'toolbox' to align with our true self. Every era has a very distinct expression, identity and flavor. We have the opportunity, the technologies and intelligence to identify, question and research the relevant principles to invent new toolboxes. The cyclical potential of transformations between periods is led by paradigm shifts. *Carpe diem* is the order.

Technology, philosophy, and culture (Body, Mind and Spirit) evolve with enduring principles in tow. Recognizing that we are part of 'movements' and resulting 'consciousness shifts' is "The essence of Transformations." Transformative thinking, or 'Structural Philosophy', is the first step in understanding how to create 'thought forms.' The highest form of energy we know is thought. Ideas, new form vocabularies, technologies and inventions tell the stories of mankind. The shift is already here. Are we ready to embrace it to 'reinvent' ourselves? What tools do we have and what knowledge do we need?

Creative expressions emerge from the internal dialog using visual and mathematical processes. It starts by transforming electrical impulses and brain stimuli into sense data for thought form re-cognition. When we speak to ourselves we think. In speaking to others we communicate. What are thoughts? Do they make us who we are or vice versa? What values do we incorporate into our thought processes and into peoples' lives? What is the role of culture and aesthetics in this process? How do we define them? Do they add any value?

Culture is the blend of the artificial with the natural. 'Man' uses natural materials to make beautiful things. Another popular version describes it as 'art forms' – dance, music, art and food. *The Law of Three* defines culture as harmonizing body, mind and spirit, aligned with the 'Ray of Creation' in the Space, Time, and Energy continuum. The first definition of culture refers to the past. It is stored subconscious experiences in space, time, energy as sense data and images for recall. The present popular view reflects our prevalent contemporary attitudes. The third is the future super consciousness set to inform new paradigms. These are big picture views of the world with newly transformed ideas that rely on proven and sustainable principles. They change our thought processes, impact our language and transform our lives. Where does transforming this esoteric knowledge into practical strategies for solutions lead?

Languages change over time to correspond with evolving thought forms, rituals and rhythms we create. Science and other disciplines constantly evolve. It is nature's way of revealing new sources of 'suchness and muchness' we can revisit. The east-west cultural divide has mental boundaries, dichotomies, myths and mysteries well entrenched and intact. Oriental systems of thought are often strange and difficult to accept by western views (paradigms). Western ideas are sometimes not readily accepted by oriental cultures. These schisms lead to wars and other socio-political and religious differences with unresolved conflicts. How can there be true 'globalism' if we cannot find common ground in philosophical and cultural traditions in the present East-West schism?

'Meditation' and 'visualization' are two major contributions to the west that correlate with our endocrine system. The endocrine system, the Brain and the central nervous system is western medicine's triad. Eastern frameworks start much earlier with the understanding of the Body, Mind, and Spirit continuum built upon meditation and visualization practices. Western medical science is a space-time framework without 'spirit'. It focuses on physiology, chemistry, biology and other synthetic disciplines.

The law of polarity governs these orientations we do not comprehend. This knowledge helps transform concepts into practical solutions from a deeper understanding of the 'mechanics of consciousness', synthesizing and harmonizing new creative methodologies. Be the potter with ideas or yourself on the wheel of life. The material, the mental and creative processes interact with all the creative forces you are connected to, expressing who you are and what you make.

Start by looking at earlier stages of your life to find what you were curious about and got the most joy doing. Early first impressions become passions with life transforming creative skills and opportunities. I used to shape the tops of large milk tins into plates. Now I design ceramic dinnerware. I wanted to discover nature's secrets for making forms. I invent and patent useful vocabularies of three-dimensional forms. I love cutting and folding forms with paperboard. There is a Zen quality to it. Cutting and folding is free, fluid and graceful. I invent curved three dimensional forms while conducting geometric experiments in this relatively new 'Non Euclidean paradigm.' From a simple mindless task, I distill knowledge through an extremely complex process. Dancing 'thought-forms' in my head are manifested. Retrace your steps, find your joy and make it your theme. Explore and consume everything about it. Study, read, draw and model as many forms as possible. Drawing is a vital spatial learning skill. Growing expands your creative and critical thinking abilities. We forget these earlier clues and lessons as adults and let the world define our needs. Then there is crisis, loss or pain to motivate us to find our joy again. Early play, focus, observation and formalizing earlier passions are great experiences. I still am amazed about what causes animals to be up and running with their herds, minutes after they are born, while humans take years to complete their brain wiring, if they ever do at all.

Connect to your higher self, that version of what you want to be, to do and say to the world. Gain deeper levels of understanding of natural principles and laws by being curious again. Observe and reconnect with what interests you the most. Begin to focus your physical, mental and creative spirit or energy and begin to align with the creative intelligences we are all connected to.

You have the ability to access freely and abundantly the knowledge you want. Transform metaphysical strategies and bring real ideas into the world whether they are from your past or are new. Make this creative process your value system generator for *your* original ideas. Start with a vivid mental picture of the life you 'want' with all the things, positive feelings and power you want created by your ideas. Let the joy of that intention be your inspiration. Recognize this as mentalism in action; the dream is being realized with focused imagination and clarity of thought. Meditate (think) and visualize (imagine) clearly and precisely. Create (with energy) the reality you want and will to manifest with passion and ease of repetition. Master your focus and focus your mastery to perfection. Be open to knowledge without cultural bias or judgment. Develop your hand-mind–heart coordination to enhance your sensitivity and integrity. Apply the 'Body, Mind, and Spirit Triad' to phenomena you see clearly. Make the *Law of Three* (3) work for you. Study elements and forces of nature with your new "nanoscope." Let these principles be the cure for fear-based 'need' thinking. Become compassionate with open heart-thinking. Invite positive thoughts into your work life through your life's work. Explore new values, experiences, intuitions and insights by thinking abstractly. Rethink quality and not quantity (body), change behavior (mind) to harmonize with principles. Connect to your higher creative spirit through your creative language to communicate on the physical, psychological and creative levels through your heart thinking. Be in control of your creative destiny and freedom, live fully and be happy.

About Herb

Herbert Glenn Bennett, RA is a multi-talented Architect and Artist. He sees an Architectural future emerging with new attitudes, design perspectives, materials and technologies forged partly by the digital explosion that's redefining our creative expressions and designs. Our "Cultural education" reminds us that "Architecture is the Mother of the Arts." We have developed a visual intelligence inspiring innovative and smart technologies supported by leading building systems professions. Architects can impact the world now unlike any other time in history.

Herb is an Institute of Design and Construction and Pratt Institute graduate. He has a B. Arch degree, a New York license and is NCARB certified. He teaches at The Fashion Institute of Technology SUNY New York and directs the Loggia research and development group. He is a researcher and Inventor, an author, an Industrial Designer with several patents. He uses multiple art forms to make products and accessories energy efficient with sound economic strategies to satisfy project needs and design parameters.

Bennett Architects RA is a client-based design and technology research firm. He is the COO of Summit Development Industries LLC, NY a housing development company. He develops innovative and alternative structural systems, green technologies and full service residential communities. His patented inventions are used by industries for industrial and commercial arts, architecture, marketing, print media and packaging design. He advises cultural and business organizations with their product development needs, their corporate collateral and integrated branding development.

Herb is a curator, moderator and panelist on several 'Percent for Art' selection panels, Arts Grants panels, Source Selection Evaluation Boards for Public art and Memorial Monuments in New York City for the MTA, the African Burial Ground and Visitors' Center and "The World in Our Art", a Moderated Art panel of Caribbean artists at the Windsor Art Center in Windsor, CT. His public works experience involves consulting artists with their municipal and private commissions. His graphic and media designs are popular with a clientele of entertainers, dignitaries, cultural institutions, galleries, well established and emerging businesses. He is featured in the popular documentary *Plight of Caribbean Artists*[1] and has participated in various video productions, interviews in several New York publications. They include the *Daily News, Caribbeat;*

---

1 http://pictify.com/59309/plight-of-the-carribbean-artist

the weekend edition, *Valentine New York Fine Arts Magazine*, and *Caribbean Life*. He has cohosted a radio broadcasting art show.

As a fine artist, Herb exhibits widely and is featured in special arts projects, private collections and gallery exhibitions. He develops community development projects for arts institutions, corporations and creative professionals. Herb is a published poet, and a private pilot. He is one of America's Premier Experts™ and authors. He transforms complex geometric designs into proprietary technologies and form inventions and inventories with unique, valuable identities. His goal is to synthesize related art forms to positively impact the lives and works of people, our planet, clients, creative developers and arts professions with his new 'Non-Euclidean; curved aesthetic' that this new geometry offers us.

herb.bennett94@facebook.com
https://twitter.com/Ben3nett
www.linkedin.com/in/bennett3ra/
www.pinterest.com/herb7xyz/projects-art-works-and-industrial-designs/
www.hbennettarchitects.com

CHAPTER 55

STOP LOOKING FOR A JOB... CREATE ONE!!!! —IT'S SAFER AND EASIER THAN YOU THINK

BY DONALD HENIG

*Only those who will risk going too far can
possibly find out how far one can go.*
~ T.S. Elliot

In this chapter, you will learn how to make a list of 10 – 20 new businesses you can start immediately! And I will show you that it is smarter and safer to start a business than to look for a job, especially for the millennial generation. I will show you the way to become the boss and enjoy the luxuries that come with it, including cars, boats, and houses as well as, helping many others due to your good fortune and hard work. The opportunities in front of you are life-changing for you and for those around you. Trust me; I've done it many times.

*Every great dream begins with a dreamer. Always remember,
you have within you the strength, the patience, and the passion
to reach for the stars to change the world.*
~ Harriet Tubman

I LEFT MILLIONS ON THE TABLE WHILE I WAS SEARCHING FOR A JOB/CAREER

While in college, I was asked to create a product and then create a marketing plan for that product. This was part of an advanced marketing class. At the time in 1980, coffee was sold in Styrofoam cups and the lids were a solid, thin plastic. The product I created was a coffee cup lid with perforated edges, which enabled the consumer to easily and quickly tear off a portion of the lid, so you could drink the hot coffee and keep it hot. At the time, my lid was not available, so people tore at one corner and then another and then ripped it back.

Sometimes it came off and sometimes you had a lid that would cut your lip. My invention or product was so ingenious that within 2 years everyone used it☺. The only problem was that I didn't make any money from this brilliant idea. Someone else patented the idea after me and made a fortune! Good for them, they had the nerve and the open mind to take a shot and create their own job. I was still of the mindset that I needed a job and to work toward retirement – bad thinking. Let me show you the reasons that you should strongly consider creating your own job as opposed to looking for one and I'll show you how to do it. I recognize that being an entrepreneur may scare you, but if you take the time to read this with an open mind, maybe a few points will resonate enough for you to look deeper. And then... success!

Try not. Do... or do not. There is no try.
~ Yoda

There is GREATNESS in you!
~ Les Brown

A rising tide lifts all boats
~ Anonymous

Everyone benefits when you create a new business, product or service. People get hired by you and they buy houses, cars, carpeting, food... And you buy bigger houses, nicer cars, and you have the ability to help many people in any way you choose. Your creation will trigger other ideas and new businesses for you and others to start and cause more people to be hired and benefit. For example, Apple has roughly 47,000 employees in the USA, but accounts for roughly 514,000 jobs in the

USA and over 700,000 overseas supporting Apple (app developers, for example) (according to NYT 3/4/12)! Everyone who creates a business helps many more people than they hire. The ripples are like a pebble thrown into a lake, it goes way beyond the first ring the eye can see. So Michelangelo, create and enjoy the riches!!

EMPLOYER OR EMPLOYEE – YOUR CHOICE

- Did you know that only 25% of employees with paid time off took all of their vacation days in 2013? (according to Glassdoor.com's data of a Harris poll). And, according to the same survey, 22% of employees don't receive any paid time off at all! Is this the life you want?

- 80% of Americans are stressed out by at least one thing at work (Nielson Research for Everest College). Workloads have increased, yet pay has not kept pace. Low pay, long commutes and unreasonable workloads are the main causes of stress. This is now the definition of a job, and most people want one! This is what most people are looking for (a job).

- Pew Research reported that bosses are more likely to be satisfied with their financial situation. And they also state that bosses are more satisfied with both their home life and their job too! *If your boss is happier, why not be the boss? After all, aren't we all doing this to be happy????*

- And finally, Economist Barry Bosworth at the Brookings Institution crunched the numbers and found that *the richer you are, the longer you'll live*. And it's a gap that is widening, particularly among women! Money may not buy happiness, but it sure can give you a few extra years to find happiness.

So more time off, more money, more satisfaction with work and homelife, and live a longer life. Be the boss!

BUT I HAVE FEARS!!!

No Money? No Experience?? No Knowledge???

My message to you is to *start stupid, start poor – start today*.

> *A trip of a thousand miles begins with one small step.*
> ~ Lao Tzu

The best time to plant a tree was 20 years ago.
The second best time is now.
~ Chinese Proverb

If you start a little stupid or less informed, you will have less fear and the obstacles that you will definitely face won't scare you into quitting too soon. Let me provide a few personal examples.

I knew nothing about…

- The entertainment industry when I started the predecessor to Corner Store Entertainment, which produced Rock of Ages, the musical, the 37th longest running show on Broadway – ever!

- Residential mortgages when I started my first mortgage company and sold it ten years later.

- Franchising when I created a mortgage broker franchise and built it to 760 units nationwide and sold it.

- Owning an ice cream truck when I bought one at 19 years old and made more money than at any time before.

- The publishing industry, but started a soccer publication that became the official newspaper for New York State Junior Soccer with circulation of over 160,000 papers per month.

- I have many more examples – just start stupid.

- Oh, and I was a solid 'C' student in High School with a good personality, great passion and a lack of fear. *The younger you are, the less you have to lose.* Make it happen and enjoy the luxuries in life!

Fear is often the #1 reason people don't create new businesses. If you knew all the potential pitfalls prior to starting a business, you probably would never start one. Nobody would, not even a young Steve Jobs. There is a great principle called the *Corridor Principle* that basically states that you cannot possibly see all the doors that will be open to you until you begin to walk down the corridor. It applies to starting a new business perfectly. You cannot possibly see the answers to the obstacles that will absolutely arise after you open your business, until you take the plunge.

There are no real obstacles, just fears to overcome!

"BUT I AM NOT OLD OR SMART ENOUGH?"

Everyone else in this industry is older and smarter and more experienced. In reality, the older person is looking at you and your energy and contacts and knowledge of technology and they are scared of you! Use your advanced skills and immediately begin networking with like-minded people and grow together. In almost no time you will gain the knowledge and experience and yet still have more energy and contacts, with the power of technology in your pocket. <u>Stand back world!!!!</u> I have an idea!

Bottom line, you have nothing to fear and nobody to fear. You are just as good or better. And if they could learn it, so can you - right? Come on, face the facts – you are going to kick butt! I am just saying to do it now and don't delay.

The greatest mistake a man can make is being afraid to make one.
~ Elbert Hubbard

Here's How To Start YOUR Business Today!!!!

It always seems impossible until it's done.
~ Nelson Mandela

Find your idea. The simplest thing to do is to form a team with some like-minded friends (commonly referred to as a **mastermind group**). It must be with people you like and really, really trust. Keep the group small. The immediate goal is to list 100 ideas for a new business. There are no bad ideas (seriously, every idea gets logged for further discussion). If an idea is bad or stupid, then realize that if you think it can't be done, then everyone else will have the same thought, but if you CAN figure it out, then you have gold! *The craziest ideas are normally the best.* Okay, once you list all 100 ideas (maybe you get to 30 and stop, but I strongly suggest going to 100 – make it fun), then it is time to begin narrowing the list. Get to the top 20, then the top 10 and 5 and finally the best 3. When you get to the top 3-5, put more work into researching those ideas before making a final decision. The final decision may surprise you – it almost always does☺. A great way to research your idea and shorten the learning curve is to look at a franchise in that field/industry and learn their tactics and copy what makes sense and seems to work. If they don't have a patent on the process, it is open to all.

- Test market your top 2-3 great ideas and see which one resonates with your target market and with you. You have to love it and feel excited, otherwise do something else. If you're not excited, it's a job….. ugh!

Every great business begins as an idea or a thought and then it becomes a dream. That's when it cannot be stopped. Dreams are more powerful than anything. When you can't sleep, go for it. Don't let anything stop you. You are going to win!

10 TRIGGERS TO YOUR BIG IDEA

Discontent is the first necessity of progress.
~ Thomas Edison

Here are some very simple new business ideas that might trigger something within you or you may want to start one of these – be my guest and enjoy. Just let me know how it goes and know that you owe me nothing but a brief thank you and update. I love helping people succeed!!!

- What are you good at???? Find something that involves the things you are good at doing and enjoy. Then figure out a business related to that. Pretty simple.

  - Make a list of 20 experiences that you were passionate about as a starting point.

- If you're an athlete, train younger kids for money. In today's competitive world of children playing a single sport, they almost all need a trainer. You can help and charge good money for this service. Parents will pay! Also, once you get good at this, you might form classes to train more kids at one time (more money for you). Then you might hire other athletes your age and skill level and form a camp (big money). Go for it. Start today and see what happens.

- If you excel in a subject, tutor others. If you are good at math and you are in High School, can't you help a 7th, 8th or 9th grader in their lower level math? Think about it, their parents might pay $50 - $150 per hour for a professional, but you can help them for $25 per hour and make some money for yourself.

- Mowing lawns sounds simple, yet most services do a terrible job! Go through a neighborhood and do a survey house to house. Ask what they like and don't like about their landscaper, and how much they pay (create a form and write their responses). Then return with a plan: better services for slightly less money. Take the account and then get the next one and the next. Then hire the people to do the work and you perform the sales and the quality control functions. Be better than the others and you can eventually charge even more than them. This is a real business waiting for someone with energy, guts and a dream.

- Blog writing: yes, most businesses need a blog and they don't have the time. Charge $50 for a 150-word blog. Learn a bit about the company and write one per week. Then do it for many small companies and you have a business!

- Pick up dog crap door to door. That's right, dog crap! I hope you're not too proud to make money! Do something others don't want to do and you will have a business for life because the barrier to entry is in their mind. You can't lose!

  - @ $25 per house 2x per week, if you get 10 in a small neighborhood, you just built a business earning $500 p/w working less than 2 hours! If you get 20 in a neighborhood, then you just quickly built a business earning $52,000 per year. And that's only 20 houses. That's not even an effort yet. Go to work and make a million! Why not??

- Mobile applications

  - Hire a developer on e-lance.com and run with your idea.

- Offer your services on taskrabbit.com.

- If you're an artist, submit designs on 99designs.com.

- Clean pools: Get a job cleaning pools and learn the trade. Learn how to open and close pools. Save your money and start your business the next year. Create a niche and get 30 accounts to start. In time, you will be able to sell this business and retire.

- And # 11... Teach older people how to use the computer better.

But I don't have enough money! Here are just a few ideas that may help:

- Try preselling your services for 2 years for payment in advance. Do that with 10 to 20 clients and you may have just bridged the gap.

- Take 20% of your business and sell it to family and friends. They believe in you, so let them invest in you. This is 'angel' funding.

- Give deep discounts for quick payment to help with early cash flow.

- Use crowd funding sites – they really work.

- Partner with an older person: Your idea and passion and their cash can make a beautiful partnership.

There are so many more, but space is limited. The point is that you need to take control of your life and create a job, not work for someone else. It's your turn to earn the money and enjoy your work life, home life and live longer. Why not you? Good luck! And remember, you are worth more than $15 per hour! Make it happen!!

About Donald

Don Henig used his thirst for knowledge, his passion to be the best, and his entrepreneurial spirit to propel his career achievements to new heights multiple times. Don began his entrepreneurial career as a successful financial planner, which led to starting his own mortgage banking firm, which ultimately grew to one of the largest in New York State in just a few years. Don was called to testify before both the US House of Representatives and the US Senate on behalf of the mortgage finance industry.

In 1986, Don founded the New York Association of Mortgage Brokers and was later elected as president of the National Association of Mortgage Brokers. He was also on the Board of Governors of the Mortgage Bankers Association of America as well as their exclusive Executive Committee. After reaching this pinnacle, he sold his mortgage company and built a mortgage broker franchise—the first of its kind. He quickly built this to 760 franchise units nationwide and sold it within three years. He then started a publishing company, which created Youth Soccer, the official newspaper for NYS Junior Soccer. He built it to 167,000 copies per month with every edition earning a profit.

Don also built successful technology firms during the dot-com boom before re-entering the mortgage industry to build MortgageSelect.com to the 5th largest online only, Direct-to-Consumer mortgage company in the nation. Then, as president of Third Party Lending at American Home Mortgage (AHM:NYSE), he orchestrated the growth of American Brokers Conduit to the 6th largest wholesale mortgage lender in the nation originating over $44 billion in mortgages in just one year and earning a net profit in excess of $300 million! And although the volume and the rankings are impressive, Don is most fulfilled by the retention rate (the rate salespeople remained with the firm from year to year). ABC's retention rate was over 93%, while its next closest competitor was only at 52%. This number speaks directly to the culture and the quality of the team he helped build.

In addition to reaching the top of the mortgage lending industry multiple times and the soccer publishing industry, Don also ventured into the entertainment industry by founding the predecessor to Corner Store Entertainment (CSE). In very short order, CSE produced six major motion pictures and the Broadway musical Rock of Ages, which is currently one of the longest-running plays on Broadway of all-time according to Playbill. Some of the actors in the films that CSE produced are: Natalie Portman, Tom

Cruise, Julianne Hough, Alec Baldwin, Mark Ruffalo, Joseph Gorden Levitt, Orlando Bloom, Juliette Lewis, Chloë Sevigny, Laura Linney, Russell Brand, Catherine Zeta Jones, Paul Giamatti, and Bryan Cranston.

Among other ventures, Don also created a firm to buy, fix and sell hundreds of foreclosed properties in less than two years – selling each one for a profit. Additionally, Don is the founder of various Internet applications as well as an eyelash growth company based in Vietnam.

Outside of building businesses, Don enjoys time with his family, helping others, playing racquetball, golf, boating, exercising, travel and eating healthy.

CHAPTER 56

COMBINING SUCCESSFUL PARENTING AND BUSINESS

BY ERIK ROBERTSON

As an Educational Psychologist I have been working with professionals from all walks of life and from all over the world. For 15 years, I have been privileged to work with thousands of parents who have trusted me with their parenting challenges. When I share my parenting insights, methodology and practical tools with them they will often exclaim, "Why didn't I know this before!?"

Hereby clearly indicating the huge lack of awareness in many parents about what Parenting is really about: YOU.

This made me decide to write my first book: *Oops, The Parenting Handbook: I wish I had known this before.* I have seen thousands of problematic and challenged families flourish and become happy, dynamic, contented families. I have seen countless children and teenagers get back on track and reclaim their happiness, so I know this works.

In this new book with Brian Tracy, I am sharing some of my parenting tools that are specifically related to the theme: How to be a Successful Business Person while being a Successful Parent.

My Parenting books are also based upon my other educational work. I have been Chairman of a Dutch Educational Network, I am a keynote speaker at many Educational Conferences all over the world. I have co-developed a Mentoring Pilot at one of India's most prestigious universities.

I also give Parenting Workshops to parents all over the world, from Los Angeles to Atlanta, and from Dubai to Amsterdam and Istanbul. Parents say they feel truly inspired, supported and empowered by my parenting insights, tips and methodology.

It is my hope that you are successful in combining your parenting with your business.

You want your child to be successful, and you want them to be a great person. This chapter will discuss how you go about doing that.

In this inspiring book about how to be a great business person, we will now look at the tools needed to also be a great parent.

Being a successful business person will positively affect your parenting, as being a great parent will empower you to be even more successful as a business person.

Before we continue we need to look at a few important contextual aspects regarding parenting today.

How is it that we are trained for everything in life, yet for the most important task, that of parenting, we are expected to make do? The information that we use to carry out our parenting is largely based on advice from our parents and grandparents, various books, websites, magazines, blogs, as well as neighbors and friends. Often, most of that information will be conflicting in nature. Obviously that does not do our parenting much good.

How is it that we are living in the Information Age, or the Age of Technology, yet our educational system is a relic from the Industrial Age? Our current educational systems around the world are all modified systems from the early 1900s.

Sure, it all looks modern and high-tech, but the actual pedagogical and grading systems are dinosaurs in need of change.

Experience and research shows that when your parenting goes through moments of crisis, you will unconsciously revert back to how your parents and/or educators treated you as a child. More often than not that approach will not be what is adequate or effective in the current situation.

The quality of our parenting today will determine the future of our Great Nation. This means there is a moral aspect to our parenting. In order to rise to this wonderful and sometimes daunting challenge, it is necessary for you as a parent to critically and honestly appraise your parenting. This will make you more effective as a parent, benefitting your child(ren), your family, and yourself as a Successful Business Person.

According to research, we are living in the most rapidly changing era ever. New technology is available at a rate faster than ever before. This has implications for our parenting. It means that the home is under constant "attack" from outside sources. As a parent, you need to think about what your family values are and how to give shape to those values.

You now have a contextual framework of aspects that have a strong influence on your parenting.

The next aspect of Successful Parenting that you need to look at is YOU.

Parenting is all about YOU as a parent. We are told that good parenting is all about the child, and though that may be true, it is my experience that it is mostly about you as a parent.

Successful Parenting is about being a Successful Human Being. And being a Successful Human Being enables you to be a Successful Business Person. A win-win situation!

If you look at the "Business of Parenting," the yield or the results will depend, of course, on the input, on your investment and efforts. This is important to keep in mind!

Depending on the circumstances, you will have a limited amount of time to spend on your parenting. In an ideal world, you will want to spend as much time as possible with your child or children. If you are already a Successful Business Person in the sense that you are financially comfortable enough to determine your own work schedule. Then that will allow you a maximum time investment in your parenting.

In most cases you will be on your way to becoming a Successful Business Person, and most likely you will be investing as much of your time as possible in your work.

That means that there is a limited amount of time that you have available for your parenting.

How to optimize that time is the question that you need to keep asking yourself.

You want your parenting to be a success. You want your children to become successful in life. You want them to become great and/or good children. In order to achieve this important goal, you will need to be willing to work on yourself.

If you are in a partnership or marriage, there must also be a willingness to work with each other in facilitating each other's growth as parents. This process requires that you become conscious at all times of what you are feeling, thinking and doing.

In my 15 years of experience as an Educational Psychologist, I have discovered that those parents who are willing to enter into the above mentioned commitments, are highly successful as parents, and for those who are business people, they become very Successful Business People.

In this chapter, I will share some of the secrets that will enable you to become a successful parent, which will allow you to make your parenting into all that you need and want it to be.

TIP NUMBER 1

Prepare for your parenting as you would prepare for a 20-Year Business Project.

Now many of you are probably thinking: ''How on earth do I do that!?''

Let me tell you how:

As I said before, (Good) Parenting is all about you:

This means that you have some homework to do before you become a parent. If you are already a parent, then consider it a refresher course.

You need to take a good look at how you have experienced your own parents, caretakers, teachers and other authority figures throughout your childhood.

These people all have had a significant influence on your (subconscious) ideas and beliefs about parenting. Research and experience teach us that during your parenting, and especially so in difficult moments, you automatically and often unconsciously revert back to what your own parents did with you.

Now therein lies a problem. That behavior might have been appropriate or effective back then, but more often than not, it is not adequate in the current situation.

Becoming conscious of what your ideas and feelings are about parenting is the most important first step that you need to take. Being clear about what you can expect from your parenting will be helpful to develop a game plan for your parenting.

If you have a partner, you will need to discuss your findings about your past parenting influences so that you are aware of each other's conditionings and views. All too often parenting fails due to the partners not being aware of their possible differences or handicaps.

Positively, parents who do evaluate their own experiences together become highly effective in their combined parenting efforts. Children feel that their parents are on the same page and that makes the children feel safe and empowered. Having happy and motivated children again motivates you as parents and everybody benefits.

Part of the 20-year plan is that you ask yourself the following questions:

- What kind of person do I want my children to become?
- What values should they embody?
- What do I think constitutes a good/great human being?
- How will I go about achieving these objectives?

TIP NUMBER 2

Be real, be authentic, and be honest.

As children we were all authentic, real and honest. We showed the world how we feel. Slowly, the world started telling us that we would be rewarded for certain behaviors, and punished for others. We learnt what was considered socially-accepted behavior (according to our surroundings), and we adapted.

In doing so, all too often we learnt to be fake, not true to ourselves, but true to others, in order to get the (social) acceptance we so desperately needed.

When we become parents, or as parents, we need to realize that our (young) children are still in touch with their inner core, and are pure, loving and authentic.

That means that they see through us when we fake it. It also means that they get confused when we are not being truthful, or when we think one thing, but say something else, or-the worst, when we say "Do not do as I do, but as I say."

So, unity of thought, word and deeds is key for Successful Parenting!

TIP NUMBER 3

Think about the three major parenting styles and ask yourself which one would work best for you and why.

There are three main parenting styles:

1. Permissive

2. Authoritarian

3. Authoritative

Permissive Parenting
Permissive Parenting is often seen when parents are too easy going, when parents allow their children too much freedom. Experience shows us that children can only handle a lot of freedom and space when they have achieved a degree of maturity. When lacking that maturity, too much freedom usually leads to licentious behavior.

Authoritarian Parenting
Authoritarian Parenting was the most used parenting style of the 20th century. Parents are often harsh, punishment is doled out freely, children are allowed very little freedom, and the parents word is law. This parenting style often leads to fearful and/or rebellious children.

Authoritative Parenting
Authoritative Parenting is by far the best parenting style. It fosters mature and responsible children.

Authoritative Parenting has an optimal mix of freedom and rules. Children are seen as mature partners in the common goals of parenting. Children are given lots of freedom, while at the same time disciplined and guided by clear rules, boundaries and consequences. Just like in real life in the outside world, they learn that the home is not a hotel, but a shared place that is governed by clear rules and regulations.

This is done in a climate of love and compassion and devotion, which allows the children to feel safe and loved. Boundaries are not restrictions but useful and necessary tools.

TIP NUMBER 4

Celebrate each other. Empower each other as parents, or empower yourself as a single parent.

As a successful Business Person and as a Successful Parent, you will most likely have hectic, busy schedules, and being a Successful Parent will require for you to invest a lot of your time.

Do not delude yourself into buying in to the myth of quality time! To a child there is no such thing! There is only time! And lots of it!

Being a Successful Business Person often may mean that there will be less time available for you as parents. So if you are a couple, spend time every month on a wonderful date just the two of you. If you are a single parent, find ways to spend real "you time", where you pamper yourself and take care of your needs.

As a couple, use your time out time to enjoy, celebrate, relax, and also use it to evaluate how you are doing.

These simple but far-reaching moments together will keep you focused on your main parenting goals, and at the same time provide you with time to mentally and emotionally recharge yourself as a parent.

TIP NUMBER 5

LOVE:

Tip number 5 is the most important tip. Without love as the foundation, all others tips will become mere window dressing.

Love is all about learning to love yourself unconditionally, at the same time loving others unconditionally. Only when we love ourselves unconditionally will we be able to let our unconditional love flow towards our children. This is not the same as unconditional love of their behavior.

There can be times when you find it difficult to love them due to some unwanted or difficult behavior. At times like that it is important, that though you might not approve of their behavior, that you keep loving them unconditionally for who they are. That way both you and your child stay empowered and strong.

CONCLUSION

You are now aware of five instrumental and effective tips that will enable you to be a Successful Parent while being a Successful Business Person.

I support you unconditionally in your quest for excellence in the above.

ABOUT ERIK

Erik R. Robertson, M.A., was raised in Tokyo, Oslo, Abidjan and New York, at English/Canadian, French, Norwegian and Dutch schools. He graduated as an Educational Psychologist with honors and top of his class in (Educational) Psychology at the University of Amsterdam.

Erik first worked in the garment trade, doing millions of dollars in sales. The company he helped found then went bankrupt, an enlightening and difficult experience that made him question his life and goals. He was then signed up by one of Hollywood's most successful agents and sent to acting school in NYC. Despite this golden opportunity, Erik decided to move back to The Netherlands; he was driven by the need to help his fellow men and he did not feel a glorious acting career was the path for that goal.

In the course of the 90s, Erik worked as a psychologist for various Institutions. Erik founded his own company Corporate Health in the late 90s with an accent on coaching, vitality (and stress-prevention), (no-nonsense and goal-oriented) Teambuilding, Human Values and Corporate Social Responsibility; and also Inspiration (Reawakening the Spirit in Work). He works as a Life Coach for CEO's from many top Fortune 500 companies as well as for managers working in various profit and not-for-profit Organizations. Erik has trained most front line healthcare workers from almost every Foundation in the Netherlands.

Erik states that: "People (and this also applies to companies) are able to be in a state of what is known as 'flow'; instead of living and/or functioning in light neuroses that we regrettably refer to as our personality (or when speaking of companies: that part of the company culture that is implicit and often subconscious if you will.) Our personality (and/or the aforementioned culture) is often made up of many conditionings that in reality serve no purpose other than encapsulating our true and grand potential.

To be in a state of 'flow' can be experienced when you transcend the person you think you are, or when you transcend the existing company culture to excel even further. Needless to say the results are spectacular. Employees' performance rises, communication improves and increases and work attendance improves dramatically...to name but a few benefits.

In the case of parenting, families become happy, loving and constructive environments in which both children and parents flourish! Recently Erik co-developed a Mentoring Pilot at one of India's most prestigious International Universities.

During 15 years Erik had a successful Parenting practice as an Educational Psychologist in The Netherlands. He worked with thousands of parents from all walks of life and from all nations.

He also gave Parenting workshops at The American School of The Hague (ASH) and The International School of Amsterdam (ISA). He currently gives talks and workshops on Parenting all over the world.

Based on his extensive research and experience he has written:

Oops! The Parenting Handbook: I wish I had known this before…

(www.oopstheparentinghandbook.com)

It is Erik's mission to inspire, support and empower parents with his loving yet down-to-earth and practical book.

CHAPTER 57

PERSONAL LEADERSHIP

BY ERIC SACHETTA

Have you ever felt as though you weren't in charge of your own life? Have you ever lacked the confidence in knowing that you could "lead" yourself? Ever questioned your ability in leading others and couldn't imagine a way to make a positive difference in the world? After all, you're just one person, right?

Well, about seven years ago, I was in the same mental state that I've described above. I didn't know who I was, where I was going, or how to begin to fix this lost feeling. The good news: I found the solution. I've since experienced a life where I am in charge and have confidence to lead myself in order to pursue my mission of making a positive difference in the world.

Among other achievements within the past seven years, so far I've accomplished the following: developed an incredible relationship with friends (old and new) who I now consider my family, fallen madly in love with an irreplaceable woman (and had the honor of marrying her, too), earned a top spot in personal sales for one of the most respected sales and marketing companies in the industry, successfully ran a district office for said company where I personally mentored, coached and led a team of young sales representatives to earn a spot in the top five district offices in the New England Division, and founded life coaching and motivational speaking businesses where I mentor business owners, recent college graduates, and current college students.

You might be wondering why I'm sharing this with you. Or maybe, "How was Eric able to achieve so many great things in such a short time? What does he have that I don't and why should I care?"

Here's your answer: the biggest impact on the above achievements, without question, was when I made the simple decision to become a Personal Leader. I chose to overcome what seemed like an impossible challenge, changed my belief in the many obstacles I faced, and instead viewed them as opportunities. You can make that same decision. YOU can achieve greatness. Still having doubts? Join me for a brief look at my journey and how you can create your own pathway to success.

MY "DEFINING MOMENT"

Before I share my story, you might be wondering what I mean by "Defining Moment." Our lives are compiled of many moments; some seem minor, some incredibly significant. Moments pass by instantly; some remembered, some forgotten forever, and some we use to define a positive change. Have you ever heard a parent say, "My life changed the moment my son/daughter was born..."? In their mind, that moment holds significance as the start of a new chapter in their life; a new beginning. As I share my "Defining Moment," think of a recent time in your own life, when something changed and you knew your life would be different. It could be something like when you decided which college to attend, or when you broke up with a significant other. Whatever the moment, think back and remember the emotions you were experiencing when you were making an important choice. The choice you made, in that moment, defines a part of who you are. Now let me take you back to the "Defining Moment" that changed my life...forever.

It was December 31, 2007; New Years Eve. I was in college, doing what most college students do on the eve of a new year; celebrating with friends. We began the night at a friend's dorm room, starting with the traditional snacks, drinks and confetti. When we left to head to Boston Common for the midnight celebration, I felt detached and deep down I felt uneasy and uncomfortable with my situation. Initially, I ignored the feeling. It bothered me to think that someone with an incredibly supportive family, and who was attending Bentley University (one of the top 20 business schools in the country) could feel the way I felt. So I brushed it off and continued making my way through the streets of Boston, trailing behind my group of friends.

All of a sudden, my world froze. To this day, I couldn't tell you if it was the alcohol, the emotion, the people around me, the time of year, or a combination of everything, that caused me to do what I did next. It's difficult for me to specify the amount of time it took for me to realize that I was separated from my friends, but when I did, it was nearly too late.

I stood alone in the middle of Boston Common, and the detached, uneasy feeling flooded my being. The first three strokes of midnight filled my ears and vibrated to my core. Rather than joining the celebration, I simply stood and stared blankly at the crowds of people huddled around me. Couples held each other preparing for their first kiss of the New Year. Groups of friends held their drinks high and families with beaming smiles chanted the countdown methodically. I felt as though I was invisible; as if I was literally watching my life pass by without me.

Overwhelmed with unhappiness, the fourth stroke of the clock chimed and I looked down at my hands to verify my existence. A surge of energy came over me and I felt as though I was going to faint. "EIGHT, SEVEN, SIX...!" the crowd chanted, continuing the traditional countdown. On the seventh stroke of the clock, the buildings, lights, and streets of Boston Common began to spin uncontrollably. So much so, that I dropped to one knee and stared at the ground in an attempt to gain control of my thoughts and confirm that the cobblestone beneath me was solid and motionless. "FOUR, THREE, TWO...!"

I looked up at the clock and shook my head as if I was shaking away any feelings of unhappiness that remained. In the seconds it took for the clock to strike midnight and the crowd to erupt, I abruptly jumped up, closed my eyes and shouted at the top of my lungs, "NOT ANOTHER MINUTE, NOT ANOTHER SECOND, I WON'T STAND FOR THIS!" My thoughts started coming in waves: *I have a supporting and loving family, I'm attending a respectable college, and I have friends who care about me. This feeling of nonexistence is GOING to stop and it's my CHOICE!*

From that moment forward, I was a different person; I experienced different emotions, different levels of positive energy, and an increased enjoyment of life that I'd never felt up until that point. To others around me, based on appearance alone, nothing had changed. I was the same Eric they had always known and loved. That's because some of the most important decisions in life are personal ones that define who we are on the inside. The decision I made to begin living life with passion and purpose, defines who I am as a person, son, brother, cousin, nephew, grandson, husband, friend, colleague, mentor, speaker, and life coach.

Had I not experienced my "Defining Moment" at midnight on January 1, 2008, I'm not sure where or who I would be today. What I do know, from what I've learned and experienced since that moment, is that my ability to guide others along their journey to living a life of fulfillment is stronger now because of it.

You may be thinking, "Eric, your life couldn't have switched from negative to positive in a single moment." You're right. My "Defining Moment" provided an opening and opportunity to start the process of living life on my terms. All the "real decisions" we make in our lives confirm our commitment to a process. What is this "process" I'm referring to? Personal Leadership. Over the past seven years I've been able to develop the process to take charge of my life, lead myself, and make a positive difference in the world. It's a process I choose to live on a daily basis to help me achieve extraordinary results and with commitment it can do the same for you.

WHAT IS PERSONAL LEADERSHIP?

Personal Leadership is a way of life based on a commitment to personal development while exemplifying the characteristics of a leader.

When I first learned about leadership from popular books, guides, and programs, I made the assumption that all I needed to do to get started in becoming a leader was to have a mission or vision for my life or business. The problem: I didn't have a strong reason for having a mission. As I grew and gained skills over the years, I slowly discovered my own understanding of leadership. Eventually, I developed the process called The 8 Mandates of Personal Leadership as a tool for others who were in my position to clarify their understanding of leadership faster than I was able.

If you don't understand why you should be a leader, why you should take responsibly for your life, and therefore don't believe you can add value to other's lives, then having a mission holds no significance. In my process called The 8 Mandates of Personal Leadership, I've learned about and describe mission as the seventh mandate. If I continued practicing my initial understanding of being a leader, and searched for a mission first, I wouldn't be in the position I am today.

In no way am I discrediting other leadership books, guides and programs. Many of my current teachings are based on what I've learned from those incredible resources. My process was created to offer a unique guide in teaching students, business owners and young professionals a step-by-step process to become Personal Leaders. It's specifically designed to guide you in your transformation in becoming an irreplaceable employee, a visionary business owner, and/or a dynamic family leader.

THE EIGHT MANDATES OF PERSONAL LEADERSHIP

1. Perspective
2. Responsibility
3. Accountability
4. Growth
5. Love
6. Lessons
7. Mission
8. Dreams

Most young adults, like my former self, have a general understanding of each mandate on its own. The *order* of the mandates is actually the most important aspect to understand. This is one of the reasons why a lot of young adults, including my former self, get confused along their journey. It's common to think, "Once I get what I want in life, that's when I will serve and give to other people." Below you'll see the skewed order of the eight mandates, which is where that thought derives from.

1. Dreams
2. Mission
3. Lessons

4. Love

5. Growth

6. Accountability

7. Responsibility

8. Perspective

At age 18, if I had studied the 8 mandates in reverse chronological order, this is probably how I would summarize what I learned: "If I first achieve my *dreams*, I will then create a *mission*, and be able to teach *lessons* to others. Only then will I decide I'm worthy of being loved, giving me the ability to *love* myself, which would then provide me with the means to *grow* as a person. I will then let people hold me *accountable* for my actions, and I will take *responsibility* for those actions. Overall, I will hold a new and improved *perspective*. As a result of my perspective, I will believe 100% in myself and others, and I will be grateful and happy."

As you've probably predicted, life just doesn't work out in the way I've described above. It's unfortunate when I see individuals struggle with trusting me on this because the above scenario is the very reason why so many people give up on their dreams when they're faced with their first obstacle.

When appropriately using the chronological order of the 8 mandates, the life summary changes dramatically. Here's how the 8 mandates should be taught and learned: "When I believe in myself, others will also believe in my ability. When I then begin taking *responsibility* for my actions I learn to ask others to hold me *accountable* for my actions. When I ask others to hold me accountable, my fear slowly diminishes while executing important steps in reaching my goals. I decide to *love* myself regardless of my past because if I cannot love myself, few others will. Loving myself will increase my capacity to offer love to others. I'm then able to care for others and feel positive emotions, allowing me to teach others valuable *lessons* I've learned because of the decisions I've made. My *mission* is then created and fueled by the passion I have found as a result of initially believing in myself. I'm willing and able to add value to the lives of others and I'm then able to achieve my wildest *dreams*."

YOU CAN CHOOSE TO BE A PERSONAL LEADER

The eight Mandates of Personal Leadership sound simple, right? Most of the time, taking different action steps (mandates) to improve an aspect of your life is very simple. The mandates *are* simple, but don't confuse something being simple with it being *easy*. If being rich and physically fit were easy, everyone would be rich and physically fit. Taking the appropriate action steps and committing to follow through until you've reached your desired goal is one of the most valuable lessons anyone can learn. The mandates are simple; committing is the challenge and also the reason why most people quit when obstacles present themselves. You are clearly not "most" people, or you would've stopped reading already.

Regardless of your current situation; your social status, your present family circumstances, or your level of belief in yourself—you must know the following facts. *You* can change your social status. *You* have an impact on your relationship with members of your family. *You* can change your belief in yourself to accomplish all of those things. Make the commitment today to start the process of becoming a Personal Leader. All it takes is one moment, one decision, and one initial action step to begin your own journey. What will you decide?

About Eric

Eric Sachetta is a Leadership Expert and devotes much of his time helping college students, young professionals, and business owners understand the value of Personal Leadership. Eric is the author of The 8 Mandates of Personal Leadership. He is a motivational speaker for colleges and universities throughout the nation where he spreads his knowledge and insight to the members of "The Next Generation of Leaders." Creator and founder of the *Eric Live The Movie Crew*," life coaching program, Eric has a unique passion for helping "The Next Generation of Leaders," become irreplaceable employees, visionary business owners, and dynamic family leaders.

Eric is also a former district manager for Vector Marketing. During his time as district manager, he interviewed thousands of graduating high school seniors, college students, and recent college graduates, eventually fueling his desire for teaching and helping others succeed at a high level. His goal of helping "The Next Generation of Leaders" shorten the learning curve between where they stand today, and who they aspire to become, was primarily inspired by his own personal experience. He started his journey to becoming a Leadership Expert as a shy, introverted college student who lacked confidence and motivation. Today, he enjoys spending time with family and friends and dedicates himself to helping the younger generation reach a level of success they had only dreamed of.

For details on how to bring Eric to your next event, conference, or meeting please call: 781-898-2009 or email: info@ericsachetta.com

To receive more information from Eric including newsletters, videos, books, and other resources go to: www.ericsachetta.com

For information on Eric's life coaching program, visit his website at: www.ericlivethemoviecrew.com

CHAPTER 58

GET OUT OF YOUR WAY: 4 STEPS TO IMPROVING YOUR LIFE

BY DEBRA WAISNER

Do you feel lost, stuck, powerless, worthless, unappreciated, under-employed, unhappy, like you lost a loved one or in a general malaise? I can relate. I've had most of those same thoughts, feelings and emotions. I have overcome them all and you can too.

Four years ago, someone asked me how I could be happy and upbeat all the time in the face of so many challenges, issues and problems. I had to sit down and examine what I was doing. I discovered I had developed a series of procedures, practices, exercises, or rituals. Many of the practices required years and years of refinement.

I'm developing a multi-step course to help people overcome their negative thoughts, feelings, and emotions to lead a happier, more productive and fulfilling life.

Imagine it's the mid-summer of 2008; you're working as an Independent Consultant. You receive an e-mail informing you that your position is being filled by a recent college graduate and you're asked to train your replacement. It's a blow, but you have 2 other clients.

A few of months later, you learn that another client has run out of money and he is closing his company. The remaining client has expressed interest in expanding your hours. It appears that you will be working 30 hours a week for the remaining client.

You sit down in a meeting with the VP of Operations for the last client. You're informed that you won't be able to keep your current hours or expand them because of threats made by a current client of theirs. They're sorry, but they can't afford to lose the business. You have no clients, no current or future income, and no prospects for new clients in an economy that has crashed. This happened to me.

For a couple of days, I wasn't the happiest of person as I pondered the future. I made plans. I scheduled time to look for part and full-time employment. I asked myself a question: "What do I want to do when I grow up?" The answer was instantaneous: a writer. I was not employed; had no money coming in to pay the bills; no work prospects on the horizon; not eligible for unemployment compensation, and yet I was grateful.

You may be perplexed at my gratitude. "What do I have to be grateful for?" I was grateful for a new adventure, challenge and opportunity. I knew it would not be easy. I would have to overcome obstacles, persist in this new vision, and do whatever was necessary to survive and thrive.

Yes, many items in my life are sideways or even upside down. I struggle to pay bills. I ask my parents for help. I work part time as a receiving and stocking clerk for a giant store; as an administrative assistant; grade standardized tests and finally back into a laboratory setting doing developmental work. I have self-published several short books on Kindle under a pen name. My life is far from perfect, and I have my own sets of struggles and challenges, but I'm grateful.

GRATITUDE LIST

The first step is to make your own gratitude list. Grab a notebook, journal or open your favorite electronic device. Review your world.

- What works in your life?
- Who makes you smile or laugh?
- What do you like?
- What are your dreams?

- Who has made a positive impact in your life?
- Who would you miss if they moved away or died?

Do the following:

- In the next 10 minutes write down a list of eight items or more for which you're grateful.
- Add one item to this list daily for the next 26 to 30 days.
- Read your gratitude list twice daily.

Here is a short list of the things I am grateful for:

- Being alive
- Family and friends
- My pets
- To be peaceful, calm and be of help to others
- Music
- Good book
- Sunshine and gentle breezes
- Good night's sleep
- Quiet time

Gratitude is a conscious choice and decision to focus your attention on what is right and good in your life. You have the opportunity to look at the world through new eyes. The mistake many people make is to focus on lack or what is missing, or what they don't like or want. People will say something like, "I don't have this or if I had that, then everything would be great. I hate this job." The emphasis is negative and their lives don't improve. Choosing gratitude focuses on what's good instead of lack or shortcomings.

Each item on your list is a seed that you plant in your garden. Focusing on your gratitude list is like adding water and sunshine to a garden. You are cultivating a garden of gratitude. Become the Master Gardener of your life.

If a fellow isn't thankful for what he's got, he isn't likely
to be thankful for what he's going to get.
~ Frank A. Clark

HOW DO YOU VIEW YOURSELF?

The average person has 40,000 to 120,000 thoughts a day depending on which research you read. Generally, you have the same thoughts day after day. Up to 70% of people's thoughts are negative. You live in an ocean of emotion and negative thoughts. Your negative self-talk has major impact on how you see yourself. When you don't control your negative self-talk, you're swimming in shark-infested waters. The sharks are darting closer and closer until one shark grabs your leg and pulls you under. There's a way to overcome this negative self-talk. Think about the answer to the following questions:

- Do You Like Yourself?
- Do You Love Yourself?
- Do You Have Faith in Your Abilities?

Would you be surprised that many people would answer no to two out of three questions? If you don't like or love yourself and don't have faith in your abilities, who will? Can you give what you don't have? There is a procedure, practice or exercise that you can follow.

First thing in the morning, go into the bathroom and make eye contact in the mirror. Repeat the following phrases:

- I like myself.
- I love myself.
- I have trust in my abilities.
- Now give yourself a big hug.

Repeat these phrases three to eight times with the hugs. It should take about 15 seconds to one minute.

Do this practice two to three times a day for the next 26 to 30 days.

I can hear some resistance about the hug. The hug is important. Hugs release oxytocin. Oxytocin is also known as the "love molecule." Research shows it helps increase self-esteem, feelings of optimism, builds trust and help people overcome fears.

You are consciously making a choice to begin to see yourself in a more positive light. You are installing a new program and overwriting bad scripts; planting seeds of self-esteem; charting a new course by acting as the captain or pilot of your life. *If you take no action, then nothing changes.*

FORGIVENESS

Forgiveness is tough for many people. If you refuse to forgive, why should anyone forgive you? Do you enjoy being angry, hurt, upset, wallowing in negative emotions, stressed, and lack of sleep?

Forgiveness is about healing you. Love yourself more than the anger, disgust and hurt for the perpetrator. Forgiveness frees you. You are not standing in judgment any longer. You no longer live there. Your perception of the event or people changes with forgiveness. You aren't time traveling to the past to visit the incident. You are living in the present. You can concentrate on your life, family and work. Forgive yourself first and then everyone else.

Remember Mr. Miyagi in the *Karate Kid*. He single handedly defeated five attackers by side-stepping their attacks. Mr. Miyagi knew the energy of the attacker would boomerang on the attacker. His power was to remain nonreactive. Forgiving works in the same manner. If you chose to attack back, then a war of words and negative feelings begin that no one can win.

The people that upset you most can also be great teachers. Was the other person striking out in fear or pain? Does yelling and screaming change a thing? Will they be defensive, shut down or change? Can you replace your anger, upset and fear with forgiveness? If you can, a new and different relationship will be born. You do not have to like them, hangout or even be friends. By not forgiving you reinforce their misconduct and will only experience more of the same.

When you're angry, your judgment is clouded and poor decisions are made. Look inward. Learn to let go of the grievances, turmoil, hurt or how not to get upset in the first place. Forgiveness improves your health and well-being. Forgive to help rid your body of dis-ease (disease).

Forgiving doesn't mean forgetting or condoning the actions. Your brain is wired to protect you and forgetting is problematic. Forgiving means you are no longer the victim. You take responsibility for your emotions and feelings.

Is there someone you should forgive? They're several methods, but the one I chose is to write about it. Put it all down on paper and don't censor yourself. Place the writing in a safe place for several days. Take it out and read what you wrote. How does it read? I realized that the anger, fury and hurt were gone. I held a small ceremony where I burned the paper; the flames consumed the words; changed into smoke and were carried away by a breeze. I was free. You can do the same practice too.

OVERCOMING FEAR

How do you feel when you're afraid? Do you stand tall, breathe deeply and active? Fear, being fearful and afraid causes you to shrink and fall back. Your posture is bad. Your breathing is shallow and you fail to take action. What is fear? Fear is the absence of love. How do you overcome fear? Find a way to restore love.

Fear kept people alive. Fear is different today. It paralyzes people. Understand that the barriers are your own thoughts that reside in your mind. Conquer and vanquish your fears by pouring light into the corners of your mind. Fear could be written as follows:

- False
- Evidence
- Appears
- Real

Most people's fear today falls into several categories:

- Fear of failure
- Fear of embarrassment
- Fear of change
- Fear of loss
- Fear of pain

Fear is the worst kind of grave, because it buries one alive.
~ Beth Fantaskey

When confronted with fear, ask the following questions:

- What you have to gain from overcoming your fear?
- How does your life improve?

- How does your life change for the better?
- What are the benefits you gain from overpowering your fear? Name and describe the benefits.

Where does the "Boogie Monster" reside? What happens when you try to avoid the "monster"? The "monster" grows bigger and fiercer. Parents vanquish the "monster" by shining a flashlight in all the dark spaces: under the bed, in the corners and in the closet. Shining light dissolves, disintegrates, and makes the "monster" disappear.

The cave you fear to enter holds the treasure you seek.
~ Joseph Campbell

Facing your fears takes determination, persistence and belief that the gain is worth the effort. Conquering fear builds a stronger foundation for your life. There is no courage without fear.

One of the most common fears is the fear of failure. I embrace failure. Working in research and development, failure is a constant companion. I fail daily; sometimes multiple times in a single day. Learning what doesn't work can be as important as what does work. Keep an open mind and be persistent. Fail your way to success. Adversity, obstacles, and problems are opportunities in disguise. Solve your problem and you can help others overcome the same fear or obstacle.

Thomas Edison failed more than 9,999 times to make a commercial light bulb. Michael Jordan failed by missing 9,000 shots, 26 game winning shots, and lost 300 games. Babe Ruth is remembered for his home runs, but struck out 1330 times. They did not let fear of failure stop them. Fear is an opportunity to learn more, be more, and grow into a more complete and whole person.

Your call to action is to list three to eight items where you let fear stop you. Answer the questions listed above for at least one item on your list. Challenge yourself to overcome one item on your list.

Use the steps discussed above consistently and persistently to improve the quality of your life.

About Debra

Debra Waisner helps friends and clients to overcome negative thoughts, feelings and emotions so they can lead happier, more fulfilled and productive lives. She has spent over 10 years as a Consultant trouble-shooting, problem-solving, in product development and Quality Control and has developed long term care food products to help those suffering from swallowing problems. Loss of clients in 2008 during the economic collapse, lead her to re-examine what she wanted to do and how best to help. That examination began a career transition that is taking place today.

Debra's new career as a writer, course developer and speaker is to help others to redefine or define themselves in a more powerful and positive light. She has self-published 4 books under a pen name dealing with gratitude, forgiveness, food labels, and a children's book. Debra is also the co-author with Brian Tracy of the book *Transform.*

Debra is a graduate of Purdue University. She was also selected as one of American's PremierExperts™. She is currently finishing developing course based on the chapter from the book *Transform.* The course will include eight sections that will delve deeper into improving and redefining negative thoughts, feelings and emotions to transform your life for the better.

CHAPTER 59

REAL ESTATE:
FOUNDATION TO
YOUR DREAMS

BY SHANE WILLIS
MBA, MARKETING AND FLORIDA REAL ESTATE BROKER

I sat there at 9:00 pm looking at my computer screen. In my right hand I had a very strong Bacardi™ and coke. The computer was relaying what was happening in the stock market, and more importantly to me, what was happening in the real estate market. I was witnessing a crash like the country had not seen since the Great Depression. Just to clarify when I say I was sitting at home, I mean a home that I could no longer afford, and with my family in the other room. I had to find a way to let them know the business has now failed. There would be no way to keep up the house payment. There would be no way for me to earn the amount of income we were used to. I felt like I had hit rock bottom. I blamed real estate for failing me. What I did not realize is that I had hit a much needed transformation moment. It wasn't real estate that was failing me, I failed real estate.

In the movie *Wall Street 2: Money Never Sleeps,* Gordon Gekko – played by Michael Douglas – explains to Shia LaBeouf's character Jake Moore, a story about the tulip bulbs and how they were used as a currency. The entire country had gone crazy and started using these bulbs as currency to buy things they could not afford. "You could buy a beautiful house on a canal in Amsterdam for a few bulbs." This is one of the first crashes that we've seen. Real estate is supposed to be that rock solid investment that avoids crashes. I'm here to tell you IT IS.

I'm sure many people reading this book would start to raise an eyebrow at me right now, considering the recent downturn that we just finished. Real estate took a beating at that point. If I had read this book when I was sitting in that room in January 2008, I would've said the same thing. "You are crazy!" Real estate has been the worst investment for the last five years. Or has it? What had to transform in me was the way I viewed real estate. Once you learn how to view it correctly, it can transform many areas in your life, as it is a good, solid vehicle for financial independence. Of course, not having to worry about paying the bills changes everything. It changes how you look at your business. It changes the decisions you make in life like where you vacation and who you can help as a charity. Before this transformation happened in the year 2008, I saw a lot of those nights with a strong rum-based beverage in my hand trying to figure out what I did wrong, and how to avoid it. I'm glad to say that transformation did happen, and I can now share it with you so maybe you too can avoid as many adult beverages as I did, and should be able to avoid half the stress.

CASH FLOW

Cash flow is the only way to look at real estate as an investment. There are a lot of television shows showing how you can make money trading real estate – like flipping a house. But that's no different than trading a stock – buying it at six dollars a share and selling it at $12 a share. The problem is this still requires a lot of your time and effort. If we want to use real estate as a vehicle that can transform our financial success, we need to look for cash flow.

This revelation really came to me as I was talking with a mentor of mine who bought another investment property at the peak in 2007. I asked him how that property was doing and if he had sold it at a loss. Ron gave me the strangest look ever and I knew that he knew something I did not. He asked a simple question, "Why in the world would I sell that property?" Of course my response was simple, "You paid $100,000 for this property and now it's worth $50,000. Why do you still hold onto it if you already lost half of your value?" Again my friend gave me a strange look, took another sip of his tea, which he then placed down slowly and told me these words that I have yet to forget. "You and I look at real estate investment differently." Well, that was a d-u-h-h moment for me since obviously he was not upset about it, and I was stressing over losing my home earlier in the year. Ron told me, "I only buy investment properties for cash flow. Who says I have lost anything?" Of course, my curiosity was built at that point, so I asked him to explain. He told me, "You're correct. I paid $100,000 for that property in 2008. It's now 2012. I rented that property immediately for $1000 a month, so I make $12,000 a year in revenue from that property. That means I have already received $48,000 of my hundred thousand dollars back." Of course I knew that, and also knew about tax incentives he received for owning the real estate. My friend took another sip of this tea and said, "Shane, again you're looking for appreciation and depreciation only. I'm only looking at cash flow. I paid $100,000 cash and I have received $48,000 back. The property is still worth $60,000. But I have no intention of selling the property. I will continue to collect my $12,000 a year. In 8½ to 9 years I will have all of my money back. The purpose of this investment was for the monthly cash flow, not appreciation or depreciation." The next thing he said to me changed how I thought. He said, "Appreciation and depreciation of real estate investing is just a bonus, never invest for the bonus, only invest for the cash flow."

My friend is not a real estate guy. As a matter of fact he owns a fishing company here in Florida. He has 4 to 5 charter boats and he enjoys captaining one of them. Ron uses real estate as an investment tool so that he can concentrate on his business. He told me that when he started investing in real estate before he owned his company, the goal was to have enough cash flow to where he did not have to take a check from his business. This is what he told me was the success of his business. Once his real estate investments were able to pay his bills, he could concentrate on his business and make business decisions for the business not worrying about if he had enough money for his household. He then shared with me how he looked at an investment property in very simple terms. These terms that I will share with you now.

I. NET OPERATING INCOME

Net Operating Income or NOI is what he was looking for when he evaluated any piece of real estate. So what is his formula for net operating income? Really simple, you take the gross rental income and subtract out the following:

a. Taxes

b. Insurance

c. Association dues (if any)

d. A Vacancy Factor (usually 1 month's rent)

e. A Maintenance Number

Property Price	$100,000	Gross Annual Rent	$12,000
Taxes	$138	Utilities & Trash	$0
Insurance	$58	Lawn Service	$50
HOA	$0	Maintenance	$50
Management	$104	Vacancy Reserve	$63
Monthly Expenses =	$463	Annual Expenses =	$5,556

Gross Annual Rent	$12,000
Annual Expenses	$5,556
NOI =	$6,444

This should give you your net operating income. Divide that into the purchase price and you should get your rate of return. As long as that operating income is in the double-digit returns then it should be evaluated closely and a due diligence should be completed.

I immediately looked at Ron and stated, "Well, that's great for you since you had $100,000 to buy a piece of real estate at that point, but I don't have anything right now. I've lost my home, my business, and I am just scraping by at the present moment." He took another long sip of his tea, which was honestly starting to aggravate me, and said very calmly, "That's exactly where I started. I had to transform my way of thinking. That I only invest in real estate for cash flow does not mean that I didn't trade real estate to begin with."

I had asked two different questions:

1. How financing changes the evaluation of an investment property.
2. Coming up with the capital to start investing.

Ron explained that to continue evaluating a potential investment with financing, just continue as follows: You take the net operating income and subtract out your debt payments. As long as the property is a positive cash flow, you may want to invest more time and due diligence into the property. If at this point it does not have a positive cash flow, stop your due diligence and go find one that will. The ease with which he seemed to evaluate properties even took me by surprise (and I am in the business). It is truly not an emotional thing at all. He really did let the numbers make the decision 100% of the time.

We finished our meeting, and I asked if we could meet again as I really needed to think about the conversation. He said of course, and jokingly added, "But next time you're buying." I agreed.

Over the next few days, I really tried to put a process together so that I could be as calm about real estate as my friend was. It really boiled down to digging into real estate and I was able to break down the cycle into two simple steps. Okay, one of the steps has two ways of accomplishing it, but it is still only two steps. If you are anything like me, you wrestled with it really being that easy, but I can assure you it is.

II.(A) STEP 1: TRADING OR WHOLESALING

Gathering the capital needed
This step involves the purchase of a property with the purpose of rehabbing the property and reselling the property for a profit. The reason I put it at step 1 is because this is the way to earn the capital needed to invest.

There are many programs out there that can discuss how to "flip" a house, and most of them say the same thing. What I found was that getting in with an experienced rehabber was the best way to learn. I asked a local rehabber here if I could shadow him for 3 "flips" just to learn the process. I volunteered some of my time as well to ensure he got something out of the deal. I did this to LEARN, not for money. Once I had a handle on what a rehabber was looking for, I then went out and found a property. Negotiations are a strong suit of mine, so I was able to negotiate a good price on the deal, by working it backwards from the rehabber's mindset. (This is where that learning comes in handy. If you know what they want you can negotiate from a position of strength). After I got the property under contract, I went back to the rehabber I had studied under and negotiated a higher price for the same property. I was able to accomplish this because I knew what profit margins he wanted, and I gave it to him. This netted me a $7,284 profit. I did this three more times and that accomplished my getting a down payment for my first rental.

The other option would have been for me to rehab one of these properties myself for an even bigger profit, but I did not want that risk yet, as I was still growing in the field and was anxious to get an investment.

II.(B) STEP 2: INVEST

Use Financing to Leverage the Investment
Next I used the same formula Ron had given me for evaluating properties based on cash flow. I found one that gave me a 14% rate of return. I used the money I had accumulated wholesaling to put as a down payment. Then the cycle started all over again.

I know it seems over simplistic, but it really is that simple. There are many hours of learning that happens in each of these steps, but the end goal for me and for Ron is to have enough cash flow from real estate to be financially independent. This allows me the opportunity to work on other businesses and projects I enjoy, without having to worry about paying my bills or taking a paycheck.

There is a reason many of the wealthiest people in the world either made or hold a major part of their portfolio in real estate. Understanding NOI and using it to evaluate real estate is a path to financial freedom.

About Shane

As an award-winning REALTOR and BROKER, Shane Willis understands real estate and is a respected leader in the real estate industry. Shane has been helping homeowners and real estate investors grow their net worth for over 20 years. Prior to his career in real estate, Shane owned and operated a successful mortgage company. He also has an extensive background in financial services, which started while he was still serving in the U.S. Army. His diverse background enables him to bring fresh and creative ideas to your real estate needs.

As a Florida resident and homeowner, as well as an income property owner and manager, Shane understands the challenges his clients face when making important real estate decisions. Shane blends his marketing savvy and education with his real estate and financial knowledge to help you maximize the investment potential of your home or other real estate.

A recognized expert in his field, Shane Willis is frequently called on to teach conferences and workshops for agents and investors. He has even been asked by the local state college to work as an adjunct professor in their business department. Shane is highly involved in the community, sitting on multiple boards to help different non-profit organizations. As an ex-soldier, he is involved in helping raise awareness and funds for the *Wounded Warrior* project.

Shane holds a Bachelor's in Marketing and a Master's in Business – with a specialization in marketing. He loves spending time with his wife and 2 children.

To connect with Shane on Twitter, visit: http://twitter.com/shanewillis10

Or listen for his podcast: Real Estate, Money, and More at: www.realestatemoneyandmore.com or on iTunes

CHAPTER 60

THE ART OF EVALUATING YOURSELF

BY ABEL MAXWELL

More people with specific goals on a personal or organizational level are going to save a tremendous amount of time and make a lot more money in the next few years than ever being made in human history, and you have to be part of them.

In the lines to follow, my purpose is to show you how to start in order to make it happen.

That being said, let me introduce to you "The Art of Evaluating Yourself" and what it entails to make your ambition a reality and be transformed. The evaluation is the first step of the process of reaching any objective or goal. It is a critical stage that is unfortunately undermined despite its decisive purpose to help your most profound aspirations.

An evaluation is the fact of making a judgement about something; it refers to an assessment, a rating or estimation. It is an essential part in the process of reaching your goals and objectives. Without it, it is difficult to have a clear idea of where you stand, how you do in your market, in order to better position yourself in the future or maintain your core competencies in your area of expertise.

I have identified three key points that will help you with your evaluation whether it is undertaken on a personal or professional level.

I - Know who you are

II - Know where you are

III - Know how you are

I - KNOW WHO YOU ARE

Being aware of who you truly are and what you do needs to be clearly identified and evaluated. Every human being is good at something and your job is to find out what's your God-given or innate gift or talent to be fruitful. I have singled out in the next lines some key points to be observed for a close evaluation.

- How clear is your intent?

Clarity refers to what you want to achieve; this is absolutely fundamental in order to have a clear sense of direction of the transformation process. Hence, you should have in writing **your vision** (know where you're going) and **your mission**, which will become the blueprint of the whole path to follow to reach the target.

Your vision refers to your faculty to foresee your future or the future of your organization – whereas your mission indicates your function or your vocation.

Other than informing on your values and what you do, both your vision and your mission's purpose is to help you keep on track with your reason of existence and the drive motivating you to reach your goal.

Just for a thinking purpose, have you notice that a giraffe does not have the same vision as a turtle? Indeed, a turtle eats from the grass whereas a giraffe eats from the top of the tree. This means that the altitude of your vision will determine how clearly you see and therefore how much you can get accomplished on a personal or organizational level.

- Are you proficient in what you are doing?

"In what are you good at?" or "Are you good at what you're doing?" is the question to ask yourself here, because competence alludes to the level of your skill. Your talent or gift needs to be sharpened and perfected to become a proven skill to be competitive in the marketplace.

"What are your core competencies?" "How committed are you to continuous improvement?" are valid questions to assess your current state.

- How creative are you?

It's impossible to have been created by a Creator and not be creative as implied by TD Jake's findings. As a result, as we cannot be creative without being connected to a Higher force or a Higher inspiration, it's important to be connected to that Higher Source through our inner guts and intuitions.

Successful people are people who follow their intuition; they are not necessarily the smartest, but they just dare to follow their inner guts. For instance, most people have had an experience of creating something and procrastinating to develop their idea before somebody else does it before their very eyes.

II - KNOW WHERE YOU ARE

Having a clear understanding of your situation in the present moment is the first key because it refers to the beginning of the whole process.

a) SWOT

You can complete a SWOT analysis, which will help you highlight your Strengths, Weaknesses, Opportunities and your Threats.

You might want to have them in a table for visual purposes to maximize your efficiency and effectiveness in this step; this is the SWOT analysis of the current situation:

- Your **S**trengths are characteristics that give you or your organization an advantage over others.

- Your **W**eaknesses are characteristics that place you at a disadvantage relative to others.

- Your **O**pportunities are elements where your competition is not performing well.

- Your **T**hreats are elements where your competition is performing well and elements in the environment you cannot control – that could cause you trouble.

Your **S**trengths and your **W**eaknesses are from internal origins whereas your **O**pportunities and your **T**hreats are from external origins.

The reason why the SWOT analysis is important is due to the fact that its purpose is to inform you of later steps in planning to achieve your goal.

b) STEEEP

You can also examine the STEEEP analysis, which refers to Social, Technological, Economic, Environmental, Ethical and Political factors that could affect you or impact you or your organization:

- On the **S**ocial level: it's essential to reflect on how your objective or goals will socially affect the social environment taking into account population demographics of the target market.

- On the **T**echnological level: the online world is huge and enables you or your organization to reach even more prospects. It's important to ponder on how you can make use of the technological advances with tools, such as social media and software available, to help you boost your visibility in the e-marketplace.

- On the **E**conomic level: ask yourself if your target market is economically reachable to purchase your services or products at a profitable price.

- On the **E**nvironmental level: are you having a positive or a negative impact on the environment (environmentally-friendly or not) – as this is becoming an increasing concern nowadays.

- On an **E**thical level: depending on the value system and principles that govern the culture of the target market, your practices should not come across as offensive and illegal as far as the country's laws and regulations are concerned.

- On the **P**olitical level: ask yourself if the political environment is favourable for what you or your organization is planning to undertake.

The purpose of knowing where you are is a prerequisite to knowing the direction in which you are going.

By setting your goals and objectives, it's easier to set your action plan. By having it in writing, you become more accountable to yourself and to your organization to where you are going. By proceeding with a step-by step "pros and cons" analysis and methodically following through will propel you forward and eventually bring you closer to your intended goal.

III - KNOW HOW YOU ARE

- How confident are you?

Self-esteem is the prerequisite to quality of relationships and is the key ingredient of your confidence magnitude. Unfortunately, it is not possible to learn confidence in a seminar or in a book. However, you can improve your confidence level by doing certain things over and over again because self-doubt is the great paralyzer of achievement. Confidence comes from not always being right, but not fearing to be wrong as Peter McIntyre indicated.

Your confident walk in the direction of your transformation, and acting as if it was impossible to fail will qualify you for your ultimate success. Your true beliefs are always expressed in your actions and rarely in what you solely say.

- Are you considering the quality of your relationships?

Life is all about relationships. In my view, the quality of your interactions will determine your level of happiness and success. You need to develop your people skills – which encompass effective listening communication skills. You can increase the extent of your vocabulary and become a better thinker, which leads to better communication.

For example, if you decide to learn one single word everyday, you will learn 365 words per year. What's fantastic is that every word will introduce you to ten more other words and if you continue this method, you'll become the most educated person in history in the next couple years.

As a matter of fact, the average child learns five thousands words in his first five years of life in comparison to the average adult learning less than five words per year. Thus, the more words you have, the better is your thinking, just like the more tools a mechanic has in his tool box, the better equipped he is to solve mechanical problems.

- Are you consistent in your efforts to reach your goals?

It is commonplace to realize that every great success was at one time a failure and that every success is the accumulation of thousands of little things that were invisible to most people.

Let me use an anecdote to illustrate consistency; there were frogs lining up for a race to climb the Eiffel tower in Paris. Many frogs were at the bottom and started the race, while way more other frogs were cheering the most courageous at the beginning of the race.

As soon as the race started, some of the frogs in the crowd started discouraging those climbing by saying "you better stop because you might fall down from the tower and it's too dangerous."

As they kept on racing, one frog was still going on slowly but steadily, while few of them in front started slowing down and eventually stopped the race as the discouragement grew more and more intense.

At some point, that one frog still climbing went ahead of the other frogs despite the dissuading comments of the entire crowd, and ended up winning the race. That frog became the winner and it's only when he got interviewed that the rest of the frogs discovered he was deaf. So, surprisingly, he could not hear the demoralizing utterances of the crowd. That winning frog was simply consistent in his efforts until his victory. This amusing story demonstrates the power of consistency.

In the same line of thinking, as a basketball fan, I noted Michael Jordan quoting: "I've missed 9000 shots in my career. I've lost almost 300 games. 26 times, I've been trusted to take the game winning shot and missed. I've failed over and over and over again in my life. And that is why I succeed." This reinforces the idea that he was just consistent in his efforts to make great things happen in his basketball career.

- How committed are you?

Being committed is one of the hardest things to do for human beings, and finding the work you can get committed to is key in your transformation. In fact, commitment is closely connected to your loyalty to your objectives and goals.

As a result, whether it is for your family, your company or your relationships, your commitment counts a great deal towards your transformation.

- How are you using common sense?

Some people fail to think things through before acting, that's why you should train your mind not only to think, but also to listen to your God-given or innate instinct. It has being discovered that women in general have the courage to listen to their intuition, that's why they are perceived smarter than men.

In addition to that, by learning from your setbacks and your shortcomings, you'll develop the capacity to think intelligently and to feel instinctively – as action without thinking is the cause of failure.

Socrates quoted "the unexamined life is not worth living" which emphasizes that you need to pause and take time to reflect on your experiences and think about the past valuable lessons and get wisdom.

- How focused are you?

It is more and more easy to be distracted by all kind of things especially with the heavy demands of current society, but by developing a sense of urgency, you can make better use of your time and complete steps required to reach your goals faster. This will eliminate procrastination because the sense that immediate action is necessary to avoid a negative outcome will catalyze your ability to perform right away.

By concentrating on what is challenging and necessary, instead of what is fun and easy, you can focus on results and not on activities that are not relevant to your transformation.

- How courageous are you?

Being courageous is not the absence of fear, but instead, the decision to take action despite the fear of the adversity. You need to develop your ability to resist fear and engage yourself in the activity in line with your transformation goals. In reality, without obstacles, there would be no need to be courageous.

If you resolve to never quit no matter what life throws at you, then you become unstoppable. At that point, you can be assured to be in a position to achieve your goal.

CONCLUSION

Self-evaluation is a crucial part of the process of reaching your goals and objectives and be transformed. An effective transformation will not happen unless these steps and sub-steps are successfully observed and completed. In a nutshell, by covering key questions on your level of clarity, competence, creativity, confidence, consideration, consistency, commitment, common sense, concentration and courage, you can bring your potential to fruition.

Personally, I would even recommend a regular evaluation after a pre-established period of time to reinforce the initial vision and mission you have set for yourself and your organization. Furthermore, maximize your core competencies more than working on your weaknesses, because that what's giving you or your organization a clear competitive advantage.

Being transformed will be even more remarkable by taking notes of the changes occurring – first with a methodical comparison of what was and what is new, then what is new and works effectively.

When you have a dream, it's your responsibility to protect it from discouragement and pessimists. Always remember that you cannot eat an elephant in a single bite, so you have to cultivate patience through the whole process, because as Aubrey Hepburn stated it accurately, "Nothing is impossible; even the word impossible says, "I'm possible."

That being said, complete your evaluation and confidently reach your aspirations to live in peace, prosperity and purpose.

Blessings,

Abel Maxwell

#AMinspirations

About Abel

Abel Maxwell helps his clients (professionals, mid-sized organizations in educational, health & spiritual sectors) gain greater value through consulting services using Entertainment and Inspirational speaking. With his passion for arts and culture, he inspires beginners and professionals to excel in what they do.

He studied in three different continents (Africa, Europe and North America - National Conservatories of Dakar, Lyon, Amsterdam and the Royal Conservatory of Toronto) and holds a degree in Business Administration with a concentration in Finances/Marketing from Université Professionnelle Internationale René Cassin (CEFAM Lyon, France) in 2005.

Abel Maxwell worked with a Forbes Fortune 500 company in the field of finance and consulting with over $298 millions in assets; he also founded the Lyon Gospel Mass Choir (130 vocalists), a choir still performing at several international functions and also released in 2006 his first album produced under the Alter Ego Music record label (France).

Ever since he moved to Ontario in 2007, Abel has inspired a number of people through the arts and has a great deal of influence on different organizations (National Association of Music Industry - A.N.I.M, Connexion Jeunesse Afrique Canada - C.J.C.A, Centre Reveil International, Professional Association of Music Professionals - A.P.C.M) and business projects in Ontario as a Director and Producer at B.O.D.B Entertainment Corporation.

With his appearances in prestigious entertainment venues and TV platforms such as National Arts Center, Radio Canada, Rogers, CBS in North America, he made a great impression on the media as a rising artist (Abel Maxwell's music available on iTunes). Abel Maxwell performed or met with celebrities including Bobby Mc Ferrin, Lionel Louéké, Esperanza Spalding, Miguel de Armas and Kirk Franklin to name a few.

Abel Maxwell speaks five languages (including French and Holland Dutch), and with his tremendous influence especially on the francophone platform, not only is he a successful performer and producer, but he is also an inspirational keynote speaker who delivers a message about reaching out for your dreams with a passion for excellence.

You can connect with Abel Maxwell at:
abel@bodbent.com, www.twitter.com/abelmaxwell,
www.facebook.com/abelmaxwell
#AMinspirations

CHAPTER 61

SHARE FIRST
THEN SUCCEED

BY BRIAN BECK

At my heaviest, I was 487 pounds. I was laid off from my radio job as a Talk Show Host in Dallas, TX at the beginning of 2003. In June of that same year, I had an opportunity to travel to Orlando to interview at another station. I was told as I boarded the plane that I was too big and needed another seat. I couldn't afford to buy another full-priced seat and I didn't have the time to see if the company I was interviewing with would pay for it. Completely decimated, I wasn't allowed to fly and I lost out on my interview. That is when I decided to have gastric bypass surgery. I truly believed it would be my cure. It did temporarily save my life, but it didn't change my way of thinking. I lost 200 pounds! Amazing, right? Over them next 6 years, I would manage to gain back 150 pounds and stretch my stomach back to my normal size. I tell you this, because I still hadn't taken responsibility for my actions, nor had I accepted the fact that I was in control, if I wanted to be. I wasn't ready for change.

June 20, 2009. That is the Saturday I hit rock bottom. Everyone has a different "rock bottom." I was driving home from my job as a Radio Traffic Reporter and really frustrated with life. I had nearly gained all the weight back that I lost from gastric bypass surgery. "Over 400 pounds again!" I repeated that phrase over and over in my head while on the service road of the Dallas North Tollway heading home to Plano, TX. Driving my Saturn Ion and nearly in tears, I was run off the road by a new Lexus sedan. In reality, the driver of the Lexus just wasn't paying attention, but I took this personally!

My car wasn't damaged, so I pulled into a strip mall parking lot. I was 37 years old, making $25,000 a year and my health was abysmal. I was married to the love of my life, but even that couldn't bring a smile to my face. I called my wife and just yelled in frustration at the top of my lungs. I hated my job, my income, my health, really my entire life! I blamed everyone. It was my company's fault. It was my former coworkers' fault. It was the fault of every former radio person that I thought screwed me over. It was the government's fault. No way was all of this misery "my fault"!

Arriving at home was no better. Sure we owned our condo, but life was out of control. Back up to a size 52 waist, I couldn't even sit on the couch comfortably in sweatpants. I didn't talk for a couple of hours. My wife was crying and begging me to snap out of it. I didn't know what to do. I felt that I had no control over anything in my life whatsoever. I couldn't afford to quit my job. Who else was going to hire a 400 plus pound Traffic Reporter? TV was out of the question. There are only three real radio companies and they were laying off, not hiring. I was stuck.

It literally took me all weekend before I ate anything. I wasn't trying to starve myself; it was depression really sinking in. Sunday evening it came to me. If I can keep from eating all weekend, not something I recommend mind you, there is something I have control over! I can control what I put in my mouth! Nobody has control over my nutrition but me!

In reality, you have control over much more than you realize. Your employers, government, parents, friends, landlords, doctors, and just about anyone else in your life don't want you to know that. It's truer now than ever! You have control over everything. How do you take control of your life back? You do it one step at a time.

1. Find one thing that you want to take back control of. In my case, it was my nutrition. For you, it could be leaving a bad relationship, finding a new job, leaving a treacherous friendship behind, working out, going after that goal that's been on the backburner for years, or not being afraid to talk to people! Find one goal and a way to

conquer it! If you're having trouble finding a goal to go after, use nutrition. It's something everyone can do!

2. Get out a piece of paper and brainstorm. I'll be using nutrition from here on out, but you can replace nutrition with anything. First, you need to figure out exactly what you want to change. It can be weight, measurement, or just feeling better. I couldn't weigh myself at the beginning because my scale didn't measure above 300 pounds. Therefore, I wanted to just feel better and go down in clothing sizes.

3. Put a short-term goal and plan together. I don't count calories. We all know that eating five to six times a day and eating the right stuff works.

4. What is the right stuff? I'm not a Medical Doctor or a Nutritionist, I can only tell you what worked for me. No processed foods. Outside of supplements, if it came in a box or wrapper, I didn't eat it. Fresh meat, vegetables, and fruits. Simple huh? Not until you TRY to make it hard. Before you ask me if something is ok to eat, I am going to tell you no. If you don't know, don't eat it. There were a few exceptions to my "no packaging" rule. I do eat real butter, olive oil, coconut oil, roasted/unsalted almonds, and occasionally brown rice or plain oatmeal. Notice that bread IS NOT on the list!

5. Plan your meals out! Know exactly what you are going to have for each meal the next day. Get a soft cooler to carry with you. If you drive a lot, get a plug in cooler for your car. Everyone can do this. If you have your food planned out, you are far less likely to make bad choices.

6. Forget about yesterday. So you fell "off the wagon". That was yesterday. This is TODAY! You can't do anything about the past, but you can learn from it. So don't let yesterday's bad decisions determine what today's decisions will be. Every decision you make right now WILL determine your future.

7. Do NOT EVER go through a drive-through window. I don't care if it is something healthy you are ordering. Get off your butt and go into the restaurant and order it from a person at the counter. Or better yet, don't go into a fast food restaurant!

8. Eating right is too expensive? Try eating what's in season. Read the grocery store advertisements. Summer is berry and melon season.

Winter is squash and citrus season. You get the idea. When produce is in season, it's cheaper!

So, we have the food and nutrition covered. Now, how do we change our mindset? I set a plan together to be able to afford to quit my job. I started saving money and training people on the side for extra income. More for experience, because I decided I wanted to become a Personal Trainer! You may not realize this, but you do not need to be certified to be a Personal Trainer. It's an unregulated industry. I did want to get certified and do things right. I had a background in Sports Medicine from the early 1990's in college, and I decided things would come full circle! I did earn my certification and started my business. The radio traffic company I worked with purchased their competition and laid off most of them. While I was promised a raise, my new boss refused to honor it, so I was stuck making $25,000/yr. Plus, I was now doing over 80 traffic reports in 8 hours in 6 different cities! I was told to use different names in every city as well. This was not fun in the least. They were all recorded into a computer and just sent to stations in Austin, San Antonio, Houston, Oklahoma City, Tulsa, and Phoenix. This was when I turned in my 2 weeks notice.

When you make a decision like that, you better be ready to work your butt off in your new business because being successful is all up to YOU! Now, I had a new goal and it was time to fight for myself again! This is how I started from literally no clients to having a waiting list today. This will work for any person wanting to improve their business outlook.

1. How much sports radio, music radio, or news radio do you listen to on your commute? I worked in media for a long time as a Radio Talk Show Host, Music DJ, Traffic Reporter, and many other jobs. The only things they care about are ratings. It's ALL entertainment! "If it bleeds, it leads," was a phrase I heard many times. Inherently, there is nothing wrong with that. But when you listen to people angry, yelling, making negative comments, and doing whatever they can to keep you tuned in, what do you think that does to your head? I'm a firm believer in reading and listening to books on tape. Even when I work out, I listen to books on tape. I pick books about positive thinking and growing my business. I find that to be much more motivating than any song could ever be. We need to bombard ourselves with positive words instead of the commercials and

negativity we see on the TV or hear on the radio every day. Do that for 2 weeks and you'll see a noticeable improvement.

2. Cut out TV. Yes I said it. Maybe keep basic cable around for emergency updates, but cut the rest out of your life. Treat it like I said to do with cheat meals. Pick one program a week to watch. When you do that, you will make sure it's a fantastic program! Think about it for a second, when did watching the NFL ever pay you a dime or help you improve your business or life? It doesn't! Unless your business is sports or you have a very important client that loves sports, it does nothing but eat up your time. I prefer playing sports now! Find a softball league, soccer league, or even a running/walking group. Not only do you get exercise, but you also get to make business connections. The more people you're around, the more opportunity you have.

3. Be mindful of the people you spend the most time with. I have lost most of my friends and colleagues that I had up until a few years ago. My best friend and radio show co-host for a decade is no longer in my life. It was my choice. He chose to stay negative and it carried over into social media as well as my new business. Instead of being supportive, he took every opportunity to bring me back down. Again, it was my wife who told me to decide what's best for my life. I knew it was the right decision to part ways with my best friend, but it hurt. He was the closest thing to a brother I had at the time. The old saying is true, take the top 10 people you spend time with, average them together, and that's you!

4. Find people that inspire YOU! They are everywhere, but we usually don't see or know them. The way you find them is striking up conversations with anyone who you find yourself next to. I don't recommend that if you are on a street corner and a prostitute walks up to you, but just about anyone else, go for it! You never know what you could learn! Use every second to your advantage. Talk to the checkout clerk at the grocery store, the gas station, the fast food restaurant (you really shouldn't be going there), the person next to you at the gym you will now join, or the businessperson sitting next to you on the subway. Everyone really does have an amazing story to tell and they all want to share it! Smile at them and genuinely listen to them. When that happens, you may have found your next business partner! At the least, maybe they would

be interested in what you do and it very well could turn into a business relationship.

One last nugget I want to leave you with. YOU are in charge of setting your own limitations. Everything that has happened to you, up to this point, is because of choices you've made. You will never be successful in your health or business until you take responsibility for where you are. Once you do that, you're on your way! Build other people up. Even if someone doesn't believe in himself or herself, instill in them how important they are and what they are capable of. It's amazing, in return, how that will also make you feel! I'm greedy that way. I help other people because it makes me feel good doing it. Try it; you'll probably feel the same way! Now go be awesome!

About Brian

Brian weighed 487 pounds at his heaviest. He lost 300 pounds and is now a Certified Personal Trainer and Weight Loss Specialist. From 6 months old, doctors put him on a "diet" because of weight. After yo-yoing for decades, Brian finally figured out what worked for him and lost 300 pounds. He tried surgery, but gained every ounce of weight back. Once he realized that the perfect mix for him was eating right, supplements, and exercise, his weight loss was unstoppable! Now he passes his knowledge on to anyone who wants it through his company "Train Me Brian".

As a Certified Personal Trainer, Brian has helped hundreds of people lose thousands of pounds in the last few years. He not only trains people at his gym in Plano, Texas, he helps people all over the country lose weight and feel better than they ever have in their lives. By giving meal plans, supplementation, and exercise programs, he's helped people in nearly every state in the country. He guarantees that if you follow his program completely, you will notice a significant change.

Now, Brian makes his clients promise to "Pass it on," meaning they will find people where they live to help just like Brian did for them. He believes that one person can make a difference, but many can start a revolution in being healthy! Once this really gets going, Brian feels that the Untied States can become the healthiest country in the world!

Brian studied Sports Medicine at Texas State University. He also studied Radio/TV/Film at the University of North Texas. He was a Radio Talk Show Host for 105.3 FM in Dallas, TX. Now as a Certified Personal Trainer, he's been featured on *Good Morning America, Good Morning Texas, USA Today, ABC News, The Huffington Post, KTCK 1310AM The Ticket,* and *1080AM KRLD Radio* sharing his knowledge on not only weight loss, but self confidence, nutrition, exercise, and overall health. Brian is also a national speaker and has spoken before crowds from 200 to 30,000 people! He wants every opportunity to spread his passion of being healthy to the entire world!

CHAPTER 62

KNOW YOUR NUMBERS

BY ADAM WEBER

I spend a considerable amount of my time educating and counseling appraisal business owners and real estate investors, all of whom cherish a dream of business success.

Having an understanding of your business's finances or numbers is one of the most important tasks is in keeping your business healthy. Nevertheless, many business owners do not pay attention to this extremely important task, and, as a result, their businesses pay the price.

If you have a tough time dealing with the finances of your business, you are not alone. There are lots of successful business owners that loathe dealing with numbers. They regard managing their finances with anxiety, fear, and insecurity. Typically, the argument that is raised is that they are simply too busy running their businesses to deal with tracking numbers on their financial statements.

According to the United States Census Bureau, over one-half of all new businesses fail within the first five years. The leading causes of such failure are:

1. Business owners often fail to manage their cash flow.

2. Business owners do not understand their financial statements.

The first step as a business owner is to acquire a good knowledge of what your financial or "money" reports are really telling you.

The crucial part is determining which ones are important for monitoring and improving your business's performance and avoiding disaster, like the half of new businesses that fail in the first five years of operation and the others that fail after the five-year time horizon.

The profit and loss statement is your best starting point. Information from your business's income statement can be used to make better-informed decisions about your company's pricing, margin maintenance and expense control.

When you "know your numbers," you can analyze past trends and make estimations for the future. Having a clear idea of how your business is doing in terms of revenues and profits can tell you if you are on track to achieving your goals, and you can make preemptive adjustments if you are not.

Remember that numbers are the language of your business.

Instead of having a month of poor sales and contemplating on what went wrong, you can track your numbers to see underlying issues and fix your problems early on.

But how do you know if your numbers are good or bad?

A good example would be your marketing. If your latest direct mail campaign generated a 2 percent response rate when all your other direct mail campaigns generated double digit response rates, then that is a good indication that you need to look closer at your copy or your offer.

Many companies have seasonal sales cycles and the relevant comparison is how you did over that period of time with the same period in prior years. This will help you reach what should be every business owner's goal, being more profitable every year. Additionally, you would want to compare your results with others in the same industry. Your best resource for that is a trade association for your business. When that is not available, other resources are accessible at most libraries.

As a business owner, knowing your numbers is the single greatest skill you need in order to launch and grow a successful business and to maintain your profitability. By knowing your financial numbers, you will detect problems quickly and that will allow you to take action promptly. You can have the greatest business idea, but, if the numbers don't work, it just doesn't matter. Let me expand.

Successful business owners understand that knowing your numbers is a necessity to survive when running a business. Knowing your numbers virtually guarantees you greater success and multiplied profits.

Here are some numbers that every business owner needs to track.

Working Capital – Your working capital is the cash or capital that you have on hand to manage your business on a day-to-day basis.

Revenue – Your sales represent the vital source of income for your business. This is the money that your business generates from sales activity, whether it is on a weekly, monthly or annual basis.

Gross Profit – This is your sales revenue minus the direct costs of producing your product or service. (These costs are your cost of goods sold.)

Operating Expenses – No matter what you sell, whether it is a product or a service, if you do not track your expenses, then your profits will be minimal and unimpressive. Your operating expenses are the costs that you bear to pay your expenses – including rent, insurance, and taxes. You not only need to track, but also to control your costs.

Net Profit – Your net profit is calculated by deducting operating and other expenses (such as depreciation) from your gross profit.

Now that we have covered the basis of knowing your numbers, we can look at the essentials that business owners need for effective money management.

Budgets and forecasts go a long way in helping you manage your numbers effectively. Many people overlook the benefits of forecasting business expenditure for a given time period. In a similar vein, you also need to make saving plans. Not to spread pessimism, but there is always an element of unpredictability in a new business; so having some resources to bank on when things get rough is a wise idea.

Keep an eye on your expenses. This cannot be stressed enough. You need to account even for the smallest expense that your company makes. Of course, this requires a lot of work, but nowadays you have various financial tools that have made this job easier

This is important if you plan to increase revenue by selling additional items with your main product. For instance, if you sell mini sound systems for $120 each, marketing headsets worth $59 to go with the system will result in a 24% increase in revenue per sale.

Let's say you spent $800 on web design and SEO. You get 500 hits on the new website and 200 of these visitors actually make a purchase. So bringing in new customers into your business costs you $4.00 each. But you will also have to ensure that each purchase is more than $4.00 if you want to make a profit. This strategy helps you to formulate your marketing budget.

Calculating what it costs to bring in new customers can be further expanded into the following categories.

Conversions - Conversion happens when viewers/listeners of your ads (or visitors to your website) actually become paying customers. Following on from the above example, 200 out of every 500 website visitors become customers, so the conversion rate is 40% (200/500). Is this rate good? It depends on what difference these conversions are making to your bottom line.

Response Rates - In traditional direct marketing, i.e., catalogues, mailing, and fliers, the average response rates varied from 1% to 5%, depending on whether the company acquired the mailing list from a broker or marketed it to its existing customer base. In online email campaigns, the average response rates tend to be much lower, at around 0.1%. So to get 20 responses, you'll need a mailing list of 20,000 contacts.

Finally, you should also calculate how many leads (potential buyers) make you a sale. This is especially beneficial if you are in the B2B industry. For example, if you are selling security systems to banks and producing one client takes you 20 prospects, you need to get 2000 leads to get 100 clients.

While the above mentioned help create the mindset for effective numbers management, they are general in nature and can be applied to other areas of your business as well. So here are some advanced tips on getting your numbers under control.

LIFETIME CUSTOMER VALUE

In marketing, Lifetime Customer Value (LCV) is a prediction of the net profit attributed to the entire future relationship with a customer. The prediction model can have varying levels of sophistication and accuracy, ranging from a crude heuristic to the use of complex predictive analytics techniques.

Lifetime Customer Value is an important concept in that it encourages businesses, both large and small, to shift their focus to the long-term health of their customer relationships. It represents an upper limit on spending to acquire new customers. For this reason, it is an important element in calculating payback of the marketing mix modeling.

In simple terms, you have to calculate how many purchases a customer makes in money value per year, and then see how long they stay in your business. So if a customer shops from you twice a year, paying $150 each time, and continues to do that for three years, he/she is worth $900 to your business. This will further help you to create goals like how many customers you need to acquire to meet the next financial target, etc.

Some businesses neglect to look closely at their employee costs. The only reason to have an employee is to generate profits for your business, and many business owners look at one figure – what they pay the employee on an hourly basis. This is an ineffective way to analyze your employee costs. It is not just the wages that you pay, but taxes, benefits, including health care costs, and in some cases, contributions to retirement, and bonuses. The costs do not end there. Do you know what your employee costs really are? Is there any wonder why the use of contract employees and VA's or virtual assistants have grown? If you have not read it yet and you are a small business owner, read Tim Ferris' book, *The 4-Hour Work Week*.

Another number to pay attention to is your "Do-Over Number." Simply put, it is the costs that are attributed to the mistakes you make. For real estate investors that I counsel, it can be the cost of scrimping on costs associated with repairs and renovations leading to the need to do the work over. If you own a restaurant, it can be the cost of having to prepare a second dish for a patron because the food was overcooked and the first dish ends up in the trash.

I believe that the second most relevant number is the **ROI or Return On Investment**. This is best defined as a measure of the amount gained or lost on an investment, expressed as a percentage of the initial investment. Whether you are a real estate investor or an appraisal business owner, it matters.

ROI serves as a tool to help business owners determine the profitability of a business venture. More specifically, it reveals the earnings the business owner receives for each dollar invested in the business.

There are several ways to determine ROI, but the most frequently used method is to divide the net profit by the total business assets. If the businesses' net profit is $1,000,000 and the total assets are $3,000,000, your ROI would be 33 percent.

Return on investment isn't necessarily the same as profit. ROI deals with the money that you invest in the business opportunity and the return you receive on that money based on the net profit of the business. The profit measures the performance of the business.

YOUR TIME IS YOUR MOST IMPORTANT NUMBER

The most important number in your business is your time. You can get more money through various avenues but once time is gone, it's gone forever. You can't buy more or borrow more time, so time is a limited resource that expires every day. As a business owner, you have to be very careful with this precious resource.

With my appraisal coaching clients, we pay close attention to this number because they may quote a fee to complete a job in two days and it ends up taking a week. This concept goes for all business types. Your most relevant number in business is the number of hours that you spend on and in your business or, more easily defined, your time.

The wealthiest business owners know that having some structure to their schedule creates a routine of success. Create a daily blueprint for yourself. If you invest the time in planning, you can add at least an hour to your "productive" time every day. That translates to at least five extra hours a week, probably more.

If you don't already, you should apply the Pareto Principal or 80/20 Rule to your time and schedule.

When applied to work, it means that approximately 20 percent of your efforts produce 80 percent of the results. Learning to recognize and then focus on that 20 percent is the key to making the most effective use of your time.

You have 10 things you need to do today. The odds are that one item is worth 10 times more than the rest.

In time management terms, it suggests that unless we actually try to do something about it then, for most of us for most of the time around 80% of what we achieve comes from just 20% of what we do. In other words, there is a huge imbalance between effort and results.

It's like saying that in the equivalent of just one day, we achieve the bulk of what we do that is worth doing in the whole week. Our contribution in the other four days merely adds up to a small fraction of what matters. It's an appalling statistic but, generally, it has far more than just a core of truth behind it.

However, if you learn from it - this natural imbalance - and start to apply standard time management ideas, then you can blow the 80/20 Rule apart. You can, indeed you should, spend far more than 20% of your time and effort on what matters. You will then achieve far more than what you have been used to; not a little bit more, but far more. From 80/20 you can move to something like 160/50 or even better.

Now that you have a clear understanding of how you can manage your business numbers better, here is a summary of what this implies for your company:

Clear Goal Setting - You can analyze past trends and make estimations for the future. Research suggests that organizations that set goals are much more likely to achieve them. Moreover, by having a clear idea of how your business is doing in terms of revenues and profits (even on a daily basis), you can tell if you're on track to achieve your goals, and you can make preemptive adjustments if you're not.

Instead of having a month of poor sales and contemplating on what went wrong, you can use your numbers to track underlying issues and fix problems early on.

By simply keeping track of things like the value of each sale, number of proposals given, and number of leads, you can instantly know which area needs to be worked upon.

About Adam

Adam J. Weber, MAI, SRA, MRICS is a nationally-recognized real estate valuation expert and the owner of Weber Advisory Group, a New York-based real estate valuation and consultation firm. Adam serves his clients by providing solutions to complex real estate valuation problems.

Adam is also the creator of Appraisal Profits, which teaches appraisers how to implement procedures, systems and high profit marketing that enable appraisal business owners to produce extraordinary business results.

Adam attended The Ohio State University and majored in Business Management with a concentration in Real Estate. He has also earned the prestigious MAI and SRA designations from the Appraisal Institute, and the MRICS designation from the Royal Institute of Chartered Surveyors. Adam is the author of the book: *Getting Back to Basics – The Ultimate Success Blueprint.*

You can connect with Adam at:
adam@weberadvisorygroup.com
www.facebook.com/adam.weber.maisra
www.linkedin.com/in/adamwebermaisra
www.twitter.com/weberswisdom
www.AppraisalProfits.com

CHAPTER 63

NEW CHOICE TRANSFORMATION

BY LAURA CLANCY

While training at ComedySportz DC, a short-form Improv Troupe, we play lots of games to entertain our audience. To make it more fun for our "loyal fans", we play as teams who compete against one another. In a battle of wits, it's the Blue Team vs. the Red Team, but nobody really cares who wins.

One of the games we play is called "**NEW CHOICE**."

This game works as follows: characters, scenes and conflicts are quickly created from scratch, and a referee intently watches the scene unfold as each word or physical action is uttered by the actor. The referee then finds some word or action that would be funny to change and blows the whistle and says, "**NEW CHOICE!**" The actor is then forced to find a new word or action to replace the original idea. Once they land on a final choice, the scene continues on with the "NEW CHOICE" idea intact.

Well, you can imagine, hilarity ensues and new choices make all actors on stage change the scene on a dime. It's SO MUCH FUN for the audience, actors and referee!

Here's an abbreviated example of the game: Hal and Sue walk into a grocery store...

Hal (sappily): "Sue, I feel lucky that you're part of my life now, since you were quite the catch. ☺ And now that we're married, I just

563

love grocery shopping with you - it's really gratifying!!"

Sue (happily): "Thanks Hal. I feel it keeps us more bonded as a couple."

Hal: "I agree, Sue."

Referee: "New Choice!"

Hal: "I disagree, Sue"

Referee: "New Choice!"

Hal: "Like a ball and chain, Sue."

Sue: "Speaking of shackles, have you heard of that new vitamin and mineral cereal called 'Golden Iron'?"

Referee: "New Choice!"

Sue: "Speaking of shackles, have you heard of that new fish called manacle?"

Referee: "New Choice!"

Sue: "Speaking of shackles, have you heard of that new adult beverage called Unfettered?"

Hal: "No, I haven't. But, about now, I'd love to release a cold one!"

Referee: "New Choice!"

Hal: "No I haven't. But you've sure become a cold one."

Referee: "New Choice!"

Hal: "Nope. But, I'd like to make you part of the catch-and-release program."

With the best punch line delivered and the audience howling with the twists and turns that have been taken...the referee calls the end of that scene...

You may be asking yourself, how does an improv game apply to **TRANSFORMATION**? How can this seemingly nonsensical idea change *me* and help me transform something in my life?

Here's my vision:

LIFE is the Ultimate Improv Stage and every time you seize on a NEW CHOICE, Adaptation and Transformation ensue . . .

After all, transformation is about making **NEW CHOICES** when the old choices are keeping you stuck and are only getting you muddy.

As a professional speaker, I've learned more than how to make people laugh by practicing this art form. I've actually garnered many valuable ideas and concepts. For example, I've experienced:

- Saying "Yes, and" is the answer to successful outcomes.

- Complacency should be feared more than failure, in order to grow personally and professionally.

- Making perfect decisions *is not* what life is about; it's about making the best out of any decisions that are made.

I've watched improv classes transform shy people into budding comedians who change the way audience members see some of their own life scenarios. It's the 21st century's comedic solutions to real problems...Strife, Levity and the Pursuit of Excellence. Isn't that cool?

As a Professional AND Multi-dimensional Transformer, I've learned that in order to transform, we must push ourselves to look at the same scenario through a different lens and take different actions to get what we most desire. We must make **NEW CHOICES**.

Real Life is full of New Choices practically every minute of every day. The choices we make for most things have an impact on everything we do.

There are seven ways in which I think we can meaningfully transform ourselves:

1. Spiritually

2. Physically

3. Mentally

4. Emotionally

5. Relationally

6. Financially and…

7. Vocationally

Real life New Choice(s) transformed my life. For me, over the years, when one avenue didn't work as anticipated, it was time for me to make a **NEW CHOICE**. I often think that my life is proof that there are more than four traditional dimensions. Let's put it this way, IMAX would need some serious innovation to make the glasses. Ha! Here's a 3-D version of my transformations…

I've gone from being a…

- stay-at-home mom to founder and CEO of the successful MuffinToppled® Enterprises, Inc.
- wallflower to an award-winning speaker
- couch potato to a 100% Raw Powerlifting Federation World Record Holder.

But, perhaps the best NEW CHOICE I made in life was the first NEW CHOICE I made in my multi-dimensional transformation. That NEW CHOICE was deciding to go from being a yo-yo dieter to a long-term lean-bodied athlete.

And, from that first NEW CHOICE that I made…

my saying 'yes and…' to opportunities…my fear of complacency…my realization that moving forward with imperfect action was better than standing still with perfect inaction

…came my best idea to help you _transform your health into wellness_.

In my opinion, of all the transformations we can make, creating our healthful wellbeing is the anchor from which all other transformation can occur. "Well"-being, whether it's moving well, feeling well, and/or eating well, is when our quality of life allows other NEW CHOICES to be made with ease.

I'd like to share with you the **NEW CHOICES** needed to create long-term healthful transformation…Improv Style:

Eddie and Tilly bump into one another …

Eddie (lumbering into Comic Con in a Shrek costume) - "Whoa, sorry about that buddy. Hey, you look to be in great shape...YOU must be a trainer! Can you get me ready for the Mr. Universe challenge in two weeks?"

Referee: "New Choice!"

Eddie (waddling around Comic Con in a Baby Huey costume) - "Hey There Tills! Can you help me win the Marine Corp marathon next week?"

Referee: "New Choice!"

Eddie (plodding into a gym)—"Hi Tilly. Appreciate you gettin' me ready for my 20th High School Reunion in twelve weeks."

Tilly (guffawing without restraint)—"HAHAHAHA... HOHOHOHO...are ya kidding me?!? Forget about it, will ya? "

Referee: "New Choice!"

Tilly— "Howdy Eddie! Yes I can. And as a person who rid myself and my clients of unwanted cankles and muffin tops, I've learned how to help people successfully reach their ideal weight goals. My fat loss system uses three cross-functional components: Mindset, Nutrition and physical Fitness. First, let's work on changing your Mindset."

Eddie (gasping)—"Do I need to, ...like, move into a monastery cell?..."

Referee: "New Choice!"

Eddie—"Okay mate...ya think a walkabout might be a good idea? It'd kill two birds with one stone...to get my mindset *there* and to burn calories..."

Referee: "New Choice!"

Eddie—"AHA, *I GET IT*! Healthy weight is a lifetime journey, not a scale destination."

Tilly—"Yesiree! That's the mindset that'll set you up for success!"

Eddie—"Yay! Score one for Eddie boy!"

Tilly—"Now, for your nutrition plan, I recommend 'air gobbling'…it's like air guitar without the guitar."

Referee: "New Choice!"

Tilly— "Nutrition's easy to learn! You see, eating well for fat loss means eating small meals-every two to four hours—comprised of natural foods—a lean protein and a natural carbohydrate."

Eddie—"Fantastic! I guess the police force will inherit my daily donut forage. I'll substitute a handful of grapes for my small meal."

Tilly—"Not exactly…where's the natural carbohydrate <u>and</u> protein?"

Eddie—"Okay, I'll have a beer with sausage…"

Referee: "New Choice!"

Eddie— "I'll have an egg and an apple for a snack."

Tilly—"Ladies and gentlemen…we have a winna' !!!"

Eddie—"For exercise, how'z about I commit to run 10 miles every day enshrining myself in a heavy duty sauna suit?"

Tilly—"With that plan, I think you need to ditch the reunion and join Looney Tunes."

Referee: "New Choice!"

Tilly–"No matter how far you run, it ain't gonna get you there."

Referee: "New Choice!"

Tilly–"Ha! For fat loss, I offer a time-saving and buck-banging exercise plan. If you Weight Train two to three times a week and do interval cardio two to three days a week, you WILL be ripped for that reunion!"

Eddie–"Well, that's *not good news*…that's scary and unbelievable…I don't know anything about dumbbells. I only want to look INCREDIBLY ripped for the reunion, not HULKY… your ideas are not only scary, *they're making me angry*. You wouldn't like me when I'm angry…."

Tilly—"Complacency will get you nowhere. <u>Never Fear! Failure</u> to reach your goals isn't likely. You'll need to be brave and believe that strength training yields better fat loss results than running."

Eddie— "That's MARVELous but, I'm outta here…"

Referee: "New Choice!"

Eddie—"Okay…I'll <u>make the best out of my decision</u> to bust through my fears about strength training…what should I expect in 12 weeks?"

Tilly—"You'll be a lean ripped machine and will make your High School friends GREEN with envy… Stepping out of your comfort zone to reach your goals is something of which to be proud. Committing to better health through proper Mindset, Nutrition and physical Fitness, will yield BANNER results…"

The Referee blows a long whistle calling the end of scene!

In 2008, my internal referee called the end of my own dramatic yo-yo dieting scene, and in the process I found the answer to my client's and my long term wellness. This long term wellness is what I refer to as "Black Dress" or "Black Tie" Ready. It's an easy philosophy to learn and includes three components: **MINDSET**, **NUTRITION** and Physical **FITNESS**. Each of these components represents the **NEW CHOICES** that must be made to become healthy overall.

© Copyright 2012 Laura Clancy

The first **NEW CHOICE** is to take charge of your MINDSET. You must understand that "to get a different result, you must have different actions." This NEW CHOICE is SO important; it represents 100% of the equation. You need to shift your thinking to the new mindset that maintaining ideal weight and health are a **life-long journey not just**

a scale destination. Without the proper mindset, it's very difficult to achieve long term results. You MUST become completely dedicated to this journey for the long haul…and then take daily action steps every hour, day, week and year to accomplish those goals. Get ready to commit to fighting the "bad habits" that have taken your health down a less than ideal path.

The second **NEW CHOICE**, representing 80% of the equation, is NUTRITION. Yes, another 80% IS an imprecise factor to get to 100%, but I don't care. I'm trying to illuminate that Mindset is the first important NEW CHOICE that you make. Once your mindset is 100% *'there'*, 80% of your weight loss and health gain will come from proper nutrition. Here are the NEW CHOICE eating habits you need to incorporate into your Transformed Life: Eat every two to four hours - "small meals" - each small meal should include a lean protein plus natural carbohydrate (fruit and/or vegetable OR starchy carbohydrate). Overall daily caloric intake for fat loss should generally be between 1500-1750 calories for females and between 3000 and 3500 calories for males. Proper nutrition entails eating food that is "clean", meaning from nature and not processed. It's that simple. Very few people will gain weight or get unhealthy eating natural proteins and natural carbohydrates.

And the final **NEW CHOICE**, representing 20% of the equation, is physical FITNESS. This NEW CHOICE will have you prioritize strength training as your number one exercise choice (also known as weight training or resistance training). Strength training is your best answer for getting and staying lean. It helps you get stronger, build muscle tone, and look awesome all the while increasing your quality of life and increasing overall metabolism. Many 21st century dwellers lead sedentary lives due to their jobs and long driving distances to and from their activities. They become weaker over time so getting stronger is the answer to many things that ail them. Strength training is the best bang for your buck for a fat-free body and provides optimal health and wellness…it's the elixir of youth!

When you add it up, that comes to 200%. I'm okay with that gross miscalculation if it helps you find your "forever health" and wellness! 200% *is the* **NEW CHOICE**!

Long Term Wellness through Mindset, proper Nutrition and physical Fitness is the professional or personal transformation tool that will help serve you most for all the other remodels you need to make. From my experience, I have found that once you commit to making these Black Dress/Black Tie **NEW CHOICES**, you will begin to transform your life into a healthier and therefore more content one.

What's really 'neato torpedo' is that once you get your choices right in one area of your life, you'll be able to tackle a new part of your life –with the game of **NEW CHOICE** busting through and conquering any professional and other personal plateaus that may still be lurking in your life.

It's a **_NEW CHOICE LIFESTYLE_** - how 'awesome possum' is that?

After all, none of us should get too complacent...

About Laura

Laura Clancy is the proud owner of Muffin Toppled® Enterprises Inc. (www.muffintoppled.com) and Wit and Fit® Seminar Productions. In other ventures, she's a co-author of the Best-Selling Books *Results Fitness* and *New Rules of Success.*

As writer and creator of the book *Wit and Fit®*, she also launched Wit and Fit® Baker's Dozen corporate and group speaking engagements; a system designed to get participants whole health well.

Her newest project is an Internet subscription-based program, Wit and Fit®: The UnMess Kit. This system is designed to create concrete heath transformation for participants. Found at: www.WitandFit.com, this Un-Mess Kit™ will be the subscriber's tool in their ongoing health odyssey, and is based on the underlying philosophy that healthy weight is a lifestyle Journey not a scale Destination. The slogan for this UnMess Kit's says it all: "When your weight and health are the pits, get this WIT and FIT®: The Un-Mess Kit!"

In another life, Laura counted beans; she holds a B.S. (that's telling) in Accounting from George Mason University. Before 1999, the only weight that she had ever lifted was a fork fully loaded with sweet food. With her 20th High School Reunion looming, she began weight-lifting with a personal trainer to get to her magic weight. But when the party ended, her High School Crush receded from consciousness and the pounds came back.

Recognizing the short-lived nature of the High School Crush Diet Plan and so many others, Laura got serious and re-toppled her own muffin, leaping from amateur status to professional. By 2009, Laura had become a Certified Personal Trainer and Certified Nutrition Consultant at the National Personal Training Institute. Laura has never looked back and has plenty to share from all she's learned along the way.

In addition to training others to lift weights and conquer fat, Laura is a competitive power lifter and held six world records at the end of 2012 and 2013. She proudly lifts with Team Force (www.teamforcepowerlifting.com). As a fitness professional living, loving, and laughing in Northern Virginia, Laura shares stories from her well-stocked humor arsenal to educate, inspire and entertain people everywhere to get healthier through Mindset, Nutrition and physical Fitness.

Laura can be reached at: Laura@MuffinToppled.com! Feel free to send her an email with your thoughts and dreams!

CHAPTER 64

SECOND TIME AROUND: ATTRACTING YOUR IDEAL PARTNER

BY MANJ WEERASEKERA
THE FRESH START GUY

Are you aware that the divorce rate for second marriages is 33% higher than the divorce rate for marriages in general? With over one-third ending within five years. It's clear that people do not learn from their marital mistakes!

If you are looking for your ideal partner the second or even third time around, this quick read will help give you a better chance of finding love, happiness and peace of mind. Imagine that? Really feeling happy, with the freedom to express yourself in a relationship that could help define you even further. And with a partner that supports and nourishes you and your goals. So much so that it becomes the springboard to success in different areas of your life. Is that possible? Well it was for me and continues to be so. And I genuinely believe it can be the same for you. Sound good?

I was married to a beautiful, caring and giving woman and after 17 years of marriage and two fabulous teenage boys, we separated. The first year was tough; very tough, and I guess that's understandable. My business suffered and emotionally I was pulled apart. Throughout all this though, I knew that it was for the best.

I now have a relationship with yet another beautiful, caring and giving woman; and this time it's in a different way. I'm now a different man and because of the positive changes I've made, I have attracted a woman who is totally right for me at this stage of my life. The relationship is synergistic, where the sum is much greater than the two parts, and we are creating a space where each of us can grow and fulfil our potential. This has in turn had dramatic effects in several other areas of my life, including my health and my business—which continues to grow despite the worst recession in history. I have a great relationship with my ex-wife and our two sons, and continue to love and support them in the best way I can. I can honestly say that I now have a sense of freedom to be myself and to express myself as fully as possible. This places me in a stronger position to be able to support myself in every sense and to support those closest to me.

I was a performance coach working successfully with some of the biggest organisations in the world before I turned my skills to this area. And what I'm about to share with you now is one step of my five-step process: *The 5 Deadly Mistakes Divorced Men Make When Looking For Mrs Right*. And although this is clearly aimed at divorced men, the principles are the same whether you are male or female, divorced or otherwise.

I believe too many men leave meeting their perfect partner to wishful thinking, and I'm urging you not to make that mistake and to actually design the type of person you would like to attract into your life.

You wouldn't go on a major holiday without planning in advance what you would like to experience: adventure, relaxation, city tours, beach, water sports, type of accommodation, etc. You certainly wouldn't buy a car without considering looks, functionality, colour, additional options, etc. And many would consider these things less important than the person they spend the rest of their life with.

Designing and planning end outcomes are common practice with regards to goal achievement in business coaching and in sports psychology. And the mechanics behind them are no different to what we are looking at here.

So here comes the science bit.

Please allow me to introduce you to the *Reticular Activating System* (RAS), also known as the *Extrathalamic Control Modulatory System*. The RAS is a part of your brain that, amongst other things, is responsible for regulating arousal. It also oversees what you concentrate on and is the receiver for what you take in through your five senses. More importantly, it is the RAS that decides what you become cognitively aware of, i.e., it works as a filter within your mind.

Studies, including at McGill University in Montreal, show that we have neurons at the front of our brains that act as filters for information, letting in only the most important of the trillions of signals that we receive and that constantly battle for our attention. Research shows that the average person does not have enough capacity to process all the information that bombards our senses. We therefore need 'gatekeepers', such as the RAS, to stop us overloading on data and to bring our attention to what we deem to be important.

So what's all this got to do with my next date, you may be asking?

Well, what should interest you is how your mind decides on what data is important enough to filter. Other than some of the fundamentals that we appear to have hard-wired into us already (Central Governor Theory by Archibald Hill), we can 'programme' our mental filters with what we would like to attract, so that the RAS can draw our attention to it. Just like programming a computer. That then becomes our important data. This conditioning happens at the level of the unconscious mind; however, the 'commands' are made at the level of the conscious mind.

Therefore, the good news is that you can purposefully programme your mind for who you would like to attract into your life. How great is that?

I use an extremely powerful and highly effective process for this type of work with my clients and I will guide you through that now. And believe me, it works!

PART ONE – DESIGN

You will need some paper and a pen.

Get yourself into a relaxed and positive state by whichever means works for you – this is important and if you are tense, worried or upset about something, this may impact the exercise in a negative way. A relaxed mind works at an optimum level.

Write a heading at the top of the page. Something like, 'My Ideal Life Partner.'

Now list out all the things that are important to you about the person you want to attract into your life. Start with anything you like; there is no particular order. The list does not have to be perfect either.

Here are some example areas:

- What they look like physically – hair colour, height, size, shape, eye colour, etc.
- How they sound – tone of voice, volume, pitch, etc.
- What they are like emotionally.
- What interests they have and what they like doing.
- What beliefs and values they have.
- How you are physically together.
- Their spirituality.

PART TWO – CONDITION

Here I will show you how to condition your unconscious mind to enable you to filter for your ideal mate.

Generally, we take in information through our five senses and there are six elements overall:

1. Visual = What we See
2. Auditory = What we Hear
3. Kinaesthetic Physical = What we Feel Physically
4. Kinaesthetic Emotional = What we Feel Emotionally
5. Olfactory = What we Smell
6. Gustatory = What we Taste

You will need to be aware of each of these elements as we progress through several simple steps:

1. Think of a 'future memory' where you are with the partner you have 'designed'. Think of something you are doing together that

you both enjoy and is important to you. Just to help illustrate and give you a feel for this, we will use the classic example of walking along a beach together. It could instead be a night at the theatre, skiing down a mountain, trekking across a hill or taking a dance class together. Use something you love to do or would love to do, but never got the chance to.

2. On a fresh page, write out what you are experiencing in this future memory using the five senses.

Two very important things to note:

- You must write this out in the *present tense,* i.e., as if it is happening now;

- When you are describing the Visual element, you must describe what you are seeing *through your own eyes,* i.e., you do not see yourself in the picture, unless it is in a reflection.

Using the beach walk example:

Visual – *"Looking through my own eyes, I see the golden beach stretching out before me. The ocean is turquoise in colour and the waves are gently lapping the shore. Palm trees are swaying in the breeze and the orange sun hangs high as birds fly across the cloudless blue sky. I turn my head to watch a sail boat in the distance and see my partner smiling at me as we walk hand-in-hand together."*

Auditory – *"I hear the waves lapping the shore and the distinct sound of birds overhead. When I look at my partner, I hear "isn't this perfect?" said to me in a gentle, loving way."*

Kinaesthetic Physical – *"I feel the warmth of the sun on my face and body. There is also a very gentle breeze, which has a mildly cooling effect. I feel my partner's hand in mine, and as we walk on the soft sand, I feel tiny grains of sand in between my toes."*

Olfactory – *"I smell the sea breeze and the faint aroma of my partner's perfume."*

Gustatory – *"I taste the salt air mingled with the delicious drink we shared moments ago."*

Kinaesthetic Emotional – *"I experience a sense of love, being loved and the freedom to be myself. I feel very happy, fulfilled and grateful."*

3. Read what you have written in step 2 several times so you become familiar with it.

4. In a relaxed state, sit or lie down somewhere comfortable and close your eyes; breathe normally and track your breathing for a few seconds.

5. Now bring up in your mind each of the six elements of your 'future memory', as listed in step 2. Start with the Visual element first and then the others one after the other in whichever order you remember. You need only spend a few seconds on each one and the whole experience need last no longer than sixty seconds. However, you *must* participate *fully* as if you are *actually there* enjoying the experience – *this is vitally important*.

Some guidelines that will help you:

Visual – Make the picture life-size, panoramic, colourful, bright and in focus.

Kinaesthetic Physical – Once you get used to doing this exercise, you may actually mimic the physical actions, e.g., for the walk on the beach, you can stand up and pretend to walk with your partner, etc.

Kinaesthetic Emotional – You *must* participate with *emotional intensity*. So really feel the emotions you are going through and make this truly compelling.

Make sure you experience the other senses intensely too.

Repeat this exercise as often as you can, preferably twice a day every day for a minimum of 21 days without fail. An optimal time to do it is just before you go to sleep at night. You can enhance or re-design your 'future memory' at any time, and indeed condition additional 'future memories' into your unconscious mind, as long as they all support the same outcome and do not contradict each other in any way.

Because this is a closed-eye process, I am duty bound to state that you must not do this exercise whilst operating any equipment, driving a vehicle or performing any other activity that may place you or other persons in any danger.

Visualisation as a tool in performance psychology has been around for decades; however, this approach of using all of your senses takes it to another level. It is based on psychological studies and is designed to activate the right filters in your mind to bring about the right situations for you to attract your ideal partner. Once these situations come your way, it is up to you to take the next steps. A great coach will help you to identify and implement those next steps; and it is of the utmost importance that you choose that type of professional very wisely.

Good luck!

About Manj

Manj Weerasekera is a highly-regarded international coach for divorced men and a transformational speaker. He has an in-depth understanding of human behaviour; how the mind is conditioned for either success or failure, and uses his skills to help his clients achieve truly inspiring results.

Whilst working as a highly successful Executive Business Coach, Manj found himself also supporting his clients in their personal relationships and saw first-hand how the pressures of managing a career or business can take its toll. This, along with his own personal experience and his desire to make the vital difference, made Manj the 'Go To' coach in this area – *The Fresh Start Guy.*

Manj's targeted coaching programmes help divorced men take the right steps to attract their ideal partner. He is passionate about his work, as the boosted levels of confidence he sees his clients subsequently operate from have a remarkable impact on different areas of their lives. This includes their happiness, health, shape, vigour, career, business and peace of mind.

He has been featured on radio and television, and in newspaper and lifestyle magazine articles. He is an expert in personal communication and a Life Skills Mentor to high net worth individuals (including some honoured by the Queen of England) and their families.

Manj has a world-class skills set that includes Humanistic Neuro-Linguistic Psychology, Performance Mindset Conditioning and the Psychology of Attention. He has worked with the UK House of Lords, co-produced a series of audio books published by the BBC and is the author of *The 5 Deadly Mistakes Divorced Men Make When Looking For Mrs. Right* and *The Merlin Approach™*. Manj is also sought-after by other professionals in his field and mentors several coaches.

He believes that we are all capable of much more than we imagine, and has a deep interest in the humanistic aspect of life, self-expression and the potential we all have to positively impact our own lives and the lives of those around us. Manj is based in London, England.

Please connect with Manj via:
Web: www.freshstartguy.com
Email: info@freshstartguy.com

CHAPTER 65

NEVER GIVE UP

BY STEVE RENNER

If you would have told me in my younger years where my life would lead me in the future, I'm sure I wouldn't have believed you. I never had any formal education after high school. I did however have a musical talent when I was younger, and spent a lot of time playing in musical groups traveling around the country. That's how I made my living until I got older and decided that wasn't the type of life I wanted. I eventually found my niche in the real world as a painter. But to go from musician/painter to Internet business expert would require a tremendous amount of growth and transformation.

My painting years were at the onset of the Internet. Discussion about this new virtual phenomenon called the Internet was just beginning and it fascinated me. Even though I lacked a formal college education, I was always thinking and learning and I was especially intrigued by this new discovery. I remember sitting at a coffee shop reading an article about companies trying to figure out how to make money on the Internet. At that time, no one had yet started making money on it. That's when the wheels began turning and ideas began flowing. Even though I knew very little at that time, I knew enough to know that the Internet was something I wanted to learn more about and I was sure there would eventually be a way to make money with it. I thought if I could become a service provider that would be the way to go because I could have customers and monthly income from those customers based on the services I provided. However, at the time I didn't even have a computer. I would go to the library to use the computers provided to the public and Internet connection was so slow it would sometimes take several minutes for a page to load.

Because of how expensive computers were at that time, they were unaffordable for me. However, I was able to barter with someone to do some work for them in exchange for a computer they owned. So, in 1996, with my bartered computer, I began an aggressive campaign to teach myself everything I could learn about the operation of the Internet. But my love interest with the Internet would be put on hold when, in 1997, I was involved in a construction accident and fell from the third floor of a building when the ladder collapsed. I broke my back and shattered my ankles among other injuries. The doctors weren't sure if I would ever walk again. I spent a month in the hospital and another year in rehab in a wheelchair. During my recovery time at home, I would go to the computer whenever I was physically able and taught myself how to do web design and everything I could about the Internet. As I got physically stronger and got back up on my feet, I kept moving toward my dream of starting an Internet business and actually formed my first Internet service company in 1998.

The day I started the business, I was online promoting it through email and word began to spread. I didn't know how to sell anything on the Internet at that time, so I was giving away the service at no charge. I gave away free websites, offered a free website builder, and free email. In 1998 email was a big deal because there were only a few email providers. At that time it was exciting just to get an email. (Unlike today when most people wish they could stop getting so many emails.)

I then connected with a company I heard about who was providing free Internet access. So, I added that service to my portfolio and was offering all the services I mentioned above plus free Internet access. Since I was giving everything away, I decided to call my company Ezze.net. Back then .net was indicative of a service provider.

I think the smartest thing I did at that time was to develop a program enabling me to track all the people who signed up for the Internet related services I was providing. I remember sitting in the living room in my wheel chair. Whenever an email came in, I was alerted by a distinct chime. I had the program set up to notify me whenever anyone signed up for services through my company. I heard the chime and went to my computer to look at the message. Someone had signed up for Ezze.net. I remember looking at my wife and saying, "Look at that! Someone signed up!" That was an exciting time! Then, a little while later I heard another chime. Sure enough, another sign up occurred. Then the chimes kept rolling; 24 hours a day, 7 days a week. 15,000 people signed up in the first 2 weeks. An unbelievable start!

I began emailing and tracking our members and eventually figured a way to monetize it so I could begin making money from the business. In 2000 I began an affiliate program giving people the opportunity to earn money by reselling the service. I sent a check to one of our affiliates in New Zealand for $30 and it took about 3 weeks for him to receive it and for the check to clear; and he lost about 30% in the currency exchange. I thought, "There has to be a better way than this." That's when I came up with the idea to pay people on a debit card. I actually got the idea from another company who had attempted something similar.

As I became more involved in payment processing, the company actually evolved into a provider of affiliate payment services as our core business. This was before PayPal. We kind of pioneered the affiliate payment service and for quite a while we were the leading provider in that niche. The name of that company was Cash Cards International. So, the company evolved from Ezze.net to Cash Cards International and became the number one provider of online affiliate payments through debit cards. With over 100,000 participants, that became my core business for about 6 years.

Eventually, many other companies began to enter that space and PayPal became a dominant player in that industry. While exploring new directions for my company, I began attending various Internet seminars. I saw people making presentations and selling their courses about how to make money on the Internet. I knew the presenters actually never made anything close to what I had made on the Internet. It caused me to think, "If these guys can do this, so can I." That experience caused me to realize there was a market where people were willing to pay for someone to teach them how to market their business on the Internet.

I started an affiliate training program, but quickly realized I was teaching them much more than that. I was teaching them how to make money on the Internet. So we became an Internet marketing training company. People would attend the online seminars for free, and would then pay to come to my office and I would show them firsthand how to make money on the Internet. That's when I started Millionaire Internet Training (MIT) seminars.

After doing those trainings for a while, I realized if people were going to market on the Internet, they were going to need things such as domains, hosting, shopping cart service, mailing list service, payment services, etc. Since I already provided all of that through Ezze.net and Cash Cards, I already had everything in place. So, it was quite easy to put it all together. The only missing ingredient was traffic. So I came up with an idea to provide traffic for people and created a traffic platform where I did a revenue-share with people that view and rate ads. So, through our platform, people could sit at home and view and rate ads and earn rewards. Advertisers can actually earn money to help offset the cost of their own ads plus earn credits to advertise more. It was a revolutionary concept.

Adding this new traffic platform really completed the business. Then I decided to put all the services under one roof and called it InetGlobal because we had become a truly global Internet services provider. That business took off like you wouldn't believe. It was like lightning struck for the third time. We quickly expanded to a couple hundred thousand members and it's been growing ever since.

Previously it took me 10 years to do $100 million in online sales. But in 2012 the company did roughly $100 million in online sales in one year alone. In 2013 the company sales tripled that and we did roughly $300 million in online sales. In 2014 we are on track to do $1 billion in online sales. We have members in 120 countries, we are in the top 300 highest traffic websites in the world, and we are on the brink of becoming one of the biggest Internet companies in the world.

However, all of this didn't come easy. There have been definite setbacks along the way. In 2009 I had a dispute with the government regarding the accuracy of my tax returns. Despite the best efforts of my attorneys, I went to court and lost. As a result, in 2010 I spent a year in jail. My attorneys and I still believe my tax return was correct and I was not evading taxes as I was accused. Unfortunately, it all comes down to who has the better representation in court. The government has really great attorneys and got the upper hand on my legal team, and the IRS ultimately won the day in court.

The great tragedy is that I never did anything wrong. I've paid millions of dollars in taxes over the years. Unfortunately, the stigma associated with that court ruling is a situation with which I now have to live. I could have become bitter and stayed down after I lost in court, but I didn't. In spite of having to deal with that tragedy and set back, I now have one of the most successful Internet companies in the world simply because I refused to give up.

2010 actually was the year of the double whammy. That same year the government suspected my company might be running some kind of Ponzi scheme. At that time, there seemed to be a rash of Ponzi scheme investigations. Ponzi schemes seemed to be running rampant with several high profile cases in the news. The US President actually commissioned a special task force in every major city in America with the task of weeding out corruption surrounding Ponzi schemes. For some unknown reason, the government looked at us and decided we looked like a Ponzi scheme. They raided our company offices, took all our books and records, and took $25 million of our money without any charges, just a suspicion.

That was another time I could have thrown in the towel and given up. But I didn't give up because I knew I was right and we weren't doing anything illegal. We fought the government and fought them hard. We kept the business going even though it was on life support for a while. After two and a half years of investigation, an order came down from a Federal Judge that ended the investigation and they gave us back all of our money. It was the first time in history that any of our attorneys could ever recall that a company had their money seized and then had it returned to them. It just validated what we are doing and made us stronger than ever. We went from that setback in 2010, barely surviving because of the government investigation, to a magnificent comeback in just 3 years.

Beginning the rebuilding process in 2011, I was able to turn the company around to become one of the most successful Internet companies in the world. We went from barely surviving in 2010 to being a leader in the industry in just 3 years, and it's all because I refused to give up. Those circumstances would have defeated many people, but I was unwilling to let that happen, and *I Never Give Up*.

Below are eight very specific keys to what has transformed me from a painter to a successful international Internet expert and executive. They are simple points, but powerful:

1) **Have a Dream** – My dream began at a coffee shop when I read an article about people trying to understand how they can make money on the Internet. My Dream was to start my own successful Internet service company. With hard work I turned that dream into a reality. If you have a dream, why not dream big. You can make your dreams come true.

2) **Believe in Yourself** – I am convinced you can accomplish anything you want in this world as long as you believe it and you don't give up on your dreams. Believe in yourself and you can achieve your dreams.

3) **Surround Yourself with the Right People** – I surround myself with really smart people and I have some of the smartest people in the world working with me. We have an incredible executive team and we employ over 100 people in the US and another 50 people offshore doing contract work for us. They are key to my company's success.

4) **Be Laser Focused** – You start with a vision and set your goals. You can make it happen if you get focused with laser precision. If it's something you're passionate about, you can do things you didn't think you were capable of doing. Create your plan, work the plan, and don't be distracted by circumstances or negative people, and just focus like a laser beam on your goals.

5) **The Attraction Factor** – There is something special that happens to focused people that I can't explain. They attract the right things and the right people. You may be surprised when the right people come into your life at the right time. It has happened over and over again in my life. No matter what I've gone through. When the time is right, the right person is going to walk through the door to help you do what you need to do. It's amazing. It has happened to me so many times

I've come to expect it. It's not a magical or big surprise anymore, it's just that real.

6) **Work Hard** – No matter what, there's no free lunch. You have to put the work in. If you don't take action, it's not going to happen. The most successful people that I know are people that aren't afraid to work hard and take action.

7) **It's Not All About the Money** – It's not all about the money; it's more about making a difference in people's lives. My company started and funds the Acesse Foundation, a professionally managed non-profit organization that helps various people in need. Helping others and giving something back is what really matters in this life.

8) **Never Give Up** – You can accomplish anything you want in this life, as long as you believe, and never give up on your dreams. And if you get knocked down, just get back up on your feet and keep fighting... and *Never Give Up*.

About Steve

Steve Renner, a pioneer on the Internet, started his first Internet Service Company in 1998. From his humble beginnings, Steve has built one of the most successful Internet Companies in the world, through sheer determination, and a "Never Give Up" attitude, against all odds.

Steve's company Acesse provides affordable Web and Mobile services for Small Business. By focusing on Small Business, Acesse has become the champion of the "Little Guy." Steve believes in treating every Acesse Member like Family, and "Acesse Members Get Priority" in pricing and placement in the Acesse search results. By providing affordable services, Acesse helps its Members to compete effectively on the Internet.

Success hasn't come easy for Steve, as he has had more than his share of adversity. In 2009 Steve had a dispute with the IRS, and went to court to stand up for what he believed to be right. Rather than plead guilty, Steve chose to fight. He ended up spending a year in jail, rather than admit to something he was innocent of.

On top of this, the US Government raided Steve's business, claiming to suspect him of running a Ponzi Scheme. They seized all his books and records, and over $25 Million dollars. After 2½ years of exhaustive investigation, the Government could find "No Wrong Doing." No charges were ever filed and the investigation was officially ended by order of a Federal Judge. The Government returned the entire $25 Million.

For most people, this type of devastating blow would have put them under, but not Steve. His "Never Give Up" attitude has brought him back from the brink of failure to become one most successful people in the world today.

Steve is living proof that you can achieve your dreams, as long as you believe in yourself, and Never Give Up!

Steve adds, "And yes, I do pay an incredible amount of Taxes!"

As Steve says, "It's not just about making money, it about making a difference in peoples lives." This is why Steve created the Acesse Foundation. The Acesse Foundation is a professionally managed non-profit organization that will fund worthwhile charitable causes; that includes providing *food and health care* for underprivileged children, an educational Scholarship Fund, to help talented Technology students, and aid for individuals who were *wrongfully convicted*. Steve's Company Acesse will donate 5% of its Pre-Tax profits annually to the Acesse Foundation.

Steve now travels the world promoting Acesse to new Small Business Customers and attracting new Sales Consultants.

Steve is a powerful, charismatic speaker, appearing in front of audiences of thousands at live events around the world.

Here are a few quotes from Steve:

- "My *Secret To Success* is to have some of the most brilliant minds in the world, on my team." *"Success Is A Team Sport."*

- "You can accomplish anything in life you want, as long as you believe, and *Never Give Up On Your Dreams."*

- Working together we can make a difference in peoples lives around the world.

- "Together We Can Change The World."

To find out more about Steve:
never-give-up.acesse.com

CHAPTER 66

DON'T F.A.I.L! UPGRADE YOUR OPERATING SYSTEM

BY PAUL MANTELLO

– WHAT WILL YOUR TRANSFORMATION LOOK LIKE?
– HOW WILL YOU KNOW THAT IT HAS BEGUN?

Transformations begin with the journey of life and are affected by the level of one's awareness, desire, passion, commitment, knowledge and discipline; however, everyone's journey is unique and that's what allows them to reach their own transformations. Some of the most powerful transformations occur after experiencing a very painful event or a series of painful events. Events so powerful, that they will force you to challenge everything that you once believed to be true. Allow me to show you a better way, one that will allow you to gain control.

My journey of transformation was no different than most, it was one that was filled with many challenges and heartache. I had many challenges that tested me at every twist and turn of my journey, each providing a lesson that I needed to learn, in order to advance to the next stage of my life. On many occasions, I faced numerous difficulties that would cause me to consider giving up and walking away from my dreams. It was definitely not easy to stay on course, especially when nothing seemed to go right. My challenges became tougher and more painful each time that I did not learn the intended lessons.

I was definitely not aware of this; until my most powerful lesson had almost become my last.

There I was just sitting in my car, stopped in traffic on the highway, feeling frustrated and angry about the lack of progress that I was making in life. It just wasn't working out the way that I had planned, it was all taking too long. As I looked up and glanced at my rear view mirror; that's when I saw it, and within seconds, it happened. Bam! My car was struck from behind by an SUV that was traveling at over 75 mph. I remember thinking to myself; in those few seconds before impact that: I would never see my wife and my son again and how I would never even have a chance to meet my unborn child, who was due to arrive in less than 8 weeks. When I regained consciousness, I remembered making a promise to God; that if I would be lucky enough to have another chance: that I would live life to my fullest, love everyone with my all, and that I would help others understand what I had discovered from my journey, awakening and transformation.

ARE YOU READY TO DISCOVER A BETTER WAY OF CREATING YOUR TRANSFORMATION?

Great, let's begin.

In order to control and create the transformation that you desire, you must first understand how your mind operates and then you must learn how to upgrade it. This is the secret that has led to all of the success stories that you have ever heard about: including Thomas Edison, Andrew Carnegie, Abraham Lincoln, Steve Jobs, etc. They all discovered what I am about to share with you and that is: that we are all born as creators. Our Creator has given us the ability to create anything that we desire, and it all begins with a simple thought, followed by an action which is sealed by faith. Once you understand this, you will be able to create anything that you desire. You have done this from the very moment that you were created. Your first creation was in the form of the changes that you caused your mother to experience in her pregnancy. You created new emotions along with physical changes in her and you also created emotional changes in everyone that you would soon know, as family. You have always been more powerful than you could have ever imagined; even before you could have given it any thought. You have been, are and always will be a creator.

Wow; so if it's that easy: what happened?
Why isn't my life perfect?

That's where the programming or operating system comes in; we've all been programmed to operate on what I call the **F.A.I.L. O**perating System. Although we all operate on this same exact **OS**, we have not all operated under the same exact environmental conditions, nor are we identical and that's why we all experience different results. We all have our own special gifts; which make us who we are.

As a creator, you have the ability to update your operating system and create one that will serve you.

WHERE DID YOUR OS COME FROM?

Everyone is born knowing the same exact things and everything else is additional programing. You are born knowing the basics for survival; breathing occurs just as naturally as your heart pumps on its own, without you giving it a thought.

Your programming has been developed and is still affected by those whom you have been and still are surrounded by. Although you were born without the **F.A.I.L. OS;** it was subtly programmed into you. You unknowingly made updates whenever you challenged certain things, while just accepting others; simply because you didn't know better.

HOW DID THIS HAPPEN?

It is just a part of life that is handed down from one generation to the next, simply by default. Think about it, where did you learn about the basics of life? Most, if not all of us; have learned these things from the people who have helped raise us and they too learned the same way: from their programmers (parents, teachers, society, etc.). The problem is that while you were young, your programming was vulnerable and not operating at its fullest, you only knew basic survival skills. So, you took most of what you learned without questioning it because you trusted your teachers and simply didn't know any better.

As you grew older and wiser, you began to challenge some of the programming, but as life began to take its toll on you, you may have decided that it would be easier to step aside and allow your life to be dictated by the "mind hackers"(outside forces that infiltrate your **OS**). But those who challenged their **F.A.I.L. OS** are the ones that broke free and regained their creator status. This is the **secret** that has allowed them to reach their ultimate success. Success has many different meanings, and only you can determine what it means to you – money, love, purpose, fame, etc.

UNDERSTANDING AND UPDATING THE F.A.I.L. OS

So, what is the **F.A.I.L. O**perating System? The **F.A.I.L. OS** is a program that is made up of **F**ears, **A**ssumptions, **I**nterpretations and **L**imiting beliefs.

Fear only has the power that you allow it to have. Fear is just a simple four-letter word, but yet it can cripple anyone in an instant.

Let's assume that fear makes up only 5% of who you are; that means that you are allowing 5% (fear) of you to take over and control the other 95%, when you are operating out of fear. What would happen if you could control your fear and use that 5% of energy towards being who you are? Think about that for a moment… how powerful will you become when you learn to harness this 5% of energy that is being used to hold you down and cripple you? Think about that, only 5% is holding back the other 95% of you. This is why it is vital for you to take control of your fears; you must do this in order to live a truly happy, successful and completely joyful life.

Fear is the avoidance of pain; which is created in your mind as a safety mechanism – to prevent or avoid painful experiences. These are either painful experiences that you've already lived through, or those of which you have seen or heard of another experiencing.

Here's a tip: Keep challenging your fears and never back down – the more that you challenge them, the more in control you will become. You decide whether your FEARS grow or shrink. Control your fears by constantly questioning and challenging them. I know that you can do this; I believe in you and now you must believe in yourself.

Assumptions are things that you believe to be true, based on your past experience or knowledge of someone else's experience. This can cause problems by creating a tunnel-vision effect – meaning that you have already decided on an outcome based on your prior experiences or knowledge; so therefore, you will only see what you want to see. Once you can learn to control your assumptions, you will begin to see more opportunities. To control your assumptions; you must first know when you're making one, then question it and see it for what it is and not what you think it is.

DON'T F.A.I.L! UPGRADE YOUR OPERATING SYSTEM

<u>I</u><u>nterpretations</u> are the meanings that you give to something that someone has said or done. You feel that there is a motive behind the other person's action(s). In other words, you create interpretations about people, situations and experiences based upon what you believe to be true. The way that you interpret something is determined by the way that you perceive the world and everything in it. It is important to realize that most interpretations are being made automatically, based on past events, which are stored in your mind. You decide what interpretation to give something based upon past events that have occurred in your life, which is why you automatically respond without a second thought. Interpretations are easily skewed by feelings that are connected to the subject at hand.

<u>Limiting beliefs</u> are things that you believe to be true and therefore limit you in some way. These beliefs shape the way that you see the world, other people and yourself. Limiting beliefs are a big part of why you will not attempt certain things – which leads to that feeling of being stuck. It's these Limiting Beliefs that holds you back from achieving more in life.

What does a limiting belief sound like and how could it be so powerful?

"I DON'T HAVE A DEGREE; THEREFORE I'M NOT SMART ENOUGH TO…"

This is a strong limiting belief; one that will affect you for as long as you believe it to be true. Therefore, you will never allow yourself to go after what you want because of a **limit** that **you** have placed upon yourself. Remember, that as a creator you will manifest whatever you think about the most, so why concentrate on what you believe is a limitation, when you could just as easily concentrate on and manifest being limitless?

WHO IS YOUR MOST POWERFUL ENEMY AND HOW CAN YOU FIND THEM?

This may be a tough answer to swallow, but an easy one to answer and it involves a top-secret tool. Are you sure that you are ready for this? If so, I want you to find a mirror (top secret tool) and take a good hard look at the person starring right back at you, that's your most powerful enemy. No one can do more harm to you than you can do to yourself. But the opposite is also true and can be achieved by learning to love yourself and not being so hard on yourself. How many friends would you have if you treated them as badly as you treat yourself? Give yourself a break.

My journey has been dictated by my passion to help others, and my transformation has led me to the creation of the **F.A.I.L. OS** which has allowed me to help shape the lives and success of others, as well as myself. Once you learn the proper techniques and begin to update your **F.A.I.L. OS**, you too will begin to unlock your true potential. In order to correct or change something, you must first know what that something is, and secondly you must know how it operates before you can devise a successful plan of action. You have been operating under this **OS** your entire life and therefore cannot expect instant changes. However, now that you have the formula and understanding of how your **OS** works, you too can begin a successful transformation. This is a life changing process that you must follow and be committed to. Just as with anything else in life, you will get from this what you put into it. I have put all of these pieces together so that you too can experience the transformation of your dreams. Now that you know and understand your operating system, you should constantly challenge and reprogram any parts of the F.A.I.L.'s that no longer serve you.

Successful transformations occur for those who are motivated, passionate and always searching for ways to improve their skills effectively – because they understand that time is not only money, but also the most precious and limited commodity that any of us have. That's why all successful individuals hire the best people when building their team(s), from coaches, attorneys and accountants to consultants. They understand that becoming the best requires dedication, discipline, training, learning, implementation and positive constructive feedback in order to shorten the learning curve, and to achieve the best results with the least amount of pain. You can see this from professional athletes to very successful entrepreneurs and executives. They understand the importance of having help and that's why they all have a coach on their team of experts. Do you have a team or are you still waiting for that one big lesson that could possibly become your last? No one ever said that you couldn't ask for help; seek and you shall find.

It's your turn to Live to your Fullest, go out and Create your Own Life, as all Creators do.

About Paul

Paul Mantello is a certified professional coach, speaker and creator of the F.A.I.L. Operating System. Paul is very passionate about helping his clients and is dedicated to helping them break the vicious cycle of programming and financial poverty that is continuously being passed down from one generation to the next.

Paul empowers his clients by teaching them the proper tools, tips and techniques that are necessary for improving their core way of thinking, leading and managing. He also uses his top secret tool, called the "S" Factor. The "S" Factor is a powerful tool that allows clients the ability to see exactly what is limiting their "S"uccess; therefore allowing for greater results in less time.

Paul also brings his experience and wisdom from his real estate & business ventures, as well as from his former Wall Street career as a licensed stockbroker. He earned his coaching and energy leadership certifications while attending one of the top leading coaching schools in the world: IPEC – Institute for Professional Excellence in Coaching.

Paul is a passionate and dedicated family man; he is the father of two boys and a loving husband to his wife Laura, of 14 years. Paul was born and raised in New York before moving to New Jersey with his wife in 2002. He enjoys giving back to the community and is a local volunteer firefighter. Paul loves to coach little league baseball as well as to help empower children to dream big and expand their minds and possibilities.

Paul believes that everyone is born with the ability to create their own lives; which can be accomplished with the proper training and knowledge.

Contact Paul at:
www.UntappedBrainPower.com
www.PaulMantello.com
www.twitter.com/PaulMantello
www.facebook.com/coachingforlifesuccess

CHAPTER 67

DEMAND

BY TRAVIS LANAGHAN

My father instilled the thought into me at a very young age, "Travis, you will be great at everything you ever do." This is what he would tell me, constantly, up to the point where I believed it. Still, to this day, I trust that I am the best man for the job. This mindset procured from my father's wise words have evolved into something more; something that has changed my life and still to this day changes my life. I am here today writing this chapter about how to transform you and your WORK habits to best serve you, all the while teaching you how to become a valued asset, rather than just a number on a payroll sheet.

My past has proven to me, as I am sure many of you are aware, that our JOBS for the most part, will continue with or without us. This aspect is terrifying in its own sense, as this simple idea can hinder us from unlocking our full potential. I have heard over and over again, "You are expendable, why are you trying so hard?" "All of you, (your positions here), you are a dime a dozen, we don't need you." These negative connotations are designed to keep you depressed and thinking, "I'm a nobody." I am here to tell you that you are not replaceable, you are unique, and your skills are in high demand. All that you need is the right mindset, the correct mentality. Then I can promise you, the people saying you are expendable are ultimately looking at your success, and knowing that they are the ones that are truly replaceable.

Let's begin with the simple word "Work." What does work mean exactly? If we take a look at the definition according to Webster's dictionary, it's "a job or activity that you do regularly especially in order to earn money." Based on that definition, work sounds like a job. Let's try another definition, "Activity in which one exerts strength or faculties to do or perform something." Again these definitions are cold and objective. In my earlier years, I always associated the word "work" as something I didn't want to do because of those very definitions. "Work" is hard, boring, and takes up all of our time. And let's face it, we all can find something better to do than "work."

Many people have a belief that they don't have the opportunities that others have, making up excuses as to why or why not. These negative beliefs will harbor resentment towards others' success and hinder one from being truly successful. We all have the choice to become whoever we want to be, but it all begins with your mindset.

Are you ready?

In this Chapter, I want to delve into exactly what "work" means, how our work affects us personally, as well as the people around us. How can it formulate who you are as a spouse, a father, a mother, and a friend? There are three distinct types of people-traits: DEMAND, MOTION, and MANAGE. People with MOTION traits tend to go with the flow, they aren't your typical leaders; they are happy going through the motions and would rather be told what to do rather than figuring it out themselves. People with MANAGE traits tend to be very organized, and find it difficult to think outside the box. They manage their mind, their goals, and only do what is needed to finish the task with minimal effort.

Throughout this chapter we are going to break down and learn the six key attributes of the DEMAND personality that are necessary for becoming successful in the work place. There is nothing wrong with any of these types of people, but whether you know it or not, your work habits are what make you the person you are today. These habits can stop you from becoming something bigger than yourself. While we may point fingers and place blame on others for our own shortcomings, in reality, it is our own work beliefs that can hold us down.

Many of us wake up earlier then we would prefer, travel somewhere, and proceed to trade our time for money. This is known to most as a job, like the definition of work. For every day of every week, we know that regardless of our efforts, the wheels and gears will continue to turn even when we are not around. Or so society has taught us. This is true in most jobs, whether you work at home or for yourself. If you stop working, the money stops. Knowing that our lives, for the most part, revolve around our JOB, how can we use work to better ourselves, to build that drive, to make us into the most valuable asset we can be?

Growing up, I played a lot of sports and was very active within my community. My parents made a deal with me. As long as I stayed active with extra-curricular activities and my grades in school stayed up, I wouldn't have to get a job. Now this sounded like a pretty sweet deal, until I started driving. Soon I found a girl who I wanted to impress, so I needed a job. Mom and Dad weren't going to fork out cash for their son to spend on sweet nothings. If I wanted to take my girlfriend/future wife out, I needed a job. I got my first job at a local hardware store. They weren't hiring, but I applied anyways. They told me they would get back to me. Well, that wasn't good enough; I needed money, and didn't really wish to flip burgers at the fast food joint. So the next day I returned, and the next day and the next, until finally after over a week of this, I earned a position on the team. Unbeknownst to me at the time, I had just learned the first lesson of a DEMAND-type personality.

Dedicated
I was dedicated enough to keep going back, day after day, showing up the same time every day, talking to the same people every day, letting them know I was serious and I wanted to work for them. When you become dedicated to an idea, a thought, a position, nothing should hold you back. People may ridicule you and tell you to stop wasting your time, but no matter how insignificant an idea or goal, if you are dedicated to seeing it through not much can truly stop you. Dedication isn't just showing up every day, it's showing up with purpose, goals, and energy.

Energetic
Coming to work every day seemed to be an exciting new challenge, am I going to help someone fix their leaky sink or sell three chainsaws? Will I have the opportunity to leave the store and install some new locks on a home? Either way, I was consistently setting personal goals. How can I outperform myself? What can I do better than I did yesterday? Having energy every day when coming to work is the key to success. Instead of looking at tasks as mindless and boring, create challenges for yourself, take that task and make it your own. Find another better

way to complete it. Even something that has been done over a thousand times can be done better. It just needs your abilities.

Motivated

Staying motivated is the most difficult mindset to overcome. When your job involves repetitive motions, it is easy to become complacent. You show up at the same place, you take your breaks at the same time – work life is putting you into a mindless motion movement. It is very easy to fall into the MOTION-personality characteristics. The most obvious question that comes to mind is, how do you stay motivated? How do you stay motivated when you are turning the same wrench or flipping the same burger, or typing up the same spread sheet for the millionth time? Where is your mind, why are you turning that wrench or typing that spreadsheet? The answer is found deep inside each of us. Is it money, power, or recognition?

Let's face it, most of us have or have had bosses who don't know the first thing about motivation, simply because they're not leaders. In order to be motivated, **YOU** need to motivate, inspire and become that leader. If you start shrugging off your responsibility, those around you are sure to follow. However, if you are the one who buckles down and encourages others to work and perform better, you will find staying motivated isn't as difficult as you once thought.

Anticipate

Not one person can predict the future, but everyone can prepare for any possible outcome. Successful people in the workplace or in life look at all possible outcomes they might encounter before moving forth with a task or a job. Anticipation means preplanning, having a course of action, and having proper contingency plans in place. Anticipating all aspects beforehand leaves little room for unnecessary stress and hardships; they can save you or someone else a great deal of time and money. These events more than likely won't happen, but you will be comforted to know that you had taken the time to anticipate such possibilities, so that you can focus your time and attention on the important details, and not leaving the unknown to chance. It is truly freeing to have anticipated and planned for a problem that arises and handle it without hesitation.

Nobility

The state of being noble in character, quality, honor, and integrity. Character defines who we are as a person; quality defines how much we believe in what do. Believing in what we do in our day-to-day work life comes down to what we do when people are not watching. How we manage situations and stand true to what is expected of us when the camera isn't looking is a sign of true nobility.

We must believe in honor and integrity to do the right thing regardless of the outcome. Make no mistake; we all fall short of these noble ideals. Your mistakes will be used as ammunition against you. Women and men of nobility believe in acceptance and responsibility, not only for their actions, but also for the actions taking place under their watch; these acts of humility and forgiveness are signs of true nobility.

Determination

The last of the DEMAND characteristics is determination. This can come in all shapes and sizes. Being truly and fully determined to seeing a project through or a job finished is probably the single most important attribute in the Demand category. Determination isn't something that naturally occurs for most, it's built up over time. Only when we fail can we truly become determined to succeed. Failure is key to the success of the determined; many say, "fail your way to success." That saying couldn't be truer for the determined. Always strive to be better, always put in that extra time, the extra effort, the extra nobility and humility. The rewards won't always be easy to spot. Perhaps there won't be any rewards; therein lies the fallacy. The reward doesn't come from someone else, the reward lies solely inside. Recognition for an achievement is nice, but if you DEMAND it of yourself, if you strive for the best, there was something you could have done better, there will always be room from improvement. Be determined to get better every day of every week of every year.

These six Demand characteristics aren't just quick tips for climbing the corporate ladder, but rather life lessons that can be put to use in every aspect of your every day. When you start applying these attributes to your lifestyle, you will notice a change, perhaps a beginning to your true purpose, but you will never know until you start to DEMAND more of yourself everyday without hesitation.

About Travis

Travis Lanaghan has always been told since he was young that "you can be the best at whatever you put your mind to," and he has done just that. He is a hard-working husband and father who has sacrificed time away from his family to support them...wanting the best for them. Family is very important to him as that is his reason why he has such a desire and need for helping people today.

He is a man that sets out to be the best person on the job because of a relentless dedication that he found obtaining his first job. Travis is someone that will never surrender and will not settle for second best, he might fall short but he never stops. To him the day-to-day challenge of learning something new thrills him as it's a way to be better than he was yesterday.

Travis is transitioning from working for someone to working for himself as an entrepreneur, the President of his company he has founded with his wife. Travis wants to make a difference in this world, in our work society; he makes sure everywhere he goes, every job he is at, that he makes a name for himself, that he leaves with everyone knowing him as the best, everyone wanting him.

Travis found his passion for objective writing at the young age of 15 years old, always set out to tell the truth, not going along with what others wanted him to write. He writes from the heart, his writing has passion, it's real and it's raw. He's been locally published and written about.

Life has not always been easy for Travis as he moved miles away from what was comfortable to him at a young age, his marriage has had more downs than ups but leaning on his Faith and in pursuit of being the best he can be, he is now able to do what he loves, sharing what he knows with you – to make you a better person in whatever situation you might find yourself in.

You can connect with Travis at:
www.facebook.com/tlanaghan
www.travislanaghan.com
TravisLanaghan@yahoo.com

CHAPTER 68

TRANSFORMING TO A QUINTESSENTIAL LIFE

BY TRISH McCARTY

Quintessential: The fifth and highest element in ancient philosophy that permeates all nature and is the substance composing the celestial bodies; the essence of a thing in its purest and most concentrated form.
~ Merriam-Webster

You are a success. You've made it. You are reading this book, always improving. You are financially strong, popular, probably own your own business, you have friends, you go on great trips, you might be considered religious, you are where you want to be…according to what others think and say about you. You are in the top 2% of the world's most influential. You know there is more, not only to give, but to feel. You have had amazing experiences and you have met amazing people and yet something else seems to be calling you. When you go to bed at night; when you wake up in the middle of the night or in the early morning, something or some things feel unresolved or perhaps are calling you.

God has tethered you to your highest calling and until you reach it, you will be wandering and wondering. And it is not defined by others, maybe not even by you. Since the day you were very, young, you have been told; and even told yourself, "You have so much potential." … Potential for what? …Potential to make money? …Potential to have a doctorate degree? …Potential to be a sports leader? …Potential to teach others? …Potential to be a writer or a scientist?

Potential is a glass ceiling, defined by someone or something because you have shown a particular talent or tendency to do well, and you have achieved that talent, that potential. But what is trying to cause a transformation toward your highest calling is so deep inside of you, trying so quietly to get your attention, and yet covered by so much noise? It becomes persistent throughout the years, as a constant, muddled, unresolved stirring, deep inside of you, wanting you to realize.

I help kids to transform. Kindergarten through twelfth grade kids begin to look for their "highest calling" as they grow, beginning in Kindergarten. And they learn that life changes constantly to call you time and time again to be more, to do more and to calm down and trust more. We don't talk about the student's potential; we discuss their dreams and find out what they love.

I formed StarShine Academy International Charter Schools in 2002, pushed by the disasters of 9/11, the Columbine Shootings and observing schools teaching kids everything BUT how to become transformational leaders and thinkers. I have been involved in transformational leadership, even as a young child, growing up in Tokyo, I was honored to serve as a child delegate to the Children's United Nations meetings in Tokyo, Japan. Later, working for AT&T, I watched and participated in transformational leadership effecting world change. While working for AT&T, developing my career, I became deeply interested in studying religion, yoga and how the brain works. In my early twenties, I began to teach yoga and to teach executives how to become transformational leaders at the time, two very different subjects. I also gave birth to a daughter with Autism, further driving my thirst for understanding more about the brain. They talked about her having less "potential." I learned that having Autism brings about some extraordinary attributes and possibilities rather than the "disabilities." In my thirties, I began a banking career with Mellon Bank, a part of the World Bank. I learned how one person could cause a world of difference to happen.

I am in another "calling" now in my life and that is to help to influence the world's most influential women, and the men who support them. Women have an extraordinary ability to bring continuity and flow back into their communities, families, businesses, cities and countries. At no time in history have women been this connected, and this powerful. My priorities are to help women to connect at the highest levels, and support and use those connections as a means to discover their ultimate collective influential power, while connecting back to their own inner wisdom, love and peace. We are witnessing the world transforming, right before our eyes, as the top 2% of the most influential women begin to work gently on themselves while working in a more collaborative way with other women leaders.

Money has driven most of the decisions and/or outcomes of the world we have experienced so far. Money is energy and flows automatically when products and decisions are based on doing the most good. Money cannot be forced into becoming sustainable. It is a natural outcome of doing things right.

The top influential women leaders of today are driven by passion, love, purpose and winning by doing "Right" and making money because of it. If we look at the top women influencers on Facebook, the Forbes List or LinkedIn, we see similarities. They run companies, they have employees, and most of them share their success through speaking, writing books and presenting at conferences. Women are perfectly positioned to shift world leadership and world business, for the first time in history.

I was asked to train eight hundred teachers in Liberia a few years ago and learned of the ordinary, unlikely, woman named Leymah Gboweeo who led a revolution to create peace in a war torn country of a twenty-year civil war with nothing more than sheer determination. The press called her pathetic. A press release describing the documentary, *Pray The Devil Back to Hell* about these few, one hundred women, can be found on the Internet and is a remarkable story few people have heard.

Pray the Devil Back to Hell is the extraordinary story of a small band of Liberian women who came together in the midst of a bloody civil war, took on the violent warlords and corrupt Charles Taylor regime, and won a long-awaited peace for their shattered country in 2003.

As the rebel noose tightened upon Monrovia, and peace talks faced collapse, the women of Liberia – Christian and Muslims united - formed a thin but unshakable white line between the opposing forces, and successfully demanded an end to the fighting– armed only with white T-shirts and the courage of their convictions.

In one remarkable scene, the women barricaded the site of stalled peace talks in Ghana, and announced they would not move until a deal was done. Faced with eviction, they invoked the most powerful weapon in their arsenal – threatening to remove their clothes. It worked.

The women of Liberia are living proof that moral courage and non-violent resistance can succeed, even where the best efforts of traditional diplomacy have failed. Their demonstrations culminated in election of Ellen Johnson Sirleaf, Africa's first female head of state, and marked a new wave of women taking control of their political destiny around the world.

This remarkable chapter of world history was on its way to being lost forever. The Liberian war and peace movement were largely ignored as the international press focused on Iraq.

There are three main points to discuss as I look at how women leaders reach heights far beyond their "potential."

BELIEF IN SELF

1. Extraordinary women believe in their abilities and are urged by at least one other person, while others do not believe they can accomplish the thing they are after.

Overcoming adversity requires great courage. In my work with the most outstanding women, I have yet to meet anyone who has not had to overcome obstacles that others looked at as "impossible." Even at very young ages, some of their stories have propelled extraordinary women to have the strength to go beyond what others would even think possible at all. This "sisterhood" of women determined to stay focused and positive – in spite of all sorts of difficulties – is a common factor.

What causes super successful women to remain positive? They learn how to be positive and they practice it and continue to learn, until they automatically demonstrate solutions. Just knowing how to begin to practice positive solutions has a transformative effect on being able to do it.

I am reminded of a woman I have worked with recently who was in a successful career and wanted to become a best-selling author. The thing I enjoy most about connecting and working with the top 2% of women leaders is that they take advice quickly and they stay focused and methodical on purpose. I told her to form a small, five-person MasterMind Group and gave her specific instructions on who to put into the group and how being a part of the group and practicing it in a well-defined way would propel everyone's success. I taught her how to get her goal of becoming an author down into her heart, from her head, by practicing very specific meditation and breathing techniques. She developed her skills, she practiced affirmations and exercises without fail, and she connected with others for mutual support…and she exceeded her dream.

PASSION AND CARING

2. Global influential women care deeply, not only about the thing(s) they want to accomplish; they care deeply about most things.
They are passionate.

Many quantum physicists today are discovering the truth about energy. *The Secret* and *What the Bleep Do We Know!?* movies taught us to be diligent in our thoughts and words. In *What the Bleep…* we actually witnessed water crystals changing as people spoke various words. The emotion behind the words carries the energy, causing the effect. Everyday more discoveries are being unveiled to show the mind-heart connection in manifesting.

These top 2% women leaders are opinionated about most things and yet are such accomplished learners, they are continually curious and ready to listen to other's ideas and opinions. They have spent their lives learning and practicing confidence-building and caring for the right reasons.

Ernest Holmes, a thought leader of the 1950's and founder of the Science of Mind Church, said, "Is it any different to say that there is one law governing all physical phenomena?"…or to say with Emerson, "There is one mind common to all individuals?" The universe is a spiritual system. It is a manifestation of Divine Intelligence. Another scientist has said that we can think of the universe in the terms of an infinite Thinker thinking mathematically, which means that faith acts as a law, and this is why prayer can be answered. Dr. Einstein said that space and light curve back upon themselves. This means that everything moves in circles. Jesus said, 'Give and it shall be given unto you; good measure, pressed down, and shaken together, and running over.' Jesus also said that they that take up the sword shall perish by it. It really means that what goes out will again return; that the inner action of our minds decides what is going to happen to us, for 'as a man thinketh in his heart, so is he.' Thoughts are things that mental states cause to produce definite results. This is why we meditate, pray and affirm the presence of good in our lives.

TRUST, CONNECTING AND MENTORS

3. Women in the top 2% of influence understand the power of trust and of connecting to others through trust, …toward a greater good for all.

When I was a very young girl, my mom gave me many pearls of advice. One piece of wisdom was to always make friends with people who don't look like me. She said my life would be a whole lot more interesting. And to this day, when I walk into a room full of strangers, to build my confidence and pay back my promise to Mom, I will look for someone interesting and I walk over to introduce myself.

My mom told me to make lifelong girlfriends and mentors as they would stick with me throughout my life successes and pick me up from failures. Learning to unconditionally trust others for advice has propelled my success faster. When I am a speaker at conferences, especially in a female-dominated audience, I am asked about this idea more than others. Women are typically slower to trust others immediately, not trusting their own gut reaction, causing delayed success. Compare some men to some women. I have been present in several meetings in my life when a man has told another man to give a large sum of money to help another's business or charity. Without too many questions, the money will be given, without knowing the third person or business very well. I can think of only one time when this has happened with women in my presence. Perhaps women are too cautious, rather than leading with their own gut-feel of intuition, they try to out-think the problem. Using spirit-filled intuition will almost always trump thinking too much.

Anyone wanting to create amazing success needs a mentor, paid and/ or unpaid. The ones you pay for, you will probably follow the advice of quicker. The ones unpaid usually end up being lifelong friends, but sometimes don't tell you the very thing you need to hear to get you to act. The Global Women of Influence Network which I started for the top 2% is a powerful group of co-mentors. These women want to be together, they want to help one another and want to be a force for shaping the future.

A TRANSFORMATIONAL LIST:

1. Wake up earlier.
2. Drink a glass of pure water and say thank you for ten things while you drink it to quick start your brain cells.
3. Drink a glass of water with juice from a fresh one-half of a lemon.
4. Sit down on the floor and meditate quietly for ten to sixty minutes. This will transform you.
5. Write in a journal.
6. Exercise your body in some way you like and read something positive.
7. Look for synergy and stay open to opportunity…they are your angel's way of leading you to a transformative life.
8. You are an average of the five people in your head…choose wisely.
9. You will repeat your last thirty minutes of your day all throughout your night's sleep.
10. Go to sleep with a grateful and loving heart.

The meaning of life is to have a life of meaning.
~ JoAnn Holland

Life is one transformational, magical ride, when you choose to follow it.

Tribute and Thank You to Mom, Ruby Sanders:

As I was writing this chapter, my most influential, spiritual, transformational female leader, my best friend and sweet Mom went back home to Heaven, where she was from. She taught me so many important, meaningful lessons. One I will use my entire life, "Life is interesting, sometimes unbearable. Sometimes life is completely magical. In every moment, you will become better or bitter. Try really hard to keep the 'I' out."

About Trish

Trish McCarty is one of America's leading business strategy and education experts on developing peak performance in schools through school management, technology and processes, shared brand marketing and cutting-edge student resources in brain-based training, self-discipline, self-esteem, motivation, and results. She has inspired thousands with her lectures, interviews, published articles and books. She has been an impassioned leader for K-12 education reinvention – alongside her corporate banking and technology backgrounds – serving on many children's charity boards throughout her life. Trish McCarty helps education superstars and professionals have more power and income for reinventing K-12 education. She has democratized the best schools and brought innovation to an audience who traditionally found it difficult to get involved.

Ms. McCarty came into the world with a global view; born in Frankfurt, Germany, as a U.S. Air Force military "brat" and as a child in Tokyo, Japan, where she served on the United Nations Board of Children. She attended Fort Lewis College, in her family's home town of Durango, Colorado with a human biology and neuroscience major and was recruited from there as an executive for AT&T. After five years, she was recruited by the President of Mellon Bank to develop national banking centers. An avid entrepreneur, she subsequently started a bank that grew to $128M in five years and won awards and highlights in national news including *INC. Magazine.*

Her company opened her first charity charter school, STARSHINE ACADEMY.

INTERNATIONAL SCHOOLS, in the fall of 2002, for K-12 disadvantaged children, on a crime-ridden street in Arizona. The highly acclaimed academic "School Eco-Village" is a replicable model for success based on the holistic education of a child in health, wealth, happiness, body, mind, and spirit. It integrates the environment and personal health with a community garden and the spirit with music, art and technology. All of the children participate in community service projects integrated into the curriculum to learn economic development and patriotism. She has created partnerships with the United Nations by hosting 11 Days of Peace and Sustainability each year from 9-11 to 9-21. The school prototype model integrates the best practices for human growth and spiritual transformation, Human resources management, sustainability, professional development, data collection and business management. Ms. McCarty is a Lincoln Center Fellow for Arizona State University for Education Leadership and is a partner at ASU Skysong Innovation Center. Yoga is an integral part of the StarShine student curriculum as Ms. McCarty has studied and taught yoga for nearly thirty years.

Trish McCarty is a constant community activist for peace, women in global leadership, and child advocacy. She is married to guitarist and platinum recording artist, Steve McCarty. She has four children and eight grandchildren. Steve and Trish frequently combine their talents in workshops and lectures to spread their message of empowerment, love, harmony, and unity.

To contact Trish McCarty:
Trish@TrishMcCarty.com
TrishMcCarty.com
www.starshineacademy.org
www.eduresources.com